TWELVE STUDIES OF
THE ORGANIZATION OF CONGRESS

Cornelius P. Cotter
Wichita State University

Heinz Eulau
Stanford University

Roger H. Davidson
Dartmouth College

Kenneth Janda
Northwestern University

Charles R. Dechert
Purdue University

Kenneth G. Olson
The George Washington University

Edward de Grazia
Georgetown University

James A. Robinson
Ohio State University

Lewis Anthony Dexter
University of Maryland

Aaron Wildavsky
University of California at Berkeley

Alfred de Grazia, Coordinator of the Project
New York University

CONDUCTED UNDER THE AUSPICES OF

THE AMERICAN ENTERPRISE INSTITUTE
FOR PUBLIC POLICY RESEARCH
WASHINGTON, D. C.
1966

The Coordinator of the project, on behalf of the other authors and himself, wishes to express gratitude to the staff of the Joint Committee on the Organization of the Congress for good advice liberally proffered in the course of the studies; to Betty Benswanger, Anita Horwich, John Appel, and Suzanne Farkas for their editorial assistance; and to Dr. Thomas F. Johnson and Mr. Earl H. Voss of the American Enterprise Institute for Public Policy Research for their continuously effective help throughout the course of the study.

AMERICAN ENTERPRISE INSTITUTE
for Public Policy Research

The American Enterprise Institute for Public Policy Research is a nonpartisan research and educational organization making studies of national policy problems. AEI's purpose is to assist the nation's policymakers, legislators, and educational leaders by providing them—and making available to the public—factual analyses and studies of important current issues of national significance.

From time to time AEI organizes symposia to consider topics of current major national interest. The symposia bring together outstanding authorities on the subject for an open exchange of opinions and views. Following each symposium the proceedings are published by AEI for public distribution.

The Institute, with the counsel of its Advisory Board, utilizes the services of competent scholars, but the viewpoints expressed are those of the participants and represent no policy position on the part of the Institute.

AEI's operations as a nonprofit tax-exempt educational organization are supported by the financial contributions of several hundred leading business firms, foundations, and the general public.

The American Enterprise Institute for Public Policy Research initiated a series of studies by a group of political and behavioral scientists in June 1965 to examine the foundations of government by legislature in the national government of the United States. Eleven scholars, working through the coordinating efforts of Professor Alfred de Grazia of New York University, met together and in smaller groups several times in the summer of 1965 to take up the problem.

The purpose of the AEI special study group was to describe how Congress functions and how it might be aided in its work to achieve a good society, counting as part of that good society the legislative way of life itself. The work was undertaken with an eye to the needs of the currently operative Joint Committee on the Organization of the Congress. For this reason the cutoff date for completion of the papers was set in September 1965.

Each scholar pursued his separate study with the common objective of organizing changes in Congress according to a model of a strong legislature. Each also studied the papers of the other contributors to ensure that the total collection of reforms proposed would create a consistent model of legislative government. Each author has expressed a general approval of the efforts of his colleagues, although he can accept final responsibility only for his own paper.

The American Enterprise Institute which, of course, neither endorses nor disapproves the findings of the study group, published eleven individual contributions serially.

CONTENTS

PROFESSOR ALFRED DE GRAZIA, of New York University, is editor and publisher of the *American Behavioral Scientist* and director of the Universal Reference Service, an information retrieval system in the social and behavioral sciences. His latest book, published in 1965, is *Republic in Crisis: Congress Against the Executive Force* (Federal Legal Publications, Inc., 95 Morton Street, New York, N.Y.). Among his earlier works are: *Public and Republic, The American Way of Government,* and *Apportionment and Representative Government.*

Toward a New Model of Congress

Alfred de Grazia

HE Congress of the United States of America has been the subject of countless studies, debates, and discussions. It takes a certain nerve to engage in its study with any hope that what will be said will be more than a few drops of water falling into a flood. Nevertheless the authors of this paper and of those that follow it proceed with some confidence, for several reasons.

One is that the rapid flux of society and the world create new problems of Congress for each generation to define and solve. Also, many behavioral studies of legislatures and Congress have been printed but not yet incorporated into reflection and action; they should now be brought to bear on the issues facing the country in respect to Congress. Finally, and most importantly, it is possible to conceive of Congress today in a new light, neither in the classical glow of the constitutional period of the late eighteenth century nor in the harsh glare of the last generation's administrative mechanics, but rather in the luminosity of an operational and sympathetic social theory.

1

The Classical Model of Congress

T HE eighteenth century Congress was the product of the Enlightenment Mind and of the political forces born of that Mind. It contained in its design several distinctive principles.

First of all, the legislature should be the First Branch of Government. It should have the supreme power to legislate and to intervene in the government whenever and wherever individuals were done injustice.

The legislature should operate as an assembly of laymen, men as intelligent as anybody else but not necessarily experts. Expertness was not conceived to be a serious problem.

Representation of geographically distinct interests and of individuals as such was regarded as the primary function of the legislature.

The success of revolutionary movements in America and elsewhere fostered a general optimism about the potential of legislatures for controlling the executive branch of government.

In short, the Age of Legislatures had arrived. The basic problem of representative government had been solved; what remained for the future was to unfold the plan in detail.

But one ominous word was missing from the vocabulary of the founders of the American republic and of their counterparts abroad. This was the word "mass." When they spoke of people acting politically in large groups, they talked of the "mob." The early designers of the legislative way of life did not think of "mass armies." They did not know of "masses of workers." They were not familiar with "mass production" or the "mass media." Nor had they considered "mass suffrage," nor the "mass political party." To this day, indeed, American politicians are loath to use the word, fearing

2

that it would imply an unsightly vision of America and offend the people.

The techniques of organizing, disciplining, and directing the large-scale institutions of modern society were strange to the early leaders. They had, by present-day standards, a pathetic incomprehension of the potential of the "masses." They could not perceive how a "mass society" could function. Although, to be sure, a foreshadowing of most of our problems and customs of today can be discovered in their words and writings, still they were not designing a Congress for a "mass society."

They were hostile to the personal rule of kings and military dictators, and to the officialdom that infested customhouses and printing shops. To counter these forces, which were linked together in the traditional state, they devised a Congress that had full legislative authority in respect to those affairs of man that government was entitled to govern. Most of the old problems that the Congress was to cope with—kings and officials—were submerged for a long time and have only recently broken the surface again, in different guises. They present themselves today as problems of efficiency in government, as the merit system and the permanent bureaucracy, as prolonged legislative sessions under heavy pressures, as enormous organizations and a great population that do not expect limited results from a limited government. The Congress of the early Republic had only to include men of independent mind and spirit, possessed of power. It did not require the spelling out of the science of operating a mass society democratically. The classical design of Congress was sufficient for its times.

The Old Model of Congress

IN the nineteenth century began the science of administration. First came the mass phenomena alluded to above—mass armies, mass production, masses of workers, mass suffrage, mass parties, and mass media; then came the science to deal with them.

Essentially, the science of organizing the mass-dominated age was the science of the work gang and the military machine, where the concept of hierarchy first prospered. The science of administration, as it developed, claimed of course to make the organization and management of all masses possible. By regimentation and standardization of equipment, large armies could be put into the field. Clothing and vehicles could be manufactured, and foodstuffs processed in vast numbers of equal units. Workers might be organized; socialism, especially of the Marxist type, was racing so fast to its logical conclusion that, where the masses did not exist, it invented them. Marx has been aptly called "the Red Prussian."

When the suffrage was widely extended, parties of a new type had to follow, as machines for the organization of the electorate. The publics were gathered into troops. The civil service could be organized according to the principles of hierarchy, impersonality, and permanent careers. And ultimately the whole society could be planned in the manner of a giant bureaucracy.

In all of the scientific thought about administration, much of which was of a high order, there was little place for the concept of government by legislature. How could one organize a legislature to "get things done" according to the principles of hierarchy, subordination, efficiency, integration, delegation with strict accountability, and so on, with the jargon of the new science? And how could one do so

4

without taking the heart and soul out of the legislature? It could not be.

Yet the attempt was made, forcibly, and through an ideology that permeated the very perceptions that men had of government, and it produced what must now be called the "old model of Congress." In the end, many men who were devoted to the ideal of a strong Congress, including members of the institution of Congress itself, were intellectually hamstrung and thus prevented from moving toward their goal of insuring the preeminence of the first branch of government.

It is the belief generally of the authors of this series of papers on Congress that it has been this old model of Congress that has excessively occupied the thoughts of political scientists of this generation and the last two before it. Authoritative, expert, and lay circles have come to think that the way towards good government lies by way of the predominance of the President, the presidency, the civil service, and the centralized political party. Since the late nineteenth century, thought and action have driven toward a military-type centralized civil service carrying on an ever-enlarging share of all social activities under ever-increasing and efficient centralized control, directed by a national political party under the personal supervision of the President. Consequently, many proposals for a more effective Congress which have been offered in the past and are being offered at this time are, consciously or unconsciously, aimed at reducing its role in government and expanding the role of the executive branch still further.

Even when a set of recommendations is intended to be favorable to Congress, the ingrained modes of thought favorable to executive centralism tip the balance in that direction. A recent example of this is provided by the report and recommendations of the American Assembly's conference on Congress, published early in 1965. The distinguished experts and civic leaders who gathered at the conference offered many proposals. Although a certain sympathy was voiced for not restricting the case work a congressman undertakes for his constituents, the majority of the participants favored the executive in its dealings with Congress.

For instance, an appeal was made for the House of Representatives to be elected to four-year terms and for these elections to be held at the same time as the presidential election. Tied-in elections would go far toward putting the Congress at the political mercy of the President. Together with other recommendations to create greater "party responsibility" in Congress, it would subject every congress-man to the domination of the political party. Only if by strengthen-ing Congress is meant weakening it as an autonomous branch of government can such proposals be credited with lending strength to the legislature.

The New Model of Congress

DISSATISFACTION with many previous approaches led this writer and others to the conclusion that it is time to elaborate a contrasting model. This legislative model became the focus of all the essays.

Congress is the central institution of the American democratic republic. Unless it functions well and powerfully, much more so than it has in the past, the road to a bureaucratic state and a kind of monarchic government will be opened up. Without a strong Congress the basic structures of voluntary associations, federalism, and autonomous enterprise will tend to dissolve into centralism. Without a strong Congress, the major problems of the country will be handled in ways that will become excessively majoritarian, often arbitrary, usually collectivist, and in the end suppressive of the American ideal of individuality.

Congress is helped to perform its crucial role in American democracy by the presidency when that institution is properly construed, by a judicial power that is appropriately respectful of representative government, by the autonomous states of the Union, and by the multitude of voluntary associations and private companies; and each in turn is helped to flourish by the existence of a powerful Congress. Congress affects all other institutions and in turn is affected by them. Together they represent the different forces that are part of a general dynamic equilibrium in which no force acts independently of the others.

7

Major Problems of the Present Age

IT is within this equilibrium that the current problems of society must be solved. There would probably be general agreement on a list of the basic issues with which the American government is presently confronted. Material poverty—the often unbearable difficulty that many people have in finding the means of keeping themselves and family in jobs, food, clothing, and shelter—troubles one out of ten persons. Health and safety are related preoccupations—whether by this is meant medical care, air purification, highway safety, or general law and order. The provision and guarantee of civil rights to members of various exposed citizen groupings are of primary importance. So is the improvement of education at all levels of instruction. And so is the betterment of the physical and spiritual conditions of neighborhood life. Lastly, the problems of foreign relations—in particular, the enduring crisis in Southeast Asia and the conflicts within the European alliance—are of pressing concern.

Such problems are forever present; they have been, are now, and will continue to be the grist of the mills of government. No one should be so unhistorical as to believe that similar issues did not gravely trouble the first Congresses of the United States. Year in and year out, men and women worried over the equivalent of our own problems; and quite as much as the present generation, they wondered whether the institutions of the land would be adequate to the task of solving them. Sometimes the institutions proved to be adequate, and sometimes they did not.

But just as the particular form of the eternal problems of men in society and their incidence change, so also must the form of the institutions that handle them. *It is in the matching of the institu-*

8

tions to the changing issues of the times that the genius of each generation is tested. All is not well in this regard today. It is the consensus of the men who have undertaken the present study of Congress that the institutions of American government are currently being changed in a manner that is unsatisfactory. They believe, indeed, that in the course of the very attempt to cope with the major issues of our age three additional problems have been created.

The first of these is the danger represented by an excessive reliance for the handling of all issues on an escalating bureaucracy, consisting of huge agencies of permanent civil servants who are not made effectively responsible to the larger society. The second is the danger of the kind of militarism that arises in the course of efforts to solve the issues of foreign affairs and their related domestic aspects. The third problem results from the increase of presidential personalism: the exaltation of an office above its stated powers and the capacities of the incumbent, which poses a veritable threat of dictatorship—or whatever one may wish to call the phenomenon of the people's overly great dependence upon the magical qualities of a person occupying an outstandingly prominent office.

Thus to the list of the major problems of our age must be added these three problems of government, which are uniquely characteristic of contemporary times. As these problems worsen, the fate of Congress and the whole concept of the legislative way of life are thrown into jeopardy. But on the other hand, the very solution to these problems lies in the strengthening of Congress. For if Congress can be made to work well—that is, if it can be sufficiently powered, properly staffed and financed, and rationally directed— then not only will the American democratic republic continue to stand, but it will prove fully adequate to its tasks of government both now and in the future.

Operating Principles for Congress

To resolve these internal problems of government and to attack definitively the substantive problems of poverty, health, education, and foreign affairs, more than wistfulness is required. To uncover the faults and to condemn them will not suffice to preserve the representative or congressional system. Explicit principles to work with are required, principles of thought and action that can guide both the reorganization of Congress and the nature of the legislation designed to correct social ills. At least 11 guiding principles can be named. A Congress needs to be sought that will, despite opposition and obstacles, perform regularly in accord with them.

Under the terms of these principles, Congress should:

1. Espouse a central view of American political society by sympathizing and identifying with all people to a significant degree.

2. Seek to acquire a prestige as enduring and broadbased in the society as that of the presidency.

3. Enhance individual and group senses of social responsibility and altruism.

4. Foster many independent publics and voluntarism in social relations generally.

5. Devolve governmental functions in increasing numbers onto socially responsible functional components of society—in education, science, economic production, welfare, etc.

6. Seek new modes of autonomous territorial and functional decentralization, i.e., a new federalism taking into account the urbanization of the American people.

7. Arrive at decisions in as rational a manner as is possible,

granted the political obstacles that make even ordinary care and foresight difficult.

8. Limit the processes of industrial bureaucratization and monopoly.

9. Limit the presidency in respect to its control of legislation, its monopoly of news and publicity, and its control over the size, shape, substance, and longevity of the executive agencies.

10. Control and supervise the executive agencies more thoroughly and in more respects.

11. Supervise foreign policies and the work of the Departments of State and Defense more closely, and publicly present alternatives and critiques of foreign policy.

Some Proposals for Reform

BEARING these principles in mind, it is easier to comprehend the kinds of reforms that the members of the present study group are proposing. Practically all the writers have evaluated new means of strengthening the constituency base of Congress so as to create richer and deeper publics independently supporting each congressman. Practically all have recommended expanded intervention by Congress in the activities of the executive branch below the level of the White House. Practically all have approved the idea of the decentralized party system and recommended that there should be no increase of central party control through the President. Nor have the members of the project recommended any increase in the President's control of the budget. The congressional seniority system, the *bête noir* of so many congressional reformers, has been subjected to some reformulation. The number of committees, campaign expenditures, lobbying controls, and other subjects typical of reform proposals in the past have not been the central concerns of the group.

However, in their reports, the authors have been able to recommend numerous practices and changes of an unprecedented character. Anticipating their fuller development in the papers to come, an indication is given here of the scope of some of the individual suggestions.

On Checks and Balances: Lewis Dexter seeks to restore the balance of powers by co-opting a variety of interests and experts to work with congressional committees: "Congress must have its own experts and use them for its own tasks and purposes." He also sees the need for a "Joint Committee on Legislative-Executive Relations." He espouses the adversary char-

12

acter of congressional intervention: conflict is not only inevitable, it is a positive technique.

On Automated Information Systems: Kenneth Janda describes the possibilities for Congress of an automated information system, whose capabilities range from instantaneously locating where given bills stand to delving in micro-time units into the recesses of administrative agencies. Each congressman should have the intelligence capabilities of the highest civil and military officers of the executive branch.

On Budgeting: Aaron Wildavsky proposes a new overall format for budgeting the vast federal government. "The power of Congress to control budgetary decisions," he says, "depends on the power of its appropriation committees." The incremental approach (rather than the comprehensive approach) to budgeting is to be preferred: "The process should be taken as far as it will go and then should be corrected for its worst deficiencies." He urges a "radical incrementalism," which means the abandonment of the annual budgetary process, and the substitution of "a continuous consideration of incremental changes to the existing base." Each activity with its unique history, character, and phasing should have its own budgetary process. Executive monopoly of the budget process is to be diligently avoided.

On Supervision of the Executive: Cornelius Cotter records that the need to ensure administrative response to congressional directives is especially an important problem out in the field, and recommends a "Resident Agent of Congress, suitably staffed and officed" in a number of districts of the country. The congressional hand should be continuously present where a great many problems of big government arise.

On Representation: Roger Davidson foresees a need for "congressional task forces that would range widely in their subject matter areas, commissioning research, holding seminars, and making trips into the field where appropriate. ... Such task forces might have their most immediate impact on present geographic interests which are inadequately served by the drawing of state and legislative district boundaries." Both new research technique and reorganization are to be the response to the need for a Congress that functionally as well as geographically represents the country.

On the Committees: Heinz Eulau would greatly strengthen the research arm of committees and introduce additional flexibility into the selection of committee chairmen, in keeping with their extraordinary powers.

On Liaison: Edward de Grazia suggests examining the adequacy of congressional access to the independent executive agencies, where it is felt that congressional influence is reduced to a low point; he seeks in general a stronger counter-liaison to the rapidly developing, integrated presidential liaison system.

On Decision Making: James Robinson would disperse among other leadership elements the agenda control now in the hands of the Rules Committee. He would also restructure the research facilities of Congress so that members could get full adversary types of briefings and reports on controversial questions.

On The Service Function: Kenneth Olson would aid the facilities for casework of the individual congressmen, viewing this function as a vital base for public support and for improving surveillance of the administration; he envisions creation of special expert staff facilities in a central office of Congress that could add knowledge and energy to the congressman's pursuit of difficult individual cases.

On Access to Executive Information: Charles Dechert proposes, among other devices, a Commission of Notables who would make semi-judicial findings in cases of executive departments and agencies withholding information from the Congress. In cases of improper denial of information necessary to congressional activities, there would be an automatic imposition of sanctions in the form of subsequent denial of appropriations for the specific budget item(s) involved.

It will be readily grasped that these proposals, representing but a sample of the numerous proposals prepared by the group, are set apart from the great majority of proposals found in the usual discussions of congressional reorganization and also from the views of many scholars. They represent a New Model of a strong legislature adapted to the needs of these times, as opposed to the Old Model or even the Classical Model.

The present writer has put forward an extensive program for the supreme legislature in his recently published book, *Republic in Crisis: Congress Against the Executive Force* (New York: Federal Legal Publications, 1965). His proposals are listed below in summary form. They can thereupon be placed in the context of the other proposals of his colleagues. They are grouped into propositions concerning the constituency, the political party, the presidency, the courts, the bureaucracy, and the internal governance of Congress.

Propositions on the Organization of Congress

I. The Constituency and Political Parties

1. Via a Central Office of Congress, congressional activities are to be reported non-controversially to the press and public in popular language. Television and radio are to be more extensively and imaginatively employed on the behalf of the Congress as an institutional whole.

2. Halls of Congress will be set up in a central city of every state to explain the history and activities of Congress in tangible and graphic terms.

3. A National Civic Service may be formed to preserve and enlarge the independent public, which is essential to the survival of Congress; the same Service will help enlarge and recruit members for the active constituencies that congressmen need.

4. A constitutional amendment is advisable to permit the states to experiment with theories of apportionment going beyond the sheer idea of equal-population districts, and to experiment also with other elements of providing representation for the future society.

5. All representative-type bodies formed by executive agencies should have the direct authorization of Congress and all members of the hundreds of such agencies in the executive branch should be considered subrogated for Congress and should pass tests to assure their comprehension of the principles of government by legislature.

6. The American political party serves its country best in its traditional weak and decentralized form; the party should not be construed as a military machine whose aim is the totalitarian government of its members and the eradication of opposition; it acts well as a catchall, a carryall, and coverall.

7. The political organizations within Congress are not to be changed to strengthen party discipline in voting; their present state is satisfactory.

II. The Presidency

8. The President would serve for a term of six years and would not be eligible to succeed himself at any time.

9. Limits are to be set on the direct material benefits which the executive agencies are permitted to give any group of people in the period of six months prior to an election.

10. Powers of the presidency attributable to past national emergencies will be reviewed and largely withdrawn.

11. Congress would present nonpartisan messages to the nation corresponding in time and scope to the President's State of the Union Message; Congress will employ special messages from time to time.

III. The Courts

12. A Supreme Court of the Union, composed of members of the Supreme Court of the United States and of the several states, is needed to decide issues of constitutional law affecting the nature of the federal union.

13. The appellate jurisdiction of the Supreme Court requires review with regard to expediting the work of the Court on sheerly legal problems and in order to determine whether the Court can employ better types of social research in reconciling decisions with judicial objectivity.

14. The membership of the Supreme Court should be increased and divided into panels in order to increase its efficiency and discourage its participation in political affairs.

IV. The Bureaucracy

15. Congress must insure itself access to the operations and materials of the executive agencies, employing however some responsible internal machinery to screen its activities against abuse.

16. Stern laws against secrecy are in order where secrecy cannot clearly be demonstrated to be vital to national security, as that term is defined by Congress.

17. The practice of permitting questions to be asked on occasion from the floor of either house and requiring their answer by agency chiefs then and there has little effect on the ultimate place of Congress in the government.

18. Congressional Tribunes, designated from a panel of quali-

fied persons serving under Congress, would be assigned to each agency of government and, each year, would assume the role of devil's advocate, proposing to the appropriate congressional committees that the agencies' activities, personnel, jurisdiction, and budget be eliminated, devolved to local governments or non-governmental groups, or otherwise reorganized.

19. All officials to whom has been delegated considerable legislative power, are to be constituted into a Sub-Legislative Corps, certificated by Congress as to their qualifications for such offices, and required to acknowledge and act in terms of the legislative capacities of their office under Congress.

20. Legislation can be passed to require the canceling of an old activity whenever a new activity is begun, and to effectuate this policy, a periodical balancing of activities on a zero-sum basis can be performed.

21. A Central Office of Congress, among its several functions, can command an array of talents to assist individual members of Congress in handling difficult cases of intervention with executive agencies.

22. Exemplary Legislation, to be made a regular feature of each session of Congress, consists of laws with minimum scope and substance, but with vital principles asserting constantly congressional rights to employ a large range of devices—such as the legislative veto—in the full exercise of its powers and control of the executive branch.

23. A General Counsel of Congress is the preferred instrument for expounding congressional intent and prerogatives at the bar; executive attorneys cannot be always relied upon for full support of congressional rationale.

24. Congress has to engage in long-range planning of the government by means of a better organized leadership working through a Central Office of both houses of Congress.

V. The Internal Government of Congress

25. The internal process of lawmaking needs to be viewed and taught as the Process of Successive Majorities whereby every collective decision of Congress is passed through a multi-faceted representation of the nation.

26. A Charter of Legislative Authority should declare the prin-

ciple of legislative supremacy of Congress and the position of Congress with respect to the executive branch, and this Charter should be disseminated widely within and outside of the government.

27. Academies of Congress are to be established in association with universities throughout the country to prepare students for work in connection with legislatures and to do research on legislative problems. Freshmen congressmen can enter such academies for special courses directly upon election and before taking office.

28. First-term congressmen should be tendered greater orientation, apprenticing, and responsibilities in the operations of Congress.

29. The size of congressional staffs should be increased to provide necessary case-work, legislative liaison, and committee agents for each congressman.

30. Planning of committee staff work should be periodically accomplished, at which time proposals for action and research may be submitted by members, discussed and designated to receive aid.

31. Qualifying tests to insure compatability with congressional principles and suitable technical skills should be required of committee staff, but the direct responsibility of staff members to committee chairmen should not be disrupted.

32. A panel of expert consultants on a full range of legislative subject matter, maintained by the Legislative Reference Service of the Library of Congress can be established, and congressmen authorized to call upon them for services.

33. A Social and Behavioral Sciences Institute ought to be set up with grants from Congress to foster the development of pure and applied social science, with respect to topics unconnected to immediate legislative needs.

34. An Inventory of Freedom and Restrictions can be built up and continuously maintained to keep accounts on how individual liberties of Americans are subtracted from or added to by governmental and non-governmental actions.

35. A Sanctions Institute should study and recommend legislative and administrative practice in connection with the host of penalties that Congress and the agencies are constantly employing, often without scientific knowledge, to exact conformity to public policy.

36. Germaneness is not to be sought in Senate debate to the preclusion of the filibuster, which, whether its verbiage is relevant or not, is the source of much of the power of Congress with respect to the President.

37. The number of committees of Congress and their names do not relate to any universal rule; an important activity, recognized as such, can find a committee home or achieve a new committee without much delay.

38. A more formal designation of general representatives on all committees to prevent excessive special-interest representation on the committee rosters is desirable.

39. Where minority-party staffing on committees is inadequate and the principle of checks and balances is therefore threatened, provision for giving over at least one-third of staff and facilities to the minority party as the convenient vehicle of honest opposition should be made.

40. Committees should be encouraged to produce policy and program statements on subjects within their jurisdiction, and to elevate these messages to the level of public reporting which has been achieved by many White House conferences, task force reports of executive and foundation groups, and agency studies.

41. Congress as a whole may structure and restructure all agencies, down to their last unit, and can give and recapture all initiatives that it believes important to have.

42. A congressman or committee can justifiably intervene as advocate of a person being harmed by the executive branch in any way, or as advocate of a person receiving treatment that reveals corruption or abuse of administration. Penalties should be prescribed for officials wrongfully making allegations of conflict of interests against legislators.

43. The personnel of the General Accounting Office might be organized into an independent or congressional civil service to accentuate their special congressional status.

44. The fiscal interventions of Congress are justifiable at several stages of financing and spending and in whatever depth of the executive hierarchy is needed to insure the achievement of congressional goals.

45. The total committee process, including the special cases of committees of investigation, should be reviewed, not to limit them, but to derive principles of procedure more in accord with scientific research and the rules of legal discovery.

46. The selection of committee chairmen is accomplished by procedures far more complicated and defensible than are generally understood, and the seniority principle that plays a large part in the selection should not be put aside for any other method that directly or indirectly would increase presidential or political-party control of Congress.

47. The poor image from which Congress suffers is the product of many causes other than its alleged "passivity" and "provincialism," most of said causes being the by-products of the forces universally operating against the legislative way of life; the sense of inferiority that many congressmen have acquired in the face of the problems of contemporary society is quite unfounded in fact; but the performance of Congress suffers throughout, in consequence. All other recommendations should tend to reform this self-image.

Good policies, planned as such, depend upon good, skillful, persistent leaders. No set of institutions, no matter how rationally engineered, can automatically and uninterruptedly produce good laws. At best, the structure can recruit good leaders and assist leaders to be good. At worst, it can recruit and foster bad leadership. When we insist that Congress must be strengthened so as to maintain an important role in American society, we must simultaneously warn that many uncontrolled and informal conditions go to make up the character of Congress as they do the character of the presidency. No assurance can be given that good reforms will guarantee that good polices will necessarily issue forth from either Congress or the executive. Structure is an important factor but unless the people are to be deluded by some mystique of power, they must expect to be frequently disappointed by the recurring policies produced by individual institutions.

By the same token, it is the patient adherence to the fundamental principles of constitutionalism, in the face of all setbacks, that marks a well-ordered and stable political community. If, whenever some single injustice or disaster befalls, people cry out, "You see, it won't work!" then the Constitution surely will not work.

Alternative to Congress

F EW persons are heard to recommend outright the dissolution of Congress as a branch of government. Probably a good many more would be pleased if Congress would wither away of its own accord or at least be so completely subjected to the executive will that it might perform a mere ceremonial function. There is a good deal of comfortable hypocrisy in this position but the issue is too important to tolerate it. What, in fact, would American government be like if Congress were abolished or, what is practically the same thing, if it had no power except simply to subsist?

The President, at first elected, would in time *cause* himself to be elected. As with the Soviet government, he would be chosen from within the presidency. Since hereditary rule is not considered rational in modern times, a monarchy would be avoided. But the President would be emperor of the republic (as Napoleon I had himself titled). All the features of a monarchy that disgusted generations of Americans would appear, but would be Americanized and therefore be rendered palatable.

Every business, including the smallest shop, and every occupation would be vested with a public interest and regulated in detail by the central civil service. Big business would be readily convertible into agencies of big government.

The civil service and the military would be the most highly prestiged classes in the nation.

The states would be vestiges, inefficiently constructed administrative districts, tolerated out of sentiment. Governors and state legislators would be controlled out of national party headquarters. All important laws would be approved in advance by the national

21

executive branch in order to insure their "desirability" and conformity to national policy.

The political parties would be very strong until such time as it became obvious that one party could do the job of two, since neither party could establish a true alternative to the then-existing political order without risking national disaster.

The press, the universities, and the intellectuals would not be harshly suppressed. They would exist in a kind of kaiserdom, or early fascism, or de Gaullism: free up to a point, said point being defined by the leaders of the central government.

The stimulus for practically all kinds of voluntary activity, including the performing arts and scientific research, would be provided by the central bureaucracy, under occasional prodding from the presidency.

Such would be some of the more important features of the American political landscape with the Congress removed. The more independent, powerful, resourceful, and self-confident Congress is, the less likely is it that those conditions would come about. Good government is a function of an independent set of publics operating through a network of decentralized and autonomous institutions of governmental and non-governmental type, the node of which is the congressional system. The reform of Congress should therefore be guided by this proposition, and proposal for change evaluated in its light.

Contrary to the belief of many, history offers a favorable prognosis for the long run. Men aspiring to a cooperative and equal state will seek to be ruled in accord with their dignity. Such rule is rule by law and mutual consultation. A publicly controlled decision-making council—when free from major superstitions and magical interventions—is the highest form of government that men have yet devised. It can express itself in the family, in the school, in business, in the church, and in the state. So long as men wish a voice about their social destiny, they will seek to be ruled by congresses. They may change the system in many respects: practically no component need retain its particular form and manner. But in the end, it must still be the congressional system in substance that will prevail among a self-respecting citizenry.

CORNELIUS P. COTTER studied at Stanford University (A.B., 1949), Harvard University (M.P.A., 1951; Ph.D., 1953), and the London School of Economics. He has taught at Columbia University and Stanford University. Presently, he is Chairman of the Political Science Department at Wichita State University.

Cotter was the recipient of a Sheldon Travelling Fellowship while at Harvard. He served on a National Committee Faculty Fellowship at the Republican National Committee in 1959, remaining on in a staff capacity for half of 1960. From 1960 to 1963, with a brief intermission at Stanford, he served as assistant staff director with the United States Commission on Civil Rights.

Cotter is author of *Government and Private Enterprise* (1960), and co-author of a number of other books and articles, including a study of the national committees, *Politics Without Power: The National Party Committees* (Bernard C. Hennessy, co-author, 1964).

Legislative Oversight

Cornelius P. Cotter

> . . . the proper office of a representative assembly is to watch and control the government. . . . J. S. Mill, *Representative Government*

Introduction

SEPARATION and balance of powers is one of the hallowed, one of the vitally influencing, and one of the more trite principles of American government. It was developed, so John Dewey once quipped, "to the end it may be a government of lawyers and not of men." [1] Like many of the relationships, or absence thereof, defined in the Constitution it is ambivalently stated—to the extent to which it is stated at all—and has been coated with a gloss of historical practice which might effectively disguise it from the framers who originally formulated it. But the doctrine is nonetheless important in its impact upon development and behavior of institutions.

As Neil MacNeil has written:

> The President of the United States, by a strict interpretation of the Constitution, could have but little effect on the drafting and enactment of American law. That was a function specifically granted to the House of Representatives and the Senate, in Congress assembled. . . . In theory, the House and the Senate were to be scrupulously independent and remote from the President, whose chief function was to execute, or administer, not to determine, the laws that Congress enacted.

> In practice, however, the theory broke down, and broke down almost at the very beginning of the American Republic.[2]

The theory broke down completely. Today the President is commonly regarded by public and Congress alike as the principal initiator of important legislation; and his party's leaders in the House and in the Senate are commonly regarded as *his* leaders. Indeed

[1] Thomas Reed Powell, *Vagaries and Varieties in Constitutional Interpretation* (New York: Columbia University Press, 1956), p. 25.

[2] Neil MacNeil, *Forge of Democracy: The House of Representatives* (New York: David McKay Co., Inc., 1963) pp. 235-36.

such has been the relationship between the President and the Congress in recent times that it has even transcended party lines. One is reminded of the Herblock cartoon commenting upon the Democratic majority leadership in the first session of the 86th Congress. Speaker Rayburn and Majority Leader Johnson are depicted standing before the President's desk at the White House. Eisenhower is put in the ungrateful position of quoting to the legislative leaders Grant's words to Lee at Appomattox, "Tell the men they may keep their horses; they will need them for the Spring plowing." In effect, of course, Herblock was attributing to Eisenhower the feat of having cowed the Democratic leadership of the House and Senate in that session of Congress. In reality, however, for a substantial portion of the President's program, the Democratic leadership of the Senate and House had willingly chosen to be the President's spokesmen or at least to cooperate with the President in ushering his program through Congress. Again, persons familiar with the 89th Congress have been known to query whether Everett McKinley Dirksen is Minority Leader or Majority Leader, because of his recent tendency to go along with the legislative wishes of the Democratic incumbent of the White House.

Contemporary presidential-legislative relations contrast strangely with those which prevailed before and in the decades immediately following the framing of the Constitution. One commentator has suggested that:

The espousal of the doctrine [of separation of powers] by the "Framers" and by the leaders on the American scene during the nineteenth century was inevitable. The very simplicity and symmetry of the threefold division of governmental functions and organs suited their rationalist approach. Most important, the doctrine fitted in well with their conception of the role of government and their analysis of its operations. The concept of separation of powers and its corollary, checks and balances, appealed to men who distrusted representative bodies, feared all-powerful executives, espoused the mechanical theory of the judicial function, and believed in *laissez-faire* philosophy—"that government is best which governs least." These political ideas suited the temper and needs of the country and especially the economically dominant groups.[3]

If legislative jealousy of administration, and preference for a *laissez-*

---

[3] David M. Levitan, "The Responsibility of Administrative Officials in a Democratic Society," *Political Science Quarterly,* 61, 1946, pp. 562, 563.

faire philosophy, were forces militating against strong executive government, they were offset in significant degree by an earlier and unsuccessful legislative effort to go it alone.

Congress had from 1775 to 1781 sought to administer the government first through congressional committees, and then through boards selected by Congress and containing congressional representation.[4] The transition from committee administration to boards began with the establishment of the Board of War and Ordinance in 1776, followed by the Boards of Treasury and of Admiralty in 1779. After 1780, however, Congress, in the light of its unsatisfactory experience with administration by boards, tended to create departments headed by a single man. Hence the Department of Foreign Affairs in 1781 with the Secretary of Foreign Affairs at its head, and shortly thereafter the Departments of War, Finance, and Marine, and lastly a Treasury Department headed by a Superintendent of Finance. But so great was the legislature's reluctance to surrender direct administrative responsibility, that by 1789 only the Departments of War and Foreign Affairs remained under the supervision of a single head. Samuel Adams' preference for committee administration had prevailed for the time being over Hamilton's advocacy of administration by executive departments.[5]

Since 1789 we have experienced a trend toward strong executive government. Commenting upon contemporary reaction to the trend, David Truman has said that "the shift of initiative toward the executive" has been "unwelcome in many quarters and regarded as insufficient in others." [6] Historically, it has been uneven and ambiguous. And, of course, it is with the shift of responsibility for direct administration from legislative committee to executive department that the need for legislative oversight arises.

The trend is given off-handed sanction in the Constitution with its Article II clause permitting the President to "require the Opinion, in writing, of the principal Officer in each of the executive Depart-

---

[4] The colonists, of course, had been accustomed to being ruled by boards. Indeed the British Board of Trade was, at various times, the principal governing agency of the Colonies. Lloyd M. Short, *The Development of National Administrative Organizations in the United States* (Baltimore, Md.: The Johns Hopkins Press, 1923), Chapter II *passim*. It is also interesting to note that what many commentators have regarded as uniquely characteristic of the American legislative process, namely the committee system, has been with us from the very start, and we first attempted to govern ourselves directly through congressional committees.

[5] *Ibid.*

[6] *The Congressional Party: A Case Study* (New York: John Wiley & Sons, Inc., 1959), p. 7.

ments, upon any Subject relating to the Duties of their respective offices." But if the President could require the opinion in writing of the heads of departments, the Congress assumed exclusive authority to create such departments. In doing so, it continued to display a grudging attitude toward turning responsibility for supervision of executive departments over to the President. In its early organic acts creating executive departments, Congress recognized the responsibility of department heads to the President only in those cases, such as the Departments of State, War, and Navy, where they dealt with functions which were assigned to the President under the Constitution. In the cases of the Treasury Department, the Post Office, and as late as 1849, the Interior Department, the department heads were subjected to congressional direction.[7]

These historical allusions are relevant to a discussion of the theory of legislative oversight principally because they show Congress groping its way toward an elaboration of the various alternative patterns of legislative-executive relations within the context of a system of distributed powers.[8] At varying times and to varying degrees, Congress has (1) indicated a preference for administering its own laws, (2) appeared willing to rely upon executive agencies for such administration, subject to congressional supervision and even day-to-day participation, and (3) seemed to recognize the desirability of making executive agencies directly responsible to the President and subject to retrospective review by the Congress.

---

[7] Edward S. Corwin, *The President: Office and Powers, 1787-1957* (4th rev. ed; New York: New York University Press, 1957), pp. 31, and 83-84.

[8] It is not with any thought of introducing a profundity that the point is made that it may be more useful to talk of distributed powers than to talk of separation and balance of powers. In talking of distributed powers we employ a generic term which encompasses the federalist principle as well as that of separation and balance of powers, an analytical convenience, for any theory of legislative oversight must pay heed to both. It is necessary only to compare the distributing clause, Article 30 of Part One of the Massachusetts Constitution of 1780 with the Madisonian definition of the basic criterion of separation of powers in *Federalist No. 47* in order to see that the framers did not intend the wall separating the three branches of government to be either excessively high or impregnable. Article 30 reads: "In the government of this Commonwealth, the legislative department shall never exercise the executive and judicial powers, or either of them: the executive shall never exercise the legislative and judicial powers, or either of them: the judicial shall never exercise the legislative and executive powers, or either of them: to the end it may be a government of laws and not of men." This contrast with Madison's well-known statement to the effect that "The accumulation of all powers, legislative, executive, and judiciary, in the same hands, whether of one, a few, or many, and whether hereditary, self-appointed, or elective, may justly be pronounced the very definition of tyranny."

The Concept of Legislative Oversight

Forms of oversight

THE contemporary Congress has been called by Allen Drury a "bill-machine." [9] Undeniably, a vital function of all democratic legislatures is "the authoritative allocation of values for ... society." [10] Equally vital, and intimately related to the function of allocating values, is the function of oversight—"Making certain the legislative programs are properly administered by the executive branch." [11] Still a third function is that of representation, which, as Friedrich and Finer emphasize, is closely linked with the concept of responsible government.[12] In other words, it is the function of modern legislatures both to sense and to represent the "will" of the people—whether they act as agents, as virtual, or as actual repre-

---

[9] Allen Drury, *A Senate Journal, 1943-45* (New York: McGraw-Hill Book Company, Inc., 1963), p. 12.

[10] David Easton, *The Political System: An Inquiry into the State of Political Science* (New York: Alfred A. Knopf, 1953), p. 129.

[11] Joseph S. Clark, *Congress: The Sapless Branch* (New York: Harper & Row, Publishers, 1964), pp. 82-83.

[12] ". . . [R]epresentation is closely linked to responsible conduct. If A represents B, he is presumed to be responsible *to* B, that is to say, he is answerable to B for what he says and does. In modern parlance, responsible government and representative government have therefore almost come to be synonymous." Carl J. Friedrich, *Constitutional Government and Democracy* (rev. ed.; Boston: Ginn and Co., 1950), pp. 263-64. ". . . [G]enerally speaking, democratic theorists have sought something labeled alternatively 'responsible government' or 'representative government.' These are not coincident, but are very nearly so. It is not merely pedantry which requires it to be emphasized that responsibility is the chief and wider aim, and representativeness merely a convenient means to attain this. There are governments in which representative assemblies participate, but are so hampered in various ways that governments cannot be called responsible." Herman Finer, *Theory and Practice of Modern Government* (rev. ed.; New York: Henry Holt and Co., 1949), p. 219.

sentatives [13]—and also to be responsible to the people not only for their own conduct but also for that of the administrative units which they themselves have created and designated to carry out specific tasks.

A necessary concomitant of a democracy's reliance upon legislatively created executive agencies to fulfill legislatively defined policies is a concept of administrative responsibility. "The problem of the responsibility of administrative officials in a democracy is the very crux of the problem of the maintenance of the democratic system." [14] One of the most persistently vexatious questions in American political experience has been to determine the desirable positions of the President and the Congress in relation to each other, with respect to policymaking, to the performance of the representational function, and more especially to the maintenance of responsible administration.[15] It has not yet been answered and probably never will be answered definitively.

We have distinguished what might be called the legislative, the representational, and the oversight functions of Congress. We have also indicated the three historical approaches which Congress has from time to time evidenced in its relations with the executive. While it is feasible to distinguish the three approaches conceptually, in practice they necessarily overlap. Indeed the function of legislative oversight may be conducted in part through the actual process of legislation. Note, for example, Hyneman's view to the effect that insofar as legislation "regulates the conduct of administration," it constitutes a form of oversight.

The determination of what the government shall do involves the definition of the tasks which the bureaucracy shall perform. The definition and assignment of these tasks may be regarded as the most important form of direction and control to which the bureaucracy is subjected.[16]

Thus a taxonomy of techniques of legislative oversight, employing as the principal discriminating factor the degree to which each technique takes the form of formal patterned institutional behavior,

---

[13] Alfred de Grazia, *Public and Republic* (New York: Alfred Knopf, 1951).

[14] Levitan, *op. cit.,* p. 566.

[15] "Administration which is responsible is lacking in the elements of bad faith, arbitrariness, or capriciousness. It constitutes a reasoned effort, in good faith, to approximate the legislative intent." Cornelius P. Cotter and J. Malcolm Smith, "Administrative Accountability to Congress: The Concurrent Resolution," *The Western Political Quarterly,* 9, 1956, pp. 955, 966.

[16] Charles S. Hyneman, *Bureaucracy in a Democracy* (New York: Harper & Brothers, 1950), pp. 137, 78.

might be anchored at one end by formal legislation.   At the other we might find highly informal but influential contacts between individual legislators or their staff and administrative agencies; and on occasion we might even find the agencies anticipating the preferences of Congress and patterning their conduct accordingly.[17]

If we were to attempt briefly and incompletely to fill the void between the two extremes of congressional oversight, we would include such methods as the following: the grant or withholding of senatorial consent to appointments or to treaties; the introduction and possibly debate of resolutions censoring or attempting to check the behavior of an administrative agency, or to "correct" what the Congress regards as an "erroneous" interpretation of legislative intent by an agency or by the Supreme Court; the introduction, debate, and possibly adoption of a concurrent or simple resolution enabling the executive to act, or withholding approval for executive action, as provided for in a parent statute such as the Reorganization Acts; performance of formal control function assigned to committee by legislation (such as the power to approve or disapprove the projected sale of military property); investigation and report by a select committee; hearings and reports by standing legislative committees

---

[17] Such efforts to anticipate and cater to, or ward off, legislative reactions can, of course, lead to highly irresponsible behavior. Joseph W. Bishop, Jr., writes, "It is one thing for a cabinet office to defend a decision which, however just, offends the prejudices of a powerful Congressman and, very probably, a highly vocal section of the public; it is quite another thing for a middle aged, middle-ranking civil servant, who needs his job, to do so." "The Executive's Right of Privacy: An Unresolved Question," *Yale Law Journal*, 66, 1957, pp. 487-88.

One example of an administrator's willingness to perjure himself and do injustice to another in order to avoid senatorial wrath came to light in 1955. William A. Gallagher, a Justice Department attorney, it developed, had gone before a federal grand jury and secured the indictment of a State Department employee on grounds of perjury. The employee had testified under oath before a Loyalty Security Board that he had never been a Communist party member or carried a Communist party card, or held Communist party meetings in his home. Gallagher secured the indictment by informing the grand jury that the Justice Department had confidential informants who confirmed the testimony of the single witness before the jury. There was no basis for Mr. Gallagher's assertion. Gallagher subsequently was fired in consequence of this behavior.

In a letter to Senator William Langer, who at the time was chairman of the Judiciary Committee, Attorney General Herbert Brownell attempted to account for Gallagher's motives: "Mr. Gallagher indicated that he felt it was better to indict Mr. Lorwin on slight evidence rather than appear before a Senate committee to explain why he had not obtained an indictment." See U.S., Congress, House, *Appropriations Committee, Subcommittee on Department of Justice Appropriations, Hearings, Fiscal 1956*, 1955, pp. 85 ff., p. 89.

and appropriations subcommittees; speech or floor debate unaccompanied by proposed legislation; correspondence, telephone calls, visits by committee chairmen or staff on behalf of committees; similar behavior by individual members of the legislature acting independently.

Oversight and "interference"

This is the range of techniques which may be employed by Congress to influence administrative behavior. Many political scientists and legislators consider it important to examine the legislative purpose in employing such techniques. Their premise is that it is possible to identify improper legislative purposes, the pursuit of which through legislative oversight of administration, is wrong. Thus, as we shall see below, distinctions are drawn between oversight, on the one hand, and "control," "supervision," or "interference," on the other. We briefly review this mode of analysis, although with no thought that the dichotomy between "proper" and "improper" motives, purposes, or objectives of legislative review or administration has operational utility.

There is a further premise underlying criticism of congressional "control," "supervision," and "interference." It is that the proper function of a legislature is to accept and respond to executive leadership. Adherents to this view—which we designate the "executive force" model of executive-legislative relations—would have legislative bodies make minimal changes in the bills and budget requests submitted by the executive. They would restrict legislative initiative in policymaking, and hold within very narrow limits legislative efforts to influence administration. The recommendations which are offered in this symposium are, of course, an effort toward constructing an alternative to the "executive force" model—one in which there is room for a strong executive and a strong legislature.

Joseph Harris states the traditional understanding of the difference between "control" and "oversight."

A distinction is sometimes made between legislative "control" and legislative "oversight" of administration. "Control" in the narrow sense refers to legislative decisions or activities prior to the relevant administrative action. Thus it includes legislative determinations about departmental policies and activities, examination of proposed executive actions in view of a possible legislative veto, and the issuance of authoritative instructions to guide executive officers in the performance of assigned functions. . . . "Oversight," strictly speaking refers to review after the fact. It includes inquiries about policies that are or have been in effect, investigations of past administrative actions, and the calling of executive officers to account for their financial transactions.[18]

Other purposes which legislators individually and collectively may pursue through such action include interfering with, hindering the pursuit, or frustrating the accomplishment of a legislative or administrative policy. Senator Joseph Clark of Pennsylvania tells the story of a southern senator, a subcommittee chairman, who upon learning of a department's intention to withhold federal funds from segregated activities decided that:

. . . there are a good many questions indeed, including the basic one of whether an executive department is entitled to its budget appropriations when it makes such decisions. The Southern chairman of the appropriations subcommittee handling the agency's budget decided that its budget needed a careful and slow examination and that it was asking for all kinds of new programs of dubious merit. In a relatively brief time, the department made a new decision regarding its attitude toward the use of money in segregated programs.[19]

Thus individual legislators, committees, or Congress itself may act "to embarrass and demean . . . officials," or to express disapproval of their behavior, "as when the USIA budget was slashed to bits in 1957 because Arthur Larson, the administrator, made a speech in which—no doubt unwisely—he said, 'Throughout the New and Fair Deals this country was in the grips of a some-what alien philosophy imported from Europe.' " [20] The Hiss Pension Act, and the legislation prohibiting the payment of compensation to certain named government employees are examples of congressional oversight candidly aimed at working retribution upon specific categories of administrative officials or individual officials. The latter piece of legislation, of course, was declared unconstitutional as a bill of attainder in *United States* v. *Lovett*.[21]

Students of the legislative process entertain and freely express pronounced views as to what constitutes proper and improper behavior with respect to legislative-administrative relations. Joseph Harris,

---

[18] *Congressional Control of Administration,* (Washington, D. C.: The Brookings Institution, 1964), p. 9.

[19] *Op. cit.,* p. 88.

[20] *Ibid.,* p. 86.

[21] 328 U.S. 303 (1946).

34

for instance, after distinguishing between legislative oversight and legislative control, goes on to express his disapproval of congressional efforts to control or supervise administration, as distinguished from passing judgment upon it after the fact. In this opinion he enjoys the company of Senator Clark who casts his analysis in terms of the alternatives of legislative oversight or legislative "interference":

> . . . The President's responsibility under the Constitution for the operations of the executive departments and agencies is sometimes disrupted and interfered with to the point of direct challenge. Congressional committees, which can never be held directly accountable, individually or jointly, for the performance of the executive bureaucracy, try to direct administration officials in the day-to-day management of their duties. This tendency to interfere in the details of administration should be resisted by Congress.[22]

Harris provides a list of seven criteria for judging "the suitability, effectiveness, and wisdom of various types of Congressional control of administration."[23] They include: (1) "The test of constitutionality. . . ." (2) "Do the controls provide Congress with the information it needs to discharge its basic responsibilities?" (3) "Are legislative controls effective in bringing to light administrative abuses of arbitrary actions that have occurred in the past, and in preventing them in the future?" (4) "Do the controls operate in a way that allows executive officers the discretion and flexibility they need if they are to administer government activity effectively and be held responsible for results?" (5) "Do the controls as applied in specific cases reflect the policies and wishes of Congress as a body rather than the wishes of a small segment of Congress?" (6) "Do the controls tend to strengthen and enforce the internal disciplines of the Executive branch, or do they duplicate and weaken them?" (7) ". . . is a specific control a suitable one to be exercised by a legislative body?"

It is probably safe to assume that most political scientists are as exacting as Professor Harris and Senator Clark in stipulating what constitutes proper and improper efforts on the part of Congress to influence the course of administration. There is, however, a vocal minority. Charles Hyneman, while recognizing and regretting the

---

[22] *Op. cit.*, pp. 87-88.

[23] *Op. cit.*, pp. 11-13. Lest the reader be confused, although Harris introduces the distinction between control and oversight, disapproving of the former as he defines it, he chooses to use the two terms interchangeably.

abuses and faults of legislative oversight as presently conducted, nonetheless reports with obvious equanimity that Congress:

> . . . participates in day-to-day direction and control of the bureaucracy. It supplies direction and control to the administrative branch by enacting laws; but it also gives direction and control in ways that do not involve the enactment of laws. Some of the things that Congress does differ in no significant way from acts of the President that we commonly call executive or administrative direction and control. The framers of the Constitution clearly intended this to be the case, for they provided that the President should secure the Senate's approval in appointing men to high offices and they gave the two houses authority to remove men from administrative positions by the process of impeachment.[24]

He finds "great advantages to be gained from the continuation of day-to-day direction and control by Congress." [25]

Hyneman stresses a crucial factor that is generally ignored by the advocates of the executive force model, who would have the Congress, at the most, attempt to reinforce the President's efforts to enforce administrative responsibility to himself. That factor pertains to the nature of the pressures which play upon administrative agencies in our form of government. Remove from the equation independent efforts by Congress to influence agency action, and you have merely *altered* the forces operating upon the agency. You have not eliminated them, and there is no reason to believe that you have improved their composition, by whatever standard judgment is made. The agency would still be subject to pressures—from private interest groups, from individuals, and from its constituency or constituencies, not to mention its own conception of its appropriate role. You would merely have deprived Congress of an opportunity to exert countervailing influence. This is, of course, precisely the objective of adherents to the executive force model.

One is reminded of the administrative Elysium described by Lewis J. Caldwell, the first general counsel of the Federal Radio Commission. He humorously proposed the following statute as "my dream of a perfect radio statute":

> Be it enacted by the Senate and House of Representatives of the United States of America in Congress assembled:
>
> Section 1. That a licensing authority is hereby created and established to be known as the Radio Czar of America.

---

24 *Op. cit.*, pp. 158-59.
25 *Ibid.*, p. 170.

Section 2. The Radio Czar created by Section 1 shall do the best he can.

Section 3. For the purpose of this Act the United States is divided into two zones, as follows:

The first zone shall embrace the area comprised within a circle having a radius of one block to be drawn around the office of the Radio Czar; the second zone shall comprise the rest of the United States, its territories and possessions.

Section 4. It is hereby expressly forbidden that any Senator, Congressman, politician, president of a women's club, or broadcaster shall set foot within the first zone, under penalty of capital punishment.[26]

None of the critics of legislative superintendence or control, as distinguished from legislative oversight, take Caldwell's view, either in humor or in earnest. Nevertheless, it does illustrate the ridiculous extremes to which it is in theory possible to go in pursuing the ideal of an administration free from day-to-day pressures exerted by Congress.

Oversight and legislative role perceptions

Interested as individual members and some committees of Congress may be in overseeing administration—albeit in an episodic and sometimes capricious manner—the fact is that legislators themselves generally do not tend to define the function of oversight as a principal legislative role.

Wahlke, Eulau, and associates, found ample confirmation of this fact with regard to state legislatures:

> In the four legislatures we are studying [California, New Jersey, Ohio, Tennessee], the major "object of the game" is recognized to be "legislation," the making of certain types of authoritative decisions. Other purposes, functions, and objectives of legislative activity subsidiary, complementary, or independent of this there may be. But in these states the individual governing his actions wholly by these incidental objectives and not at all by the principal task of lawmaking is not considered to be acting as a legislator at all.[27]

Recognizing the allowances which have to be made for the varying

---

[26] "The Standard of Public Interest, Convenience or Necessity as Used in Radio Act 1927," *Air Law Review*, 1, 1930, p. 259.

[27] John C. Wahlke, Heinz Eulau, William Buchanan, and LeRoy C. Ferguson, *The Legislative System: Exploration in Legislative Behavior* (New York: John Wiley and Sons, Inc., 1962), p. 136.

constituencies of national and state legislators, and the fact that the former is a full-time and the latter a part-time position, we hazard the guess that this finding would be confirmed for the national legislature were a study made—which only goes to reinforce Drury's view of the contemporary Congress as a "bill machine."

Ironically, if Hyneman is correct in his surmise that Congress exercises more influence over administrative agencies on a day-to-day basis than does the President, Congress nevertheless tends to look to the President for legislative leadership to an extent which tends to undermine its independence in defining the tasks of administration and supervising the work of the agencies. Matthews found that:

> Modern presidents are expected to lead Congress. This expectation, with all of its ambiguities, is as widespread on Capitol Hill as anywhere else. . . . [F]ew, if any, senators expressed opposition to presidential leadership as such, rather, if they objected at all, it was to the direction, ineffectiveness, or lack of legislative "leadership" from the White House.[28]

Thus any proposals for a "legislative force" model of oversight must deal with the problem of legislative role perception with particular reference to Congress' view of its relationship with the President.

Wahlke and Eulau point out that "historical conceptions of what is appropriate legislative behavior may be at variance with actual requirements of the contemporary position of the legislature in the structure of power."[29] The principal problem of reform may well turn out to have little to do with the existence or innovation of appropriate techniques. Rather, it may be to endow the legislator with the awareness that precisely because it is necessary in modern times to vest broad discretion in administrative officials, it is all the more necessary for him to exercise regularized and continuous oversight over their activities if we are to avoid "uncontrolled and unaccountable power."[30]

A two-player, zero-sum game?

Presumably presidential-congressional relationships are not subject to interpretation as a two-player, zero-sum game. Strengthening the legislature will not necessarily detract from the power and effectiveness of the President—indeed it may enhance both.

---

[28] Donald R. Matthews, *U.S. Senators and Their World* (Chapel Hill: The University of North Carolina Press, 1960), pp. 140-41.

[29] *Op. cit.*, p. 263.

[30] Levitan, *op. cit.*, p. 579.

Employing a simile which antedates the day of game theory but approximates the notions expressed in game theory, Lawrence Chamberlain concluded on the basis of his study of the legislative process that it "is not like a seesaw where as one end goes down the other must automatically go up. It is, rather, like a gasoline engine which operates most efficiently when all of its cylinders are functioning. When the President becomes unusually active, there is a tendency to assume that the congressional cylinder has ceased to function. Such is not necessarily the case." [31] The concept of legislative oversight of administration, with its implications of legislative "control," "supervision," and the like is all too readily evocative of notions of legislature *versus* executive—by no means the most fruitful approach to dealing with legislative-executive relationships.

Joseph Harris, in the most authoritative book thus far produced on the topic of legislative oversight of administration in the United States, invokes the idea that one cannot serve two masters to support his proposition that the Congress cannot legitimately ask the Bureau of the Budget to help it to perform its job of legislative oversight. Also, he has based upon the parliamentary model the suggestion that if the legislature significantly alters the President's budget recommendations, it hardly can call the Chief Executive to account for his administration of the resultant programs. It would seem to follow that if a President cannot be held accountable to the legislature for a program which it has chosen to approve only in modified form, the President must then either resign or else have power to dismiss the legislature.

But in practice all men serve more than one master. Indeed, life as we know it, or tend to prefer it, is not characterized by the existence of masters whose overweening jealousy is such that a man cannot serve more than one. Thus a member of the Bureau of the Budget is really performing an anticipatory task for the legislature when he reviews—with a view to reduction—the budget estimates of a given department. The Bureau of the Budget may be regarded as intermediary between the line operating administrative agencies and Congress, while the General Accounting Office is seen as fulfilling a function that is not quite legislative nor completely administrative. Thus it is evident that in a complex political system such as our own it would be unnecessarily dogmatic to insist that agencies

---

[31] Lawrence H. Chamberlain, "The President, Congress, and Legislation," *Political Science Quarterly*, 61, 1946, pp. 43-44.

under the aegis of one branch of government cannot occasionally serve another simultaneously.

Oversight and party politics

Legislators are partisans; the President and his retinue usually are politicians, not so much by force of circumstances, as by choice, instinct, and long experience. Evaluation of the conduct of programs within the administration, whether made by individual legislators, committees, or one or both houses of Congress, cannot therefore be shorn of intended or unintended partisan overtones.

The President's party adherents in the Congress may, as Truman finds, be given coherence "because of and in response to [his] initiatives." [32] Yet this does not mean that he will not experience bitter opposition to elements of his program from factions of his own party. Nor does it mean that those supporting his legislative program [33] among his party's delegation on the Hill, will refrain from conducting a potentially or intentionally embarrassing scrutiny of the administration.

The oversight role of the opposition party, when the President's party dominates both houses of Congress, remains murky in practice and in theory. And, of course, whatever the appropriate role may be, it is presumed by many to vary for foreign programs and for domestic. Moreover, the interests, areas of tolerance, and vigor of activity of legislators will in some degree reflect their perception of constituency interests—further complicating efforts to discern durable patterns.

Thus it is that a President must juggle a number of variables in order to achieve his legislative program. Not only will he develop and seek to employ his party's leadership on the Hill toward that end, but, on occasion at least, he will seek common cause with the opposition leadership toward forging a transitory majority.

---

[32] *Op. cit.*, pp. 289-90. Eisenhower wryly commented on CBS Reports, in October 1961, that when he came into office "there was not a single Republican in the Senate . . . who ever served under a Republican President." As a result, he found that they were so "raised in the tradition of antagonism between the Executive and the Legislature" that it was "very, very difficult for Republican Senators, at first, to remember that their job was now to cooperate with the President and he with them." Arthur B. Tourtellot, *The Presidents on Presidency* (Garden City: Doubleday & Company, Inc., 1964), p. 261.

[33] The concept of the President's legislative program, taken for granted today, is of relatively recent origin. It would be digressive to attempt to narrate its development in this chapter, but see Richard E. Neustadt, "Presidency and Legislation: The Growth of Central Clearance," *The American Political Science Review*, September 1954, and Richard E. Neustadt, "Presidency and Legislation: Planning the President's Program," *The American Political Science Review*, December 1955.

In addition to reliance upon party leadership in Congress, Presidents in recent decades have increased the number of assistants for legislative liaison; their duties involve not merely the cultivation of members of the President's party in Congress, but of all members of Congress. The Kennedy experience is illustrative. Lawrence F. O'Brien, then the President's assistant for liaison, found that his initial job and his "most difficult chore was to learn the political tendencies and problems" of the 435 members of the House and the 100 members of the Senate. It was not a mere matter of conveying presidential preference to the party leadership in the House and the Senate and of relying upon them to whip the party troops into line. "In February, 1961, just a few weeks after Kennedy became President, O'Brien met privately in a suite at the Mayflower Hotel in downtown Washington with Bolling, Thompson, and Carl Elliott of Alabama for a detailed discussion of the House members." This group arrived at a reckoning to the effect that "of the 435 members of the House, roughly 180 could be safely counted as favoring the President's domestic legislation. Another 180 could just as surely be counted as opposed to it. In doubt were the remaining seventy-odd Representatives. They could be persuaded; they were the same group counted by the lobbyists as 'negotiable.'" At this point the Democrats controlled the House by a 263 to 174 margin, "but party designation did not accurately indicate the political tendencies of the individual members." A President's legislative chief could not neglect the opportunity to forge any kind of *ad hoc* coalition that would enable him to gain legislative favor for any element of the President's program. This picture is anathema to the "responsible party government" bloc of political scientists. But it is the prevailing system.[34]

Various schemes have been offered to formalize and institutionalize the relationship between the President and the House leadership beyond that of the relatively informal Big Four or Big Six meetings of today. The Legislative Reorganization Act of 1946 approved policy committees for each party to be maintained at public expense in the Senate. But at the instigation of the Democratic and Republican leaders of the House it did not make similar provision for that body. To remedy this defect, Robert LaFollette writing in the *American Political Science Review* in 1947 proposed a "Joint Legislative-Executive Council" composed of party policy committees in each house, the leaders of the President's party on the Hill and the

---

[34] MacNeil, *op. cit.*, pp. 257-59.

Chief Executive himself. He hoped that this would set up a stronger bond of policy by acquainting the legislative leaders with the views of the executive. He could permit Cabinet members to sit in on council discussions of proposed legislative programs.

The "policy" committees in the Senate have not developed as policy-formulating bodies for the two parties.[35] Yet, in the absence of statutory support and government funds, the Republican young Turks in the House have developed a Republican Policy Committee through which they seek to define party positions and to provide the basis for a "loyal opposition" type of partisan oversight of administration. Northern and liberal Democrats in the House have established a Democratic Study Group which may prove parallel in purpose and activity to the Republican Policy Committee.[36] These developments are in embryonic stage, and it would be rash to extrapolate from them. The national committees of the two parties have neither acknowledged any responsibility nor evidenced any talent for supplementing the marginal efforts at partisan oversight in the legislature.

Thus we conclude that party has not proved to be a systematic and continuing fulcrum for legislative oversight of administration. Domination of the Congress by the President's party does not afford him substantial protection against potentially embarrasing, albeit episodic and unsystematic legislative inquiries into the conduct of administration. Conversely, domination of either or both houses by the opposition party does not pose a particular threat in this regard. To the extent to which he chooses to attempt to ward off legislative efforts at oversight of facets of his administration, the President is left with the same partially structured and partially chaotic avenues of appeal that lie before him as he pursues his legislative program in Congress.

---

[35] Hugh A. Bone, *Party Committees and National Politics* (Seattle: University of Washington Press, 1958).

[36] On the development of the Republican Policy Committee in the House, see Charles O. Jones, *Party and Policy-Making* (New Brunswick: Rutgers University Press, 1964). Hugh A. Bone comments on the Democratic Study, Group in his *American Politics and the Party System* (3rd ed.; New York: McGraw-Hill Book Company), pp. 255-56.

Varieties of Legislative Oversight

Impeachment

VARIOUS authors have singled out various specific constitutional grants of power to Congress as a basis for legislative oversight. Neil MacNeil reports that the house has impeached only 12 men, and the Senate convicted but four of them, in the 170 years of the history of the House of Representatives, and that no impeachment has been voted since 1936. Nevertheless, he holds that "the power to impeach has been implicit in the House's right to investigate the whole of the federal bureaucracy." [37]

Congress' power to impeach can be applied only to the President, Vice President, and members of the federal judiciary. Thus it would seem that any use of the impeachment process to check the behavior of administrative agencies would have to rest upon charging the President or Vice President with high crimes and misdemeanors as they relate to those agencies. If, therefore, impeachment is of importance as a vehicle for legislative oversight it is only as a Damocles sword hanging over the heads of but one or two members of the executive branch. Perhaps the simile which Lord Bryce used is more appropriate. "Impeachment," he wrote, "is the heaviest piece of artillery in the congressional arsenal, but because it is so heavy it is unfit for ordinary use. It is like a hundred-ton gun which needs complex machinery to bring it into position, an enormous charge of powder to fire it, and a large mark to aim at." [38]

Organizing the government

Again, it has been said that the implicit constitutional power of Congress to organize the executive branch of the government pro-

---

[37] James Bryce, *The American Commonwealth* (3rd ed.; New York: The Macmillan Company, 1901), Vol. 1, p. 211.

[38] *Op cit.,* p. 179.

vides the fundamental basis for the practice of legislative oversight. This view was vehemently denied by Presidents Jackson and Cleveland, both of whom defied congressional action based upon the premise. It was also, of course, the source of the disagreement between Congress and the President leading to the impeachment of Andrew Johnson; Congress took the position that if it could create and abolish offices, it could stipulate the conditions of appointment and removal. As late as 1920, President Wilson vetoed legislation because it provided for removal of an agency head and his deputy by concurrent resolution, [39] and in the case of *Myers* v. *United States,* 272 U.S. 52 (1926) the Supreme Court seemingly laid to rest the proposition that Congress may constitutionally lay limits upon the right of the President to remove a person from executive office.

The chief way in which Congress in recent years has exercised legislative oversight under its power to organize the executive branch has been through the process of reviewing the organization and functioning of the administrative agencies of the government with the view to formulating recommendations for change. In recent decades this has taken the form of congressional enactment of reorganization legislation bringing into being study groups such as the two Hoover Commissions and permitting the President to submit reorganization plans to the Congress. The plans become valid unless disapproved within the prescribed time by concurrent resolution or by simple resolution of one house—the statutes have at various times provided for either. But note that while this has proved to be an effective way for the legislature to study with relative objectivity the performance of federal agencies and the need for change, it has been accompanied by a tendency to permit the President to frame the basic recommendations and submit them to Congress. Thus the initiative remains in the White House. This pattern has not developed to the exclusion of direct legislation reorganizing or creating new agencies, such as the Department of Health, Education, and Welfare, and the Department of Housing and Urban Development.

While reorganization acts tends to look to the executive for initiative, they provide Congress with secondary opportunities for oversight beyond the investigations carried out by the reorganization commission. These opportunities come when the President submits his recommendations in the form of reorganization plans. Congress has been highly selective in approving and disapproving reorganiza-

---

[39] Budget and Accounting Act of 1920, 59 *Congressional Record,* pp. 7660, 7662.

tion plans. Legislative disapproval of proposed policy or of personalities can determine the fate of reorganization plans. It is quite clear, for example, that President Truman was denied approval for his plan to elevate the then Federal Security Agency to the status of a cabinet department because Congress disapproved of Federal Security Administrator Oscar R. Ewing's activities on behalf of a national health insurance plan.

Advice and consent

We have referred to the removal power as it relates to those powers of oversight which Congress derives by virtue of its power to organize the government. There is also, of course, the Senate's power of advice and consent on certain executive appointments, which gives that body and its committees a degree of influence over executive choices. In effect this might be called "pre-oversight," for denial of consent presumably is indicative of legislative apprehension that the prospective appointee might perform in office in a manner displeasing to it.

The importance of this opportunity for pre-review is indicated by David J. Danelski's study of the appointment of Justice Pierce Butler.[40] It is also indicated by the care with which the Senate Judiciary Committee reviewed the qualifications of Lewis D. Brandeis for office and the Senate debated them. In 1930 the Senate refused to confirm the appointment of Judge Parker to the Supreme Court in response, as Schmidhauser puts it, to his "faithful adherence as lower court magistrate to the 'anti-labor' doctrines of the highest court of the land." [41] Perhaps the most dramatic recent exercise of the senatorial power occurred when Lewis L. Strauss was nominated by President Eisenhower in 1959, for appointment as

---

[40] *A Supreme Court Justice Is Appointed* (New York: Random House, 1964), see particularly Chapter 7.

[41] John R. Schmidhauser, *Constitutional Law in the Political Process* (Chicago: Rand McNally & Co., 1963), p. 81. Further discussion of this subject is provided by Corwin, who writes "if the President in nominating to an office within a state fails to consult the preferences of the Senator or Senators of his own party from that state, he is very likely to see the appointment defeated on an appeal to the Senate by the slighted member or members. Reciprocally, the Senate will ordinarily interpose no objection to the President's nominees for Cabinet or diplomatic posts. While any attempt to find basis in the written Constitution for this interesting understanding would be disappointing, since it is the advice and consent of the Senate that the Constitution requires and not that of individual Senators, yet no usage of the Constitution affecting the powers of the President is more venerable." *Op. cit.,* p. 73.

Secretary of Commerce. This was the first, and thus far the only, rejection of a nomination to cabinet status in the post-World War II era.

While the power to withhold consent would seem to be rather heavy artillery, in Bryce's terms, it can be employed with great versatility. David Farnsworth reports that:

Even though the Senate does not often strike down appointments made by the executive, the controversy that occasionally develops over a nomination and the rare case of a rejection of a nomination by the Committee serve to remind the executive that it is not a free agent in making nominations. Moreover, in evaluating the extent to which the Committee and the Senate are a restraint upon the executive, it is unrealistic to consider only the number of nominations rejected and the number of nominations not reported by the Committee. From 1947 to 1956, three nominations of ambassadors sent to the Senate were withdrawn by the executive before any conclusive action could be taken by the Committee or the Senate. . . .

The nomination of Mark Clark as ambassador to the Vatican was withdrawn after opposition developed on two points. First, opponents of the nomination pointed out that an 1870 law stated that no military officer on active duty could hold a civilian post. An amendment to this law would have been necessary before Clark could have qualified for the post. The second point of opposition was on the grounds that an ambassador to the Vatican was, in effect, the support of a religion, which is expressly prohibited by the Constitution. After two months of such controversy, Clark requested and received the withdrawal of his nomination.

The executive thus on occasion has used the technique of withdrawing nominations having difficulty in the Senate to avoid the embarrassing and status-damaging situation of a rejected nomination or, if it should be approved, the show of open opposition to an executive nominee. The executive does not, of course, always use this technique when opposition develops, but it is available. Such withdrawals must also be considered as a part of the Senate's and the Committee's restraint on the nominating power of the executive.[42]

---

[42] David N. Farnsworth, *The Senate Committee on Foreign Relations* (Urbana, Illinois: University of Illinois Press, 1961), pp. 58-59.

Further, the *Congressional Quarterly* provides a "box-score of nominations" for 1947 through 1963, which suggests that the number of withdrawn nominations and the total of unconfirmed nominations can be significant, although the total number of nominations actually refused is miniscule.[43] Hearings and debate on executive nominations may provide occasion for expressing personal objections to the individual concerned, for alleging conflict of interest, for opposing the nominee on the grounds that he entertains policy preferences which are too "liberal" or too "conservative," or for reviewing and expressing objection to the administration's policies. Also, a Senate dominated by the party in opposition to that of an outgoing President may, as occurred in 1960, hold up large numbers of appointments in order to reserve them for his successor.[44]

The appropriations process

It has been reliably estimated that upwards of nine-tenths of the work of Congress is concerned with spending issues.[45] This estimate suggests that the greatest potential for congressional oversight of administration lies in the appropriations process and indeed, the history of congressional exercises of the so-called spending power also suggests that legislative oversight of administrative spending has been one of the most recurrent and vexatious issues in American government.[46]

Section 7. All Bills for raising Revenue shall originate in the House of Representatives; but the Senate may propose or concur with amendments as on other Bills.

*   *   *

Section 9. No money shall be drawn from the Treasury but in Consequence of Appropriations made by Law; and the regular Statement and Account of the Receipts and Expenditures of all public Money shall be published from time to time.

---

43 Congressional Quarterly, Inc., *Congress and the Nation 1955-1964: A Review of Government and Politics* (Washington, D. C.: Congressional Quarterly Service, 1965), Part II, p. 102a.

44 In *Congress and the Nation*, Part II, pp. 103a-111a, the *Congressional Quarterly* discusses briefly each of the major controversial nominations of 1945-63.

45 This estimate is attributed to George Galloway by Robert Ash Wallace in *Congressional Control of Federal Spending* (Detroit: Wayne State University Press, 1960), p. vii.

46 See Lucius Wilmerding, Jr., *The Spending Power: A History of the Efforts of Congress to Control Expenditures* (New Haven: Yale University Press, 1943).

Two related problems with respect to appropriations have plagued us since the first Congress met in March 1789, and they show no signs of going away. One is the definition of standards (in terms of object and procedure) for expenditure of appropriated funds; the second is to hold the executive to the expenditure of funds solely for the purpose for which they have been appropriated.[47] With respect to the first problem, we continue today to echo the Hamiltonian-Madisonian dispute as to the specificity with which Congress should appropriate funds. Hamilton preferred appropriations under broad heads, giving large discretion to the executive; Madison and Gallatin, taking the Republican view, preferred detailed appropriations.[48] There has always been considerable dispute as to which of the two approaches results in the more responsible executive expenditure of funds.

On the second problem, we have the extreme examples of Lincoln's expenditure of unappropriated funds, and Eisenhower's refusal to expend appropriated funds on at least one occasion when he disagreed with Congress as to the wisdom of such expenditure. In recent decades Congress has aggravated the problem of executive accountability by appropriating funds with the terms of expenditure so vaguely stated as to give the executive carte blanche; by making initial appropriations for agencies which are to become self-supporting; and by permitting agency borrowing from the Treasury for self-supporting programs.[49]

Wilmerding makes the sweeping, but seemingly well-documented, statement that the devices used by Congress as instruments of control of expenditure have failed, and that Congress has never had adequate means of determining whether its financial authority has been respected. "Congress has not yet succeeded in devising a system of procedure stringent enough to render efficacious its unquestioned right to control the public expenditure. I say procedure, for it seems clear that what is needed is not a new right but a prompt and searching remedy." [50]

If this is true, it is not for lack of effort. As early as 1795 we find the national legislature requiring that any sum remaining unexpended for more than two years after the expiration of the calendar year in which it was appropriated was to go into a surplus

---

[47] *Ibid.*, pp. 4-7.
[48] *Ibid.*, Chapter 3, especially pp. 48-51.
[49] Cf. Government Corporation Control Act of 1945, 59 Stat. 597.
[50] *Ibid.*, p. 307.

fund. The purpose of this legislation was to put an end to the executive practice of carrying over unexpended, but appropriated, funds from one year to succeeding years, and thus supplementing current appropriations to suit executive convenience. The next object of legislative attack was the administrative practice of using funds for purposes other than those for which they were appropriated. A law of 1809 required that "the sum appropriated by law for each branch of expenditures in the several departments shall be solely applied to the objects for which they are respectively appropriated, and to no other." But this requirement was more breached than honored.

New legislation seemed merely to invite new administrative efforts at circumvention. This, taken with a rudimentary theory and practice of legislative oversight of spending, which persisted throughout the entire century, spelled the inevitable breakdown in the system of specific appropriations obviously intended by Congress. To the extent to which Congress put an end to the mingling of funds and the carrying forward of balances, department heads came to rely upon requests for deficiency appropriations, on the assumption that Congress was not going to permit essential functions to lapse for want of funds. Difficulties in estimating the actual needs of departments, and the tendency to exhaust prematurely one year's appropriation to pay the preceding year's deficiency caused even well-behaved agencies to run short. Delays in passing the annual appropriations bills aggravated the financial situation of executive departments, and drove them to borrowing private funds in anticipation of congressional appropriations. This was done in secret, and Congress was deceived by such concealments, all in the name of necessity.

The situation did not radically improve after the Civil War. New legislation in 1868 and 1878 was more reassuring to the Congress than influential upon executive action. And efforts at retrospective review of executive spending practices was episodic and partisan.[51]

More adequate reform lay in the next century. It is a measure of the consistency of the problem of rationalizing executive requests for funds, and legislative review, both of those requests and the subsequent expenditure of appropriated funds, that any President of the nineteenth century could have uttered the admonition which President Taft sent to Congress in 1912:

The reports of expenditures required by law are unsystematic, lack uniformity of classification, and are incapable of being sum-

[51] *Ibid.*, pp. 118-36.

marized so as to give to the Congress, to the President, or to the people a picture of what has been done, and of costs in terms either of economy of purchase or efficiency of organization in obtaining results.

The summaries of expenditures required by law to be submitted by the Secretary of the Treasury, with estimates, not only do not provide the data necessary to the consideration of questions of policy, but they are not summarized and classified on the same basis as the estimates.

* * *

Instead of the President being made responsible for estimates of expenditures, the heads of departments and establishments are made the ministerial agents of the Congress, the President being called on only to advise the Congress how, in his opinion, expenditures may be reduced or revenues may be increased in case estimated expenditures exceed estimated revenue.

* * *

So long as the method at present prescribed obtains, neither the Congress nor the country can have laid before it a definite understandable program of business, or of governmental work to be financed; nor can it have a well-defined, clearly expressed financial program to be followed; nor can either the Congress or the Executive get before the country the proposals of each in such a manner as to locate responsibility for plans submitted or for results.[52]

Taft's message was based upon a report of the Commission on Economy and Efficiency which Congress financed and the President appointed in 1911. It was to review budgetary procedures abroad and in the United States, and make recommendations for improvements in the budgetary process at the national level. The Commission recommended that Congress enact legislation establishing a budgetary system whereby the President would submit to Congress early in each session a budget for the executive branch. This budget document would be accompanied by a message "setting forth in brief the significance of the proposals to which attention is invited." The law would also require the head of each department or independent agency to submit to the Secretary of the Treasury and Congress "annual reports which . . . would contain detailed accounts of expendi-

---

[52] U.S., Congress, House, *The Need for a National Budget, Message from the President of the United States Transmitting Report of the Commission on Economy and Efficiency,* 62d Congress, 2d Session, House Document 854, pp. 2-4.

tures so classified as to show amounts expended by appropriations, as well as by classes of work [as listed in the budget]." Thus the President would be given control of the budget and the Secretary of the Treasury and Congress would be equipped with the necessary data to audit expenditures for consistency with appropriations.[53]

Such a statute finally was put on the books in 1921. The Budget and Accounting Act of that year created a central budget agency located in the Treasury Department but responsible to the President. The Director and Assistant Director of this new agency—the Bureau of the Budget—were appointed by the President without the requirement of senatorial approval. The Act required the submission of budget estimates to the Bureau, and granted it a right of access to the books and records of executive agencies. It required that the President annually submit the executive budget to Congress on the first day of each regular (annual) session.

The auditing function was to be preformed by the newly established General Accounting Office, independent of the executive branch. The Comptroller General who heads it is appointed by the President with the consent of the Senate. His 15-year term of office and the provision that he may not succeed himself are calculated to render him immune from executive pressure. It is his function to develop suitable accounting methods, to sign warrants covering money into and out of the Treasury, to audit the accounts of the executive agencies, and to be a financial adviser to Congress.[54]

In separate studies Wilmerding and Wallace have enumerated some of the conventions or assumptions which are taken for granted with respect to the appropriation power of Congress. According to Wilmerding (1) "it is the exclusive right of Congress to specify the several objects to which the grants for the year may be applied and to limit the amounts which may be applied to each object"; (2) "it is the duty of the Executive, *except* in cases of urgent necessity, to apply the Congressional grants only to the objects and within the amounts voted"; (3) "in cases of urgent necessity it is the duty of the high offices of government to risk themselves for the public good and, having transcended the appropriation laws, to throw themselves upon the justice of Congress." He finds that the first of these has been recognized throughout the course of American history; the second since the days of Jefferson; and concludes that "the third has

[53] *Ibid.*, pp. 7-8.
[54] Harvey C. Mansfield, *The Comptroller General* (New Haven, Conn.: Yale University Press, 1939).

been prejudiced by some recent doubts—doubts, however, which could arise only in quiet times and then only in minds not fully alive to the responsibilities of executive government." [55]

Wallace, in his study of the appropriations process, assumes the following powers to be associated with congressional control of the purse: (1) "congressional determination of a desirable volume, range, and direction of program activity"; (2) "congressional exercise of independent judgment concerning the financial resources, required by administrative agencies to support effectively such volume, range, and direction of program activity"; (3) "availability of congressional sources of information and analyses as a basis for exercise of independent and informed judgment." [56] In effect, Wallace's assumptions would appear to be an elaboration of the first convention which is listed by Wilmerding. The assumptions voiced by both Wilmerding and Wallace contrast interestingly with Harris' strictures concerning the obligation of Congress to accept the President's budget recommendations if it expects to be entitled to hold him responsible for administration.

A good deal of the criticism which is heaped upon congressional performance of the oversight function through appropriations process relates to the effectiveness with which it performs the functions enumerated by Wallace. Congress is said, for instance, to pass on the President's budget in such a "piecemeal" fashion as to provide "no occasion for a 'great debate' on fiscal policies which would inform and educate the public and fully establish the President's responsibility for his financial program." [57] It is, of course, a classic criticism of the appropriations process that individual subcommittees attempt to review the budget estimates in excessive detail. A concomitant complaint—and both are warranted—is that Congress is asked by the subcommittees to deal with trivia in one realm, while approving uncritically items costing billions of dollars in other realms. Wallace is undoubtedly correct in suggesting that "the idea that Congress should avoid administrative detail is wishful thinking." He goes on to indicate that such ideas probably stem "from havoc wrought, on occasion, by members of Congress who have injuriously meddled in administrative detail purely for partisan or selfish reasons or for reasons based strictly on local interests which are at odds with the national interest." [58]

---

[55] Wilmerding, *op. cit.*, p. 193.
[56] Wallace, *op. cit.*, p. 5.
[57] Harris, *op. cit.*, p. 68.
[58] *Op. cit.*, pp. 15-16.

There are political scientists who are tolerant of the ways of Congress—"the first branch"—to the point of approving the *status quo*. Charles Hyneman, for example, confesses to the view that Congress "does well" those very things concerning which the vast majority of his colleagues agree that it does poorly.[59] There is an alternative view, consistent with what we take to be a pro-legislative bias on Hyneman's part, and that is that Congress might function more effectively by its own standards if it would spend more time and effort defining them, and then apply them. On the matter of legislative scrutiny of detail, for example, the important consideration is whether that scrutiny is systematic and balanced—whether and how such review fits into an overall scheme of legislative purpose.

Inadequate staffing is popularly regarded as one of the chief weaknesses of the appropriations subcommittees. The legislature, we are told, and especially the appropriations subcommittees, do not have staff available adequate to enable collection of the information required for effective functioning. Nevertheless there is a serious question whether there is not a point of diminishing returns in providing increased staff. Kofmehl concludes:

> With a heavy burden of legislative and nonlegislative business, Congress needs staff assistance. Yet the problem of staffing the members and committees of Congress is especially perplexing because of the diffuseness, diversity, and changeability of the internal power structures of Congress and because of the comparatively unique nature of the policymaking and representative functions of members of Congress. Moreover, it is a task fraught with dangerous potentialities not only for Congress but also for the entire governmental system.

> During the period covered, experience amply confirmed the philosophy of the Legislative Reorganization Act of having only a few highly competent professional aides for each standing committee. Keeping the committee staffs small conduced to confining them to their proper sphere and to maintaining their quality and efficiency. Most of the pathologies of staffing appeared among the inflated committee staffs. The statutory allotment of professional staff members for the standing committees seemed to be adequate for most of them.[60]

---

[59] *Bureaucracy in a Democracy, op. cit.,* p. 125, fn. 2.

[60] Kenneth Kofmehl, *Professional Staffs of Congress* (West Lafayette, Indiana: Purdue Research Foundation, 1962), pp. 203, 205.

Two further criticisms of Congress' use of the appropriations process as a means of legislative oversight are germane to the present discussion. First, it is said that Congress is unduly preoccupied with reducing the budget as distinguished from considering its merits. If such reductions are across-the-board they are criticized as too undiscriminating; if accompanied by increases in some programs, they are criticized as invading the executive prerogative.[61] The second criticism is directed at the tendency for appropriations committees to become populated not merely by persons who develop a substantial competence in the area for which the subcommittee is responsible but by congressmen with axes to grind. Thus the tendency for a person eligible for appropriations subcommittee membership and having a naval base in his district is likely to be assigned to the appropriations subcommittee handling Defense requests. There would appear to be need for some set of rules of the game to be applied to decrease incentives to place constituency interest against national, without simultaneously incurring the sacrifice of substantive familiarity with the field.

We have gradually come to the realization that the budget document is "the work plan of the nation." We must belatedly come to an awareness that the process of reviewing that work plan and putting it on the path to realization, is assigned to a Model-T appropriations process operating in an age of digital computers and space missiles. It may be that the group contributing to this symposium do not, collectively, possess the knowledge and competence to frame specific recommendations for reforms of the appropriations process to bring it into step with contemporary needs and opportunities. Such reform is essential, however, and should be the subject of intensive and, if necessary, prolonged inquiry by Congress and students of the legislative process having knowledge of contemporary data collection, storing, and retrieval systems.

For example, it might be possible to computerize the budgetary and appropriations processes. It might also be possible and desirable to depart from the present method of making one-year fiscal July 1-June 30 appropriations on a selective basis; this would permit the appropriations process to mesh more closely with programs, such as weapons development, which are not adaptable to 12-month cycles. These are but two of many changes with which it might be profitable to experiment.

---

[61] See e.g., Senator Clark's expression of concern, *op. cit.*, p. 82.

Congressional access to information from the executive

In 1934, attorneys for the Petroleum Board, an obscure agency within the Interior Department charged with the enforcement of the Petroleum Code under the National Industrial Recovery Act, took action against the Panama and Amazon oil companies for violation of Section 4 of Article III of the Petroleum Code. The government attorneys appealed an unfavorable district court opinion to the Supreme Court.

In the course of preparing the Government's memorandum in connection with the petition for certiorari in the Amazon case, a careful attorney in the Department of Justice took the unusual precaution of checking the published copies of the Petroleum Code, used by both the Government and the industry, with the original copies of the Executive Orders filed in the State Department. To his horror he discovered that when Section 4 of Article III of the Code had been amended in some minor details, the amending order, which stated that "Section 4 is amended to read as follows," was followed by only the first paragraph of the Section. The second paragraph contained the vital provisions making violation of production quotas unlawful. This omission, which, it may be noted, was largely responsible for the subsequent creation of the Federal Register as a publication in which the official version of federal administration orders could. be authoritatively found, was called to the attention of the Court in the Government's memorandum.[62]

The Federal Register Act of 1935 and the Federal Reports Act of 1942 are examples of belated recognition on the part of the federal government of the need to publicize the standards which it is going to apply to private persons and firms. Today some agencies of the federal government, such as the Agricultural Marketing Service in the Department of Agriculture and the Extension Service are primarily concerned with collecting and propagating information. Further, virtually every agency of government is now concerned with its "image"—the agency press officer antedates the congressional liaison officer. But, of course, the government influences the ordinary citizen's perception of his universe as much in the "information" which it withholds as in the information which it propagates. Much of the information which is suppressed is suppressed in accordance with statutes permitting such action.[63] Thus we find the

---

[62] Robert L. Stern, "The Commerce Clause and the National Economy, 1933-1946," *The Harvard Law Review*, 59, 1946, pp. 656-57.
[63] *Ibid.*

federal government vitally influencing the content of the press and. the news periodicals on which congressmen as well as the ordinary citizen inevitably base much of their perception of what contemporary problems are and what are the alternative ways to cope with them.

We have already commented upon the relative inadequacy of sources of information available to congressmen as compared with the executive. Even though the subpoena power is available, and assuming witnesses are well informed and will not plead the Fifth Amendment, a congressman's intuition about the areas in which to inquire may be less sophisticated than that of the administrator whose daily preoccupation is with a much more restricted range of policy-making and whose constituency is almost certainly much less demanding of his time and much less of a periodic threat to his office. But beyond this, from the administration of George Washington on to the present, the executive traditionally has taken the view that it is entitled to refuse to divulge certain information to Congress, revelation being a violation of the confidentiality of the relationship which the President is entitled to enjoy with his subordinates, or would not be in the national interest. Occasionally the Chief Executive will respond to a request for information from a congressional source on a conditional basis, stipulating that it be offered in executive session of a committee, or on a confidential basis.

President Jackson offered one of the early rationalizations of the executive's right to refuse information to Congress:

The executive is a coordinate and independent branch of the Government equally with the Senate, and I have yet to learn under what constitutional authority that branch of the Legislature has a right to require of me an account of any communication, either verbally or in writing, made to the heads of Departments acting as a Cabinet council. As well might I be required to detail to the Senate the free and private conversations I have held with those officers on any subject relating to their duties and my own.

Feeling my responsibility to the American people, I am willing upon all occasions to explain to them the grounds of my conduct, and I am willing upon all proper occasions to give to either branch of the Legislature any information in my possession that can be useful in the execution of the appropriate duties confided to them.

Knowing the constitutional rights of the Senate, I shall be the last man under any circumstances to interfere with them. Knowing those of the Executive, I shall at all times endeavor to maintain them agreeably to the provisions of the Constitution and the solemn oath I have taken to support and defend it.[64]

In an exchange of letters which was included in the hearings of the Subcommittee on Constitutional Rights in 1958, Attorney General William P. Rogers and Congressman George Meader gave classic expression to the opposing executive and legislative views on the right of the executive to withhold information. Rogers argued that on the theory of separation and balance of powers, the executive is a distinct branch of the government with rights that neither of the other two branches may transgress. The President has the exclusive right—indeed the responsibility—to determine what information can be released and what cannot be released to the public or to the Congress on the grounds of national interest. In the view of Representative Meader, the power to decide whether information should be produced is in the hands of Congress, not the President. The argument that the executive has superior insight as to what is and what is not in the public interest is not tenable, and there is, moreover no constitutional authorization for the so-called executive privilege. Executive agencies are supposed to be the servants and not the masters of the people. The power of inquiry is essential to the power of legislating, and if the executive claims the right to withhold information, in effect it is claiming the right to frustrate the legislative power of Congress.[65]

Secrecy in government is a concern not only to legislators but to those associated with the mass media—hence the recurrent congressional investigations of this issue.[66] Testifying before the Constitutional Rights Subcommittee in 1958, Attorney General Rogers distinguished between the right of the public to know and the right of

[64] Special Message to Senate, December 18, 1833, Richardson, III:36; quoted in Tourtellot, *op. cit.*, pp. 202-03.

[65] U.S., Congress, Senate, Committee on the Judiciary, Subcommittee on Constitutional Rights, *Freedom of Information and Secrecy in Government,* Hearings, 85th Congress, 2d Session, March 6, 1958, Part 1, pp. 56-61.

[66] See, for example, U.S., Congress, Senate, Committee on the Judiciary, Subcommittee on Constitutional Rights, *Freedom of Information and Secrecy in Government,* Hearings, 86th Congress, 1st Session, 1959. See also Francis Rourke, "Administrative Secrecy: A Congressional Dilemma," *American Political Science Review,* 54, 1960, pp. 684-85. "Among recent instances where Congress has found executive secrecy a handicap in its efforts to oversee administration, none has gained more publicity that the Dixon-Yates affair. In 1955, Congressional critics of the administration's proposals to finance private construction of a utility plant in the Tennessee Valley for the benefit of the

Congress to know, and codified what he took to be the governing principles with respect to each. With regard to the right of the people to know, he found four principles to prevail:

1. While the people are entitled to the fullest disclosure possible, this right like freedom of speech or press, is not absolute or without limitations. Disclosure must always be consistent with the national security and the public interest.

2. In recognizing a right to withhold information, the approach must be not how much can legitimately be withheld, but rather how little must necessarily be withheld. We injure no one but ourselves if we do not make thoughtful judgment in the classification process.

3. A determination that certain information should be withheld must be premised upon valid reasons and disclosure should promptly be made when it appears that the factors justifying non-disclosure no longer pertain.

4. Non-disclosure can never be justified as a means of covering mistakes, avoiding embarrassment, or for political, personal or pecuniary reasons.[67]

With respect to the legislature's right to know he enumerated eight principles which had been established during the Washington, the Jefferson, and the Tyler administrations:

Washington

1. That the Constitution fixes boundaries between the three branches of the Government: Legislative, Executive, and Judicial.

2. That the documents of the Executive Branch are within the control of that branch, not of all branches.

3. That the Legislative Branch can make inquiry of the Executive for its documents, but in response to Congressional requests

---

AEC were exercised to discover that a Bureau of the Budget consultant, Adolphe H. Wenzell, had simultaneously been an officer of the First Boston Corporation. This was the investment house that had represented Dixon-Yates in negotiations with the AEC and the Budget Bureau."

[67] William P. Rogers, Attorney General of the United States, statement on "Inquiry by the Legislative Branch Concerning the Decision Making Process and Documents of the Executive Branch," before a Subcommittee on Constitutional Rights of the Senate Judiciary Committee, March 6, 1958, p. 2 (mimeo).

for documents, the Executive should exercise a discretion as to whether their production would serve a public good or would be contrary to the public interest.

4.   That the authority of the President for the conduct of foreign affairs does not oblige him to produce the instructions which had been given to his representatives in negotiating a treaty. It seems clear that they constituted advice within the Executive Branch on official matters. The official action of the Executive was embodied in the Treaty which was submitted to the Senate for its advice and consent.[68]

Jefferson

1.   That documents containing information of uncertain reliability apparently reflecting adversely on individuals should not be disclosed.

2.   That documents containing information given in confidence to the Executive Branch should not be disclosed by that Branch.[69]

Tyler

1.   That it would be contrary to the public interest for the Executive Branch to produce documents which might affect its settlement of pending claims against the United States.

2.   That it would be contrary to the public interest for the Executive Branch to produce documents on official matters before they had been embodied in official actions.[70]

On the basis of these principles, then, it would appear that at best the right of Congress to compel the production of information by the executive branch remains cloudy. Corwin reports further that as of 1957, he knows of no instance in which a high official in the executive branch has appeared before a congressional committee in response to a subpoena.[71]

---

[68] *Ibid.*, p. 11.

[69] *Ibid.*, p. 12.

[70] *Ibid.*, p. 13.

[71] *Op. cit.*, p. 113. "In the many years that have rolled by since Jefferson's presidency there have been hundreds of congressional investigations. But I know of no instance in which a head of department has testified before a congressional committee in response to a subpoena or been held for contempt for refusal to testify. All appearances by these high officials seem to have been voluntary. The rule of immunity is, however, regarded with special deference as affecting the Secretary of State. When early in 1947 a green Congressman, whose head had possibly been turned by his finding himself a member of a subcommittee of the House on the Merchant Marine, issued a

Checking the executive by concurrent resolution [72]

One of the least ambiguous provisions of the Constitution is the requirement that:

Every Order, Resolution, or Vote to which the Concurrence of the Senate and House of Representatives may be necessary . . . shall be presented to the President of the United States; and before the Same shall take Effect, shall be approved by him or being disapproved by him, shall be repassed by two thirds of the Senate and House of Representatives, according to the Rules and Limitations prescribed in the Case of a Bill.

This would appear to stipulate the need for presidential assent to concurrent resolutions adopted by both houses of Congress. The record, however, indicates that in fact such resolutions have never been submitted for presidential approval.[73] The practice is based upon the theory that concurrent resolutions are not legislative in nature and have no effect beyond the confines of the Capitol.[74] It

---

subpoena to Secretary Marshall, his embarrassed associates promptly recalled the document and gave their brash colleague a little lecture on the 'protocol' pertaining in such matters. Likewise, while other heads of departments may be 'directed' by Congress or one of its committees to furnish needed documents, the Secretary of State is invariably 'requested' to furnish them; and in both instances the call is usually qualified by the softening phrase 'if the public interest permits.' "

[72] This and the next section on "Reporting," are drawn, largely verbatim, from Cornelius P. Cotter and J. Malcolm Smith, "Administrative Accountability to Congress: The Concurrent Resolution," and "Administrative Accountability: Reporting to Congress," *The Western Political Quarterly,* 9 & 10, 1956, pp. 955-66 and 1957, pp. 405-15. Documentation has largely been eliminated, but can be found in the original source.

[73] *Hinds' Precedents,* IV (1907), p. 3483, based upon Senate Report No. 1335, 54th Congress, 2d Session, January 27, 1897. "The Committee found that in the first twelve Congresses there were one or two instances of simple resolutions being approved by the President; and that, with one or two exceptions, all joint resolutions were approved." Passage of concurrent resolutions "began immediately upon the organization of the Government, but their use has been, not for the purpose of enacting legislation, but to express the sense of Congress upon a given subject, to adjourn longer than three days, to make, amend, or suspend joint rules, and to accomplish similar purposes, in which both Houses have a common interest, but with which the President has no concern."

[74] *Cannon's Precedents,* VII (1935), p. 1037. On February 28, 1908, the House of Representatives considered Senate Concurrent Resolution 5, extending invitations to foreign governments to participate in an international Congress. "Mr. James R. Mann, of Illinois, submitted that a concurrent resolution was without effect beyond the confines of the Capitol and would confer no authority on the Secretary of State, and that a joint resolution and not a concurrent resolution was the proper vehicle for the purpose." An amendment was offered and agreed to changing the concurrent resolution into a joint resolution.

is only necessary to run a finger down the list of concurrent resolutions in any recent volume of United States statutes to attest to the housekeeping or purely advisory nature of the preponderance of these resolutions. Thus, in 1955 Congress by concurrent resolution regulated parking on the Capitol grounds, congratulated Michigan State College on its centennial year, and provided for congressional participation in the NATO Parliamentary Conference.[75]

Nevertheless, the art of insinuating into a delegatory statute a congressional power to legislate or to influence and participate in administration by means of the concurrent resolution has become highly refined in recent decades. In so doing, Congress appears to have pursued a variety of objectives: (a) In some instances it has reserved power to terminate a statute or program. (b) It has asserted power to enable or require executive action. (c) Finally, it has made administrative exercise of delegated power subject to congressional approval or disapproval by concurrent or simple resolution.

Some of the main features of resolutions in each category are enlarged upon below.

(a) *Terminating Programs.* Use of the concurrent resolution to terminate delegations of power to the executive branch may take two forms. The first is congressional reservation of a power to repeal the statute. The standard phrasing for this type of resolution is as follows: "The provisions of this Act, . . . shall terminate on June 30, 1943, or upon the date of a proclamation by the President, or upon the date specified in a concurrent resolution. . . ." [76] A similar provision is contained in at least 23 emergency statutes enacted since 1941.[77] The Mutual Defense Assistance Act of 1949 secured to the Congress a kind of item veto, through reserving to it the power by concurrent resolution to terminate assistance to "any nation" under the Act.[78]

The second type in this category is congressional reservation of the right, by concurrent resolution, to declare an end to conditions which authorize the President to take contingent action. Instances of this form of terminating resolution are relatively few. In a 1941

---

[75] Senate Concurrent Resolution 3; House Concurrent Resolution 6; House Concurrent Resolution 109, 69 Stat. B3, B10.

[76] Emergency Price Control Act of 1942, 56 Stat. 23, Sec. 1 (b) (January 30, 1942).

[77] See Cornelius P. Cotter and J. Malcolm Smith, "Administrative Accountability to Congress: The Concurrent Resolution," *The Western Political Quarterly*, December 1956, p. 959, footnote 25.

[78] 63 Stat. 714, Sec. 405 (d) (1949).

statute, the Secretary of the Navy was authorized to establish a plant protection force for naval shore establishments "and to maintain and operate the same until June 1943, unless Congress shall have, in the meantime, by concurrent resolution, declared such a force no longer necessary." [79] Again a 1942 amendment to the Communications Act of 1934 gave the President certain powers to control wire communication facilities "upon proclamation by the President that there exists a state or threat of war involving the United States" and for a period "ending not later than six months after the termination of such state or threat of war and not later than such earlier date as the Congress by concurrent resolution may designate." [80] And, more generally, Congress has also reserved the right, although not on an exclusive basis, to declare by concurrent resolution the "dates of commencement and termination of an armed conflict." [81]

However, legislative efforts to employ the power to terminate statutes by concurrent resolution prove anticlimactic, in view of the many instances in which the power to accomplish this was included in the delegatory statute, and all were unsuccessful.

(b) *Enabling or Requiring Executive Action.* An example of the use of the concurrent resolution as an enabling device is the provision of the Neutrality Act of 1939,[82] which imposed rigorous limitations upon United States carriage to belligerents "whenever the President, or the Congress by concurrent resolution, shall find that there exists a state of war between foreign states." This Act provides the only recent instance of congressional effort to reserve a power by concurrent resolution to *require* executive action. On the theory that the Act "places on the Congress a responsibility corresponding with that which has been placed on the President in the matter of finding a condition of war to exist," individual members introduced concurrent resolutions declaring the existence of war between the U.S.S.R. and Finland, Japan and China, and Germany and the U.S.S.R. These were decently interred in committee.[83]

The Federal-Aid Highway Act of 1944 authorized appropriation of $500 million a year for each of the first three postwar years for

---

[79] 55 Stat. 616, Sec. 1 (August 11, 1941).

[80] 56 Stat. 18 (January 26, 1942).

[81] E.g., amendment to the Military Personnel Claims Act of 1945, 67 Stat. 317 (August 1, 1953). As is usual, the President might establish such inclusive dates by proclamation.

[82] 54 Stat. 4 (November 4, 1939).

[83] The words are those of Senator Gillette at 76 *Congressional Record*, p. 355 (1940). Senate Concurrent Resolution 35 (1940); Senate Concurrent Resolution 36, and House Concurrent Resolution 44 (1940); House Concurrent Resolution 44 (1941).

highway construction. The President, by proclamation, or the Congress, by concurrent resolution, could determine when these years began.[84] Senate and House concurrent resolutions were introduced in the 79th Congress in 1945 fixing the first postwar fiscal year under the Act as the year ending June 30, 1946. Introduced in the House, the resolution passed in that chamber and was agreed to by the Senate.[85]

(c) *The Legislative Veto.* The Reorganization Acts of 1939, 1945, and 1949 [86] provide interesting illustrations of the use of the simple and concurrent resolution to approve or disapprove administrative action. All three Acts had the purpose of reorganizing the government to enable it better to cope with emergency conditions. The 1939 Act stipulated that the President's reorganization plans should take effect:

> . . . upon the expiration of sixty calendar days after the date on which the plan is transmitted to the Congress, but only if during such sixty-day period there has not been passed by the two Houses a concurrent resolution stating in substance that the Congress does not favor the reorganization plan.[87]

A similar provision was contained in the 1945 Act which had the expressed purpose of facilitating "orderly transition from war to peace." [88] The 1949 Act provided for one-house veto of reorganization plans. The plan would have effect:

> . . . upon the expiration of the first period of sixty calendar days, of continuous session of the Congress, following the date on which the plan is transmitted to it; but only if, between the date of transmittal and the expiration of such sixty-day period there has not been passed by either of the two Houses, by the affirmative vote of a majority of the authorized membership of that House, a resolution stating in substance that that House does not favor the reorganization plan.[89]

Although the first Reorganization Act providing for a legislative veto of reorganization plans was enacted in 1939, concurrent resolutions disapproving such plans were introduced in vain until 1946. However, in July of that year, both houses agreed to House Concur-

---

[84] 58 Stat. 838, Sec. 2 (1944).

[85] 92 *Congressional Record*, pp. 9099, 9217; 59 Stat. 846 (1945).

[86] 53 Stat. 561, Sec. 5 (1939); 59 Stat. 613 (1945); 63 Stat. 203 (1949).

[87] 53 Stat. 561, Sec. 5 (a) (1939).

[88] 59 Stat. 613, Sec. 2 (a) (1945).

[89] Despite this provision, the Congress chose to approve Reorganization Plan No. 1 of 1953 by joint resolution, in order that it might, in the course of approving it, also amend it. 67 Stat. 18 (April 1, 1953).

rent Resolution 155 disapproving President Truman's Reorganization Plan No. 1. The next May a new Congress disapproved Reorganization Plan No. 2 of 1947. The third and last reorganization plan to be defeated by concurrent resolution was Plan No. 1, 1948, which incurred congressional disapproval in March of that year. Because the Reorganization Act of 1949 permitted veto of the President's plans by simple resolution of one house, the Senate was able to frustrate President Truman's efforts to elevate the Federal Security Agency to departmental status in Senate Resolution 147 of that year.

The Federal Civil Defense Act of 1950, in an apparently unique provision, adapts the concurrent resolution to the vetoing of interstate civil defense compacts.

> The consent of the Congress shall be granted to each such compact, upon the expiration of the first period of sixty calendar days of continuous session of the Congress following the date on which the compact is transmitted to it; but only if, between the date of transmittal and expiration of such sixty-day period, there has not been passed a concurrent resolution stating in substance that the Congress does not approve the compact.[90]

It only remains to indicate the manner in which concurrent resolutions have been used for the purpose of securing for the Congress intimate participation in the administration of selected programs— principally in the field of immigration and naturalization. In the Alien Registration Act, 1940, Congress provided for the "deportation of additional classes of aliens." "Aliens of proved good moral character" might "at the discretion of the Attorney General . . . have deportation suspended" under certain conditions. However, if deportation were suspended for more than six months:

> . . . all of the facts and pertinent provisions of law in the case shall be reported to the Congress within ten days after the beginning of its next regular session, with the reasons for such suspension. . . . If during that session the two Houses pass a concurrent resolution stating in substance that the Congress does not favor the suspension of such deportation, the Attorney General shall thereupon deport such alien in the manner provided by law. If during that session the two Houses do not pass such a resolution, the Attorney General shall cancel deportation proceedings upon the termination of such session. . . .[91]

---

[90] 64 Stat. 1245, Sec. 201 (g) (January 12, 1951).
[91] 54 Stat. 670, Sec. 20 (June 28, 1940).

In subsequent legislation Congress reserved the right by concurrent resolution to suspend deportation or to grant permanent residence,[92] and a considerable proportion of the concurrent resolutions enacted each year now constitute directives to the Attorney General in this regard.

Statutory provisions for committee oversight

In the course of signing H.R. 6042, the Defense Appropriations Bill, on July 13, 1955, President Eisenhower rebuked Congress for including in the bill Section 638, requiring the Secretary of Defense to secure prior consent of the House and Senate Appropriations Committees, before separating from his department functions which he thought could better be performed by private industry. The President averred that "the Congress has no right to confer upon its committees the power to veto Executive action or to prevent Executive action from becoming effective." Invoking the constitutional principle of separation of powers he indicated that he would ignore the provisions.[93]

The bill which President Eisenhower reluctantly signed is not wholly without precedent. Indeed a survey of legislation in the fields of foreign affairs and economic or military emergency since 1933 indicates numerous attempts by Congress to secure for its committees some degree of continuing influence over the executive. This may take the form of requiring periodic or special reports to policy committees instead of the full houses, or requiring compulsory consultation with committees; or, somewhat rare to date, the committee may be granted a suspensive, enabling, or veto power over administrative action.

We have earlier indicated an aversion to judging the potential for good or evil of various kinds of congressional efforts to share in the burdens of administration on the basis of conjectures as to the legislative purpose. We have also argued that Congress might profitably reassess its purposes in embarking upon a variety of efforts at control of administration, to look for coherence and effectiveness. There would seem to be considerable ambiguity of purpose in the various congressional requirements for administrative reporting to committees. For instance, the requirement may be completely devoid of a purpose to control administration and may aim merely at securing technical information or advice to aid in policy formulation. But

---

[92] *Ibid.*
[93] *New York Times,* July 14, 1955, pp. 1, 8.

equally, it may be intended to provide a basis for the closest possible scrutiny and control. For when executive agencies must report in detail and frequently on the discharge of delegated functions, they find it necessary either to attempt to mislead the Congress—a dangerous pastime—or else to play the role of meticulous surrogate of the legislature, perhaps even acting in anticipation of committee wishes in the smallest detail.

Thus it would be difficult to distinguish the informative and control purposes of, say, the provision of the Supplemental National Defense Appropriations Act of 1948, requiring that the Secretary of Defense report quarterly "to the Committees on Appropriations and Armed Services of the Congress . . . the amounts obligated" for the construction of aircraft and equipment. The reports were to "include a statement of finding by the President that the contracts let are necessary in the interest of the national defense and that the contract specifications insure the maximum utilization of improvements in aircraft and equipment consistent with the defense needs of the United States." [94]

In the Mutual Defense Assistance Act of 1951, which established "an embargo on the shipment of arms, ammunition, and implements of war . . . to any nation or combination of nations threatening the security of the United States," Congress gave the administration power to "determine . . . which items are, for the purpose of this Act, arms, ammunition, and implements of war . . . which should be embargoed." [95] Aid to any nation "knowingly" permitting shipment of such materials or equipment to the U.S.S.R. and its satellites was to be suspended, unless the President found that "unusual circumstances indicate that the cessation of aid would clearly be detrimental to the security of the United States." Upon making such a decision, the President must "immediately report" it "with reasons therefor to the Appropriations and Armed Services Committees of the Senate and of the House of Representatives, the Committee on Foreign Relations of the Senate, and the Committee on Foreign Affairs of the House of Representatives." Further, he must "at least once each quarter review all determinations made previously and . . . report his conclusions to the foregoing committees." [96]

These are but two examples of what might best be described as legislative adaptations of Carl J. Friedrich's so-called "rule of antici-

[94] 62 Stat. 258 (May 21, 1948).
[95] 65 Stat. 644, Sec. 101, 103 (a) (October 26, 1951).
[96] *Ibid.*, Sec. 103 (b).

pated reaction." [97] In this context the rule implies that administrative officers, aware of the imminent necessity of reporting to the legislature the details of their exercises of discretion under delegatory statutes, will attempt to pattern their action so as to maximize the likelihood of legislative approval.

The element of coercion is less obvious—though nonetheless present—in statutes which, instead of requiring detailed reporting of administrative discharge of delegated functions, provide for periodic or continuous administrative consultation with congressional committees. The line between "consultation" and "coercion" can be drawn only by one who has carefully studied the day-to-day relationships between individuals and groups. The Economic Cooperation Act of 1948, for instance, created a Joint Committee on Foreign Economic Cooperation consisting of ten members from the Foreign Relations and Appropriations Committees of the Senate, and the Foreign Affairs and Appropriations Committees of the House. The Economic Cooperation Administrator was, "at the request of the committee," to "consult with the committee from time to time." [98] In 1950 the Secretary of Defense was empowered "after consultation with the respective Armed Services Committees of the Congress" to "acquire . . . construct," etc., facilities necessary "for the administration and training of the Reserve components of the Armed Forces." [99]

The Defense Production Act of 1950 established a Joint Committee of Defense Production "to make a continuous study of the programs authorized by this Act, and to review the progress achieved in the execution and administration of such programs." It required all agencies and officials administering programs authorized by the Act, "at the request of the committee" to "consult with the committee, from time to time, with respect to their activities under this Act." [100] Again a Joint Committee on Immigration and Nationality Policy was created "to make a continuous study of . . . the administration of" the Immigration and Nationality Act of 1952.[101] The Act instructed the Attorney General and the Secretary of State to "submit to the Committee all regulations, instructions, and all other information as requested by the Committee relative to the administration of this Act; and the Secretary of State and the Attorney General shall con-

---

[97] *Constitutional Government and Politics* (New York: Harper, 1937), p. 16. Also see Herbert A. Simon's analysis in *Administrative Behavior* (New York: Macmillan, 1954), pp. 129 ff.

[98] 62 Stat. 137, Sec. 124 (b) (April 3, 1948).

[99] 64 Stat. 829, Sec. 3, 11 (September 11, 1950).

[100] 64 Stat. 798, Sec. 712 (b) (September 8, 1950).

[101] 66 Stat. 163, Sec. 401 (a) (June 27, 1952).

sult with the Committee from time to time with respect to their activities under this Act." [102]

The history of recent use of the "legislative veto" might lead one to expect that, in those instances where it seeks to retain a power of continuous oversight of administrative action, Congress would be prone to locate this function in either or both houses and not to delegate it to committees. In fact, careful study might reveal that compulsory executive consultation with the committees and joint committees-agency decision making are more the rule than the exception.[103]

Certainly Congress in requiring the Atomic Energy Commission to report to the Joint Committee on Atomic Energy in instances where it imparts atomic secrets to other nations contemplated committee control of such action. Arrangements with other nations were not to be consummated until "the Joint Committee on Atomic Energy has been fully informed for a period of thirty days in which the Congress was in session." [104] If the Committee disapproved the arrangement and found the Commission unresponsive to its influence, it would have time in which to report on these facts to Congress.

When it authorized the establishment of a long-range proving ground for guided missiles in 1949, Congress stipulated: "Prior to the acquisition under the authority of this section of any lands or rights or other interests pertaining thereto, the Secretary of the Air Force shall come into agreement with the Armed Services Committees of the Senate and the House of Representatives with respect to the acquisition of such lands." [105] This provision candidly established a joint committee-agency decision-making arrangement. A 1951 statute required the Secretaries of the Army, Air Force, and Navy, and the Federal Civil Defense Administrator, to "come into agreement with" the two Armed Services Committees "with respect to those real-estate actions by or for the use of the military departments or the Federal Civil Defense Administration." [106] The Emergency Powers Interim Continuation Act of April 1952, continued this provision in force.[107]

---

[102] *Ibid.*, Sec. 401 (f).

[103] See J. Lieper Freeman, *The Political Process: Executive Bureau—Legislative Committee Relations* (Garden City: Doubleday, 1955); and, Harold P. Green and Alan Rosenthal, *Government of the Atom: The Integration of Powers* (New York: Atherton Press, 1963).

[104] 65 Stat. 692, Sec. 10 (a); (October 30, 1951), and Green and Rosenthal, *op. cit.*

[105] 63 Stat. 66, Sec. 2 (May 11, 1949).

[106] 65 Stat. 365, Sec. 601 (September 28, 1951).

[107] 66 Stat. 54, Sec. 3 (April 14, 1952).

68

In conclusion we mention a device for providing congressional committees a kind of suspensive power over administrative action. This is the familiar provision for suspension of deportation orders where the Immigration and Naturalization Subcommittees of the House or of the Senate have "favorably acted on" a bill for the relief of the alien in question. The Act cited here was restricted in effect to the 75th Congress. Stays in deportation made under its terms were to "be terminated not later than the date of adjournment of the first regular session of the Seventy-sixth Congress." [108]

Legislative procedure and oversight

We frequently hear of the disillusionment with which the visitor to Capitol Hill looks down upon the near empty wells of the House and the Senate where a legislator may drone inaudible comment to the eight or ten colleagues present. Neither house, as a rule, presents the public with a spectacle of great debate on the major issues of the day. While the Senate rules permit more flexibility and greater length in debate, each house has come to be something other than a deliberative body. Many factors account for this, and not all are recent by any means.

It may be that we are witnessing a transition from legislative initiation to legislation validation of policy (all the more reason to emphasize oversight). But the rise of presidential leadership does not suffice to account for the relative paucity of outstanding debate in the two houses which indeed far antedates the rise of the twentieth century presidency. Lord Bryce complained in 1890 "that the debates of the House of Representatives were scarcely mentioned in the national press and they did little to instruct or influence national opinion." [109] MacNeil vividly reports some of the environmental factors which until recently discouraged whatever inclination there might have been toward "great" debate in the House:

> The very size of the Hall of the House, and the large number of Representatives crowded into it, conspired to produce confusion and chaos. For a century and a half, until the 1930's, the members had to suffer excruciating personal discomfort. The acoustics of the old Hall, now used to exhibit statues, and of the new Hall as well were appalling. So was the ventilation. Unless a Representative had a great voice—of one loud-voiced member, John P. Hale of New Hampshire, it was said that he could stand atop Mount Washington and address his entire native state—he

---

[108] 52 Stat. 1249 (June 29, 1938).
[109] MacNeil, *op. cit.,* p. 305.

could not be heard beyond the immediate vicinity on the floor from which he spoke. Before the construction of the first office building for Representatives, the members had no other place to transact their business than from their desks on the floor. There they read their local newspapers, answered their constituents' letters, and consulted with their colleagues. The clatter from the slamming desk drawers, the rustling of paper, the hurly-burly of pages scampering about the Hall, and the hum of many voices raised a din through which only an exceptional voice could penetrate. "If ever anything worthwhile is said," commented a Washington reporter in 1931 on House debate, "few can hear it and still fewer pay any attention." Speaking to the House, said another reporter in 1878, was "like trying to address the people in the Broadway omnibuses from the curbstone in front of the Astor House." [110]

Such mundane improvements as expanded office space, air conditioning of the chambers of the two houses, and installation of amplifying equipment (both as late as 1938) have contributed toward creating a physical environment more hospitable to debate than that which existed but a few score years ago. However, the congested calendar of the House, and its very size, make for the continuance of stringent limitations on debate, regardless of physical accommodations. The institution of "revise and extend" has come to be a substitution for debate. The hour restriction per individual member on general debate is largely an illusion, since important bills come up under special rules which provide for a maximum period for the total debate that falls far short of the time required to permit all interested representatives to voice their views at length. The rules also provide for management of the time by members of the committee having jurisdiction over the bill in question. Further militating against extended debate is the practice of considering major legislation in the Committee of the Whole House where the one-hour rule does not apply.

The title of this paper is followed by a quotation from J. S. Mill that "the proper office of a representative assembly is to watch and control the government." Perhaps it might better be said that "a major office" of such an assembly is to perform this function. Moreover it is important that the assembly perform this function on some systematized and continuing basis, through the vehicle of debate in the House. Such debate would supplement, complement, and probably very frequently would be based upon, committee action.

[110] *Ibid.*, p. 309.

It would be a rash observer who offered a scheme for drastic changes in the House rules to loosen debate. Attention may appropriately be called once again, however, to Senator Kefauver's recommendation for a Question Period in the Congress. John D. Millett has described the operation of this hoary institution in the British House of Commons:

> The first hour of every Parliamentary day except Friday is devoted to answers by Ministers of their Parliamentary Secretaries to questions which have been submitted by members of the House. Supplementary questions may be put orally, although the Speaker may rule out of order any question exceeding the scope of the original, or the Minister may ask for notice of the query. . . . There are two resorts for the member who finds an answer especially unsatisfactory. He may at the time give notice that at the "first opportunity" he will raise the matter on adjournment. Then after eleven o'clock in the evening he may bring up the issue concerning which he is dissatisfied. This recourse is infrequently used, as a member can usually obtain satisfaction privately. Or, immediately following the question period a member may ask leave of the Speaker to move adjournment of the House on the grounds of a matter of "urgent public importance." The Speaker must be convinced that it is a matter of urgent public importance before he will grant leave to make the motion.[111]

The practical utility of this device for legislative oversight has been attested to by a number of studies, and there would appear to be an unusual degree of transferability to the American legislative scene.[112]

The House finds it essential and the Senate convenient to organize their legislative work on a system of "calendars." The Senate requires but two calendars, the Executive Calendar for treaties and Nominations, and Calendar of Business, containing all bills awaiting action. The House has some five calendars, in addition to "the Speaker's Table" (presidential vetoes, conference reports).[113] In addition to this, District of Columbia business takes precedence, as

---

[111] *The British Unemployment Assistance Board* (New York: McGraw-Hill, Inc., 1940), pp. 160-61.

[112] See, e.g., *ibid.*, and Cornelius P. Cotter, "Emergency Detention in Wartime: The British Experience," *Stanford Law Review*, 6, 1954, pp. 238, 280-84.

[113] Union Calendar: public bills dealing with appropriations or revenues; House Calendar: other public bills; Private Calendar: private bills (considered on 1st and 3d Tuesday). Consent Calendar: any bill on Union or House Calendars may, if no objection, be placed on Consent Calendar (considered on 1st and 3d Monday); Discharge Calendar: when petition is served to take bill out of committee (2d and 4th Mondays).

necessary, on two days each month. It would be an appropriate recognition of the importance of the oversight function if, at least in the House, though possibly in the Senate also, an oversight calendar were established, that had priority on at least two days each month. On these days committee chairmen and ranking minority members who have matters of oversight to call to the attention of either chamber would have priority before members wishing to deal with the other business facing that house. In the lower house this use could be made of the time freed from District affairs, in the event that home rule is granted within the near future.

Oversight of the judiciary

There is a tendency to emphasize the role of the Supreme Court as interpreter of the Constitution; there is a parallel tendency to overlook the exercise of legislative oversight of judicial decision making. Insofar as the Court exercises judicial review its decisions are subject to congressionally initiated reversal by constitutional amendment. See for example *Pollack* v. *Farmers' Loan and Trust Co.*, 157 U.S. 429 (1895), which declared a federal income tax statute unconstitutional, and was reversed by the Sixteenth Amendment to the Constitution. But a great deal of Supreme Court decision making takes the form of interpreting the meaning, as distinguished from the constitutionality, of statutes of Congress. Congress is free to disagree with, and by legislation to change, legislative policy as interpreted by the Court. A pioneering article on congressional reversal of Supreme Court decisions appeared in the form of a law note in the *Harvard Law Review,* May 1958.[114] The authors of the law note found 21 instances in which Congress had reversed Supreme Court decisions during the period 1945-57. Of these 21 only "six cannot be viewed primarily as a conflict between the two branches of government. Rather, Congress was able to take into account policy factors that the Court could not properly have considered in ruling on property disputes or in applying a clear statutory directive." [115]

In several cases ranging from 1954 to 1957 the Supreme Court provoked the ire of particular factions within the Congress and thus evoked a series of legislative efforts (a) generally to circumscribe the appellate power of the Supreme Court (which is subject, of course, to legislative definition), or (b) to reverse particular decisions. One of the decisions most irritating to Congress was that of *Pennsylvania* v.

---

[114] "Congressional Reversal of Supreme Court Decisions: 1945-1957," *Harvard Law Review*, 71, 1958, pp. 1324-37.
[115] *Ibid.*, p. 1326.

Nelson, 340 U.S. 497 (1956), which held that the Smith Act pre-
empted the field of subversion to the exclusion of state legislation in
dealing with the subject. Congressional response to the *Nelson* case,
and others similar to it, was H.R. 3, which did not become law, but
was passed by the House of Representatives on July 17, 1958, and
was recommitted by the Senate in August of that year by a 41 to 40
roll call vote. "The measure would have established two new rules
governing application of the pre-emption doctrines: (1) federal laws
were to be construed as intended to invalidate laws only if Congress
had stated specifically that it wished to pre-empt the field of legislation between a state law and a federal law, and (2) existing federal
laws should not be construed as indicating Congress' intention to bar
states from passing laws punishing sedition against the Federal
Government." [116]

Another abhorrent decision handed down that year was *Slochower*
v. *Board of Education,* 340 U.S. 551 (1956), holding that a state
could not discharge an employee for pleading the Fifth Amendment
before a congressional committee where the state offered no opportunity for a review of the individual's loyalty on the merits. In 1957
in *Jencks* v. *United States,* 353 U.S. 657, the Supreme Court held
that in a federal trial the government must produce certain records
for examination by a defendant. Fourteen bills were introduced in
Congress following the Jencks case, with the purpose of clarifying
and curbing the decision. One of these became Public Law 85-269
which now "requires the government to disclose only those prior
statements of the witness which relate to his testimony, and the
defense can have access to such reports only after the witness has
testified." [117] Another unpopular decision was *Mallory* v. *United
States,* 352 U.S. 449 (1957), which ordered the release of a convicted rapist on grounds that a voluntary confession made between
an arrest and a delayed arraignment before a federal commissioner
was inadmissible at the trial.

An important legislative proposal which failed to reach the statute
books was S. 2646 (the Jenner-Butler Bill) which failed of passage
in the Senate in August of 1958 by a 49 to 41 roll call vote. The
Jenner-Butler Bill would have restricted the powers of the Supreme
Court in six ways: (1) by depriving the Supreme Court of appellate
jurisdiction in cases involving admission to state bars; (2) by providing that no past or future anti-sedition laws at the federal level

---

[116] 104 *Congressional Record*, pp. 13851, 13993, 14161 (1958). *Congress
and the Nation 1945-1964, op. cit.,* p. 1442.

[117] See Rourke, *op. cit.,* pp. 688-89.

should be construed by the courts as prohibiting enforcement of otherwise valid state laws; (3) by making each house of Congress the final judge of whether questions put to witnesses by its committees were pertinent to the authorized purpose of the committee inquiry; (4) by depriving persons being tried for contempt of Congress for refusing to answer questions before a congressional committee of the right to argue pertinency as a defense unless the issue had been raised at the time of the questioning; (5) by providing that the 1940 Smith Act made all teaching or advocacy of forcible overthrow of the U.S. government a crime, irrespective of whether it was conceived as merely an abstract doctrine or as an incitement to action; (6) by enlarging the application of the term "organize" as used in the Smith Act.[118]

The *Congressional Quarterly* reported that by 1959 the legislative trend had turned and the Congress was becoming more tolerant of the Court. This is attributed to the 1958 election which increased the number of northern Democrats in the Senate; to a series of Court cases giving wider scope to state taxation; and to two major 1959 security rulings which favored the government. "In 1959 and for the remainder of the postwar period, the Southerner-conservative Republican coalition, from time to time, did emerge to succeed in reversing specific High Court decisions. But, despite rumblings between 1962 and 1964 on Supreme Court rulings on school prayer . . . and reapportionment . . . the coalition was not successful in actually curbing the Court's powers." [119]

Some students of American politics make a fetish of the Supreme Court's alleged entitlement to complete insulation from criticism and political influence. It is difficult to see why the Supreme Court's interpretation of the meaning of a congressional statute must stand immune from legislative correction. Clearly some of the bills introduced in recent Congresses were punitive in intent, and yet, whatever their purpose, it is clear that they aimed at exercising a power which is constitutionally that of Congress, namely to determine the jurisdiction of lower federal courts and to define the appellate jurisdiction of the Supreme Court or to correct a specific judicial interpretation of a specific congressional enactment.

Recent criticism of the Court does not mark a precedent. It has been an object of attack throughout history. Of the some 5,400 constitutional amendments proposed in the Congress since 1789, a significant number have dealt with the Court. Many of these were introduced during the height of New Deal disillusionment with the

---

[118] *Congress and the Nation 1945-1964, op. cit.*
[119] *Ibid.*

judiciary. At that time it was proposed, for example, to limit the powers of the federal courts to declare federal legislation unconstitutional, and to require a two-thirds rather than majority vote of the Court to declare legislation unconstitutional, specifically to reverse certain unpopular Court decisions. One of the most interesting proposed constitutional amendments would have provided that congressional legislation declared unconstitutional by the Court would be deemed constitutional upon reenactment by Congress.[120]

At the very least, Congress should have power to reverse Supreme Court determinations that its statutes are unconstitutional—perhaps by reenactment by two-thirds vote in two consecutive sessions of the legislature. This kind of suspensive power would not undermine the strength of the Court. One is reminded of Justice Holmes' stricture to the effect that "the United States would [not] come to an end if we lost our power to declare an act of Congress void"—although he added "I do think the Union would be imperiled if we could not make that declaration as to the laws of the several states." [121] And yet, it is arguable that the union would not be imperiled if Congress, in a manner similar to that indicated above, were permitted to review Supreme Court decisions invalidating state legislation under the Constitution. Perhaps ours is a sufficiently mature federal system today that we could afford the experiment.

Presidential leadership, crisis, and oversight

It is usual in discussing the enlarged role of the presidency in modern government to attribute a part of this cause to the recurrent crises which have dominated the twentieth century. Thus David Truman refers to "the pivotal position achieved for the Presidency under a series of 'strong' Chief Executives dealing with an almost unbroken series of domestic and world crises." [122] It is also usual practice to attribute to the executive an ascendant role in time of war and assume a concurrent demise of the legislative role. Thus Senator Clark writes:

> . . . In times of peril the President can act because the Congress will recede. If he can cite statute he will, if not he will act anyway, as Lincoln and F.D.R. did. As the sense of danger recedes, Congress rises again to reassert its constitutional prerogatives. In the absence of crisis, Congress cannot and will not act

---

[120] *Proposed Amendments to the Constitution of the United States,* Senate Document No. 163, 87th Congress, 2d Session,1963.

[121] Quoted in Thomas Reed Powell, *op. cit.,* p. 21.

[122] *Congressional Party, op. cit.,* p. 9.

affirmatively except under a strong President who has a clear mandate from the people, not only because of the separation of powers and the way Congressmen and Senators come to office, but also because of the congeries of rules and customs which favor inactivity.[123]

And Pendleton Herring comments on the tendency which he perceived toward the development of a rivalry or the reawakening of a rivalry between the President and Congress in postwar periods of demobilization. He referred to the periods following the Civil War and the First World War when supposedly control of policy went to the Congress.[124]

It has come to be a part of the democratic tradition to assume that democratic governments are not capable of dealing with crises without undergoing a fundamental transition from their usual forms to something approximating authoritarianism. The chief requisite in time of emergency is assumed to be the freeing of the executive from legislative restraint. Thus John Stewart Mill concluded his ardent defense of representative government with the shattering aside "I am far from condemning in cases of extreme necessity, the assumption of absolute power in the form of a temporary dictatorship." [125] Clinton Rossiter has written a book-length study casting the problem of emergency government in terms of temporary dictatorship.[126] Carl Friedrich and others invoke this concept.[127]

It is understandable that even students of democratic government would tend to lapse into an analysis cast in terms of authoritarianism or dictatorship, however softened by use of the word "temporary." Wartime or emergency conditions would appear to demand concentration of power in the executive, while democratic governments are characterized by the distribution, even the diffusion, of powers. Thus, on the surface, emergency would seem to demand the release of the executive from the usual institutionalized restraints which play

---

[123] *Congress: The Sapless Branch, op. cit.,* p. 105. Note again the recurrent theme of presidential power *versus* legislative power.

[124] Pendleton Herring, "Executive-Legislative Responsibilities," *American Political Science Review,* 38, 1944, pp. 1155, 1157.

[125] *Representative Government* (New York: Dutton, 1950), pp. 274, 277-78.

[126] Clinton L. Rossiter, *Constitutional Dictatorship* (Princeton: Princeton University Press, 1948).

[127] *Constitutional Government and Democracy* (rev. ed.; Boston: Ginn & Co., 1950), Ch. XXVI; see also Frederick M. Watkins, *The Failure of Constitutional Emergency Powers Under the German Republic* (Cambridge: Harvard University Press, 1939). The British historian Smellie commented that "a real totalitarian state appeared" in Great Britain during the Second World War. K. B. Smellie, *A Hundred Years of English Government* (2d ed.; London: Gerald Duckworth & Co., Ltd., 1950), p. 289.

upon it. Whatever emergency would *seem* in the abstract to demand by way of metamorphosis of democratic institution, history tells us that while Great Britain and the United States vastly intensified the range of government controls during World Wars I and II, and enlarged their variety, they simultaneously retained a significant degree of legislative oversight of the executive, and a considerable diffusion of power. In wartime as in normal times the President and Congress are as likely to work cooperatively together as they are at loggerheads.

Emergency conditions perhaps provide the true test of the ability of contemporary legislative institutions to perform the function of oversight. For if ever it were likely that a President could defy Congress on a continuing basis it would be in time of threat to the existence of the nation. We have the famous example of President Franklin Roosevelt's demand to Congress on September 7, 1942, that it repeal a provision of the Emergency Price Control Act:

> I ask the Congress to take this action by the first of October. Inaction on your part by that date will leave me with an inescapable responsibility to the people of this country to see to it that the war effort is no longer imperiled by threat of economic chaos.
>
> In the event that the Congress should fail to act, and act adequately, I shall accept the responsibility, and I will act.
>
> At the same time that fair prices are stabilized, wages can and will be stabilized also. This I will do.
>
> The President has the powers, under the Constitution and under Congressional acts, to take measures necessary to avert a disaster which would interfere with the winning of the war.
>
> I have given the most thoughtful consideration to meeting this issue without further reference to the Congress. I have determined, however, on this vital matter to consult with the Congress. . . .
>
> The American people can be sure that I will use my powers with a full sense of my responsibility to the Constitution and to my country. The American people can also be sure that I shall not hesitate to use every power vested in me to accomplish the defeat of our enemies in any part of the world where our own safety demands such defeat.
>
> When the war is won, the powers under which I act automatically revert to the people—to whom they belong.[128]

Such presidential behavior is by no means the rule. Nor was it the rule for Franklin D. Roosevelt.

---

[128] Corwin, *op. cit.*, pp. 250-51.

It is not the prevalent mode of relations between President and Congress in time of peace or in time of war. This is indicated by the work of the Truman Committee in the Second World War. Donald H. Riddle in his study of that committee quotes Truman as saying "I just wanted to help the President win the war." The committee acted with high responsibility. True, it irritated administrative agencies on occasion; it probably interfered in administration on occasion; it had its nominees for particular wartime positions; it had its pet projects and its pet peeves. But its purpose at all times was to complement the activities of the executive branch in fighting the war, and to help to insure that along the way an excess of zeal did not camouflage and permit the continuance of inefficient or inadequate administrative behavior, or undermine democratic institutions.[129]

Studies of British and American wartime government such as the volumes in the remarkable British "civil history" series edited by W. K. Hancock, uniformly revealed the continuing influence and indeed control over administration which democratic legislatures can exert in wartime.[130] The fact that novel powers which are not exercised as a rule in peacetime are granted to the executive or assumed by him, and the fact that executive leadership tends to expand to fill the demand for it, create the impression that democratic institutions and practices are suspended. But upon close analysis, it will be found that the essential institutions and practices which we associate with democratic government, and perhaps especially legislative oversight, continue to function.

The pitfalls of analogizing from the parliamentary system to the congressional-presidential system should not be taken as suggesting that there is no transferability of experience between Great Britain and the United States. There has been much profitable borrowing of substantive legislative provisions between the two countries. Conceding the limitations of oversight when the executive dominates the legislature, the British have nonetheless developed and effectively employed a mode of response to recurrent domestic emergencies, such as strikes affecting the national welfare, whereby the opportunity for legislative oversight and participation is maximized. The method of oversight is generically akin to the American use of the concurrent

---

[129] Donald H. Riddle, *The Truman Committee: A Study in Congressional Responsibility* (New Brunswick, New Jersey: Rutgers University Press, 1954). p. 28.

[130] W. K. Hancock (ed.), *History of the Second World War, United Kingdom Civil Series* (London: His Majesty's Stationery Office, various dates). See especially W. K. Hancock and M. M. Gowing, *British War Economy* (London: His Majesty's Stationery Office, 1949).

resolution (the "legislative veto") to influence legislation under the Emergency Powers Act of 1920.[131]

The Emergency Powers Act empowers the government to declare an emergency when it appears to it "that any action . . . taken or . . . immediately threatened by any persons or body of persons" is "of such a nature and on so extensive a scale as to be calculated, by interfering with the supply and distribution of food, water, fuel, or light, or with the means of locomotion to deprive the community, or any substantial portion of the community, of the essentials of life." Under such a proclamation the government may by order in council make necessary regulations for securing the essentials of life to the community. Such regulations may not, however, provide for military or industrial conscription, nor may they make peaceful striking or persuasion to strike an offense.

In Britain, proclamations of emergency must be communicated to the Parliament "forthwith," and if that body is not then in session, "a proclamation shall be issued for the meeting of Parliament within five days." Emergency regulations may be promulgated but must be laid before Parliament "as soon as they may be" and expire if not approved by resolution of both houses within seven days following their receipt. They may "be added to, altered, or revoked by resolution of both houses" at any time. Proclamations of emergency have "force for [not] more than one month," and the emergency regulations expire with the proclamation. The government may, if it wishes, issue a new proclamation and new regulations at any time, but the regulations must receive parliamentary approval afresh.

The United States, which traditionally responds in *ad hoc* fashion to crippling dock, auto, steel, and rail strikes, might well consider replacing the myriad of varied and frequently ineffectual emergency statutes with generic legislation similar to that described above, and including equally clear and forceful provisions for legislative oversight.

---

[131] 10 and 11 Geo. 5, Ch. 55 (1920).

Conclusions and Recommendations

WE have had experience, in history, with an extreme "legislative force" model characterized by a legislature which directly administers its own programs. It did not work. Some critics are fearful of the inevitable transformation of the pattern of executive-legislative relations toward what we may call the extreme "executive force" model. This would be characterized by a kind of executive domination of the legislature that would make of the latter a virtual rubber stamp. The authors of these papers do not herald the imminent arrival of such a situation. Either of the two extremes is the negation of oversight. Neither has room for it—in the first it is superfluous, in the second impracticable.

Insofar as the argument concerning the proper pattern of executive-legislative relations is conducted by reasonable and informed students, it is an argument cast in terms of balance. As, in adopting a federal form of government, we sought to preserve strong states while creating a strong national government—thus achieving "union without unity"—so we seek today, in the arena of the relations between Congress and the President, to maintain a national legislature which is functional and strong, consistent with a President who is strong and independent in those spheres in which he ought to be.

There is a kind of "adversary" approach to skirting the difficulties imminent in defining the ingredients of the "balance" just referred to. That is to take the position that the legislature should be encouraged to pursue any avenues it wishes toward influencing administrative conduct, in any manner that it wishes, and toward whatever ends it wishes. Then, let the executive resist "encroachment" as it has the motive, weapons, and the stamina to do so. This is a plague-on-both-your-houses approach, and a substitute for analysis.

We think that striking a balance between executive and legislative power should be guided by a number of considerations. (a) The

79

legislature is entitled to legislate when as and if it pleases, consistently with constitutional limitations. It is equally entitled to accept executive effort at leadership in this process of policy formation as it is to disregard it. (b) The appropriations process is the obverse side of the coin of policymaking, and Congress should vigorously employ it toward expressing approval of, toward modifying, or toward negating executive policy proposals as expressed in budget requests. There are sufficient avenues of communication and opportunities for executive influence with legislators to enable the executive to protect its program against arbitrary legislative action. (c) Congress has available to it a variety of devices to permit it to conduct retrospective review of the administration of programs approved and financed by it. The evidence thus far collected would indicate that these devices are not employed as methodically and effectively as they might be. We suggest that effective legislative oversight can complement the President's attempts to keep his own administration responsible. (d) Congress has evidenced a desire to influence administration in a manner which is prospective, continuing, and detailed, with regard to a restricted number of programs in which it has a special constituency or other commitment. One can look with equanimity upon this phenomenon—it does not spell the doom of separation and balance of powers—so long as it does not multiply in the absence of occasional critical scrutiny.

The foregoing is not to suggest an absence of need for institutional and attitudinal change to strengthen Congress as an independent force overseeing the administration. This we attempt in conclusion. The recommendations are meant to be experimental and incremental, and are offered in no didactic spirit. What we are dealing with is largely a matter of legislative perception of its appropriate role. Institutional changes will be recommended below, but they are worth the effort only insofar as they facilitate a change of attitude toward the oversight function.

It is important that the full body of the House and of the Senate better equip itself to perform an oversight function. To this end, hoary as the recommendation may be, I would revive the late Senator Estes Kefauver's recommendation of a question period.

There should be greater use—indeed, perhaps exclusive use—of joint legislative committees, with the legislative committees perhaps performing the budget review process in addition to the authorization process for agencies within their purview.

The Bureau of the Budget should be made a joint agency of the President and Congress. The objection in terms of serving two masters does not necessarily hold water, and in any case this would be preferable to building up petty bureaucracies on the Hill. Short of this, Congress should establish its own budget office, responsible to whatever officer of Congress, committee, or committees appears most logical.

The House and the Senate should establish oversight calendars, giving precedence at least two days in each month to committee reports pertaining to oversight of administration. Home rule for the District of Columbia would help to free legislative time for this purpose and for more effective and sustained oversight, generally.

Steps should be taken to (a) computerize the budgetary and appropriations processes, and (b) to depart, on a selective basis, from the one-year, fiscal July 1-June 30, appropriation for programs which are not suited to this cycle.

Congress could be assured of more effective oversight of emergency executive action, and the President assured more flexibility to respond to emergency, if a generic statute applicable to all types of emergency were adopted; one provision of the statute would require that presidential proclamations of emergency and rules and regulations promulgated under such proclamations be subject to congressional veto by concurrent resolution.

The Supreme Court engages in two levels of review of congressional legislation. At the first level, involving judicial interpretation of the *meaning* of statutes, Congress freely and frequently reverses such interpretation by enacting new legislation, clarifying its legislative intent. At the second level, that at which the Court interprets the *constitutionality* of congressional legislation, the Congress should similarly, although perhaps through a more extended procedure, have power to reverse the Court. We therefore recommend a constitutional amendment to permit Congress, on re-enactment by a two-thirds vote of both Houses in two consecutive sessions, to render constitutional statutes which the Court has found to be in violation. The extension of this authority to enable Congress to validate state statutes declared unconstitutional by the U.S. Supreme Court is also worthy of consideration; Congress by legislation incorporating reference to the state statute involved could reverse the Court and render the statute valid.

LEWIS ANTHONY DEXTER is Lecturer in Social Science, Massachusetts Institute of Technology, engaged in three-year study of the politics of health, education, welfare and labor programs in state governments, and has had an extensive background in legislative matters.

He has participated in congressional campaigns in Illinois, upstate New York, Pennsylvania, Maryland, Missouri, and Massachusetts. He was also Elections and Nationalities Group Analyst for the Democratic National Committee in 1952. In 1956 and 1960 he was research director to the successful candidates for governor in Massachusetts. In 1957 and 1961 he helped set up that state's new governor's office. Over the last 30 years he has taken part in many campaigns for local office. He has been employed on Capitol Hill as a special adviser on civil defense and foreign trade legislation. He has also been connected with several lobbying organizations as a consultant for one of which he wrote a several-hundred-page manual of lobbying procedures.

The American Political Science Association awarded him and his co-authors, Raymond Bauer and Ithiel Pool, the Woodrow Wilson award given annually for the best book published in the U.S. in political science, for *American Business and Public Policy* (New York: Atherton Press, 1963). He has also prepared a series of articles on the Congress, including "The Representative and His District" (Bobbs-Merrill reprint series, PS-63), and "What Does Congress Resemble in What Respect?" read at the American Political Science Association meetings in September 1965. At present, Dr. Dexter is preparing a book to be edited by A. Biderman and E. Crawford discussing the uses and non-uses of social science by congressmen.

He is perhaps best known for his book *The Tyranny of Schooling, An Inquiry into the Problem of "Stupidity"* (New York: Basic Books, 1964).

"Check and Balance" Today: What Does It Mean for Congress and Congressmen?

Lewis Anthony Dexter

Introduction

POLITICAL and social institutions depend, ultimately, upon ideas in the minds of men—ideas about the way people should or will act. Frequently there is a slippage between fundamental ideals, on the one hand, and the effects of actions on the other: so that what men believe ought to happen does not coincide at all with the way things are actually done.

When such discrepancies occur in an institution people nowadays often start looking into the basic theory by which it is guided. So they set up commissions and committees on reorganization. Perhaps the feeling that there has been such a slippage between what Congress *ought* to do and what it *is* doing explains the establishment of the Joint Committee on the Organization of the Congress—and this symposium of papers. At any rate, one reason why I personally wanted to take part in the symposium was my feeling that Congress is not really checking and balancing the President and the executive departments as much as it should, and could.

Congress is not as effective in checking and balancing as it ought to be because of the absence of a relevant contemporary development of the doctrine. Most people in the United States today have no clear notion as to why there should be a Congress which is separate from and independent of the other two branches of government. To be sure, they know this is the way things have always been; but if asked to justify or explain the American system of separate powers, they will generally talk in terms of out-of-date eighteenth century notions and problems. Members of Congress themselves, of course, usually come to recognize the full significance of their job; but they do not articulate it to the public in terms of modern life as much as is desirable. And partly because they do not speak up for themselves, there is no general climate of opinion or informed public support to back Congress when, on occasion, it does carry out its job of checking — and sometimes blocking — the programs of the executive departments.

What is needed most, then, is a restatement of the doctrine of check and balance in terms of the current social and political conditions. Certainly there are various ways in which Congress could reorganize itself so as to check and balance more efficiently. Part II of this paper suggests changes in procedure, structure, and regulation which would, I believe, help Congress to carry out its traditional task today. However, these changes will be helpful only if there is a revitalization of the whole check-and-balance doctrine; by themselves they will not lead to the results we want.

Checks and Balances:
The Current Value of the Doctrine

Check and balance in government means one branch thwarting, hampering, interfering with, criticizing, and opposing the activities of the other so as to counteract the unwisdom of the "wise."

THE seventeenth century Swedish statesman Count Oxenstierna reportedly summed up the lesson of his years in government with a single sentence. "I have found," he said, "with what little wisdom the world is ruled!" This bleak judgment contains the justification for the doctrine of check and balance in general, and for congressional checking of the executive in particular.

Check and balance in government exists only under the following conditions: (1) The governmental system comprises two or more separate branches of equal legitimacy and authority, each having its own independent base of support; [1] and (2) the relationship between these branches is so defined as to render it, in normal circumstances, perfectly proper for officials of the one to thwart, hamper, interfere with, criticize, and oppose the activities of the other.

These conditions amount to what may be called "a system of separate powers." [2] It is in this context that the function of the check-

---

[1] See Philip Selznick, "Sociology of Law," prepared for the forthcoming *International Encyclopedia of the Social Sciences*, Crowell Collier. (The Selznick article is now available in mimeographed form from the Center for the Study of Law and Society, University of California at Berkeley, April 1965.)

[2] Discussions of the American system of government are usually conducted in terms of the "separation of powers." But this phrase, although much used, is misleading because it erroneously implies that the executive ought to do

and-balance doctrine in the United States government today has to be understood. For, from the point of view of the ordinary citizen, the outstanding characteristic which favorably distinguishes the American system of government from unified governments in other countries is the existence of what the late, beloved Morton Grodzins called "multiple cracks." He used this phrase to imply that in our government there are several entry points or places where a private citizen can lodge a complaint, or ask a favor, or present a viewpoint. If a petitioner or representative of an interest group gets turned down by officials at one point in the system, he has a good prospect of being heeded and supported by government officials holding a similarly powerful position somewhere else in the system, possessing an equally legitimate right to intervene in the matter in question.

Such "multiple cracks" are possible precisely because our government consists of three independent branches, each having its own separate legitimate powers. If they were ever to be effectively coordinated and integrated—say by a "responsible party system," as some have desired—then the number of entry points would automatically diminish and the principle of check and balance would be undermined.

Nowadays, when we hear a good deal about "consensus" and "cooperation" as always being desirable in government, the notion that check and balance should involve thwarting, hampering, interfering, criticizing, opposing, will naturally seem to many a little perverse and wrong-headed. But the whole point is that it is the making of mistakes which may be thus hampered, the commission of errors thwarted, the imposition of one-sided and unfair decisions interfered with, the adoption of a wrong policy opposed.

Of course, there are nicer words to describe these aspects of check and balance. Instead of thwarting and hampering, we might talk about "correcting and reorienting"; instead of interfering, we might refer to "oversight" and an "effort to help people face real situations"; instead of criticizing, we might emphasize the "contribution of constructive ideas." But I am deliberately and purposefully using the more impolite and abrasive terms, because there seems to me to be

---

nothing but administrate, the legislature legislate, the judiciary judge. Whereas in practice, as scholars are now beginning to recognize, no such clearcut division of functions exists or can be expected to exist. The executive has always done a good deal of judging and legislating, the judiciary much legislating and some administering, and the Congress at least some administering and judging. It is in this intermingling of functions by the separate co-equal branches of government that the doctrine of check and balance has its significance, and the American system of government part of its genius.

a real danger of Congress becoming too "nice" as an institution, too respectful of the experts in the bureaucracy [3] and of the "leader" in the White House. Moreover, the terms that I have used are exactly the same unpleasant terms which are hurled at the heads of those congressmen who do try to carry out their jobs.

If individual congressmen are effectively to check and balance the executive, they must inevitably expect to be criticized by those whose biases are pro-executive, and they must steel themselves against ridicule accordingly. Such criticism and ridicule is likely to come from the White House, the bureaucracy, the more intellectual journalists, and the majority of the professoriat, especially those in the fields closely identified with the bureaucracies.[4]

Congressional check and balance is necessary in this country on a day-to-day basis to offset the dominance of the specialists in the bureaucracy.

Specialists, of course, are valuable, and in a complicated, scientific world necessary. But there are grave dangers in relying upon them too much, and the maxim "specialists should always be on tap but never on top" should be remembered. Unfortunately, in modern life trained professionals are, in their particular areas of responsibility, increasingly "on top." And more often than not, even when they have a politician or businessman as their nominal boss, they tell him what decisions he is to make.

In consequence, life-and-death decisions are made by specialists

---

[3] Some evidence to support this statement is presented in Lewis A. Dexter, "Congressmen and the Making of Military Policy," in R. Peabody and N. Polsby (eds.), *New Perspectives on Congress* (Chicago: Rand McNally, 1963), pp. 305-24, republished in D. Bobrow (ed.), *Components of Defense Policy* (Chicago: Rand McNally, 1965), pp. 94-110 (longer mimeographed version available from the author); the issue is also implicit in much of the discussion of Congress in R. Bauer, I. Pool, and L. Dexter, *American Business and Public Policy* (New York: Atherton Press, 1963), particularly, pp. 401-62.

[4] One of the most valuable readings for the student of check and balance today is Herbert Spencer's cutting and clear discussion of the tendency of professionals in each field to look at things in terms only of their own occupational biases; see his discussion of professional bias in *Study of Sociology* (New York: Appleton Press, 1873), pp. 161-64, reprinted in J. Cuber and P. Haroff, *Readings in Sociology* (New York: Appleton Press, 1962), pp. 10-14. I have tried to apply Spencer's approach to some current difficulties which experts create in my "Use and Abuse of Social Science by the Practitioner," *American Behavioral Scientist*, November 1965, pp. 25-29.

who frequently have the power of government behind them, and who are easily able to outargue and overawe those actually affected by their decisions. For instance, when government orders an urban renewal program, or when a small shopkeeper or self-employed craftsman gets into trouble with the federal tax authorities, or when a group of mentally retarded adolescents are threatened with institutionalization, the experts and specialists are normally able to impose decisions upon the people involved with little attention to their views and wishes.

Naturally, specialists often make decisions which in their long-run consequences are right, correct, valuable, and admirable. But all too frequently such long-term decisions are clumsily handled and many people are avoidably hurt in the process. There needs to be some one who is rewarded for asking: "Is it really necessary to do this thing in the way that hurts these people in this fashion?" or "Although much of this program must be carried out, no doubt, how about these-and-these parts of it which are certainly going to have this ill-effect upon such-and-such kinds of persons?" or "Have these possible boomerang effects or undesirable side-products of the program been adequately considered, and have you figured out how you will deal with them if they occur?"

Some specialists ask such questions themselves. But specialists usually acquire a vested interest in their programs because prestige and reputation depend upon the programs being adopted lock, stock, and barrel. And then, too, any given group of specialists is usually recruited from a rather limited segment of society, and has usually been unconsciously indoctrinated in a whole set of assumptions and values which are not shared by the people affected by their decisions. Lastly, most specialists work in a much more hierarchical, bureaucratic system than the people whose lives they determine. All these facts make it likely that specialists, with the best will in the world, will often ignore or overlook such questions and the questions such people have in their minds.

On the whole, the *political* man, in American society the congressman or legislator, is best suited to raise such questions. Congressmen, for instance, especially congressmen who really know their districts, are made aware of many different interests and concerns. They hear many complaints, and to a certain extent they themselves can sometimes actually benefit by "making an issue." So, what is sometimes a purely selfish desire for publicity or electoral support leads them to speak out for people whose wishes the specialists would otherwise disregard. Finally, congressmen differ sharply from most other groups of professional men in that they belong to a working group (that is, the Congress itself) whose members are expected to take quite seriously and respectfully the complaints and problems of outsiders. Nearly every other professional group (including most of the groups to which experts in the bureaucracy belong) indoctrinates its members (no matter what lipservice is paid to democracy) to regard the professional as much better informed than any outsiders and therefore better equipped to judge.

Emphasis on specialization could lead to tyranny.

So far I have been talking about instances where, basically, the decisions of the specialists are in the overall public interest, but where side-effects or by-products are harmful and injurious to individuals or groups of individuals. However, there are also instances where the specialists are cruelly wrong: wrong because they identify themselves, whether deliberately or unwittingly, with a particular vested interest in society without taking into account the interests of others; wrong because at a given time all those in a given profession are indoctrinated and trained in a particular tradition that may have long since ceased to have any validity.

One example in the history of the movement for social welfare was the practically unanimous agreement of economic specialists that regulatory and remedial legislation was economically unsound. Another example was the adoption of the idea of racially-based inferiority by most specialists on poverty and immigration in the 1910 period. In more recent years, we have seen psychometrists using intelligence tests to discriminate against worthy people; the tests were useful enough for their original purpose, but organized groups of specialists misused them and people have been abused in consequence. And in the history of medicine, we can think of the original violent hostility of the medical profession to the Semmelweiss-Holmes notion that doctors spread childbed fever (which was later proved true). Or we can think of the high probability (strongly suggested by Szasz and Scheff)[5] that present commitment procedures for insanity are in many jurisdictions likely to result in the unjust incarceration of people,

---

[5] See T. Szasz, *The Myth of Mental Illness* (New York: Harper, 1961) and T. Scheff, "Social Conditions for Rationality: How Urban and Rural Courts Deal With the Mentally Ill," *American Behavioral Scientist,* March 1964, pp. 21-24, and "Societal Reactions to Deviance; Ascriptive Elements in the Psychiatric Screening of Mental Patients," *Social Problems* (11, 1963-64), pp. 211-16.

merely because they happen to offend middle class professionals biases about reasonableness and quite regardless of any considerations of the public good.

In some instances, specialists even instigate and create tyranny. To be sure, their motives are of the best, their ideals of the highest, their aspirations of the noblest. All this was true of specialist theologians, the friars who managed the Holy Inquisition; yet their treatment of heretics and lapsed Catholics was cruel. Indeed, if we ever have a really tyrannical dictatorship in this country, it will probably develop, like Michael Young's *Meritocracy* or Aldous Huxley's *Brave New World,* from glorification of the specialists.

The need for an institution which encourages its members to look into the tyrannical behavior of experts and to protect us against the development of a "meritocracy" tyranny is quite apparent. And Congress, as the separate legislative branch of our government, is the proper body to provide us with such protection.

The check-and-balance system can be used to correct the mistakes and errors of judgment of the specialists.

Imagine, for the sake of argument, that all specialists, bureaucrats, and leaders became so imaginative and kindhearted that the kind of oppression which we have been discussing simply could not happen. The biggest need for an effective system of check and balance would still remain.

Firstly, even specialists make mistakes—mistakes not at all cruel or tyrannical, but which are just plain foolish. Moreover, they keep on making the same sort of mistakes. The Polish army, for instance, according to all accounts relied upon cavalry to resist tanks during World War II; prior to 1939, prominent diplomats in the Western powers refused against all the evidence to take the Nazis seriously.

Secondly, people in the same sort of job or the same social position tend to make the same sort of mistakes, because they pay attention to the same sort of things—and overlook the same sort of things. And if they have also been schooled and trained in the same way, the similarity of foolishness is even greater. To use further military example: Between 1916 and 1940 the cavalrymen and the commanding generals in most nations could not or would not understand the importance of the tank in warfare, for reasons which well illustrate why specialists are sometimes suicidally wrong.

Professor Theodore Ropp has pointed out in this connection that "any body of organized knowledge . . . produces a pattern of thinking which influences the way people work in that field. . ."; and he goes on to explain that because of the existence of this pattern, the thinker finds problems solvable and some real problems remain concealed from him.[6] This point was summed up by Thorstein Veblen in a beautiful phrase when he said that men in any profession or line of work tend to suffer from a "trained incapacity." In other words, they develop a doctrine, a set of traditions and values, which overlooks and ignores significant aspects of reality. And as new situations and new problems arise, it turns out that something which has been overlooked or ignored is often a key element of the real problem that people actually have to face.[7]

Another consideration that has to be taken into account is the tendency within an efficiently administered bureaucracy, other things being equal, for the head of the organization to accept the views of his own specialists as final, and for these specialists to structure their views according to what they think the head of the organization wants. The result is that bureaucracies do not encourage real diver-

---

[6] See Theodore Ropp, et al., "The Process of Assimilation of New Weapons Into Effective Organization and Tactics," Annex IIIB to Historical Trends Related to Weapon Lethality (mimeographed), issued by Historical Evaluation and Research Organization, 2233 Wisconsin Avenue, Washington, D. C. 20007, 1964, pp. B-2, B-4.

[7] Actually, what happens is this: any theory or doctrine necessarily simplifies the world a great deal. It highlights some things and ignores others. For instance, both economics and physics are much simpler than "the big, blooming, buzzing confusion" of the actual world. Such simplification is essential in order to manage and grasp certain aspects of reality; and *for the initial purposes of the original theorists* a widely respected doctrine or way of thought generally proves useful, valid, and liberating. But events change, new knowledge is acquired and new problems develop—so that the doctrine which was once helpful in solving a particular kind of problem in a particular set of circumstances often hampers the solution of another. For instance, the laissez-faire economic theory of Adam Smith was liberating and substantially valid for his time, place, and purposes; but under other circumstances it was ridiculously inapplicable. Gradually as new knowledge developed and new problems sprang up, it had to be seriously modified to have any meaning for the world of 1900, where a few large corporations possessed technological resources Smith had never dreamed of. But Smith's disciples—professional economists —kept on discussing the problems of 1900 in terms of the simplifications of 1776. For this reason, they probably made adjustment to the economic costs of World War II or the Great Depression more difficult; just as in many instances the programs they imposed upon underdeveloped nations were ridiculously inapplicable to conditions there.

For a discussion of the subject of "trained incapacity," see Kenneth Burke, *Attitudes Toward History*, (rev. 2d ed.; Boston: Beacon, 1961).

sity of thought, independence of ideas, or recognition of those problems which it would be uncomfortable for the chief executive or their own professionals to face up to.

Now, one way to avoid this blindness, and the consequent serious mistakes to which it may lead, is to encourage different groups of specialists, different agencies, to fight with each other. Members of Congress whom I know have felt that bitter conflict within the Defense Department, for instance, is to the public interest, because it is only as a result of such conflict that outsiders can find out what really is going on.[8] And, it was observed that President Franklin D. Roosevelt frequently made a point of leaving jurisdictional lines unclear and of giving the same assignment to different kinds of people, so as to encourage bureaucratic infighting and the consequent clarification of issues.

Supporters of check and balance should certainly endorse the Roosevelt approach in principle and strongly resist the stress laid on harmony and consensus by Presidents like Eisenhower and Johnson. However, recent history shows the weakness of relying upon such fights within the bureaucracy as the chief source of public enlightenment—though they should be encouraged and stimulated, wherever feasible. Effective strong Presidents like Johnson and able, driving secretaries like McNamara suppress controversy since in the short run it is unfortunately in their interest to sweep departmental differences of opinion beneath the rug.

In any case, the issues about which specialists differ most sharply are not necessarily the issues of great civic importance. Jonathan Swift's account in *Gulliver's Travels* of the ferocious controversy between "big endians" and "little endians" ("which end of an egg is up?" would be our modern way of putting it) suggested the difficulty here. The specialists often agree on some fundamental points which are precisely those that men of common sense would question, and only fight ferociously about technical details within a common framework of assumptions. In other words, the real issue in Swift's story was not "which end should be up?" but whether it *mattered* which end was up. Thus, conflict between the armed services, for example, is seldom a source of real enlightenment: since all too frequently the services agree on a basic policy which may be essentially erroneous in terms of the public interest, and disagree merely about the

---

[8] See Lewis A. Dexter, "Congressmen and the Making of Military Policy," in D. Bobrow (ed.), *Components of Defense Policy* (Chicago: Rand McNally, 1965), pp. 94-110.

details of implementing it. One case when most military authorities were wrong was the Franco-British acceptance of the Fochian doctrine of all-out attack in the 1914-18 war. The few politicians who questioned this strategy—First Lord of the Admiralty Churchill and Chancellor of the Exchequer McKenna, for instance—are now generally agreed to have been right. The prevailing specialist doctrine, almost everyone who has studied the subject would now admit, killed millions of young men and in the final analysis was partly responsible for the troubles on the 1918-39 international scene.

The point I am making is *not* that we should take it for granted that most specialists are wrong. By no means. But what we need is somebody to question the specialists, to harass them into thinking through and stating their fundamental assumptions, to request that they relate their doctrines to the actual problems of ordinary people and to keep on pushing until they do, and above all to pay attention to the few specialists who question the prevailing point of view. On any issue there usually are a few specialists who see things differently from their colleagues, and among them there are occasionally one or two genuine prophets equipped to deal with the future.[9] Going back to our example of tank warfare, Liddell-Hart and General Fuller, among a few others, were military men who long before 1940 saw the tank as the future weapon of mobile warfare (included in the "few others" was that genius, Charles de Gaulle—we now forget that this was his first great claim to fame).

Naturally, the kinds of mistakes which specialists made during World Wars I and II are exceptionally dramatic.[10] Probably, most of the time the military specialists are in fact right; but this should not, for one single minute, be taken for granted in regard to large measures of policy, when there is time for forecasting and analysis.[11]

---

[9] For a good account of a maverick military expert see Elting Morrison, *Admiral Sims and the Modern American Navy* (Boston: Houghton, Mifflin, 1942).

[10] A good example of a non-dramatic mistake which could have been questioned more effectively than it was occurred when the U.S. army finally abandoned horse cavalry. It gave up, by a natural conjunction of ideas, the mule, too. But in fact, it turned out (and could have been foreseen) that mules were very useful for warfare because they could and did keep going where mechanical vehicles got bogged down. And so, after abandoning the mule, a hurry-up pressure to get mules and mule-handlers took place under the experience of actual war!

[11] An example of current military policy which should be questioned, just as the "Western" strategic attack policy should have been questioned by British leaders in 1912-16, is the reliance of most of our military leaders upon strategic bombing and guerrilla type activities, with little attention to psycho-

Harassing the specialists ought to be the paramount task of Congress today.

Obviously, a separate legislative branch is the best institution to raise questions and to harass and to chivvy specialists, and generally to force them to be more careful and considerate about what they do and recommend. Obviously, at least, until somebody thinks of a better way of achieving the same result.

Because Congress relies so heavily on the use of standing committees, check-and-balance operations must undoubtedly be performed in standing committees; in any case, standing committees are better equipped to perform the check-and-balance function than any other legislative mechanism. They permit legislators to become specialists in discovering the weakness and exaggeration of subject matter specialists. Also congressmen can make themselves specialists on the kinds of mistakes the bureaucratic specialists ought to be asked, and the kinds of explanations the specialists are likely to put forward in reply. Confronted by inexperienced legislators who are dealing with them for the first time, specialists can and do run rings around them.[12] It takes experience to learn the kinds of slogans, rationalizations, excuses, and evasions which a particular group of bureaucrats specializes in (and which many of them genuinely believe). Indeed, a good congressman must be, as one member described himself to me, a "gnawing, gnawing, gnawing so-and-so." It is only by gnawing and gnawing and gnawing that one can get at the meaning and significance behind the slogans, rationalizations, excuses, and evasions— to repeat, there is an *expertness* in checking on specialists. In becoming "gnawing, gnawing, gnawing so-and-sos" congressmen will be fulfilling their best and most significant function. In fact, there ought to be a prize for the gnawingest so-and-so in Congress, and in each state legislature too!

chemicals which are best suited to gaining the desired objective of measured retaliation. On this see B. H. Liddell-Hart, *Deterrent or Defence* (London: Stevens & Sons, 1960), Ch. 8, "Is Gas A Better Alternative?" and Lewis A. Dexter, "Conventional Death or Unconventional Survival," *Saturday Review* (Science Section), February 7, 1959, republished in the *Congressional Record* by Representative Edith Green of Oregon, February 17, 1959. On the theory of measured retaliation as against strategic bombing, see (Prime Minister) Lester Pearson, *Democracy and World Politics* (Princeton: Princeton University Press, 1955).

[12] The high turnover in state legislatures, and the consequent inexperience of many members, probably explains why they are so ineffective sometimes in checking the executive.

Senator Dirksen demonstrates the kind of humility which congressmen should scorn. In expressing his disagreement with the House Republican leadership on Vietnam he reportedly remarked: "How could I, a mere shavetail in World War I have any right to question strategy set by the generals?" And a member of the House Armed Services Committee said to me, in a very serious evaluation of his task, "The whole problem is that we are not military experts and we have to rely upon what the military people teli us. . . . Who are we to say 'no' to the military people?" To a lesser extent perhaps, but nevertheless very significantly, congressmen treat specialists in other departments of the bureaucracy with the same respect—not nearly as much as the specialists would like, of course, but far more than is desirable in terms of the view about the public interest which I have advanced.

On the other hand, at the moment, the Congress fortunately does exert influence in checking the excesses of the executive specialists and administrators. But much of this influence is latent rather than direct, stemming from the executive's fear that Congress might clamp down on it if it does thus-and-so. Moreover, as the bureaucracy grows, and as the respect for professional people in this country increases, congressmen may become less willing to criticize the executive and check its mistakes.

How can congressmen increase their capacity to check and balance?

The first necessity, far more important than any other, is for legislators to regain the belief in the concept of Congress as an independent branch of government within the system of separate powers. That is, they must renew their confidence in Congress as an institution with a definite function to perform vis-à-vis the other two branches, and particularly the executive.

A basis for such confidence is to be found in a conscious, articulated awareness of the enormous value and significance of the check-and-balance doctrine in contemporary times. This awareness will necessarily involve rejection of the call for party discipline or party responsibility [13] which is now so intellectually fashionable. It will demand a denial of the value of consensus and harmony. And

---

[13] See James Burns, *Deadlock of Democracy* (Englewood Cliffs, N.J.: Prentice Hall, 1963), for the most persuasive statement of the doctrine of party responsibility.

above all, it will mean that congressmen will have to have confidence in themselves and in their own judgment.[14]

As far as I can determine, right now many members of Congress are essentially the kind of men who do in fact trust their own judgments. Probably in their pre-congressional careers, most of them were more self-confident and independent than the average. For the kind of personal risks generally involved in running for Congress, the kind of self-reliance needed to go through gruelling campaigns of self-advertisement, would tend to suggest that in our political system we generally elect men of high self-confidence. But, since these men are dependent on public support, they need to be backed by a climate of opinion which respects and encourages the questioning of experts, the challenging of specialists, the intelligent harassing of bureaucracies. The absence of such a climate of opinion today could mean that Congress as an institution will become an anachronism—although in terms of the approach argued here, it is really the times that are out of joint not the Congress.

Can Congress and informed publics develop sufficient awareness of the meaning of check and balance?

But what are the prospects of the right climate of opinion emerging? In seeking to turn upside down the attitudes of recent years, are we simply asking for the impossible? In other words, is this demand for a change of attitude practical? Such a political change or development *is* practical when, although people at a given moment seem wholeheartedly to believe in attitudes which point one way, nevertheless at the back of their minds, they feel something quite contradictory; that is, "latently" they are experiencing attitudes that point towards a denial of the doctrines and beliefs which they think they hold.[15] In fact, a latent contradiction of this kind is already becoming evident in the current attitude towards experts and specialists in this country. Jokes about psychologists, the widespread popularity of such comics as Little Orphan Annie, the semi-sympathy which many people, half-ashamedly, appear to have felt for the Berkeley students in their strike, and the wave of recent books directed against the "meritocracy," all these things suggest that we

---

[14] Quite unexpectedly, I find an interesting parallel between my point here and the argument for "autonomous" personality development in David Riesman, *The Lonely Crowd* (New Haven: Yale University Press, 1950).

[15] I am trying to state the major points of L. Doob, *Propaganda* (New York: Holt, 1935).

may be ready to modify greatly our former wholehearted trust in experts, specialists, and leaders. A positive shift so that the back-of-the-mind attitudes become recognizably dominant and the dominant attitudes become secondary usually occurs in one of two sets of circumstances: When major problems that are not being solved within the existing framework of belief come to public attention; or when a large number of people simply become bored with prevailing doctrine. The odds of one or the other of these developments taking place seem pretty high.

Most Americans tremendously underestimate the possibility and probability of great political change. Yet, in recent times we have seen many very important changes in this country: the development of the social welfare state, the increasingly intimate relationship between the states and the federal government, the new respectability of birth control proposals, the switch from complete unconcern over mental retardation to tremendous official involvement. But they have come about in such a step-by-step way that we were hardly aware that they were going on or had taken place. In some of the states, even greater political changes have taken place, changes which five years before "everybody" said were impractical: For instance, the diminution in the power of the Executive Council in Massachusetts, the collapse of the big city machines in several states, and, again in Massachusetts, the Cardinal-Archbishop publicly declaring that the state ought not to enforce Catholic views about birth control on non-Catholics by law!

All this is not to maintain that the changes advocated in this paper, and in this symposium generally, will necessarily happen. Indeed the odds are somewhat against it. The most likely happening is the development of more and more arbitrary executive authority, with Congress becoming no more important that the British House of Lords or the Canadian Senate. However, the valid analogy here is that of a horse race. Although a good handicapper would make More-and-More-Executive-Control-on-the-de Gaullist-Model the favorite, he would nevertheless also give Return-to-Real-Check-and-Balance a fair chance—but add "it depends upon how he is fed, exercised, and trained."

Measures to Enable Congress to Check and Balance the Executive More Effectively

THERE are two major ways to increase Congress' ability to check and balance. First, more members of Congress, individually, should deliberately plan their work in such a way as to check the specialists and the administrators in the executive branch. Since congressmen have a good deal of freedom to carry on their work, this is perfectly practical.[16] Second, changes can be made in the organization of the Congress itself which will stimulate members to act more frequently and effectively in terms of the check-and-balance tradition. Many of the suggestions made by fellow participants in this symposium are highly pertinent. The proposals which follow here should be considered in conjunction with theirs.

Congress should hire its own specialists, and make sure that they are indoctrinated in a congressional check-and-balance viewpoint.

It is generally agreed that Congress needs more experts of its own. This, certainly, is essential. A parallel with the adversary tradition in our legal system will illustrate the need very clearly. When executive officers present their programs to Congress, they are supported by hundreds, sometimes thousands, of specialists, much like a giant corporation going into court with a vast array of lawyers and ac-

---

16 On this point see Lewis A. Dexter, "The Representative and His District," Bobbs-Merrill reprint series, PS63, and Ch. 29, "The Job of the Congressman," in R. Bauer, I. Pool, and L. Dexter, *American Business and Public Policy* (New York: Atherton Press, 1963).

countants. Whereas when Congress wants to find out the meaning and significance of any executive proposal, and to weigh it in terms of the public interest, it usually finds itself in the position of the small shopkeeper who for some reason is engaged in a lawsuit against a giant corporation—quite unable to match the huge resources of the other side and lucky, indeed, to have a couple of competent specialists to help!

But it is not enough for Congress just to hire specialists. Indeed, the mere provision of specialists and technical advisers for congressmen may do more harm, from our standpoint, than good. For the great majority of specialists in many fields (not in all) tend nowadays to believe in what the editor of this symposium, Professor Alfred de Grazia, has called the "executive force model." [17] That is they tend to sympathize with the notion that ordinary people need to have done for them and to them what is good for them—according to the preconceptions of the professions to which the specialists themselves belong. The mere fact that a specialist, so inclined, happens to be hired by a congressional committee does not mean that he automatically changes his viewpoint. On the contrary, he may well work with the specialists of the bureaucracy against the emphasis on congressional check and balance—because his loyalty to his profession is greater than his loyalty to Congress as an instrument of the check-and-balance process. The danger that specialists, quite unconsciously in many instances, will thus sacrifice Congress to their profession is considerably increased if either: (a) employment is more or less temporary, so that the main picture the specialist has of himself is not primarily as a congressional employee; or if (b) a number of specialists are working on the same problem together, without having been properly indoctrinated in the congressional approach—for people working in a group naturally tend to reinforce their own professional biases. [18]

---

[17] Alfred de Grazia, *Republic in Crisis* (New York: Federal Legal Publications, Inc., 1965), Appendix B. The belief in the "executive force model" and the hostility towards legislators is, as far as my observation goes, even much greater among specialists in state government, most of whom see the enhancement of the power of the governorship as the only chance of "salvation."

[18] Indeed, as a general rule, I would say that congressional committees should be extremely reluctant to hire a number of specialists in the social or physical sciences to work together and that congressional contracting out of work to research institutes, as the executive often does, is not under present circumstances likely to produce satisfactory results for Congress. For most groups of researchers nowadays tend to hold an executive force viewpoint; and the committees would have to do considerable screening to get groups holding a congressional viewpoint.

One way of avoiding the difficulties just suggested is for congressmen to realize that the suspicion with which some of them view "academic types," and "Ph.D.s" is well-founded. However, they should be very clear as to why they feel so suspicious. It is not to the Ph.D. or the professional expert as such that politicians should object, but to the contempt for check-and-balance politics which is characteristic, probably, of the majority of distinguished and articulate scholars. If they understand the reason for their distrust of scholars, then congressmen will be encouraged to search for assistance from among that minority of specialists who do not share the general academic admiration for the executive. At present, it seems to me that some congressmen (and many state legislators) reluctantly rely upon specialists whom they profoundly distrust, in the belief that not to have any specialist assistance at all would be much worse.

Developing a program of indoctrination for congressional specialists:

This would be one obvious way to ensure that the specialists hired by Congress will thoroughly understand the check-and-balance notion and know that as congressional employees they must regard executive proposals suspiciously. After all, the military services sometimes devote months to indoctrination courses. Why should not the Congress do the same? The objectives of both are similar. In order to be a really good officer in, say, the Marine Corps, a man must unlearn some of the assumptions about the way to behave which he has learned in civilian life; likewise, specialists working for Congress ought to unlearn some of their assumptions about the superiority of professional judgment and of the executive model of government, which most of them have acquired, almost unconsciously from their university training.

A program of orientation for specialists might well include reading and application of writings on check and balance such as those in the present symposium. It should also stress classic statements of the need for check and balance which appear in such works as *The Character of a Trimmer*. [19] The major emphasis in this indoctrination course should be on specific examples of the dangers of accept-

---

[19] This, probably one of the most significant and certainly the best written political pamphlet ever produced, was prepared by George Saville, Marquess of Halifax, in the reign of James II; but it has great current relevance. Although there have been many editions, it is now, so far as I can find (publishers please note!) out of print.

ing what leaders in one's own field say,[20] and the dangerous results of pushing a professionally accepted doctrine too far or failing to modify it to suit changing circumstances. It should also generally stress the wisdom of the naive and the folly of bureaucrats through consideration of simple allegories like *The Emperor's New Clothes.*

Increasing the specialists' contact with the public:

Beyond indoctrination at a verbal level, a good many staff specialists actually ought to have the same kind of contact with the public that congressmen or the local congressional secretaries experience. It is probably not necessary that every single staff specialist, or even a majority of specialists, have such experience. But each congressional committee staff ought to include several specialists with this kind of experience,[21] since it will help to create awareness of the "big, buzzing, blooming confusion" of actual life and prevent overemphasis on particular professional doctrines. Of course, the best way for the specialist to make contact with the public is in political campaigning or in actual service at a local patronage headquarters; but, if, in any given case, this experience cannot be arranged, no doubt equivalents could be planned.

Use of personality tests:

Just at present, such tests are in disrepute with Congress, but this is chiefly because ill-equipped technicians have either used the wrong tests or have used them for irrelevant purposes. With due planning and care, personality tests could be developed (or adapted from existing tests) which would help to exclude those specialists who are most hostile to the principle of Congress checking the executive. For instance, people whose personality profile shows great faith in respectable views are unlikely to challenge the leaders of their profession.

Introduction of regulations to prevent conflicts of interest:

Most specialists have close relationships with other persons in their own profession. Consequently, many congressional specialists

---

20 For natural scientists, a good text on this subject is David Lindsay Watson, *Scientists are Human* (London: Watte & Co., 1936). Social scientists could use Kenneth Burke, *Attitudes Towards History* (rev. ed.; Boston: Beacon Press, 1961).

21 What I am talking about here is "cushioning," which is the term I use in my book, *Tyranny of Schooling* (New York: Basic Books, 1964), pp. 153-55, to describe the effort to make sure that each staff group has a leaven of the desired experiences, even though not every one in the group has.

have their closest relationship with executive professionals, committed to the executive viewpoint. And since executive specialists are far more numerous, and in many professions usually far more distinguished, than the congressional specialists, the latter are not only hesitant about advancing their own emphasis but often accept the former's opinions when they ought not to do so. Besides, the congressional professional, of necessity often has in the back of his mind the awareness that advancement in his career may very likely lie in the executive bureaucracy; so whether working *with* an executive department, or working *against* an executive department or not, he may well see his future bosses there.

This situation can be partially corrected by establishing a provision to prohibit congressional staff assistants from working for the executive or being employed in liaison with the executive until, say, two years after they have left congressional employment. Various exceptions might be made, of course, such as permitting a man who has worked on veterans' affairs to be given executive employment in a totally unrelated field like the Federal Communications Commission. One of the tasks of the Joint Commission on Check and Balance Principles, suggested below, would be to administer the exceptions. Probably the regulation should also define certain lobbying organizations that always work with the executive—for example, the pro-reciprocal trade organizations—as being for these purposes parts of the executive.

The regulation could be further reinforced by paying a bonus to ex-congressional employees who continue to refrain from working, directly or indirectly, for the executive after the two-year prohibition elapses. Also, the payment of salaries or fees to ex-congressional employees for work in the executive department, or to major contractors, without approval of the Joint Commission should be declared illegal, and the money be recoverable by appropriate fiscal authorities as paid without authorization. Presumably, such prohibitions could not apply to military service; but the assignment of ex-congressional employees to policy or public relations work while in service should be equally prohibited.

Although "grandfather clauses" would have to be written in to prevent cases of real personal hardship, similar regulations should be put into effect to prohibit the spouses or dependent children of congressional employees from being hired by the executive at a professional level in Washington (there's no harm in their being hired for purely clerical jobs or jobs in the field). The principle should first be declared, and then exceptions made, where they will do no harm: For instance probably there's no reason why the wife of the staff director of a congressional committee concerned with civil defense should not work in National Archives; but she should not be employed in the policymaking units of the Defense Department, or, for that matter, of Health, Education, and Welfare.

Finally, it might be a wise precaution to prohibit employees of Congress from sharing living quarters with employees of the executive department. This is a very common Washington practice and my impression is that in general such living arrangements again benefit the executive-oriented experts, since the pressure of their numbers and professional tradition makes it difficult for congressional employees to preserve congressional attitudes in these circumstances. Accordingly, regulations to make such living arrangement difficult—perhaps by reducing the stipend of congressional employees who continue with them after some specified date—should be discussed (the mere discussion of the issue, indeed, might serve to eliminate most of the cases). Individual congressmen who are in a strong enough bargaining position should now make it a condition of employment that their staff not room with executive employees.[22]

Various measures could be taken to assist individual congressmen in their task of checking the executive.

To some extent, what has just been said about the need to protect congressional staff from overexposure to the executive viewpoint applies to congressmen themselves; although it is much less im-

---

[22] Following out this line of thought, it would also be appropriate if students of Congress, particularly when engaged in interviewing where they get confidential information, were to recognize similar ethical obligations. Perhaps the American Political Science Association could work out a code enjoining students of Congress (a) *never* simultaneously to advise or consult with the executive on any matter of legislative impact, and (b) always to establish a waiting period—say, two years—before taking up any employment with the executive having legislative import after the completion of their legislative studies (the waiting period before taking up work in executive liaison should certainly be much longer!).

Another relevant but parenthetical issue in the general question of how to insulate people from overexposure to the executive viewpoint is the matter of patronage. I am not sure how important it is in Congress, but I am sure it is significant in state legislatures. Executive departments sometimes try to buy "immunity" from legislative criticism by agreeing to accept appointees selected by legislators. How can this danger be counteracted? Perhaps by making more patronage positions available in the legislature itself? I am not satisfied with any answer to this problem as yet.

portant, because their very position and experience mean that they are necessarily less susceptible to executive blandishment. (I write this, having spent no time in Washington since John F. Kennedy became President: some reports suggest that executive blandishments or arm-twistings are more intense now than they used to be.) It is probably of no great importance to prohibit ex-congressmen from accepting executive posts; indeed this might do more to humanize the executive than weaken Congress. However, it may be desirable to have a self-denying ordinance that prevents wives and children of congressmen from working for the executive, but this so rarely happens that it is not crucial.

Use of indoctrination courses:

Programs for congressmen stressing check-and-balance principles are, of course, highly desirable. Private foundations could provide a stipend for indoctrination courses specially designed to help the "congressmen-elect" think about the principles of check and balance and how to apply them to the particular legislative issues with which they hope to be concerned. These courses would be particularly pertinent to: Those states where primaries take place in the spring or early summer, and it then becomes perfectly clear who is going to be sent to Congress; the candidates who are in fact, though not in law, congressmen-elect need not campaign, and would therefore have time to attend courses.

Provision of funds for the briefing of congressmen:

On certain political questions, the probability is that most of the people congressmen see and hear from will be connected with, or ideologically tied to, the executive. Congressmen may find that, both in office visits and on social occasions, they almost exclusively meet people who are biased in favor of the executive viewpoint.[23] Naturally, informal meetings provide a good deal of information, and they should not be eliminated. But each congressman could keep listings

---

[23] I owe this idea originally to a member of the appropriations committee concerned with military affairs. He would never see an officer or Pentagon bureaucrat on a social occasion; and to another member of Congress (still serving), who pointed out to me that the real scandals of influence never get into the press; he said: "The people who are really trying to bribe and pressure Congress are from the Department of Defense. They learn you want to go somewhere and call you up and say 'How about traveling on one of our planes?' And it just so happens there is riding along with you a pleasant, agreeable officer from the Service which gives you the ride . . . he does call attention to things from their standpoint."

of the opinions of the people he has seen and heard from on a given topic. If it turns out that most of his visitors have represented the executive viewpoint, the congressman might openly solicit offsetting, countervailing arguments. Now, of course, the employees of the executive departments are paid for any time they spend working with congressmen. Funds should therefore be provided which congressmen could use when necessary to commission visits from specialists opposed to the executive viewpoint and who could also prepare appropriate briefs if requested. To avoid the possibility of duplication—as well as a possible public outcry against apparent waste—probably the administration of these funds should be supervised by the Joint Commission on Check and Balance Principles (otherwise three or four congressmen might coincidentally commission the same job from the same people).

Congress should authorize the committee to co-opt additional members, carefully chosen so as to enhance effectiveness of check-and-balance operations.

When we think of the 535 members of Congress all at once, it seems like a large number. But when we consider the number of members of Congress in relation to the amount of work they have to do, and compare their number with the number of bureaucrats, it is really quite small. The important thing here is not the increase in the numbers in the executive departments so much as the fact that there has been a great increase in the number of *subjects* with which Congress ought to deal, without any increase in the number of members.

Some people have suggested that the Congress should be enlarged, perhaps even doubled in size. Although the idea is attractive, there are several drawbacks to it. First, the prestige of congressmen and of Congress itself might well be diminished if the number of members were materially augmented. Second, if twice as many people were given the whole set of opportunities, rights, privileges, and duties which members of the Congress now possess, it would create substantial administrative difficulties. It is much more than twice as difficult to run a large body of co-equals as to run a small one; and in a large body, the likelihood of some central executive committee (such as the Speaker and his lieutenants, for instance) securing complete, dictatorial control would be much greater.

However, there is a partial way out which has many of the advantages of enlarging the Congress without the disadvantages. I shall state the proposal in the most extreme (but I think desirable) form. In regard to proposals for immediate reorganization, it would no doubt have to be modified somewhat. But I am trying to show here the overall direction towards which we should aim in 1979 and 1989.

The congressional committees should co-opt persons to work with them and to serve in effect as members of the committees; some of these co-opted persons might be on retainer and others serve as full-time committee members. Naturally their orientation must be very clearly towards congressional check and balance.

Five categories of co-opted members proposed:

(1) *Ex-representatives, ex-senators.* Everyone who has been on Capitol Hill for some years can think of members who were extraordinarily useful on committees but who were not re-elected. The employment of some skillful ex-representatives and ex-senators as co-opted members would, incidentally, reduce the distasteful employment choices some of them face.

(2) *Members of state legislature (and possibly even a few city councils)* who have shown a talent for looking into legislative matters, or for investigation, but who are relatively unlikely to be elected to the Congress, because of the nature of their states or districts or because they are more concerned with the legislative-investigative responsibilities of the General Assembly than with conducting election campaigns. In some states where legislatures have relatively light sessions, members might keep their state legislative seats [24] and be opted on congressional committees where there is no possible conflict of interest between the federal government and their particular state government. This will mean that they will generally sit on defense and foreign affairs committees, but there is no reason why, for instance, a Maryland legislator should not help investigate some matter within the purview of the Interior Committee on Western Minerals. By way of example, the kind of person who comes to mind as being suitable for co-option is George Metcalf, until recently state senator in New York, or Mary Newman, representative in the General Court of Massachusetts.

(3) *Journalists* who have specialized in investigations.

(4) *Possibly certain types of professional specialists (for example in book reviewing, fraud investigation, medical pathology).* It might be worth thinking about this, as it would presumably encour-

---

[24] Although they probably could not serve on major committees or on the State Legislative Council, and would have to agree not to run for statewide office.

age the willingness to question the bureaucratic expert and to assume an adversary attitude towards them. Would it be of value to seek out qualified persons with such a professional background? Would they add anything to what lawyers already supply to the Congress?

(5) *Representatives of relevant special interest groups* who do not normally get a hearing in Congress. I am thinking here of groups like the American Indians which, because of accidents of congressional districting and population distribution, are hardly ever heard in Congress effectively. Indeed, we might properly go one step further. For instance, American legislation has such tremendous consequences for the Maritime Provinces of Canada that it might be wise to co-opt some outstanding statesmen from this area on certain committees (e.g., Labor, Ways and Means, Interstate and Foreign Commerce, Merchant Marine and Fisheries). Gradually, by trial and error, we might extend this principle to cover several foreign countries, and so avoid some of the boomerang effects which follow when U.S. legislation adversely affects their interests due to a misunderstanding of their needs. In fact, congressmen and Canadian politicians [25]—or for that matter congressmen and Mexican politicians—now would get along a lot better working on the same project than either of them gets along with the State Department's expert officials who are at present the intermediaries (and who in technical terms create "noise," or otherwise put, "foul up the line").

Employment procedure:

Aside from the obvious necessity of providing office facilities and pay [26] and authorizing the establishment of relevant positions, the Congress could leave the precise procedures up to individual committees. Within a general framework, variations could be tried out.

---

[25] Suppose, for instance, that the present liberal government in Canada is swept out of office. For a variety of reasons, no one in the world would be better equipped to consult with the Senate Foreign Relations Committee on a regular basis, and to speak for a large segment of both American and Canadian opinion, than the present Prime Minister of Canada, Lester Pearson. Even more exciting would be the co-opting of Prime Minister Smallwood of Newfoundland to the Interstate and Foreign Commerce Committee, should he ever decide to retire from his executive post.

[26] Probably the salary should be initially set in terms of an individual's previous rate of pay plus a travel allowance, with gradual increments until it reaches a little less than a congressman's salary. This would be preferable to setting it initially at a high level, simply to discourage people from pressuring for such an assignment as a patronage matter.

Some committees might choose not to co-opt anyone but the point that every committee should insist on if it does decide to co-opt members, is that they be given positions of respect and esteem, second only to those of congressmen themselves. In practice, the system will be of greater value if the co-opted members are given some latitude to choose issues for investigation according to their particular interests. In regard to hearings, summoning of witnesses, etc., there probably will be some matters of parliamentary law and the constitutional delegation of powers to be examined—but these can surely be handled by legal technicians.

Of course, very stringent, enforceable, prohibitions forbidding such co-opted members (except for ex-representatives) from running for Congress themselves would absolutely have to be enacted.

Special advantages of the innovation:

The immediate benefits of co-opting additional members are, hopefully, clear enough. In addition there are two important indirect advantages to be derived which could substantially contribute to the general strengthening of Congress:

(1) Some legislative bodies have in the past been weakened by a large turnover in the membership. This has not happened in the federal Congress for a long time, but if it did, and there were a lot of new members on the major committees at the same time, it would give the executive a still greater advantage in dealing with the Congress than it has now. However, if it is provided that the terms of half the co-opted members should run seven months beyond the start of a new Congress, some carryover of experience would be ensured.

(2) In view of the party system as it operates in Congress, it is also unfortunate if after elections one party or the other loses all or most of its experienced and wise men on several committees. Apparently, this actually happened to the Republicans in the House in 1934. Such an eventuality would seriously undermine the check-and-balance principle if, as is likely, the party that loses a lot of seats is not the party in the White House; for then the partisan stimulus to check and balance in Congress will work poorly. It should therefore be provided that if either party loses more than 20 percent of the seats which it had in the previous Congress, it should be permitted to designate a certain proportion of its defeated or former congressmen to serve as co-opted committee members in the new congress. Several different ways of providing for this arrange-

ment can be thought out. In a footnote, I suggest one of them,[27] but I see no strong argument for this way of doing it, as against other ways of achieving the same purpose.

Congress should set up a Joint Commission on Check and Balance Principles.

Another structural change of great value would be the establishment of a Joint Congressional Commission on Check and Balance Principles.

Two responsibilities of this commission have already been referred to: the establishment and supervision of regulations on employment of ex-congressional employees in the executive departments; and the financing and finding of experts for members of the Congress who want to get a clear statement of the case against a particular executive proposal.

The major task, however, of such a commission would be: (1) to serve as a central voice for ideas about how Congress should more effectively carry out its task of checking and balancing; and (2) to be a spokesman for congressmen who are in difficulties with the executive as a result of trying to carry out their tasks. In the nature of things, if such a committee were effective, it would come to stimulate ideas about what the Congress can best accomplish.

The commission might, from time to time, undertake investigations and studies which either do not seem to fall very appropriately within the sphere of influence of any particular committee, or else have particular bearing on the constitutional system of check and balance. It could also be assigned responsibility in regard to those aspects of congressional management which bear on the power of the Congress to check and balance and, in particular, it might be made responsible for working out the general system of co-opting members to committees, discussed above. On the other hand, it should *not* be permitted to exercise general authority on

---

[27] I would propose that when a party has lost 20 percent of its members of either house, and when over one-third of its members in the past Congress on a given committee are defeated, it shall be permitted to select additional members as follows: (in the case of the House, it would be a little simpler, so I describe only that here) three members on each major House committee, two members on other committees. On the major committees, the first minority party choice shall be elected by all the minority members of Congress in the outgoing Congress *not* on his committee; the second by all the majority party members of Congress *not* on his committee; the third by lot conducted among defeated members of the minority on the relevant committee in the outgoing Congress.

other matters of congressional administration. These should be left entirely to the committees and individuals who now handle them, since experience has shown that the constant handling of day-to-day duties tends to rob one of the chances to face big problems.

Such a commission should include co-opted members drawn both from the general public and from the two houses of Congress (as well, of course, as some distinguished ex-congressmen). If it can be possibly avoided, the majority of the commission's members should not consist of the chairmen of the important committees and subcommittees. At least half of the non-congressional members should regard their assignments as taking one-third or two-thirds of their time. But all of them should have some other work, so as to prevent any tendency to become too preoccupied with their commission assignments and to downgrade the congressional members.

The advantage of the commission having distinguished co-opted members on it, is that it can then speak for the doctrine of check and balance in general, and not just for a particular Congress. For instance, if a commission composed of sufficiently distinguished members protested executive denial to Congress of *significant and relevant* information, it would carry more weight than the protest of a purely congressional body.

It is obvious that the commission will have to have a staff. And here it will be important to see that the personnel employed are not those whose previous work orientation has been towards congressional procedures, constitutional law, or the management of legislative bodies. The function of this commission should be creative and innovative, and not concerned with the conduct of formal procedures.

Conclusion

This article is written at a time when Congress is the weakest of the three governmental agencies and when the power of the executive is increasing a good deal. So, I have been suggesting ways to increase the power of Congress; but if 25 years from now the Congress became overweeningly powerful, and the executive weak, then exactly the same arguments would apply in reverse. In any case, I am not suggesting that we jump from the executive frying pan into the congressional oven. Just as the Congress should check and balance the executive, so the executive should check and balance the Congress.[28] Since the latter aspect presents no problem at the moment, it has not been discussed in this paper.

Obviously, it would be exaggerated to maintain that the particular approach to the check-and-balance tradition advanced here is absolutely essential to decent government. All that is contended is that, if properly carried out, the doctrine can help to protect us against tyranny and mistakes; and that there is no reason for the Congress to continue as an independent body unless it seeks to implement the check-and-balance principle.

---

[28] No study has ever been made that I know of about the way in which check and balance operates historically or comparatively. And almost everyone who has considered the matter discusses check and balance in terms only of the three branches of government, executive, legislative, judicial. Actually, the different federal agencies check and balance each other (quasi-judicial commissions versus the executive departments, one of the executive departments versus another); the states or state agencies sometimes balance and check federal agencies as well as vice versa; and powerful "private" interests like newspapers and TV stations, churches, and big business, all may and do check and balance one or another of the three branches of the federal government. A serious analysis of how such checks and balances occur would permit us to be far clearer about what Congress does and what it ought to do.

In today's world, with the enormous complexities of modern life, *some* form of check and balance is necessary, some instrument for criticizing and chastising the bureaucracy, or we let legislative power lapse. James Burns in his *Deadlock of Democracy* in effect argues for what he calls a "Jeffersonian principle" (other people would call it a "radical democratic" principle), by which the rulers are able to have their way, and to act quickly, decisively and effectively. But, in fact, Jefferson thought of a very radical way of chastising the bureaucrats—he believed a revolution every 20 years would be a good thing! The Madisonian check-and-balance principle would seem to be a rather more humane method of avoiding tyranny and the excesses of pedantic bureaucracy.

If we do not reinvigorate the check-and-balance principle through the legislative branch, then we ought probably to discover other ways of implementing it. However, so far as I can see, the congressional method is more satisfying than any likely alternative. To be sure, it has its disadvantages. Professor Burns in a letter to me says:

> May I ask you whether you are not really pleased that the check-and-balance system has been suspended this year (1965) and that at last we are getting the great measures that have been held up so long? In other words, it would take a great deal of ingenuity to develop a check-and-balance system that would give Congress a more significant role but not hold up the measures that seem to have the support of the majority of the people.[29]

The real problem of democracy, to answer Professor Burns' question, is as much, or more, to find solutions which are acceptable to many different groups, rather than simply to respond to alleged majority demands or the judgment of specialists. More generally, the great civic need is not for one particular program or another but for wisdom in legislation and the taking into account of conflicting interests in both present and future problems. A genuine check-and-balance system, in which the Congress checks and balances the executive and the judiciary, as well as vice versa, seems more likely to produce reasonably sensible government than virtually exclusive rule by bureaucrats and leaders — and certainly it would be less likely to become tyrannical.[30] The greater the devel-

---

[29] Personal letter from James M. Burns to Lewis A. Dexter, August 23, 1965. Quoted by permission.

[30] Most writing like Burns' is influenced by the fact that the last five Presidents of the United States were men of considerable prudence—hopefully,

opment of "multiple cracks" in a system of government, the greater the likelihood that somehow or other a handful of wise prophets or an oppressed minority can be heard. It is this likelihood which seems to me to make check and balance rather than the dominance of any one branch of government the best choice for all of us.

Later: One point of importance has been suggested by comments received from friends and acquaintances about newspaper stories summarizing an earlier publication of several of the articles in this volume. Nearly all of these people assumed that we must be talking about *reforming* Congress. It was in most cases difficult to make the point that we are more concerned with *strengthening* Congress than *reforming* it, and was obviously surprising to several experienced Washington hands to hear that whatever reform we want is chiefly a reform of the presidency, the executive force model, and its concommitant tendency to accept specialist judgment as final. So, it is perhaps with stating again that we are hopeful chiefly of reforming the executive in this sense.

---

though as yet doubtfully, this is true of the present President. But suppose—which is by no means impossible—a couple of fire-eating chief executive men with the worst features of Andrew Jackson; suppose, for that matter, a President who treated Mexico and India as Lyndon Johnson treated the Dominican Republic; or suppose just stupid and unimaginative Presidents, then many of those who now deplore check and balance would thank God for the Congress. Had our pro-executive political science writers of today lived in the latter days of Augustus Caesar, they would have thanked the gods for the Princeps and have been grateful that the Senate was no longer a serious political instituition in Rome. But these same men could easily have lived to see Caligula and Nero govern Rome. Would they not then have wished for the revitalization of the Senate? Naturally, I do not anticipate any Caligula or Nero in the United States; but I can well imagine a President having, say, the worst qualities of several state governors whose weakness many people are aware of. (In regard to Jackson's worst qualities, I refer to his flagrant refusal to obey the Supreme Court on the Cherokee issue, "John Marshall has made his decision; now let him enforce it," and the terrible "Trail of Tears" which the persecution of the highly civilized Cherokees created.)

AARON WILDAVSKY is Associate Professor of Political Science at the University of California at Berkeley. He formerly taught at Oberlin College. He received his B.A. from Brooklyn College in 1954 and his Ph.D. from Yale University in 1959. His books include: *Studies in Australian Politics, the 1926 Referendum* (F. W. Cheshire, 1958); *Dixon-Yates: A Study in Power Politics* (Yale University Press, 1962); *Presidential Elections* (with Nelson W. Polsby) (Scribner's, 1964); *Leadership in a Small Town* (Bedminster Press, 1964); and *The Politics of the Budgetary Process* (Little, Brown & Co., 1964). He is currently engaged in constructing an empirical theory of the budgetary process and in studies of the presidency.

I have said—if it were possible for man to be so constituted, as to feel what affects others more strongly than what affects himself, or even as strongly— because, it may be well doubted, whether the stronger feeling or affection of individuals for themselves, combined with a feebler and subordinate feeling or affection for others, is not, in beings of limited reason and faculties, a constitution necessary to their preservation and existence. If reversed—if their feelings and affections were stronger for others than for themselves, or even as strong, the necessary result would seem to be, that all individuality would be lost; and boundless and remediless disorder and confusion would ensue. For each, at the same moment, intensely participating in all the conflicting emotions of those around him, would, of course, forget himself and all that concerned him immediately, in his officious intermeddling with the affairs of all others; which, from his limited reason and faculties, he could neither properly understand nor manage. Such a state of things would, as far as we can see, lead to endless disorder and confusion, not less destructive to our race than a state of anarchy. It would, besides, be remediless—for government would be impossible; or, if it could by possibility exist, its object would be reversed. Selfishness would have to be encouraged and benevolence discouraged. Individuals would have to be encouraged, by rewards, to become more selfish, and deterred, by punishments, from being too benevolent; and this, too, by a government, administered by those who, on the supposition, would have the greatest aversion for selfishness and the highest admiration for benevolence.

To the Infinite Being, the Creator of all, belongs exclusively the care and superintendence of the whole.

—JOHN C. CALHOUN, *A Disquisition on Government*
(New York: Political Science Classics, 1947),
pp. 5-6. (Brought to my attention by H. D. Price.)

Toward A Radical Incrementalism
A Proposal to Aid Congress in Reform of the Budgetary Process

Aaron Wildavsky

MY purpose in writing this paper is to aid Congress in reforming the budgetary process from the viewpoint of legislators in a representative assembly.[1] The usual proposals for helping Congress by taking its job away or by shifting its responsibilities to the executive or by recommending that it confine itself to those actions of which it is least capable will not be found here. I shall propose a radical incremental approach designed to improve the calculating capability of all governmental participants in the budgetary process. I shall also propose mechanisms for improving the essential political information on budgeting available to Congress, somewhat at the expense of the Chief Executive, though not without some compensations for him as well. Finally, I shall suggest that Congress sponsor research which, for the first time, would be directly geared to improving its ability to act on appropriations in terms best suited to its limitations and opportunities.

My approach is based on considerations (as old as political theory itself) which do not seek vainly to condemn natural political behavior, but rather to so arrange the interaction of political forces as to secure desirable results. At one point in the *Politics,*[2] Aristotle

---

[1] I wish to make it perfectly clear that I do not subscribe to the view that the executive branch is a scheming ogre gleefully squeezing the life out of our innocent and defenseless Republic. My views are quite different; I would not regard such a characterization as either accurate or helpful in the analysis of public policy. I have been asked to take the viewpoint of Congress in writing about policy. This I have gladly done, for our Congress deserves our best. As a citizen and a political scientist, I would just as gladly perform a similar service for the executive. My intention is not to disparage the great institutions of our democracy but to contribute to understanding and perfecting them.

[2] Richard McKeon (ed.), *Basic Works of Aristotle* (New York, 1941), pp. 1185-87, 1212-24.

devised a solution to a vexing political problem. It seems that the poor were so busy trying to make a living that they could not afford to attend the Assembly, while the rich found so much profit in their private activities that it did not appear worthwhile for them to participate. This violated the balance of political forces whereby justice emerges from a clash of interests. Aristotle's solution was characteristically ingenious: the poor were to be paid to attend and the rich fined if they failed to attend. We might also recall how the Greeks saw to it that men of wealth paid their subscriptions to the state. If one man claimed he could not pay, any man willing to do so could substitute his property for the property of the man who alleged he could not pay. Children recognize the considerations involved when they divide a valued object by having one of them cut it in half and the other select the piece for himself. Spinoza's *Tractatus Politicus*[3] is full of suggestions for mechanisms by which the passions of men may, by their strength and predictability, be usefully employed. He suggests, for example, that military leaders be paid from the receipts of import and export duties so that they will be motivated to defend the state but not to engage in continual wars, since this would interrupt commerce and with it their source of income. The Constitution of the United States, with its separation and sharing of powers, its federalism, its staggered elections, and overlapping constituencies, is based on this kind of consideration, as the words of the framers so clearly reveal. I would take my stand with the authors of the *Federalist* (especially in their 51st number) who argue that political practices should be so arranged "that the private interest of every individual may be a sentinel over the public rights."

In order to provide necessary background, the first section of the paper is devoted to an analysis of the nature of reform proposals. Following this is a brief description of the budgetary process in the United States. After an analysis of the major criticisms of the budgetary process, the paper ends with an exposition and defense of radical incrementalism as a desirable approach to budgeting in the United States.

---

[3] A. G. Wernham, *Benedict de Spinoza, The Political Works* (Oxford: The Clarendon Press, 1958), *inter alia*.

The Political Meaning of Budgetary Reform

A LARGE part of the literature on budgeting in the United States is concerned with reform.[4] The goals of the proposed reforms are couched in similar language—economy, efficiency, improvement, or just better budgeting. The President, the Congress and its committees, administrative agencies, even the interested citizenry are all to gain by some change in the way the budget is formulated, presented, or evaluated. There is little or no realization among the reformers, however, that any effective change in budgetary relationships must necessarily alter the outcomes of the budgetary process. Far from being a neutral matter of "better budgeting," proposed reforms inevitably contain important implications for the political system.

A crucial aspect of budgeting is whose preferences are to prevail in disputes about which activities are to be carried on and to what degree, in the light of limited resources. The problem is not only generally "how shall budgetary benefits be maximized," as if it made no difference who received them, but also specifically "who shall

---

[4] Arthur E. Buck, *Public Budgeting* (New York: Harper and Brothers, 1929); Jesse Burkhead, *Government Budgeting* (New York: John Wiley and Sons, Inc., 1956); Hoover Commission on the Organization of the Executive Branch of the Government, *Budget and Accounting* (Washington, D. C., 1949); Edward A. Kolodziej, "Congressional Responsibility for the Common Defense: The Money Problem," *The Western Political Quarterly,* XVI, 1963, pp. 149-60; Arthur Smithies, *The Budgetary Process in the United States* (New York: McGraw-Hill, 1955); Robert Ash Wallace, "Congressional Control of the Budget," *Midwest Journal of Political Science,* III, 1959, pp. 151-67; and William Franklin Willoughby, *The National Budget System* (Baltimore: Johns Hopkins Press, 1927).

receive budgetary benefits and how much." One of the central problems of social conduct consists of somehow aggregating different preferences so that a decision may emerge. How can we compare the worth of expenditures for irrigation to certain farmers with the worth to motorists of widening a highway, or the desirability of aiding old people to pay medical bills with the degree of safety provided by an expanded defense program. All this is further complicated by the necessity of taking into account the relative intensity of preference with which policies are sought by different people. The process developed for dealing with interpersonal comparisons in government is not economic but political. Conflicts are resolved (under agreed upon rules) by translating different preferences through the political system into units called votes or into types of authority like a veto power. Therefore, if the present budgetary process is rightly or wrongly deemed unsatisfactory, one must alter in some respect the political system of which the budget is an expression. It is impossible to make drastic changes in budgeting without also altering the political system and the distribution of influence within it.[5]

By far the most significant way of influencing the budget would be to introduce basic political changes (or to wait for secular changes like the growing industrialization of the South). Imagine that the electoral college were changed to favor conservatives or that the seniority system were altered to favor more liberal committee chairmen; give the President an item veto or provide him with more powers enabling him to control the votes of his party in Congress; enable a small group of congressmen to command a majority of votes on all occasions so that they can push their program through. Then you will have exerted a profound influence on the content of the budget.

Since the budget represents conflicts over whose preferences shall prevail, one cannot speak of "better budgeting" without considering who benefits and who loses or demonstrating that no one loses. Just as the supposedly objective criterion of "efficiency" has been shown to have normative implications,[6] so a "better budget" may well be a cloak for hidden policy preferences. To propose that the President be given an item veto, for example, represents an attempt to increase the influence of the particular interests which gain superior

---

[5] Aaron Wildavsky, *Politics of the Budgetary Process* (Boston: Little Brown & Co., 1964), pp. 127-44.

[6] Dwight Waldo, *The Administrative State* (New York: The Ronald Press, 1948), *inter alia;* Herbert A. Simon, *Administrative Behavior* (2d ed.; New York: Macmillan, 1957), pp. 172-97.

access to the Chief Executive rather than, say, to the Congress. Only if one could eliminate the element of conflict over expenditures could it be assumed that a reform is "good enough" if it enables an official to do a better job from his point of view; since conflict over expeditures cannot be eliminated, the policy implications for others must be taken into account.[7]

Perhaps there are reforms which promise benefits for all and deprivations for none, or benefits for some and deprivations for none. But this cannot be assumed; it must be demonstrated especially to groups which anticipate deprivations for themselves. I am proposing that we be explicit about our intentions and demonstrate some awareness of the likely consequences of our proposals. (This advice is meant for the scholars whose task presumably includes being open with their colleagues, and not for the political participants for whom it might not always be wise to reveal what they are about.) It is clear, then, that before reforms are suggested, we need some idea of how the federal budgetary process operates in its political context. Then we may get a better idea of the consequences of reform proposals in comparison with the consequences of the present budgetary process.

---

[7] Wildavsky, *op. cit.*, pp. 127-44.

The Budgetary Process

FOR our purposes, we shall conceive of budgets as attempts to allocate financial resources through political processes. If politics is regarded as conflict over whose preferences are to prevail in the determination of policy, then the budget records the outcomes of this struggle. If one asks "who gets what the (public or private) organization has to give?" then the answers for a moment in time are recorded in the budget. If organizations are viewed as political coalitions,[8] budgets are mechanisms through which sub-units bargain over conflicting goals, make side payments, and try to motivate one another to accomplish their objectives. In a study such as this, which stresses the appropriations process in Congress, the political context of budgeting can hardly be overemphasized.

The making of decisions depends upon calculation of which alternatives to consider and to choose. Calculation involves determination of how problems are identified, get broken down into manageable dimensions, are related to one another, and how choices are made as to what is relevant and who shall be taken into account. A major clue toward understanding budgeting is the extraordinary complexity of the calculations involved. In any large organization, there are a huge number of items to be considered, many of which are of considerable technical difficulty. Yet there is little or no theory in most areas of policy which would enable practitioners to predict the con-

---

[8] Richard Cyert and James March (eds.), *A Behavioral Theory of the Firm* (Englewood Cliffs, N.J.: Prentice-Hall, 1963).

sequences of alternative moves and probability of their occurring.[9]
Man's ability to calculate is severely limited; time is always in short
supply; and the number of matters which can be encompassed in
one mind at the same time is quite small.[10] Nor has anyone solved
the imposing problem of the interpersonal comparison of utilities.
Outside of the political process, there is no agreed upon way of com-
paring and evaluating the merits of different programs for different
people whose preferences vary in kind and in intensity.

Participants in budgeting deal with their overwhelming burdens
by adopting heuristic aids to calculation. They simplify in order to
get by. They make small moves, let experience accumulate, and
use the feedback from their decisions to gauge consequences. They
use actions on simpler matters that they understand as indices to
complex concerns. They attempt to judge the capacity of the men
in charge of programs even if they cannot appraise the policies
directly. They may institute across-the-board ("meat-axe") cuts to
reduce expenditures, relying on outcries from affected agencies and
interest groups to let them know if they have gone too far.[11]

By far the most important aid to calculation is the incremental
approach. Budgets are almost never actively reviewed as a whole in
the sense of considering at one time the value of all existing programs compared to all possible alternatives. Instead, this year's
budget is based on last year's budget, with special attention given to a
narrow range of increases or decreases. The greatest part of any
budget is a product of previous decisions. Long-range commitments
have been made. There are mandatory programs whose expenses
must be met. Powerful political support makes the inclusion of other
activities inevitable. Consequently, officials concerned with budgeting
restrict their attention to items and programs they can do something
about—a few new programs and possible cuts in old ones.

Incremental calculations, then, proceed from an existing base. By
"base" we refer to commonly held expectations among participants
in budgeting that programs will be carried out at close to the going
level of expenditures. The base of a budget, therefore, refers to
accepted parts of programs that will not normally be subjected to
intensive scrutiny. Since many organizational units compete for
funds, there is a tendency for the central authority to include all of
them in the benefits or deprivations to be distributed. Participants

[9] David Braybrooke and Charles Lindblom, *A Strategy of Decision* (New York: Free Press of Glencoe, 1963).

[10] Simon, *op. cit.*

[11] Wildavsky, *op. cit.*, pp. 1-13.

in budgeting often refer to expectations regarding their fair share of increases and decreases. The widespread sharing of deeply held expectations concerning the organization's base and its fair share of funds provide a powerful (although informal) means of coordination and stability in budgetary systems that appear to lack comprehensive calculations proceeding from a hierarchical center.[12]

Roles (the expectations of behavior attached to institutional positions) are parts of the division of labor. They are calculating mechanisms. In American national government, the administrative agencies act as advocates of increased expenditure, the Bureau of the Budget acts as presidential servant with a cutting bias, the House Appropriations Committee functions as a guardian of the Treasury, and the Senate Appropriations Committee as an appeals court to which agencies carry their disagreement with House action.

Possessing great expertise and large numbers, working in close proximity to their policy problems and clientele groups, and desirous of expanding their horizons, administrative agencies generate action through advocacy. But how much shall they ask for? Life would be simple if they could just estimate the costs of their ever-expanding needs and submit the total as their request. But if they ask for amounts much larger than the appropriating bodies believe is reasonable, their credibility will suffer a drastic decline. In such circumstances, the reviewing organs are likely to apply a "measure of unrealism" [13] with the result that the agency gets much less than it might have with a more moderate request. So the first decision rule for agencies is: do not come in too high. Yet the agencies must also not come in too low, for the assumption is that if the agency advocates do not ask for funds they do not need them. Since the budgetary situation is always tight, terribly tight, or impossibly tight, reviewing bodies are likely to just accept a low request with thanks and not inquire too closely into its rationale. Given the distribution of roles, cuts must be expected and taken into account. Thus, the agency decision rule might read: come in a little high (padding), but not too high (loss of confidence). But how high is too high? What agency heads usually do is to evaluate signals from the environment—last year's experience, legislative votes, executive policy statements, actions of clientele groups, reports from the field—and

---

[12] *Ibid.*, pp. 16-18.

[13] J. S. Hines (Research Officer) and R. W. Edwards (Chairman), *Budgeting in Public Authorities* (New York: A Study Group of the Royal Institute of Public Administration, 1959), p. 245.

come up with an asking price somewhat higher than they expect to get.[14]

Having decided how much to ask for, agencies engage in strategic planning to secure their budgetary goals. (Strategies are the links between the goals of the agencies and their perceptions of the kinds of actions which their political environment will make efficacious.) Budget officers in American national government uniformly act on the belief that being a good politician—cultivation of an active clientele, development of confidence by other officials (particularly the appropriations subcommittees), and skill in following strategies which exploit opportunities—is more important in obtaining funds than demonstration of efficiency. Top agency officials soon learn that the appropriations committees are very powerful; committee recommendations are accepted by Congress approximately 90 percent of the time.[15] Since budgetary calculations are so complex, the legislators must take a good deal on faith; thus, they require agency budget officers to demonstrate a high degree of integrity. If the appropriations committees believe that an agency officer has misled them, they can do grave damage to his career and to the prospects of the agency he represents. While doing a decent job may be a necessary condition for the agency's success in securing funds, the importance of having clientele and the confidence of legislators is so great that all agencies employ these strategies.[16]

In addition to these ubiquitous strategies, there are contingent strategies which depend upon time, circumstance, and place. In defending the base, for example, cuts may be made in the most popular programs so that a public outcry will result in restoration of the funds. The base may be increased within existing programs by shifting funds between categories. Substantial additions to the base may come about through proposing new programs to meet crises and through campaigns involving large doses of advertising and salesmanship.[17] The dependence of these strategies on the incremental, increase-decrease type of budgetary calculation is evident.

The Bureau of the Budget in the United States has the assigned role of helping the President realize his goals (when it can discover what they are supposed to be). This role is performed with a cutting bias, however, simply because the agencies normally push so hard in

[14] Wildavsky, op. cit., pp. 21-32.

[15] Richard F. Fenno, Jr., "The House Appropriations Committee as a Political System: The Problem of Integration," American Political Science Review, LVI, 1962, pp. 310-24.

[16] Wildavsky, op. cit., pp. 65-98.

[17] Ibid., pp. 101-23.

making requests for funds. The Bureau helps the President by making his preferences more widely known throughout the executive branch so that those who would like to go along have a chance to find out what is required of them. Since Congress usually cuts the President's budget, Bureau figures tend to be the most that agencies can get, especially when the items are not of such paramount importance as to justify intensive scrutiny by Congress. Yet the power of the purse remains actively with Congress. If the Budget Bureau continually recommended figures which were blatantly disregarded by Congress, the agencies would soon learn to pay less and less attention to the President's budget. As a result, the Bureau follows consistent congressional action.[18] It can be shown empirically that Bureau recommendations tend to follow congressional actions over a large number of cases.[19]

In deciding how much money to recommend for specific purposes, the House Appropriations Committee breaks down into largely autonomous subcommittees in which the norm of reciprocity is carefully followed.[20] Specialization is carried further as subcommittee members develop limited areas of competence and jurisdiction. Budgeting is both incremental and fragmented as the committees deal with adjustments to the historical base of each agency. Sequential decision making is the rule as problems are first attacked in the subcommittee jurisdiction in which they appear and then followed step-by-step as they manifest themselves elsewhere.[21] The subcommittee members treat budgeting as a process of making marginal monetary adjustments to existing programs rather than as a mechanism for reconsidering basic policy choices every year.[22] Fragmentation and specialization are further increased through the appeals functions of the Senate Appropriations Committee which deals with what has become (through House action) a fragment of a fragment. When the actions of subcommittees conflict, the difficulties are met by repeated attacks on the problem or through reference to the House and Senate as a whole.[23]

The members of the United States House Appropriations Committee consider themselves guardians of the Treasury who take pride

[18] *Ibid.*, pp. 4-42.
[19] Otto Davis and Aaron Wildavsky, "An Empirical Theory of Congressional Appropriations." (Mimeograph, 1965).
[20] Fenno, *op. cit.*
[21] Wildavsky, *op. cit.*, pp. 56-64.
[22] Fenno, *op. cit.*
[23] Wildavsky, *op. cit.*

in the frequency with which they reduce estimates.[24] They reconcile this role with their role as representatives of constituency interests by cutting estimates to satisfy one role and generally increasing amounts over the previous year to satisfy the other. As guardians of the public purse, committee members are expected to cast a skeptical eye on the blandishments of a bureaucracy ever anxious to increase its dominion by raising its appropriations. In order to provide an objective check on the effectiveness of the committee's orientation, Fenno [25] examined the appropriations histories of 37 bureaus concerned with domestic policies from 1947-59 and discovered that the committee reduced the estimates it received 77.2 percent of the time.

Tough as they may be in cutting the budgets of their agencies, appropriations committee members, once having made their decision, generally defend the agencies against further cuts on the floor. This kind of action is in part self-interest. The power of the appropriations subcommittees would be diminished if their recommendations were successfully challenged very often. Members believe that the House would "run wild" if "orderly procedure"—that is, acceptance of committee recommendations—were not followed. The role of defender also has its roots in the respect for expertise and specialization in Congress, and the concomitant belief that members who have not studied the subject should not exercise a deciding voice without the presence of overriding consideration. An appeal to this norm usually is sufficient to block an attempt to reduce appropriations.[26]

A member of the Senate Appropriations Committee is likely to conceive of his proper role as the responsible legislator who sees to it that the irrepressible lower house does not do too much damage either to constituency or to national interests. The senators are rather painfully aware of the House committee's pre-eminence in the field of appropriations and they know that they cannot hope to match the time and thoroughness that the House body devotes to screening requests. For this reason, the Senate committee puts a high value on having agencies carry appeals to it. The senators value their right to disagree on disputed items as a means of maintaining their influence in crucial areas while putting the least possible strain on their time and energy. The Senate role of responsible appeals court is dependent, of course, upon agency advocacy and House committee guardianship.

---

[24] Fenno, *op. cit.*
[25] *Ibid.*, p. 312.
[26] *Ibid.;* Wildavsky, *op. cit.*

The Budgetary Process Reconsidered

IN describing the budgetary process, we have identified a number of basic characteristics that have called forth a great deal of criticism from many sources. For example, the aids to calculation have been described as arbitrary and irrational. It has been said that, instead of concentrating on grand policy alternatives, the appropriations committees interfere mischievously with the administrative process through excessive concern with small details. Some critics go so far as to state that this petty intervention takes place without adequate information so that administrators are harassed for all the wrong reasons by men who lack knowledge. The specialized, incremental, fragmented, and sequential budgetary procedures have been faulted as leading to a lack of coordination and a neglect of consequences of the actions that are taken. At the same time, Congress is said to be losing its control of appropriations because its meager efforts cannot keep pace with the superior information resources of the federal bureaucracy. Nor, the critics add, are the appropriations committees willing to make the vast increase in staff which would enable them to make their will felt through intelligent decisions on broad policies. Instead, they combine dependence on the executive for information with "irrational" practices such as across-the-board cuts. The participants in budgeting have been taken to task for serving local interests rather than the national public interest. Their roles are considered to be excessively narrow, and the strategies they follow are condemned as opportunistic if not immoral. Finally, the appropriations process is deemed much too slow and too late: actions are taken on material which is out of date, and administrators are left uncertain how much money they will have until long after the previous fiscal year has ended.

It is immediately evident that many of these criticisms are contradictory. Increasing the staff of the appropriations committees hardly seems like a good way to cut down on detailed oversight of administration. Concern with local interests is one way of dealing with the differential consequences of national policy. Congress can hardly interfere less with administrators by making all the basic policy decisions for the executive agencies. That the critics of Congress are confused is an old story; let us make the best sense we can out of the criticisms and deal with the serious concerns which they raise.

The alternative budgetary process envisioned by the critics is quite different from the one we now have. Instead of aids to calculation such as the incremental method, they prefer comprehensive and simultaneous evaluation of means and ends. In their view, coordination should be made the explicit concern of a central hierarchy that should consider a wide range of alternative expenditures and investigate rather fully the consequences of each and the probability of their occurring. Each participant should seek to protect the general interest rather than the particular interests directly within his jurisdiction. Strategies should be eschewed or, at least, based on the merits of the program rather than on making the best possible case. Congressmen should avoid interferences in the administrative process and concentrate on developing superior knowledge and greatly enlarged staff assistance in order to make the most general determinations of governmental policy. The following pages deal in detail with various critical approaches.

Comprehensiveness

One prescription offered by the critics for "rationally" solving problems of calculation is to engage in comprehensive and simultaneous means-ends analysis. But budget officials soon discover that ends are rarely agreed upon, that they keep changing, that possible consequences of a single policy are too numerous to describe, and that knowledge of the chain of consequences for other policies is but dimly perceived for most conceivable alternatives. The result, as Charles Lindblom has demonstrated, is that although this comprehensive approach can be described, it cannot be practiced because it puts too great a strain by far on man's limited ability to calculate.[27]

[27] Charles Lindblom, "The Science of 'Muddling Through'," *Public Administration Review*, XIX, 1959, pp. 79-88.

What budget officials need are not injunctions to be rational but operational guides that will enable them to manage the requisite calculations. Commands like "decide according to the intrinsic merits," "consider everything relevant," "base your decision on complete understanding," are simply not helpful. They do not exclude anything; unlike the aids to calculation, they do not point to operations that can be performed to arrive at a decision.

All that is accomplished by injunctions to follow a comprehensive approach is the inculcation of guilt among good men who find that they can never come close to fulfilling this unreasonable expectation. Worse still, acceptance of an unreasonable goal inhibits discussion of the methods actually used. Thus, responsible officials may feel compelled to maintain the acceptable fiction that they review (almost) everything; and yet when they describe their actual behavior, it soon becomes apparent that they do not. The vast gulf between the theories espoused by some budget officials and their practice stems, I believe, from their adherence to a norm deeply imbedded in our culture, which holds that the very definition of rational decision is comprehensive and simultaneous examination of ends and means. In this case, however, the rational turns out to be the unreasonable. Sad experience warns me that even those who agree with the analysis thus far are prone to insist that governmental officials must "take a look at the budget as a whole," even though neither they nor anyone else has any idea of what that might mean or how it might be accomplished. Surely, considering "the budget as a whole" does not mean merely putting it between the covers of one volume, or letting one's eyes run over the pages, or merely pondering the relationship between income and expenditures. Yet, if (to take current examples) evaluating the most important relationships between the space program, the war on poverty, and aid to education appears to be extraordinarily difficult, what is the point of talking about reviewing "the budget as a whole" in the real sense of analyzing the interrelationships among all the important programs. The perpetuation of myth is an old story. What is unfortunate is that insistence on an impossible standard takes our attention away from real possibilities for change.

Failure to consider the contributions toward calculation of the existing budgetary process distorts the magnitude of the problem. New programs and substantial increases and decreases in old programs do not receive close attention when interest groups, politicians, or bureaucrats, anxious to make an issue, demand an investigation. What escapes intensive scrutiny is not the whole but only certain parts, which carry on as before. The fact that some activities do not receive intensive scrutiny is hardly sufficient reason to do everything over every year. In my recommendations, I shall deal with the problem that remains.

Coordination

The fact that the budgetary process is not comprehensive has given rise to charges that it is uncoordinated. Indeed, the very terms that we have used to describe budgetary practices—specialized, incremental, fragmented, sequential, non-programmatic—imply that at any one time the budget is not effectively considered as a whole so as to systematically relate its component parts to one another. As long as the lack of coordination is the result of ignorance of other people's activities or the complexity of organization, there is a good chance of overcoming it by dedicated staff work or some formal coordinating mechanism. But, in many cases, lack of coordination is a result of conflicting views about policy that are held by men and agencies that have independent bases of influence in society and in Congress. The only way to secure coordination in these cases is for one side to convince or coerce or bargain with the other. When it is understood that "coordination" is often just another word for "coercion," the full magnitude of the problem becomes apparent. For there is no one, the President and congressional leaders included, who is charged with the task of dealing with the "budget as a whole" and who is capable of enforcing his preferences. Vesting of formal power to coordinate the budget effectively would be tantamount to a radical change in the national political system, requiring the abolition of the separation of powers and a federally controlled party system, among other things.

What may be said about coordination, then, if we take the existing political system as not subject to drastic change? By taking as our standard of coordination the existence of a formal structure charged with the task and capable of executing it, we come up with an obvious answer: there is very little coordination excepting what the President can manage through the Budget Bureau. By accepting the possibility of informal coordination, of participants who take into account what others are doing, we can say there is a great deal of coordination that has escaped the notice of observers.

Let us pose the following question: how does an appropriations subcommittee know when things are not working out in other areas affected by its actions? Are its budgetary decisions coordinated with those decisions made by other subcommittees? Part of the answer is found in a comment by a committee member to the effect that "people can't be too badly off if they don't complain." The subcommittees do not consider themselves to be the only participants in budgeting. They expect, in accordance with sequential decision making, that committees and organizations in the affected areas will take corrective action. When an agency shouts more loudly than usual, when an interest group mounts a campaign, when other congressmen begin to complain, subcommittee members have a pretty good idea that something is wrong. If their perceptions of the array of political forces lead them astray, the appropriations subcommittees can be brought back into line by a rebellion within the full committee or by an adverse vote on the floor. For, as we noted earlier, unless members have an exceedingly intense preference, they will try to come up with appropriations that will not be reversed on the floor; to do otherwise would be to risk losing the great prestige the committee enjoys. The subcommittee may be thought of as exercising discretion over a zone of indifference, within which others are not aware enough or not concerned enough to challenge them, but beyond which others will begin to mobilize against them. In this way, a semblance of coordination is maintained. And as time passes, the participants come to develop a tacit understanding as to the general level of most appropriations, a phenomenon we have previously designated by the notion of fair shares. No one has to check up on everyone; it is sufficient that occasional marked departures from commonly held notions of fair shares would generate opposition.

Widespread acceptance of this concept of fair shares may go a long way toward accounting for the degree of coordination (the extent to which participants take into account what others do) that does exist in calculating expenditures totals. The total budget was rarely drastically out of line with expenditures before it was formalized in 1921, and even without control by a central authority today we do not usually get extraordinary increases or decreases except during national emergencies. There has been much more subtle and informal coordination by tacit agreements and accepted limits than there has previously been thought to be.

To some critics the procedure by which the agencies (as well as the appropriations committees and the Budget Bureau to a lesser extent) try to guage "what will go" may seem unfortunate. They feel that there must be a better justification for programs than the subjective interpretation of signals from the environment. Yet we live in a democracy in which a good part of the justification for programs is precisely that they are deemed desirable by others. What is over-looked is that these informal procedures are also powerful coordinating mechanisms: when one thinks of all the participants who are continuously engaged in interpreting the wishes of others, who try to feel the pulse of Congress, the President, interest groups, and special publics, it is clear that a great many adjustments are made in anticipation of what other participants are likely to do. This, it seems to me, is just another term for coordination, unless one insists that coordination be redefined to require conscious control by a single individual or group.

The interaction between appropriations committees and administrative agencies includes at least seven modes of coordination:

1. Laws commanding specific actions;
2. Committee reports demanding specific action on (implicit) pain of future penalties;
3. Exchange of indulgences;
4. Taking each other's preferences into account with direct contact;
5. Accommodations to prior actions of the other without consultation;
6. Argument in which one side convinces the other;
7. Granting of side payments by one participant in return for action by the other.

Neglect of consequences

The budgetary process is sometimes attacked for its apparent neglect of consequences, and there can be no doubt that lack of comprehensiveness in budgeting means that a participant making a specific decision will often neglect important values affected by that decision. However, Lindblom has proposed that consequences neglected by one participant may be considered by another, or by the same participant working on another problem.[28] To the extent, therefore, that all significant interests tend to be represented in a fragmented political system, decision makers may reduce their information costs, by neglecting many alternatives, in the confidence that they will be picked up by others or by themselves at another time. Thus, the budgetary process as a whole may be considered rational even though the actions of individual participants may not seem to

---

[28] See his *Decision-Making In Taxation and Expenditures, Public Finances, Needs, Sources and Utilization* (Princeton: National Bureau of Economic Research, 1961), pp. 295-336.

be because they omit from their calculations consequences important for others.

The political process in a democracy has a built-in feature that assures that some presently neglected values will be considered. This mechanism exists because politicians and interest-group leaders are motivated, by their hope of retaining or winning office, to find needs that have not been met and proposing to fulfill them in return for votes.

No doubt the neglect of some values (say those dear to Negroes) could be better avoided by increasing the weight of the appropriate interests in the political process. There is no point, it seems to me, in faulting the budgetary process for the lamentable failure of some groups to be properly represented in the political life of the nation. Political mobilization of Negroes will obviously do much more to protect their neglected interests than any change in the mechanism for considering budgets.

The most powerful coordinating mechanisms in budgeting undoubtedly are the various roles adopted by major participants in the budgetary process. Because the roles fit in with one another and set up a stable pattern of mutual expectations, they do a great deal to reduce the burden of calculations for the individual participants. The agencies need not consider in great detail how their requests will affect the President's overall program; they know that such criteria will be introduced in the Budget Bureau. The appropriations committees and the Budget Bureau know that the agencies are likely to put forth all the programs for which there is prospect of support and can concentrate on fitting them into the President's program or on paring them down. The Senate committee operates on the assumption that if important items are left out through House action the agency will carry an appeal. If the agencies suddenly reversed roles and sold themselves short, the entire pattern of mutual expectations might be upset, leaving the participants without a firm anchor in a sea of complexity. If the agency were to refuse the role of advocate, it would increase the burden on the congressmen; they would not only have to choose among desirable items placed before them with some fervor, but they would also have to discover what these items might be. This is a task ordinarily far beyond the limited time, energy, information, and competence of most congressmen.

The roles appear to be "natural" to the occupants of these institutional positions. A man who has spent many years working in, say, the natural resources area can be expected to believe that his programs are immensely worthy of support. (He may try to eliminate programs he deems unworthy, but there are always others to take their place.) Indeed, he would hardly be worth having as a governmental employee if he did not feel this way in his position. By serving as advocate in the real world, he sees to it that important values in his area are not neglected if he can help it.

The House Appropriations Committee's role of guarding the Treasury, with its emphasis on reducing requests, makes sense in the context of agency advocacy. If the congressmen can be reasonably certain that the agency has put its best foot forward, then their decisions may be viewed as choices along the margins of the top percentage of expenditures advocated by the agencies. The role of guardianship provides the congressmen with a stance that supplies reasonably clear instructions—cut the estimates—while keeping the area within which they must focus their attention (the largest increases) manageable in terms of their limited time and ability to calculate.

Some critics suggest that appropriations committee members should adopt a different role. In this "mixed" role, the congressman would be oriented toward neither cutting nor increasing but to doing both in about equal proportions. Each case would have to be considered on its own merits. To some extent, of course, this balance occurs under the present system. The difference is one of degree, but not less important for being so. For where they are in doubt or do not care to inquire in detail, the congressmen may now follow their prevailing orientation—usually to cut at the margin—expecting to receive feedback if something drastic happens. Under a "mixed" role, however, an exhaustive inquiry into all or most items would be called for. The resulting increase in amounts of calculation required would be immense. And to the extent that other participants adopted a mixed role, the pattern of role expectations upon which participants are now dependent as a calculating device would no longer prove stable. The calculation of preferences, essential in a democratic system, would become far more burdensome since inquiries would have to be instituted to find out what the various groups wanted in specific cases.

Furthermore, the adoption of a mixed role would be likely to lead to a greater neglect of values affected by decisions. Unless the ability of each participant to calculate the consequences of his actions is much more impressive than the evidence suggests, he is bound to neglect more if he attempts to do more. Yet this is precisely what a mixed role would force him to do. Instead of concentrating on a limited range of values within his jurisdiction, as his present role requires, he would have to consider the widest possible range of values in order to make a mixed role work. In place of the reasonable certainty that each participant does a good job of looking after the relatively narrow range of values entrusted to his care, there would be little certainty that any particular value would be protected because no one had been especially directed to look after it. Let us explore this question further as a fundamental problem in normative political theory.

Interests

Why, it may be asked, should the various participants take a partial view? Why should they not simply decide in accordance with what the public interest requires? Actually, this is the principle that participants think they are following now; they all believe that their version of the public interest is correct. It is their differing institutional positions, professional training, and group values that lead to perspectives producing somewhat different interpretations of the public interest. Let us, then, rephrase the question and ask whether it is better for each participant to put first the achievement of his own goals (including the goals entrusted to him by virtue of his position) when he considers what is meant by "public interest," or whether he should view the goals of others as of prime or at least equal importance to this consideration?

I am prepared to argue that the partial-view-of-the-public-interest approach is preferable to the total-view-of-the-public-interest approach, which is so often urged as being superior. First, it is much simpler for each participant to calculate his own preferences than for each to try to calculate the preferences of all. It is difficult enough for a participant to calculate how the interests he is protecting might best be served without requiring that he perform the same calculation for many others who might also be affected. The "partial" approach has the virtue of enabling others to accept as an input in their calculations the determination of each participant as to his preferences, which is not possible under the total approach. The danger of omitting important values is much greater when participants neglect the values in their immediate care in favor of what seem to them a broader view. How can anyone know what is being neglected if everyone speaks for someone else and no one for himself?

The partial approach is more efficient for resolving conflicts, a process that lies at the heart of democratic politics. Because the approach is partial, it does not require its practitioners to discover all or most possible conflicts and to work out answers to problems that may never materialize. It permits each participant to go his own way until he discovers that the activities of others interfere. Effort can then be devoted to overcoming the conflicts that arise. The formation of alliances in a political system requiring them is facilitated by the expression and pursuit of demands by those in closest touch with the social reality from which they issue. It is not, then, *noblesse oblige* but self-interest that assures that all demands insist on being heard and find the political resources to compel a hearing. A partial adversary system in which the various interests compete for control of policy (under agreed upon rules) seems more likely to result in reasonable decisions—that is, decisions that take account of the multiplicity of values involved—than one in which the best policy is assumed to be discoverable by a well-intentioned search for the public interest for all by everyone.

Strategies

If it is granted that budgetary practices based on a partial view of the public interest are desirable, then it would appear necessary to accept the use of strategies designed to secure appropriation goals. It is not surprising, however, that critics find something basically underhanded, even undemocratic, in the maneuvering of "special interests" for strategic advantage. Would not a straightforward approach based on the "merits" of each program be preferable?

Requiring that an individual commit suicide for the public good may at times have an acceptable rationale; suggesting that it become a common practice can hardly claim as much. I shall take it as understood, then, that asking participants in budgeting consistently to follow practices extremely disadvantageous to themselves and their associates is not reasonable. The participants must be able to maintain themselves in the environment.

The notion that administrators go around telling each other (or believing in secret) that the purposes for which they request funds are not valid but that they want the money anyway in order to advance themselves and build empires is not worthy of consideration. It would be exceedingly difficult to keep people in an organization if they could not justify its purposes to themselves. Such an attitude would be bound to come to the attention of other participants, who would take appropriate action. It would be bad strategically as well as morally. Attempts to reduce a complex distributive process like budgeting to the terms of a western melodrama—the good men ride white horses and advance on their merits; the bad men wear black masks and rely on strategies—do away with the great problem of deciding upon expenditures advocated by officials who are sincere believers in their proposals, and who know that all demands can be satisfied.

Budgetary strategies may generally be characterized as attempts to make the best case for the agency at the best time and thus to get as large an appropriation as possible. This behavior follows from the role of the agency as advocate. As a practical matter, we would expect any agency head worth his keep to respond to opportunities for increasing appropriations and warding off cuts. The contrary position—making the worst case at the worst time—is not likely to be greeted with enthusiasm by either congressmen or agency staff.

Seizing on the opportune moment for advancing the agency's budgetary goals has much to commend it. The nation is served by initiative in meeting the needs of the time. An element of flexibility is generated that helps ensure that opportunities for action will be taken. "Crisis" strategies belong in this category. What is the difference, we may ask, between using a crisis to increase appropriations and acting to meet the nation's requirements in an hour of need? The desire to present the agency's requests in the best light can be used in a positive sense to improve the thinking of the operating units. The budget office can play an important mediating role because it must explain and justify agency actions to the outside world. By playing devil's advocate to agency personnel, by pointing out that justifications are not clear or persuasive, by saying that the program heads have to do better to convince the Budget Bureau or the appropriations committees, the Budget office may compel or encourage thinking from diverse perspectives. In this way, a wider range of interests and values receive consideration.

Clientele and confidence strategies are desirable as well as inevitable in a democratic society. The feedback that clientele give to the participants is essential political information about who wants what programs, at what level, and with what degree of intensity. The establishment of confidence in an agency and its officers provides the trust necessary for congressmen who must live with complexity; the sanctions upon that agency that follow from lack of congressional confidence represent a great safeguard against duplicity. That morality is to some extent the handmaiden of necessity does not make it any less real or valuable.

A naked recital of strategies is bound to suggest that a certain amount of trickery is involved. Some strategies that appear to be deceitful represent amoral adjustments to an environment that does not give the participants much choice. Consider the kind of duplicity that appears to be involved in the game wherein agency people make believe that they are supporting the President's budget while actually encouraging congressmen to ask questions that will permit them to talk about what they would really like to have. Is this behavior immoral or does the immorality belong to the Executive Office directive that tries to compel agency personnel to say things that they do not believe in order to support the President? Congress has the power of the purse and it is difficult to argue that it should not have the kind of information about what the people in charge of the program think they ought to get that might help it to arrive at decisions. If one wants to get rid of Congress, then the problem solves itself. But if one accepts the separation of powers, then it may well be that it would be destructive to deny Congress information it would like to have, especially when for Congress to have it is manifestly in the interests of administrators. The Biblical injunction against excessive temptation is appropriate here.

Merits

Despite all that has been said, the very idea that strategies are employed may still appear disturbing. Why cannot programs be presented on their merits and their merits alone? The most obvious answer is that the question presupposes popular, general agreement on what constitutes merit when the real problem is that people do not agree. That is why we have politics. To lay down and enforce criteria of merit in budgeting would be, in effect, to dispense with politics in favor of deciding what the government shall do in advance.

Much of what is meant by merit turns out to be "meets my preferences" or "serves my interests" or "the interests of those with whom I identify." It would be most peculiar for a nation calling itself a democracy to announce that only the most meritorious policies were carried out despite the fact that they were not preferred by any significant group in the population. The degree to which widespread preferences are met not only *is* but *ought* to be *part* of why policies are deemed meritorious.

We all know that people do not always realize what is good for them. They are occupied with many things and may not recognize the benefits flowing from certain policies. They may find it difficult to support policies that are meritorious but not directly related to their own immediate needs. Here is where strategies come in. Where support is lacking, it may be mobilized; where attention is unfocused, it may be directed by advertising; where merits are not obvious, they may be presented in striking form. Ability to devise strategies to advance the recognition of merit is immensely more helpful than cries of indignation that political artistry should be necessary.

Merit consists, in part, of the effectiveness with which programs are formulated and carried out. No one should doubt that this criterion is recognized in the budgetary process; estimates, justifications, and presentations are directed to this end. Though effectiveness is indispensable—confidence would be lacking without it, for one thing; clientele would be dissatisfied, for another—agencies find that it does not take them far enough. An agency may be wonderfully effective in formulating and carrying out its programs and yet see its fortunes suffer because of the need for Congress to cut that year or to shift funds to some other vital area. Defense appropriations are often a function of domestic concerns; stabilization policy may be constrained by military needs; the complexity of a project or the difficulty of demonstrating immediate results may militate against it. Consequently, the agency invariably finds that in some areas its good works and best efforts are not being rewarded. Prizes are simply not distributed for good deeds alone. The agency's mode of adapting to this circumstance is to use demonstration of good works as one among a number of strategies. Forbidding agencies to use strategies designed to give its good requests a better chance, because bad requests can also be dressed up, seems inadvisable as well as unlikely to succeed.

Motivation

Instead of bewailing the use of strategies, it would be immensely more fruitful to arrange incentives within the system so as to insure that good strategies and good programs will go together as often as possible. Budgeting would be conceived of in this sense as constituting a problem in human motivation. When motivation is disregarded, it is no wonder that unsatisfactory results ensue. In order to demonstrate that this problem is by no means peculiar to the national budgetary process let us take a brief look at budgeting in Soviet and American industrial firms.

Rewards to managers in Soviet industrial firms depend on their meeting production quotas assigned in economic plans. But necessary supplies—skilled labor and financial resources—are often lacking. The first consequence of this is that the quota is not set from above but becomes the subject of bargaining as the managers seek to convince the ministries that quotas should be as low as possible. Yet the managers find it prudent not to hugely exceed their quota, for in that case next year's quota will be raised beyond attainment. The second consequence is that production is not rationalized to produce the greatest output at the lowest cost, but is geared instead to meeting specific incentives. Heavy nails are overproduced, for example, because quotas are figured by weight. Maintenance may be slighted in favor of huge effort for a short period in order to meet the quota. Funds are hidden in order to provide slack that can be used to pay "pushers" to expedite the arrival of supplies. The list of essentially deceitful practices to give the appearance of fulfilling the quota is seemingly endless: producing the wrong assortment of products, transferring current costs to capital accounts, shuffling accounts to pay for one item with funds designated for another, declaring unfinished goods finished, lowering the quality of goods, and so on.[29] The point is that the budgetary system arranges incentives in such a way that managers cannot succeed with lawful practices. When similar incentives are applied in American industrial firms, similar practices result, from running machines into the ground, to "bleeding the line," to meeting a monthly quota by doctoring the accounts.[30]

As in the Soviet Union, American firms often use budgets not to reflect or project reality but to drive managers and workers toward increased production. Budgets are conceived of as forms of pressure on inherently lazy people [31] so that (to paraphrase Mao Tse-tung) the greater the pressure the better the budget. Inevitably, managers and workers begin to perceive budgets as "perpetual needlers" or as "the hammer that's waiting to hit you on the head." [32] In some cases, this leads to discouragement because it is apparent that whatever the effort, the budget quota will be increased. Since accounting is separate for sub-units in the firm, it is not surprising that fierce negotiations take place to assign costs among them. As a result, top officials find it necessary to engage in campaigns to sell budgets to the units. Otherwise, sabotage is likely.[33] While some attention has been given

---

[29] Joseph S. Berliner, *Factory and Manager in the USSR* (Cambridge: Harvard University Press, 1957).

[30] Frank Jasinsky, "Use and Misuse of Efficiency Controls," *Harvard Business Review*, XXXIV, 1956, p. 107; Chris Argyris, *The Impact of Budgets on People* (New York: Controllership Foundation, Inc., 1952), pp. 12ff.

[31] Argyris, *op. cit.*, pp. 6ff.

[32] *Ibid.*, pp. 12-13.

[33] *Ibid., inter alia;* Bernard H. Sord and Glenn A. Welsch, *Business Budgeting: A Survey of Management Planning and Control Practices* (New York: Controllership Foundation, Inc., 1958), pp. 140-50.

to human relations in budgeting,[34] only Stedry [35] has attempted to explore the essential motivational problems of budgeting within an organizational framework. Yet, without an understanding of the impact of different goals and incenitve systems on human activity, reliable statements about the likely consequences of different budgetary incentives can hardly be made. I shall attempt to deal with this problem in my recommendations.

Power

The strategy which critics of the budgetary process find most objectionable is Congress' use of the appropriations power to alter policies of executive agencies. To say that congressmen interfere too much in the details of administration, however, is to consign them to impotence. Grand policy decisions come few and far between. Most policy is made through interpretation of statutes by administrators or through a succession of marginal adjustments in the form of legislative amendments. If by "administrative detail" one means "trivial," then it would seem that the administrators who are presumably being defended would have little to worry about. A basic analytic problem, preventing meaningful thought, is that "policy" is identified with "Congress" and "administration" with the executive branch. By definition, Congress should not tell administrators what to do, because administrators administrate and Congress is supposed only to make policy. I agree so completely with the position taken by Richard Fenno that I would like to quote his comments at some length:

> To relegate Congress to the making of broad policy decisions and to oversight in terms of broad program management is to prescribe precisely those tasks which Congress is least capable of performing. To criticize Congress for intervening in a specific and detailed fashion is to attack it for doing the only thing it can do to effectively assert its influence. Specifics and details are the indispensable handles which Congressmen use to work inductively toward broader kinds of oversight judgments. Specifics and details are what concern the constituents on whose behalf Congressmen must intervene with the bureaucracy. Specific and detailed requests from an interested Congressman to a bureau head or division chief do more to "galvanize the internal

---

[34] Arnold A. Bebling, "A Look at Budgets and People," *Business Budgeting,* X, 1961, p. 16.

[35] Andrew C. Stedry, *Budget Control and Cost Behavior* (Englewood Cliffs, N.J.: Prentice-Hall, 1960).

disciplines of administration" (Arthur Macmahon's phrase) than any broad statement of policy. The profusion of committees and subcommittees make possible a degree of specialization which gives to Congressmen the detailed and specific information they find most useful in influencing executive behavior.

Specific and detailed controls by individuals and small committees give Congressmen their maximum influence because these controls are best adapted to the realities of executive decision-making. If executive decision-making is basically piecemeal, incremental and marginal, then congressional control, if it is to be effective, must be basically piecemeal, incremental and marginal. What is or is not "appropriate" congressional control cannot be prescribed *a piori*. . . . Congressional control is or is not appropriate in the context of the realities of legislative and executive decision-making. The legislator ought not to be criticized for using those controls which are available to him and which his experience tells him bring the greatest influence over executive activity. If we do not recognize this, we will continue to prescribe impossible control tasks. . . .[36]

The power of Congress to control budgetary decisions depends on the power of its appropriations committees. For no large assembly of men can develop the expertise, self-direction, cohesiveness, and dispatch which are necessary to do the large volume of budgetary business. A good index of the power of any legislature is whether it develops and follows committees of experts in specific areas of decisions. Where such committees are absent, as in Great Britain, the power of Parliament becomes a fiction. (A common definition of a cabinet is a committee which permits no rivals.) The appropriations committees measure up exceedingly well when we consider that their recommendations are adopted by the houses of Congress approximately 90 percent of the time. Although one might contemplate with equanimity some reduction in this record of success, a drop below, say, 75 percent would seriously compromise the appropriations committees with the President and the agencies. For a great deal of the ability to have agencies follow congressional will is dependent on the knowledge that the appropriations committees are watching and that their actions will be upheld with a high degree of certainty. Once the power gets transferred to Congress as a whole, its exercise becomes so uncertain and diffuse that no one can count on it. Congress-

---

[36] Richard F. Fenno, Jr., review of Joseph P. Harris, "Congressional Control of Administration," in *American Political Science Review,* LVIII:3, 1964, p. 674.

men simply do not have the time and the knowledge to debate a very large number of appropriations with sense and then follow through. The general body of congressmen do well to keep the appropriations committees in line with an occasional defeat on the floor to remind them whom they are ultimately beholden to.

The great power of the appropriations committees consists in the extent to which agencies and the Bureau of the Budget systematically take account of their preferences. Anyone who has seen budget offices in operation knows that the unseen hand of Congress is never far from the surface. The agency practice of holding mock hearings in which some officials are assigned the role of appropriations committee members is a vivid illustration of how Congress makes its will felt indirectly.

The power of the appropriations committees depends on their ability to command regular support in Congress, support which in turn is dependent on the cohesiveness of the committees. Fenno [37] has shown that support for the House Appropriations Committee drops markedly when its subcommittees issue split recommendations. The internal norms and calculating mechanisms whereby the committee achieves a high degree of integration are therefore of extreme importance in the maintenance of congressional power. The incremental, fragmented, non-programmatic, and sequential procedures of the present budgetary process aid in securing agreement. It is much easier to agree on an addition or reduction of a few thousand or a million dollars than to agree on whether a program is good in the abstract. It is much easier to agree on a small addition or decrease than to compare the worth of one program to that of all others. Conflict is reduced by an incremental approach because the area open to dispute is reduced. Agreement comes much more readily when the items in dispute can be treated as differences in dollars instead of as basic differences in policy; calculating budgets in monetary increments facilitates bargaining and logrolling. It becomes possible to swap an increase here for a decrease there or for an increase elsewhere without always having to consider the ultimate desirability of programs blatantly in competition. Procedures that de-emphasize overt conflicts among competing programs also encourage secret deliberations, nonpartisanship, and the recruitment of personnel who feel comfortable in sidestepping policy decisions most of the time. The prospects for agreement within the House Appropriations Committee are enhanced by closed hearings and mark-up sessions, and

---

[37] Fenno, "The House Appropriations Committee as a Political System: The Problem of Integration," *op. cit.*

by a tradition against publicity. Were deliberations to take place in public—"open covenants openly arrived at"—committee members might find themselves accused of "selling out" if they made concessions. Willingness to compromise, to be flexible, is a quality sought in choosing members to serve on the appropriations committees. Party ties might be disruptive of agreement if they focused attention on the policy differences between the two political persuasions. Instead, party differences are submerged during committee deliberations, and the usual process of taking something from a program here, adding to a program there, swapping this for that, can go on.

However the committee's practices are subject to attack precisely because of their de-emphasis of large policy considerations. Manifestly, the House Appropriations Committee does not normally consider its task to lie in rehashing every year the arguments over the fundamental desirability of the legislation already considered by the substantive committees and passed by Congress. Fortunately, Richard Fenno [38] has provided us with a splendid analysis of a committee whose members took fierce partisan and ideological positions on virtually all the issues that came before them. The norm of reciprocity —accepting the recommendations of other subcommittees if they accept yours—was unknown on the House Education and Labor Committee in the years after the Second World War. The members went after each other with abandon. They appeared to glory in differences and to stress the ultimate values which divided them. As a result, the committee was supremely ineffective in getting its recommendations accepted in the House. Internal committee warfare contributed to the long delay in producing any important legislation on education. Were these norms to prevail on the appropriations committees it is doubtful that a congressional budget could be produced at all. In the presence of delay and confusion and in the absence of party majorities to resolve these matters consistently on a strict partisan basis. Congress would be faced with the choice of abandoning its budgetary prerogatives or of indulging in the grossest forms of action leading to wild and unpredictable swings in the levels of appropriations.

Reform proposals

The literature on reform is replete with suggestions for improving the rationality of the budgetary process, which turn out to have vast

---

[38] Frank Munger and Richard Fenno, Jr., *National Politics and Federal Aid to Education* (Syracuse, N.Y.: Syracuse University Press, 1962), pp. 106-36.

implications for the distribution of power. Identifying rationality with a comprehensive overview of the budget by a single person or group, Arthur Smithies despairs of the fragmented approach taken by Congress and proposes a remedy. He suggests that a Joint (congressional) Budget Policy Committee be formed and empowered to consider all proposals for revenue and expenditure in a single package and that its decisions be made binding by a concurrent resolution. He presents this reform suggestion as a moderate proposal to improve the rationality of the budget process.[39] If the proposed Joint Committee were unable to secure the passage of its recommendations, as would surely be the case, it would have gone to enormous trouble without accomplishing anything but a public revelation of futility. The impotence of the Joint Committee on the Economic Report,[40] the breakdown of the single congressional attempt to develop a comprehensive legislative budget,[41] and the failure of congressional attempts to control the Council of Economic Advisers [42] and the Budget Bureau,[43] all stem from the same cause. There is no cohesive group in Congress capable of using these devices to affect decision making by imposing its preferences on a majority of congressmen. Smithies' budgetary reform presupposes a completely different political system from the one which exists in the United States. In the guise of a procedural change in the preparation of the budget by Congress, Smithies is actually proposing a revolutionary move which would mean, if it were successful, the virtual introduction of the British Parliamentary system.

In a sophisticated advocacy of budgetary reform, John Saloma suggests a Joint (congressional) Committee of Fiscal Policy, which

---

[39] Smithies, *op. cit.,* pp. 192ff.

[40] Avery Leiserson, "Coordination of the Federal Budgetary and Appropriations Procedures Under the Legislative Reorganization Act of 1946," *National Tax Journal,* I, 1948, pp. 118-26.

[41] Wallace, *op. cit.;* Dalmas H. Nelson, "The Omnibus Appropriations Act of 1950," *Journal of Politics,* XV, 1953, pp. 274-88; John Phillips, "The Hadacol of the Budget Makers," *National Tax Journal,* IV, 1951, pp. 255-68.

[42] Roy Blough, "The Role of the Economist in Federal Policy-Making," *University of Illinois Bulletin,* 1953, p. 51; Lester Seligman, "Presidential Leadership: The Inner Circle and Institutionalization," *Journal of Politics,* XVIII, 1956, pp. 410-26; Edwin G. Nourse, *Economics in the Public Service: Administrative Aspects of the Employment Act* (New York: Harcourt Brace, 1953); Ronald C. Hood, "Reorganizing the Council of Economic Advisers," *Political Science Quarterly,* LXIX, 1954, pp. 413-37.

[43] Fritz Morstein Marx, "The Bureau of the Budget: Its Evolution and Present Role, II," *American Political Science Review,* XXXIX, 1945, pp. 869-98; Richard Neustadt, "Presidency and Legislation: The Growth of Central Clearance," *American Political Science Review,* XLVIII, 1954, pp. 641-71; Seligman, *op. cit.*

he believes can operate within the existing political system. The Joint Fiscal Committee would have a small membership drawn from leading members of the two appropriations and the two finance committees of Congress. The Joint Committee would be well staffed. According to Saloma:

> The Joint Committee should not be required to submit a formal legislative budget for congressional enactment. At most it should develop budgetary guidelines to assist the fiscal committees (guidelines that probably would be kept confidential). Primarily it should provide a forum for continuing Congressional consideration of the budget, changing economic and political assumptions on which the budget is based, and the status of authorization and appropriation measures.[44]

Saloma [45] believes that the Joint Fiscal Committee would improve communications between the houses of Congress, enable Congress "to express its sentiments on broad fiscal policy," provide a continuing picture of the budget which Congress does not have, and provide guidelines to a coordinating committee of appropriations subcommittee chairmen on levels of appropriations. Smithies' proposal has been made more realistic at the cost of emasculating it. What is the point of the Joint Fiscal Committee if, unlike the Joint Committee on Atomic Energy, it cannot make recommendations for action on the floor of Congress? Why should any other committee pay attention to its recommendations? Experience with the Joint Economic Committee suggests that advisory committees of this character have hardly any influence at all on governmental policy.[46] If the budgetary guidelines of the Joint Fiscal Committee were adopted, which is doubtful, we would have in effect a steering committee of Congress, which Saloma recognizes is unrealistic. If they were rejected, as is likely, disillusionment would be inevitable, despite Saloma's warning that expectations should not be too high. Whatever information is desired on the outstanding authorizations and appropriations can be had through the existing committees of Congress or through some simple information service. It seems to me

---

[44] John S. Saloma, "The Responsible Use of Power," in Saloma and Murray L. Weidenbaum, *Congress and the Federal Budget* (Washington, D. C.: The American Enterprise Institute for Public Policy Research, 1965), p. 182.

[45] *Ibid.,* pp. 175-93.

[46] Ralph K. Huitt, "Congressional Organization and Operations in the Field of Money and Credit," in William Fellner, *et al., Fiscal and Debt Management Policies: A Series of Research Studies prepared for the Commission on Money and Credit* (Englewood Cliffs, N. J.: Prentice-Hall, 1963), pp. 399-495.

that Saloma's proposal, a variation of the McClellan Committee bill, is simply a bow to the gods of comprehensiveness. As usual, no demonstration is made of the feasibility of a comprehensive approach; instead, the gods are appeased by providing an umbrella committee, much as if incantation of the Joint Fiscal Committee's name would reveal the divine presence of a rational view of the budget as a whole.

Summary

In appraising the budgetary process, we must deal with real men who know that, in this real world, the best they can get is to be preferred to the perfection they cannot achieve. Unwilling or unable to alter the basic features of the political system, they seek to make it work for them rather than against them in budgeting. Participants in budgeting not only work within the specified constitutional rules, they also make active use of them. Problems of calculation are mitigated by the division of labor in the separation of powers; morality is enforced by substantial external checks as well as by inner motives; a wider range of preferences is taken into account by making the institutional participants responsible for somewhat different ones. A great deal of informal coordination takes place as participants adjust to their expectation of other's behavior. An incremental approach guards against radical departures most of the time, whereas agency advocacy and strategies designed to take advantage of emergent needs help ensure flexibility. A basic conclusion of this appraisal is that the existing budgetary process works much better than is commonly supposed.

There is, however, no special magic in the *status quo*. Inertia and ignorance as well as experience and wisdom may be responsible for whatever problems exist in the present state of affairs. Improvements of many kinds are undoubtedly possible and desirable. The heart of the problem of budgetary reform lies in the inevitable tension between the practice of incrementalism and the ideology of comprehensiveness. The assumption of all previous proposals for reform has been that incrementalism must be sacrificed to comprehensiveness. But as this section has suggested formal coordination and comprehensive calculation of budgets are unfeasible, undesirable, or both. If comprehensiveness is rejected, however, there turn out to be other significant directions for reform that have not yet been tried. My view is that the present budgetary process should be taken as far as it will go and then corrected for its worst deficiencies. Proposals for reform should advocate a more thoroughgoing incremental approach, not its opposite—a more comprehensive one. There should be greater use of aids to calculation rather than less. Agencies should not be told to give up advocacy, but should be motivated to make their best case even more persuasive. There should be even less formal unity and more conflict in budgeting than there is today.

Radical Incrementalism

THE President, the agencies, and Congress are now compelled to give at least *pro forma* consideration to all the activities in the whole budget in a limited period of time. This results in a brief period characterized by frantic activity and the rote presentation of masses of information, most of which is not subject to change and of no special interest to anyone at that time. Why? Because of unthinking acceptance of the idea that there must be a budget containing all expenditures presented and considered at one time. As the federal budget grows, and life and budgeting become more complex, the demand for central direction increases. Yet the overload of information is already staggering; aids to calculation are used in a desperate attempt to simplify consideration of small parts of the budget. The time has come to cast aside the myth of comprehensiveness. Theory should be brought in line with experience so that there will be a chance of improving the experience. The budget needs to be further fragmented. Attention needs to be directed to matters of political interest which can be changed. Evaluation of budgetary requests must be spread out so that greater time and attention may be devoted to each of them. The development and refinement of further aids to calculation should assume a high research priority. The delays in the budgetary process should be markedly reduced by permitting the most immediate response to budgetary requests.

My proposal is that we abandon the annual budgetary process, as it is now known, and substitute a continuous consideration of incremental changes to the existing base. Each agency will assume that the funds for its programs will automatically be continued. All appropriations will be continuous, except for a small number designed for a limited time period. When an agency wishes to increase or decrease its funds for a program or to eliminate an old program or begin a new one, it will submit a request to Congress through the Bureau of the Budget. The President may submit requests for change to Congress, and have them considered right away. The appropriations committees may call for testimony at any time on any budgetary matter and change appropriations irrespective of the fiscal year. By altering authorizations to spend, the substantive committees may also bring reconsideration of budgetary matters. I call this proposal radical incrementalism because it is based on pushing the evident incremental tendencies in budgeting to encompass the entire process.

A basic purpose of radical incrementalism is to facilitate speedy and continuous adaptation to emergent problems. While some programs may remain in a steady state, others can be reviewed as often as any participant deems it necessary. Supplemental appropriations would become a thing of the past. Demands could be dealt with as they arise. If the latest incremental move suggests a new step requiring changes in appropriations, a decision could be made right then and there. The tyranny of the annual budget—requiring formal review of programs of little immediate interest and inhibiting action on programs which need attention at the moment—would be ended.

Suppose that a subcommittee wished to look at trends in personnel or building costs. It could simply ask for these figures and act on them as it saw fit. Should a subcommittee want to view any budgetary item in relation to an agency's total appropriations, it could request both sets of figures. In order to facilitate this procedure, the appropriations committee should require agencies to develop quick and inexpensive methods of estimating expenditures. The agencies as well as the appropriations committees need to develop better aids to calculation. It may well be the case that much agency budgetary work is far too expensive and cumbersome for the results achieved. The development of rough and ready cost estimates should make it possible for agencies to provide serviceable breakdowns of their activities from a variety of conceptual viewpoints. Instead of being stuck with a rigid set of program categories, terribly expensive to maintain under proper accounting, the agencies and the subcommittees would have the advantage of being able to look at activities from diverse perspectives.

An objection that might be raised to radical incrementalism is that certain programs could escape scrutiny over a period of years.

This potential problem may be solved by appointing people to review periodically those programs or activities that do not change very much from year to year, and would, therefore, tend to escape frequent scrutiny. Since they do not alter radically, a thorough going over every five years or so would be sufficient. Nor need any one organization do it all; the incremental approach can make use of the division of labor that is a part of the national system. Departmental budget offices, the bureaus themselves, the Bureau of the Budget, and the House and Senate appropriations subcommittees and their investigating staffs, might use sampling techniques so that each would review a few programs of this kind every year. The results could then be used to see if congressional scrutiny were warranted the next year. In this way, a large part of the problem may be met while adding only a little to the burden of the participants. Should the appropriations committees decide that they wish to review every activity as often as every five to eight years, they could make it a rule that each appropriation lapses five to eight years after the last congressional act.

Narrowing, fragmenting, and dispersing these budgetary reviews has considerable advantage from the viewpoint of encouraging experimentation and innovation: because no one organization is overburdened, the most thorough analysis is facilitated; more active participation by high level officials is encouraged because the material to be considered at any one time is not overwhelming; as the knowledge and interest of top officials is fed back down the line, the significance of the activity and the importance of those who engage in it is likely to be enhanced. If budgetary reviews can be liberated to some extent from the peak periods of the formal budgetary cycle, imagination and creativity can be given freer play. The absence of immediate deadlines may encourage speculation and experimentation, while the increased probability that hierarchical superiors have time to listen gives greater promise that the efforts may lead to tangible results. The variety of organizations involved should also lead to consideration of a broad range of values and perspectives.

At first glance, it might appear that problems of coordination would be made more difficult than they are today. I think not; unless, of course, one is prepared to define coordination as placing all appropriations within the cover of one huge book at one time. Nor does it make much sense to define coordination as a central review, since this begs the question of whether policies have actually been related to one another in a reasonable way. It is a lot easier to mesmerize oneself with talk about central coordination than it is to practice it.

Radical incrementalism, however, can be practiced. Each increment of the budget can be considered as it comes up. Attempts can be made to adapt the new policy, through successive approximation, to major features of the environment as revealed by experience. Thus, a series of rapid adjustments can be made in a budgetary system which encourages (indeed, compels) decision makers to take into account the preferences of others and to mitigate the adverse consequences that policies may have for them. Under radical incrementalism, adaptation can be undertaken with greater intelligence because: (1) the action is close in time to awareness of the problem; (2) changes are smaller, quicker, alterable, and, therefore, more easily made; (3) the decision makers are enabled to have a better grasp of where they are in relation to where they want to be; (4) each change can be separately evaluated against a general picture of the most relevant programs then in operation instead of, an immensely more complicated task, multitudes of suggested changes being pitted against each other simultaneously; (5) every change is always important in the sense that a major participant in the system wants it.

Nothing in radical incrementalism prevents any participant in the budgetary process from using any and all analytic techniques at his disposal. Everyone is permitted to be as wise as he knows how to be. If the day should come when a simultaneous comparison of all governmental programs appeared desirable, the President or Congress could consider the budget in just that way. If it appears desirable to consider all programs dealing with water or land or any other area of policy, the President or the appropriations committees can call for action. Indeed, a radical incrementalism might foster such an approach by permitting scheduling when other great matters were not up for immediate decision. The endless search for "needless duplication," "sheer waste," and "irrational decisions" could go on with as much, or as little, sense as before.

Consequences of radical incrementalism for major participants

What would happen to the President's budget? It would represent the President's preferences on any and all budgetary items on which he cared to express an opinion. It could be as complete a document as he (through the Budget Bureau) knows how to make, or it could contain positions only on selected matters. It would go to Congress as a source of information, but it would not be the action document that it is now. Instead, action on presidential requests would take place when he sent specific demands for specific items to the appropriations committees. The President's budget would be much like his State of the Union Message where he presents his legislative priorities and shopping list, but where he does not necessarily comment on policies he does not wish changed. When he wants action, he follows up his address by submitting a series of concrete proposals for action. Then, as his pending requests are acted upon, the President takes these decisions into account in submitting his next wave of requests. The President would gain flexibility he does not have now because he would not have to commit himself in advance on all appropriations requests as is the case under the annual budget approach. Nor would he and his chief advisers have to engage in the chaotic activity of the fall, when tired and overburdened men work furiously to put together all appropriations. Outgoing Presidents would not have to go through the charade of developing a budget with which to stick their successor, and incoming Presidents would not have to face the immediate task of putting together another full-scale budget to counteract the one that is then operative. The new President could deal with the most vital matters first, and then take up the rest in a more leisurely way.

The President's ability to pursue economic policies would be enhanced rather than diminished by radical incrementalism. There would be no decrease in his ability to plan for a desired relationship between revenue and expenditures. He could set out the relationship he believes desirable in his budget message or in his economic report or in any other way he deems appropriate. And he could propose action to meet his preferences through regular legislation, appropriations, or executive action. But he would not be compelled to do this at any specific time as is now the case. He could wait until he thought a change was necessary, receive the most current predictions of current revenue and expenditure, and act at once. When emergencies require increased expenditure, as in the Vietnam situation, or when long-range estimates proved to be faulty, as frequently happens, he could modify his plans. Since the possibility of substantial change in expenditures is confined to a few areas of policy, these could be re-studied when necessary. While automatic stabilizers, such as unemployment compensation, work well in guarding against depressions, voluntary action by the federal government has not proved effective.[47] Perhaps the flexibility provided by radical incrementalism will permit speedier and more appropriate adaptation to contemporary needs.

---

[47] Wilfred Lewis, Jr., *Federal Fiscal Policy in the Postwar Recessions* (Washington, D. C.: The Brookings Institution, 1962).

A possible objection to radical incrementalism might be that Congress would suffer because agencies would not have to come before the appropriations committees every year for all the appropriations that (aside from trust funds and the like) are usually included in the annual budget. However, instead of concentrating their attention on appropriations requests only in the once-a-year period when all requests are made, agencies would be continually thinking of the prospect of making their next request. On vital matters, the agencies might be called for repeated appearances. To the extent that Congress is more often on their mind its influence should grow rather than decrease.

Opinion on radical incrementalism will probably be divided in Congress. Some members who identify with a presidential constituency might object on the grounds that welfare policies would be hurt by enhancing the power of the appropriations committees to cut in crucial places. However, this would not happen, because, while conservatives now gain somewhat by the special positions they hold on committees, this advantage is rapidly disappearing.[48] There is good reason to believe that the seniority system will increasingly benefit proponents of welfare legislation. Both Presidents and the formal congressional leadership have ample means at their disposal to place members who represent preferences of the party majority on the appropriations committees, and they have already used this to good effect in the House. Deviance from the party majority is largely a southern, Democratic phenomenon and will diminish in size and importance with the growth of Negro voting, population shifts out of the deep South, and increased Democratic party representation elsewhere. Moreover, the best analysis we have of the appropriations committees in Congress (see forthcoming book by Professor Richard F. Fenno, Jr. of the University of Rochester, Rochester, New York) suggests that they do not markedly transgress on the preferences of the mass of other legislators. While it is true that service on the appropriations committees does tend to make members suspicious of executive advocacy, it is also true that the substantive committees are generally packed with legislators whose constituency interests suggest a more expensive view of governmental programs. A creative tension between the somewhat differing orientations of the two levels of committees does not appear to be a bad thing.

---

[48] Raymond E. Wolfinger and Joan Heifetz, "Safe Seats, Seniority and Power in Congress," *American Political Science Review*, LIX, 1965, pp. 337-49.

Fiscal conservatives might also oppose radical incrementalism for fear that it would result, in general, in higher governmental expenditures. Such critics might argue that, in considering programs one at a time, Congress would lose track of the implications for the total rate of expenditure. However, there would be little difficulty in arranging for a reporting service in Congress that would issue frequent statements on total approved expenditures. The solution to the problem of securing decreases, or holding down increases, in expenditure lies in the elimination of programs and not in budgetary procedures. If fiscal conservatives wish to make a drastic impact on expenditures, they will have to elect many more legislators who support their views than is now the case. Barring this unlikely development, there is no point in making the appropriations process the whipping post for developments that represent secular trends in the political system as a whole. Where appropriations subcommittees appear to stand in the way of expenditures desired by a significant majority of their colleagues, they may be out-voted on the floor, or congressional majorities may resort to backdoor spending or to other devices that take control of appropriations out of the offending subcommittees' hands. When fiscal conservatives, or liberals for that matter, are able to assert themselves in Congress, radical incrementalism should provide somewhat better opportunities for selective intervention than now exist.

In my opinion, the most serious obstacle to the acceptance of radical incrementalism is an ideological one. The proposals may not receive serious consideration because they run counter to the reigning ideologies of comprehensiveness and annual budgeting. But I still think them useful to have at hand if and when Congress gets serious about improving its capabilities as an institution.

Strategic political knowledge

By reducing the information requirements of budgetary decisions, radical incrementalism increases the possibility of reasonable action. Whatever knowledge exists can be brought to bear on the problem by some participant in the system. Knowledge may be increased in the sense that the data are more recent and the feedback from one action can be immediately used in the next appraisal. But knowledge about how to deal with problems is only one kind of knowledge. There is a prior knowledge which often assumes greater political importance: namely, what problems should be considered? A radical incrementalism provides an important aid to calculation in that it focuses attention on those changes from the status quo which are important to some participant. But there are other ways of being alerted to matters of importance which would be especially useful to congressmen.

The Budgeting and Accounting Act of 1921 provides for presidential submission of agency budgets to Congress through the Bureau of the Budget. The appropriations committees do not formally receive original agency requests but only those requests as amended or deleted by the Chief Executive. We all know, to be sure, that when ties between agencies and appropriations committee chairmen are close the original agency demands may be brought out in private or in committee hearings. But, agency officials are under restrictions in how far they can go in open advocacy. In any event, junior members of the appropriations committees may never discover this information, and the same will most certainly be true of most other members of Congress.

As political men in a representative assembly, legislators are, above all, dealers in preferences. Since they are makers, shapers, molders, brokers, and bargainers of preferences, the most important information for them to have is information about what people want. Related to this as an aid to calculation is information on where preferences of key participants differ and why, for it alerts legislators to a conflict of preferences in which they may wish to intervene. Congress could well use Franklin D. Roosevelt's well-known practice of programming for conflict, which was designed to assure him that he would be called in on important matters, that is, matters on which preferences and policies differed. This kind of strategic political knowledge is of special importance to congressmen because they appear to be more skilled in reconciling conflicting preferences than in evaluating complicated sets of budgetary figures.

Therefore, I propose that, along with radical incrementalism, there should be a legal requirement that the original requests of agencies be made public, together with a statement by the Budget Bureau giving its reasons for making changes. Congressmen would be immediately alerted to a conflict of preferences and would have the rationales of both the agency and the Budget Bureau presenting rival arguments. Both the agencies and the Budget Bureau would be highly motivated to make the best possible case for their demands. If they were also motivated to reach an agreement through bargaining, the very fact of their success would be one indicator that the matter was not of the highest priority for congressional attention. While some agencies might try to raise their demands inordinately for bargaining purposes, a series of attempts would soon reveal that consistently coming in too high would not serve their interests and would be abandoned.

Thus far I have deliberately used the general word "agency" to avoid complicating the argument with distinctions between bureaus and departments. My initial recommendation is that each department retain its present power to make secret recommendations to the President on behalf of the bureaus within its jurisdiction. In this way, general presidential influence on initial bureau requests could be maintained through his power to hire and fire cabinet members and other heads of organizations. Since department heads must maintain themselves in an environment which necessarily differs from that of the President, their recommendations may sometimes be expected to differ from his on crucial matters. (If this were not the case, the President would have much less need for a Budget Bureau and an Executive Office.) The congressional purpose of unearthing significant political matters through the airing of conflicts would be served. Should this proposal prove insufficient, Congress could go further and require department heads to present in writing their reasons for disagreements with the Budget Bureau request.

Under a system of congressional programming for conflict, the President would lose his ability to maintain the fiction that agencies uniformly support his budget. If this means that congressmen would learn more about where to intervene, there might be a corresponding decrease of the presidential influence now gained by keeping Congress in the dark. Undoubtedly, the proposal will be fought for that reason. But, in fact, the President's support would still be terribly important to the agencies. Congress would still rely on the President's figures as a starting point for their consideration and as a bench mark for making cuts or (less frequently) increases. Agencies would almost always be better off with the President's support than without it; since Congress tends to cut the President's budget, an agency would have to mount a special campaign, with no certain prospect of success, in order to have a chance for victory. It would hardly be advisable, therefore, for agencies to flaunt the Chief Executive. The President might gain in another direction through his ability, under radical incrementalism, to intervene continuously in the appropriations process rather than to confine his energy largely to consideration of the annual budget.

I have no intention of proposing a system that would interfere with the confidential relationship between the President and the Bureau of the Budget. All communications from the Budget Bureau to the President would be as privileged as they are today. Nothing would prevent the Budget Bureau from presenting one kind of argument to the President and another to Congress. The only requirement would be that the President (through the Bureau of the Budget) comment on the differences between his recommendations and those of the agency involved.

A painful adjustment on the part of the Bureau of the Budget would undoubtedly be required. It has grown up in an environment which nurtures secrecy. Its confidential relationship with the President has been used to prevent public scrutiny of its action. Rationalizations of its positions on issues, which have become partly implicit in the sub-culture of the Executive Office, would have to be raised to the surface at some point. The Bureau's claim to a more rational mode of decision making in the public interest (as opposed to irrational procedures in agencies surrounded by special interests) would become open to public examination. The Bureau of the Budget could no longer operate entirely as if it were guided by an informal version of the Official Secrets Act, which so effectively shields executive personnel in Great Britain from outside intervention. While Bureau personnel would gain by being liberated from the physically and mentally exhausting task of putting together an entire governmental budget in a few frantic weeks, they might not be happy with a radical incremental approach to budgeting.

By raising conflict to a more public and hence more visible level, interest groups may be stimulated to greater activity. In a democracy, where public knowledge is generally deemed good, this hardly appears to provide an objection to radical incrementalism. Recent scholarship has suggested that in many cases the power of interest groups in relation to public officials has been exaggerated. Where interest groups are already very powerful, as in the case of the Rivers and Harbors Congress, the chances are that they are privy to the additional information that would be made public under the new system. Thus, the proposals for increasing the availability of strategic information might work to strengthen groups presently weak while adding little or no additional power to the strong.

Knowledge about policies

Although it might be agreed that strategic political information is of the highest importance to a political body like Congress, knowledge about the fields of policy themselves is also significant. Since the specialization of subcommittee members, together with long service in particular areas of policy, undoubtedly does more to augment the substantive information of the legislators than anything which might be suggested, it follows that proposals that drastically increase the turnover of legislators or prevent them from specializing should be resisted. One minor suggestion, however, might be useful. The appropriations committees might hire one or two staff members whose purpose would be to recruit *ad hoc* teams of scholars and practitioners to give a special kind of advice. These men would produce very brief reports telling the subcommittees two things: the questions deemed to be of greatest importance in the relevant field of policy, and the best known ways of looking at the problems involved. Then, if the members of a subcommittee were interested, they could spend a few days at the beginning of the session discussing general policy considerations with their consultants. The best that could be said for this approach would be that it might sensitize congressmen to different kinds of questions and approaches divorced from the immediate need to make a decision. The worst would be that nothing useful would happen. The approach seems worth a try on a low priority basis.

Under a radical incremental approach, with programming for conflict, each organizational unit in the executive branch would be highly motivated to bring forth its best programs and to back them up with the best knowledge at its command. Congress could then use the resources in the executive branch to improve the quality of information that goes into its own decisions. It could still be possible, however, for situations to exist in which all the participants lack useful knowledge. No amount of competition or conflict or reconciliation of divergent preferences would produce reasonable decisions where everyone is poverty-stricken in regard to knowledge. One can say that in the midst of universal lack of knowledge a centrally directed and enforced policy would be by far the worst kind since its impact would be more far-reaching and its reversal would be far more difficult. Such a problem is not peculiar to Congress; universal ignorance is a defect of the society, not merely of a single institution. Yet Congress does have an obligation to increase the sum total of knowledge relevant to carrying out its policymaking functions. The best way for individual congressmen to become aware of gaps in information is to carry on intimate association with program personnel in the agencies and with experts from industry and academic life who might be most sensitive to what we do not know. Beyond this, the task force of experts described above might make suggestions for research in areas where crucial knowledge is lacking.

The aid given governmental bodies by organizations such as **RAND**, also suggests that Congress should look kindly upon the establishment of research corporations in all major areas of policy. Although these corporations would have ties to executive agencies, the increase in information which they would generate would also be useful to Congress. By increasing the number of men trained in various policy areas, research corporations like RAND also increase the possibilities for Congress to gather information from knowledgeable men during and (especially) after their term of employment has ended.

The usual solution suggested for the problem of lack of knowledge in Congress is simply to add to staff resources. In this undifferentiated form, however, the proposal is not terribly helpful. How great an increase in staff, for whom, and for what purpose? The appropriations committees now are entitled to as many staff assistants as they want. In addition, they have virtually unlimited call on the General Accounting Office and other agencies for as much help as they ask for. However, while the staff members are by and large immensely knowledgeable—they may well know more about programs than the highest executive officials—they tend to serve the subcommittee chairmen and ranking minority members rather more than the junior members. But not all junior members would want an additional staff person, responsible only to themselves, who would help out on appropriations. Some members might be tempted to engage in subterfuge by using their appropriations staff for other purposes they deem more valuable. To encourage open behavior it would be advisable to give all legislators a couple of extra staff people at high pay. Then those appropriations committee members who wanted extra assistance could use a staff man for that purpose or not as they saw fit. In this way, a few members might be helped without encouraging a direct conflict with subcommittee chairmen and regular committee staff who might view the earmarking of additional staff for appropriations work as a threat to them. Of course, some conflict over new staff is probably inevitable. A very large increase in personnel or committee staff would seem undesirable on the ground that congressmen are valuable as representatives and not as office managers.

But this discussion still begs the question of what kind of knowledge congressmen need. As a self-respecting body, Congress ought to have research carried on which is expressly designed to help its members in the context in which they work. There is no point in preparing vast volumes of general data to be added to the tomes congressmen already have no time to read. Nor is there much point in preparing comprehensive decision procedures which Congress could not and would not use. It would be most desirable, however, for researchers to study ways and means of developing and introducing scanning mechanisms which would tell congressmen what matters were worth their attention. Forcing conflicts to the surface is one such mechanism. So is increase-decrease analysis. Congressmen need more devices which gear the budgetary process toward producing signals which direct attention to important problems or to strategic opportunities for intervention at low cost in time and high payoff in control. A research group on "aids to calculation" might prove exceedingly useful in this respect.

To the best of my knowledge no one has ever undertaken a study designed to tell congressmen how they might best get compliance with their directives. The lack of knowledge of budgetary motivation has previously been mentioned. What relationship should there be between agency and Budget Bureau requests and grants of funds to secure the highest degree of sensitivity to congressional preferences? What kind of division of functions between and within agencies would maximize opportunities for congressional knowledge and intervention? What simple budgetary forms could be devised to remind executives of congressional interest? The President has found a new Machiavelli in Richard Neustadt; Congress finds no one to give it advice about its special power stake.

Increase in conflict

A predictable consequence of the adoption of the reforms proposed here would be a moderate increase in conflict within Congress over specific appropriations. By highlighting the matters that do receive consideration by the appropriations committees, a radical incremental approach should moderately increase the awareness of interested congressmen. By increasing staff possibilities for junior members of the committees, their ability to disagree with the more senior members should be enhanced somewhat. Emphasizing differences between the President and the agencies should increase political knowledge for all interested members of Congress. Since committee recommendations now receive such a high level of support in Congress, a modest increase in conflict would enable ordinary congressmen to have a little more influence without disrupting the budgetary process. The ability of the system to withstand conflict would also be enhanced by a radical incremental approach because it decreases the need to reach formal agreement on the entire budget. If conflict within Congress leads to lack of agreement and some delay, the agencies can continue to spend at the same level while waiting for a decision on proposed changes. Moreover, only incremental parts of the budget would be delayed while the rest would continue as before. By relaxing the inhibitions created by the overwhelming need to agree on a whole budget every year, the creative aspects of conflict would be given greater scope in budgetary matters as they are in other legislation.

Conclusion

THE change to radical incrementalism would not require as great a change in budgetary practices as it would in perceptions of these practices. Incremental practices are a part of the present budgetary process; but, because participants believe that the ideal budgetary process is comprehensive and coordinated hierarchically, they view incrementalism, with an attitude somewhere between desperation and contempt, as a necessary evil that was adopted only because they did not know any better. At present, incremental practices take place within the framework of annual considerations of the entire budget; this arbitrary time schedule, which is designed to give the appearance of comprehensiveness, actually serves neither the theory of comprehensiveness nor the practice of incrementalism. While comprehensiveness, which cannot be practiced, is touted as a lofty ideal, incrementalism, which could be practiced, is hidden in the scullery like an unloved but necessary Cinderella.

If Congress were willing or able to delegate its powers to an executive committee of compatible legislators, it could, of course, achieve central direction in the same limited sense as the President has: the final word on budgetary decisions would come from a single source whose unity would be visible. But, if Congress is unwilling and unable to do this, as is surely the case, then it should seek to manifest its influence in ways appropriate to a body of legislators capable of unity on an *ad hoc* basis but not consistently over a wide range of measures. Its ability to continually form and reform *ad hoc* coalitions addressed to emergent political problems should be enhanced through a radical incrementalism. Congress is in the business of correcting mistakes—consequences of decisions with adverse impact on people—and should improve its ability to do so with dispatch. The weaknesses of Congress as a highly fragmented institution are self-evident. I am suggesting that Congress could gain strength by making use of its essential nature rather than by running away from it.

Bibliography

Argyris, Chris. 1952. *The Impact of Budgets on People*. New York: Controllership Foundation, Inc.

Axelson, Charles F. 1963. "What Makes Budgeting So Obnoxious?" *Business Budgeting*, XI, pp. 22-27.

Bebling, Arnold A. 1961. "A Look at Budgets and People," *Business Budgeting*, X, pp. 16 ff.

Berliner, Joseph S. 1957. *Factory and Manager in the USSR*. Cambridge: Harvard University Press.

Blough, Roy. 1953. "The Role of the Economist in Federal Policy-Making," *University of Illinois Bulletin, 51*.

Braybrooke, David, and Charles Lindblom. 1963. *A Strategy of Decision*. New York: Free Press of Glencoe.

Buck, Arthur E. 1929. *Public Budgeting*. New York: Harper and Brothers.

Burkhead, Jesse. 1956. *Government Budgeting*. New York: John Wiley and Sons, Inc.

Cyert, Richard and James March (eds.). 1963. *A Behavioral Theory of the Firm*. Englewood Cliffs, N.J.: Prentice-Hall.

Davis, Otto, and Aaron Wildavsky, 1965. "An Empirical Theory of Congressional Appropriations." (mimeo)

Fenno, Richard F., Jr. 1962. "The House Appropriations Committee as a Political System: The Problem of Integration." *American Political Science Review*, LVI, pp. 310-24.

—————. 1964. Review of Joseph P. Harris, "Congressional Control of Administration," in *American Political Science Review*, LVIII:3, pp. 673-75.

Hines, J. S. (Research Officer), R. W. Edwards (Chairman). 1959. *Budgeting in Public Authorities*. New York: A Study Group of the Royal Institute of Public Administration.

Hood, Ronald C. 1954. "Reorganizing the Council of Economic Advisors," *Political Science Quarterly*, 69, pp. 413-37.

(Hoover) Commission on the Organization of the Executive Branch of the Government. 1949. *Budget and Accounting*. Washington, D.C.

Huitt, Ralph K. 1963. "Congressional Organization and Operations in the Field of Money and Credit," in William Fellner, *et al.*, *Fiscal and Debt Management Policies: A Series of Research Studies prepared for the Commission on Money and Credit*. Englewood Cliffs, N.J.: Prentice-Hall, pp. 399-495.

Jasinsky, Frank. 1952. "Use and Misuse of Efficiency Controls," *Harvard Business Review*, XXXIX, pp. 105-12.

Kolodziej, Edward A. 1963. "Congressional Responsibility for the Common Defense: The Money Problem," *The Western Political Quarterly*, XVI, pp. 149-60.

Leiserson, Avery. 1948. "Coordination of the Federal Budgetary and Appropriations Procedures Under the Legislative Reorganization Act of 1946," *National Tax Journal*, I, pp. 118-26.

Lewis, Wilfred, Jr. 1962. *Federal Fiscal Policy in the Postwar Recessions*. Washington, D.C.: The Brookings Institution.

Lindblom, Charles. 1961. *Decision-Making In Taxation and Expenditures, Public Finances, Needs, Sources and Utilization*. Princeton: National Bureau of Economic Research, pp. 295-336.

————. 1959. "The Science of 'Muddling Through'," *Public Administration Review*, XIX, pp. 79-88.

Marx, Fritz Morstein. 1945. "The Bureau of the Budget: Its Evolution and Present Role, II," *The American Political Science Review*, XXXIX, pp. 869-98.

McKeon, Richard (ed.). 1941. *Basic Works of Aristotle*. New York: Random House.

Munger, Frank, and Richard F. Fenno, Jr. 1962. *National Politics and Federal Aid to Education*. Syracuse, New York: Syracuse University Press.

Nelson, Dalmas H. 1953. "The Omnibus Appropriations Act of 1950," *Journal of Politics*, 15, pp. 274-88.

Neustadt, Richard. 1954. "Presidency and Legislation: The Growth of Central Clearance," *The American Political Science Review*, XLVIII, pp. 641-71.

Nourse, Edwin G. 1953. *Economics in the Public Service: Administrative Aspects of the Employment Act*. New York: Harcourt Brace.

Phillips, John. 1951. "The Hadacol of the Budget Makers," *National Tax Journal*, IV, pp. 255-68.

Saloma, John S. 1965. "The Responsible Use of Power," in Saloma and Murray L. Weidenbaum, *Congress and the Federal Budget*. Washington, D.C.: The American Enterprise Institute for Public Policy Research, pp. 103-205.

Seligman, Lester. 1956. "Presidential Leadership: The Inner Circle and Institutionalization," *Journal of Politics*, XVIII, pp. 410-26.

Simon, Herbert A. 1957. *Administrative Behavior*, 2nd edition. New York: Macmillan.

Smithies, Arthur. 1955. *The Budgetary Process in the United States*. New York: McGraw-Hill.

Sord, Bernard H., and Glenn A. Welsch. 1958. *Business Budgeting: A Survey of Management Planning and Control Practices*. New York: Controllership Foundation, Inc.

Stedry, Andrew C. 1960. *Budget Control and Cost Behavior*. Englewood Cliffs, N.J.: Prentice-Hall.

Sundelson, J. Wilner. 1938. *Budgetary Methods in National and State Governments*. Albany, New York: J. B. Lyon Co.

Waldo, Dwight. 1948. *The Administrative State*. New York: The Ronald Press.

Wallace, Robert Ash. 1959. "Congressional Control of the Budget, *Midwest Journal of Political Science*, III, pp. 151-67.

Wernham, A. G. 1958. *Benedict de Spinoza, The Political Works*. Oxford: The Clarendon Press.

Wildavsky, Aaron. 1964. *Politics of the Budgetary Process*. Boston: Little Brown and Company.

————. 1965. "Private Markets and Public Arenas," to be published in *The American Behavioral Scientist*.

Willoughby, William Franklin. 1927. *The National Budget System*. Baltimore: Johns Hopkins Press.

Wolfinger, Raymond E., and Joan Heifetz. 1965. "Safe Seats, Seniority and Power in Congress," *American Political Science Review*, LIX, pp. 337-49.

CHARLES R. DECHERT was born in Philadelphia, Pa., in 1927 and received his Ph.D. in Political Philosophy from the Catholic University of America in 1952. While in the Air Force he worked with the Human Resources Research Center at San Antonio, Texas, and later as a Psychological Warfare Officer in Washington, D. C. He left a position as analyst in the Office of the Secretary of Defense in 1956 to undertake European Area Studies and research at the Bologna Center of the Johns Hopkins University. The following year he was named Visiting Professor of Comparative Economic and Social Policy at the International University of Social Studies "Pro Deo" in Rome, Italy. Since 1959 he has been teaching at Purdue University, Lafayette, Ind., where he holds the title of Professor of Political Science. He has served as a consultant to the Joint Economic Committee, the Institute for Defense Analyses, the Italian Ministry of Justice, and a number of private organizations.

Professor Dechert has written numerous articles for both European and American professional journals. His study *Ente Nazionale Idrocarburi: Profile of a State Corporation* appeared in 1963. A volume on the social impact of cybernetics will be published in the fall of 1966 by the University of Notre Dame Press. He is currently in Italy preparing a study of Christian Democracy as an international movement.

Availability of Information for Congressional Operations

Charles R. Dechert

Introduction

IN recent years political scientists have devoted increasing attention to the role of communications in the overall political system and in the process of government itself. Indeed, the richness and sensitivity of institutional devices for the communication of the needs and wants of its citizens may be the most significant indicator of the maturity of a political system.[1] In this respect representative institutions, as they have developed in the United States, are peculiarly well adapted to the reception and conciliation of a vast range of widely disparate needs. This paper will be devoted primarily to the information requirements of the Congress in performing its basic formal functions of legislation, authorization and appropriation, and control of the implementation of the laws (oversight).

---

[1] For a general discussion of the role of communications in politics, see Gabriel Almond and James Coleman, *Politics of the Developing Areas* (Princeton: Princeton University Press, 1960); Gabriel Almond and Sidney Verba, *The Civic Culture* (Princeton: Princeton University Press, 1963); Karl Deutsch, *The Nerves of Government* (London: The Free Press of Glencoe, 1963). With regard to communications and decision processes in the U. S. Congress, see W. J. Keefe and M. S. Ogul, *The American Legislative Process: Congress and the States* (Englewood Cliffs, N. J.: Prentice-Hall, 1965); James A. Robinson, *Congress and Foreign Policy Making* (Homewood, Ill.: Dorsey, 1962); John Wahlke, Heinz Eulau, James Buchanan, Leroy Ferguson, *The Legislative System* (New York: Wiley, 1962); Richard F. Fenno, Jr., "The House Appropriations Committee as a Political System," *American Political Science Review*, June 1962, pp. 310-24; Bruce M. Russet, "International Communications and Legislative Behavior: The Senate and the House of Commons," *Journal of Conflict Resolution*, December 1962, pp. 291-307. For a basic discussion of political leadership as centrality in a communications network, see David B. Truman, *The Congressional Party* (New York: Wiley, 1959), pp. 293-94.

Clearly these functions do not encompass the whole of Congress' activity and role in the American political system. Congressmen provide a major channel for individuals' and groups' demands on the government and for the rectification of administrative abuses on a case-by-case basis. Congress can "make news," define issues, and alert public opinion to problem areas and policy alternatives in the conduct of public affairs.

The effective performance of both the formal and informal functions of the Congress requires the free flow of information both to and from the public as a whole, corporate and associational groups, the press and other media, the departments and agencies of government, and the President. The effectiveness of Congress as the principal instrument of government representing the multiplicity of geographic, functional, economic, religious, ethnic, cultural, and other interests of the pluralistic American commonwealth is dependent on the retention and reinforcement of its constitutional powers as the legislative branch of government. Perhaps the most significant institutional alternative to Congress' continuing dynamic role in American society lies in the rise of the administrative state in which increased public order and personal security may be bought at some cost in liberty, spontaneity, and openness.

From this point of view, the Congress as a corporate body within the governmental structure is essentially an information processing and decision system, characterized by an extremely complex internal network of channels and filters, with some flux in membership and communications nodes. It is responsible for satisfying a vast number and variety of demands by creating, funding, and monitoring a more or less integrated system of governmental institutions and relations. Since the output of authoritative decisions by the Congress is largely dependent on its information inputs (intelligence), the principal objective of this paper will be to examine some of the constraints on congressional function deriving from its main sources of information (especially in the executive branch) and to suggest institutional devices that Congress might employ to improve the intelligence function.

Congress' Information
Requirements and Sources

THE Congress is essentially a political arena. Hence its information requirements cannot be analyzed solely in terms of the factual inputs needed to define an issue, generate alternative solutions, select the "best" solution to meet some simple objective criteria such as cost or profit, and then control implementation in terms of "economy and efficiency."

The role of the legislature in democratic societies is to form a relational pattern whereby the individuals and corporate elements of the nation are fitted together in a meaningful and reasonably satisfying manner for the achievement of the citizens' personal and community goals and of the national goals. This values mix has traditionally been termed "the common welfare" and implies the institutional arrangement that most nearly satisfies and harmonizes the legitimate aspirations of every individual, group, and interest of the commonwealth. Sophisticated and effective representative bodies like the United States Congress have developed customs, procedures, and practices designed to compromise and adjust conflicting interests in a civilized manner that normally precludes the use of political advantage to destroy or alienate weaker interests or groups in the national society.

The information needed by Congress to fulfill these purposes is factual, analytic, and attitudinal. Information is required on individuals and groups, and on their interrelations, and it is required from both public and private sources. Further, because of the extremely complex, largely informal, yet very sophisticated division of role and

169

function between and within the houses of Congress, their respective committees and subcommittees, and their members, each congressman has varying information requirements beyond the common minimum needed to participate in corporate decisions. His individual information needs vary according to his particular constituencies, his interests, his committee assignment(s), and his own personal expertise.

Legislation defines and sanctions relationships within a society. It may originate as an external demand on the legislature either from the public or from other branches of government, or it can be self-initiated by the Congress on the basis of its members' perception of need. However, there is a growing consensus among congressional scholars that Congress' role in legislation is becoming less and less significant in the face of the President's legislative program.[2]

In theory, the Congress can perceive actual or prospective environmental situations requiring effective governmental response, and act to meet these demands prior to the articulation of institutional solutions by persons or groups external to itself. But in practice, even when members of Congress generate an initiative, the proposal often requires a lengthy period for public discussion and rallying support, and may not be acted upon until returned to the Congress as part of the President's program. The evolution of the Peace Corps illustrates the trend. Representative Reuss suggested the Peace Corps concept in 1959. After limited exploration by the Congress, the idea was espoused by an *ad hoc* bipartisan private group which suggested it to personal aides of both presidential candidates in 1960. Theodore Sorenson picked it up as a potential "kicker" in the Kennedy campaign. The Peace Corps became symbolic of the "youth and idealism" of the "new frontier." The program was initiated as an agency within the Department of State on March 3, 1961, on the basis of Executive Order 10924 of March 1, 1961. Congress officially "created" the agency with the Peace Corps Act of September 22, 1961. Similarly, the Trade Expansion Act of 1962 originated in the Herter-Clayton Report which was sponsored by

---

[2] David B. Truman (ed.), *The Congress and America's Future* (Englewood Cliffs, N. J.: Prentice-Hall, 1965), esp. the articles by S. P. Huntington and R. E. Neustadt; Raymond H. Dawson, "Congressional Innovation and Intervention in Defense Policy: Legislative Authorization of Weapons Systems," *American Political Science Review,* March 1962, pp. 42-57; Neil MacNeil, *Forge of Democracy: The House of Representatives* (New York: David McKay, 1963), see esp. pp. 235-36 on the breakdown of legislative initiative.

the Joint Economic Committee and prepared at the Washington Center for Foreign Policy Research. The report was published by the committee on November 1, 1961. In a public address on the day of publication, George Ball as Undersecretary of State made the Herter-Clayton proposals part of the executive program.

Legislation in the United States is becoming increasingly programmatic. Rather than legislation being proposed and passed on a piecemeal basis to handle specific and limited relationships, or to relieve concrete shortcomings and inequities within the society, individual items of legislation are represented as part of an overall pattern. Implicit in these programs are the faint beginnings of a "systems approach" to legislation.

A truly coherent legislative "program" would, of course, necessitate an organic interrelation of elements. But this has rarely been the case up to now and perhaps should not be. Once it is effectively operating, the machinery of government perhaps may better develop and change by small increments that are fitted over time into the overall relational web by a process of continuing interpretation of legislative intent and by developing patterns of usage that soften potential contradictions and adjust conflicts of corporate interest.

Nonetheless it is entirely feasible today to generate systemic bodies of legislation that will interrelate large numbers of elements in very complex patterns for the achievement of given goals or sets of goals. Certainly a decision to "abolish poverty" or "develop Appalachia," if defined in operational terms, could be made the subject of a complex yet coherent set of legislative provisions. Certain omnibus bills have taken on this programmatic character; for example, the National Defense Act of 1947, although even here the details were largely left to the informal give and take of administrative politics.

Congress is also concerned with the control of the implementation of the laws it has made, very frequently in the detail of specific application, but equally in the general consonance of executive action with legislative intent, and the adequacy of the agencies and the institutional norms established by law to achieve the social effects desired.[3] In addition, Congress is interested in "economy and effi-

---

[3] See Joseph P. Harris, *Congressional Control of Administration* (Washington: The Brookings Institution, 1964); Seymour Scher, "Conditions for Legislative Control," *Journal of Politics,* August 1963, pp. 526-51; "Congressional Committee Members as Independent Agency Overseers: A Case Study," *American Political Science Review,* December 1960, pp. 911-20.

ciency" in seeing that the resources employed to achieve a given end are in reasonable proportion to the end itself.

Investigations pursuant to the oversight function have been fruitful in focusing attention on the recurrent constitutional question of congressional access to information possessed by the executive agencies. Clearly adequate congressional oversight may require knowledge of rather sensitive types of information. For example, informed decisions relevant to the continuance of an advanced weapons system might require access to classified Defense Department data on performance, to CIA-generated information on Soviet capabilities and vulnerabilities, and to memoranda detailing intra-departmental disputes regarding alternative systems. Any meaningful congressional investigation of possible subversive activities in executive agencies would have to rely on sophisticated counter-espionage techniques. This would require relatively free access to FBI, CIC, ONI, OSI, and CIA files as a minimum. It should also perhaps include free access to the investigated agency's own personnel files to find who recommended whom to whom, supervisor effectiveness reports, changes in functional jurisdictions, etc. Some or all of the data needed in each instance would almost certainly be refused to a congressional investigating committee. Hence the fundamental question is this: What, if any are the limits on the Congress' oversight function? Where does it impinge on executive prerogatives?

Committees having a specialized investigative character, but which possess no routine channels (formal or informal) of access to the information they require, may have the greatest difficulty in gaining the data they need. In some cases, the investigation is foredoomed to frustration by its very nature, or by Congress' lack of analytic facilities to handle such data. The investigations conducted by Senator Joseph McCarthy, regardless of the personality and mode of address of the chairman, were essentially small-scale counter-intelligence operations utterly beyond Congress' capability, and fore-doomed to ridicule and failure under the existing rules of the game.

The argument might well be made that the Congress is already swamped by information, that its input channels and information handling machinery are simply not equipped to handle the mass of available data in a practical manner for decision making. The problem of congressional access to information might be better defined as a problem of information management. What specific elements of information are needed to make what judgments? Where are these elements located? How are they to be retrieved?

And how should they be presented in order to be meaningful?

Generally speaking, the newer and more technical a government program, the more difficult it is for the relevant committee of the Congress to determine precisely what information is needed for the fulfillment of its function. Over time, these requirements will tend to become routinized as the focus of the chairman's and members' interests become clear, and as the agency involved experiments with various presentation formats. On its side, an agency will continue to use the type of information and emphasis that proves acceptable to the committee(s), modifying the content and/or emphasis of unfavorably received reports, and increasingly relying for presentation of testimony on officials whose manner proves pleasing. An interesting series of studies on the stabilization of information expectations could be made by analyzing in terms of theme, emphasis, and personality the testimony of a new agency over a period of five or ten years. *A priori,* it might be hypothesized that successive years would demonstrate a decreasing variation in content, with occasional perturbations reflecting major changes either in the committee or agency leadership.

Much of the factual and attitudinal information available to congressional committees, members of Congress, and their staffs is derived from personal friends and acquaintances, from newspapers and magazines, from books and scholarly studies. A considerable part comes from "interested" sources such as trade associations, corporations, or other groups. Some is provided by the studies and analyses of more or less disinterested research groups such as The Brookings Institution, The Committee for Economic Development, the National Planning Association, the American Enterprise Institute for Public Policy Research, The Center for the Study of Democratic Institutions, and so forth. The Congress may call upon academicians for testimony, counsel, or contract research. Published public opinion surveys such as the Gallup Poll or Harris Survey are widely studied on the Hill; and individual members, personally or through their parties, may employ pollsters for detailed studies on special issues or of particular constituencies.[4]

The Congress' principal intelligence research facility is the Legislative Reference Service (LRS) of the Library of Congress. Congressional opinion is widely divergent on the utility of both the Service and the Library itself. One senator complained of the Library

---

[4] See Lewis A. Dexter, "What Do Congressmen Hear?" in N. W. Polsby, et al. (eds.), *Politics and Social Life* (Boston: Houghton Mifflin, 1963).

that the books he wants are never available, so he buys them at one of the better bookstores. Perhaps the Capitol should have a bookstore and members of Congress a book and periodical allowance. Of the Legislative Reference Service, it is sometimes said that it provided excellent service 15 years ago, when senior researchers would do depth studies tailored to the needs of individual members of Congress. In recent years, however, the LRS has been flooded by demands from members of Congress that it respond to constituent requests for information. A more serious burden lies in a growing demand by congressmen for depth studies which the LRS has not the capability to satisfy. A request for the half-remembered refrain of a seventeenth century ballad to be used in a speech can be met quickly and well. A request for a comparative study and evaluation of the administrative organization of the public health services in Britain, Sweden, Germany, and the U.S.S.R. might present a serious problem.[5] Yet requests of this latter type may be made by any one of 535 members of Congress and their staffs, and by the committees and subcommittees of both houses. These requests are to be answered by one of 33 specialists in a service having other functions and operating on an annual budget of $2,524,000 (1966 estimate) within a national library having a budget of $26,652,000 (1966 estimate).

The need for Congress to equip itself with an adequate intelligence system was recognized to some degree in the Legislative Reorganization Act of 1946. Prior to that Act, only the two appropriations committees and the Joint Committee on Internal Revenue Taxation had consistently employed well-trained, technically qualified staffs with continuity of tenure. Yet the staffs authorized in 1946 are small, subject to continuous work pressures, and frequently used for functions other than the collection and analysis of information.[6] Any substantial enlargement of the committee staffs carries with it a danger of bureaucratization and rigidity. But at the same time, these staffs, together with the administrative assistants of members, because of their closeness to Congress' problems and operations provide an excellent channel for information inputs and a knowledgeable source of congressional intelligence requirements.

---

[5] See U. S., Congress, *Hearings before the Joint Committee on the Organization of the Congress,* 89th Congress, 1st Session, testimony of Dr. Hugh Elsbree, Director, Legislative Reference Service, August 2, 1965; U.S., Congress, *Interim Report of the Joint Committee on the Organization of the Congress,* Senate Report No. 426, July 8, 1965, p. 15.

[6] Kenneth Kofmehl, *Professional Staffs of Congress* (West Lafayette, Ind.: Purdue University Studies, 1962), p. 4.

of such scope and variety and require such detailed technical competence that nothing short of the intellectual depth of a great university could adequately fulfill the congressional intelligence function. This is true, not only because of the need for access to precise, current, and detailed factual knowledge, but even more because of the sophisticated analytic methods and procedures that might be applied to congressional decisions and to the evaluation of executive proposals. Increasingly, the deliberations of almost every substantive committee involve, at some point, or other, questions of the impact of science and technology, or possible uses of available or prospective technologies in the resolution of a public issue.

All committees of the Congress are faced with the same problem . . . lack of continuity, technical knowledge and full understanding of the complexities, technicalities, and relationships of basic science, research and development, and applied technology, on the part of the staff and the members of the committees. Although panels of scientists and others who are qualified in the various areas of science and technology have been appointed as advisers to some of these committees, they are available to only a very limited number of Members of Congress for a limited period of time.[7]

Moreover, in terms of the relative weight and place of the different major institutions of American society, the Congress would seem to require continuing structural-functional analyses of all significant interest groups in the country, their resources, operational codes, and patterns of interaction with other groups and with the overall national political system. In view of the critical importance of attitudinal information to the Congress and to its members, it is perhaps surprising that the Congress has made no effort to provide itself with a survey research facility.

A major contribution to legislative information is supplied by the General Accounting Office (GAO) under the Comptroller General of the United States, who is directly responsible to the Congress. The GAO is the congressional watchdog on federal expenditures, confirming by independent audit that all funds are disbursed in accordance with statute, initiating actions to recover illegal or improper payments, settling accounts or claims, and making decisions that govern the details of governmental financial practices.

---

[7] U.S., Congress, Senate, Committee on Government Operations, Committee Print, *Proposed Report on Establishment of a Commission on Science and Technology,* 89th Congress, 1st Session, June 1965, pp. 5-6.

In addition to reporting to Congress on its systematic audits of executive branch operations, the GAO is required by law to undertake any particular investigation that may be requested by the Congress:

> All departments and establishments shall furnish to the Comptroller General such information regarding the powers, duties, activities, organization, financial transactions, and methods of business of their respective offices as he may from time to time require of them; and the Comptroller General, or any of his assistants or employees, when duly authorized by him, shall, for the purpose of securing information, have access to and the right to examine any books, documents, papers, or records of any such department or establishment.[8]

Traditionally the GAO has been little concerned with the overall organization and management of federal agencies. But there are indications that the GAO may now be developing a capability to study the internal operations of federal agencies in the broader terms of a "management audit" concerned with the overall adequacy and efficiency of operations in terms of the agency's statutory mission. The further development of this capability would require increased appropriations for the GAO. It should be encouraged by the Congress, and might include continuing research and development of measures of governmental effectiveness, and quantitative techniques for analyzing alternative patterns of organization and policy implementation. Such a development within the GAO would not only enhance and deepen Congress' oversight capabilities, but might well serve to suggest legislative initiatives on program authorization, expansion, or curtailment, and on agency reorganization.

The only inherent weaknesses of the GAO in this respect may lie in an organizational tradition of highly bureaucratic regulation and a bookkeeper mentality that could carry purely monetary measures of value to extremes. Also, while several congressional staff members, in conversation, have waxed enthusiastic about the accuracy and care of GAO's investigative reports to Congress, they have complained that these reports were often so out-of-date as to be ir-

---

[8] Section 313, Budget and Accounting Act. See U.S., Congress, House, Committee on Government Operations, *Submission of Agency Accounting Systems for GAO Approval,* House Report No. 179, 89th Congress, 1st Session, March 17, 1965. See also the testimony of Mr. Frank Weitzel, Acting Comptroller General of the United States before the Joint Committee on the Organization of the Congress, August 5, 1965.

relevant and had chiefly an historical value with regard to the misspent past of terminated programs.

It should also be noted that the work of the GAO and the investigations conducted by the Senate and House Government Operations Committees are largely independent of one another. The GAO's major function has been the routine and continuing financial review of federal expenditures. As a matter of practice, the GAO submits draft reports to the relevant agencies and departments for review and comment prior to preparing a final draft for the Congress. On the other hand, the government operations committees are interested primarily in the broader aspects of oversight, with an emphasis on the policy and organizational issues involved and a view to legislative action rather than financial control. The government operations committees serve as the channel through which GAO reports come to the cognizance of the Congress. On August 5, 1965, some members of the Joint Committee on the Organization of the Congress expressed the need for improved liaison between the GAO and individual members of Congress, as well as improved channels of communication between the GAO and the Congress as a whole.

In recent years the Congress has been making increasing use of the commission mechanism to provide information inputs relevant to the legislative and oversight functions. This device is particularly appropriate when the technical nature of a problem and the depth of expertise required to resolve it are beyond the normal capabilities of the members, the committees, and their staffs. In addition to conducting depth research and making legislative recommendations, a commission may also serve a political function by providing a representation of major interest groups in the problem area concerned. Thus in the very process of gathering and analyzing congressional input data, it can provide a forum for achieving a prior compromise between varying demands on the political system. The commission itself, of course, serves essentially as a policy board, supervising the research work done by a professional staff and consultants, and striving for unanimity in its report and recommendations. The functions of a commission in focusing attention on a problem area, postponing the need for congressional action, summarizing and analyzing available information, and making legislative recommendations reflecting a consensus among major interests can prove a very valuable input to the Congress.

Probably the most fruitful use of the commission device occurred in the creation of the two Commissions on the Organization of the

Executive Branch of the Government (1947-49 and 1953-55), more commonly known as The First and Second Hoover Commissions. Undoubtedly much of their effectiveness lay in the extraordinary quality, public prestige, and breadth of virtual representation found in their membership.

The task of both commissions was to investigate the executive branch and make recommendations to effectuate the congressional policies of promoting economy, efficiency, and improved public service. The commissions included representatives of the executive branch at the cabinet level and members of the President's staff, members of Congress, businessmen and financiers, representatives of the professions and the academic community. The Hoover Commissions hired staffs of about 75 persons and made extensive use of outside specialists who were formed into special task forces each having expertise in a specific field of inquiry. The first Hoover Commission submitted 19 reports, the second submitted 20 reports. The total expense of both commissions was under $5 million.

The results of the work of the two commissions were impressive.

	First Hoover Commission		Second Hoover Commission	
Total recommendations proposed	273		314	
Total recommendations adopted	196	(72%)	200½	(64%)
By administrative action		111 (41%)		146½ (47%)
By legislation		85 (31%)		54 (17%)
Total legislative enactments	77		44	

Inherent in the commissions' work was a comprehensive and integrated approach to the problems of governmental reorganization in terms of the organic interrelations involved in federal activities. The first commission ended its concluding report with an exhortation to Congress to:

> . . . give careful attention to treating the whole body of our recommendations even though the implementation may have to be done on a step-by-step basis. . . . Once the practice of exempting certain agencies and excepting particular functions has

begun, the chances of achieving substantial improvements in the efficiency of Government will speedily diminish.[9]

As part of the information input relevant to the oversight function the Congress has frequently required periodic executive reports as a legislative requirement coupled with the creation of an agency or program. The utility of these, however, has been questioned in a report of the House Committee on Government Operations:

> The contents of the annual Department and Agency reports to Congress have deteriorated to the extent that these reports are of negligible value in the assessment of the economy or efficiency of . . . operations.[10]

Representative Todd in his testimony before the Joint Committee on the Organization of the Congress (Monroney Committee) on May 24, 1965, suggested that the Legislative Reference Service should prepare abstracts of these agency reports and other relevant government publications. This would permit members of Congress to exercise greater selectivity in their choice of reading matter on subjects they will probe in depth.

Today, the mass media play a critical role in the congressional intelligence system. For most members of Congress, public media are the principal source of information on the overall national and international environments of the United States. Hence it follows that the Congress' *overall* perception is largely conditioned by these media. Only in the usually somewhat limited areas of his own functional and geographic expertise can the individual member sift the press critically. And when he does, he undoubtedly finds a systematic (though not necessarily intentional) distortion. He knows that the rest of the news he reads is probably equally distorted, but he has no systematic device for redressing the balance. Secondly, regardless of what he himself knows or believes to be true, the member of Congress is subject to the opinions of the electorate. He must act politically in terms of his image of the public's conception of reality; and in the long run, the public's overall conception of the "big picture" is itself largely the result of exposure to the mass media.

---

[9] The material on the Hoover Commissions is based on U.S., Congress, Committee on Government Operations, *Summary of the Objectives, Operations and Results of the Commissions on the Reorganization of the Executive Branch of the Government,* Committee Print, 88th Congress, 1st Session, May 1963.

[10] U.S., Congress, House, Committee on Government Operations, *Survey of Selected Activities,* Part 1, House Report No. 456, 88th Congress, 1st Session, June 25, 1963, p. 3.

The member also knows that much national and international news originates in the executive, and that certain official viewpoints will be reflected in mass media, owing to the selected channels through which such information is released. By virtue of the information it possesses, and a corresponding capacity for selection (and hence also for suppression) of what will be transmitted, the executive, and especially the President, can do much to define both the content and the relative emphasis found in the mass media. It achieves this by an expression of affective tone in news releases, in interviews, or photographs, by regulating access to persons, events, and installations, and above all by its ability to "make news" or "dominate the news."

James Reston has remarked: "But news, by its very definition, is obviously news of conflict, news of crisis, and the time when it is most necessary to report it is at the time of the crisis." [11] The consensual definition of what constitutes "news," especially by the Washington correspondents, creates both constraints and possibilities for those who control information.

Congress has become acutely aware of its own position of inferiority within the governmental system in regard to news.[12] But it has not tried to develop institutionalized sources of information, and dissemination procedures independent of the executive. Instead it has sought increased access to information in the executive both for itself and for the press and has hoped thereby to eliminate the distorting lens of selection (and repression) of data by the agencies.

Perhaps the most significant development in political communications during the postwar period has been the institutionalization of the "leak" to the press. This may be used to serve the President's purposes, or it may be employed in the interagency and interpersonal power struggle within the government itself. Douglas Cater examines this device and its functions at length in his volume *The Fourth Branch of Government*.[13] In many ways, the "leak" provides an important intelligence input to the Congress, since it can

---

[11] U.S., Congress, Committee on Government Operations, *Availability of Information from Federal Departments and Agencies* (Panel Discussion with Editors, et al.), 84th Congress, 1st Session, November 7, 1955, p. 26.

[12] See, for example, Karl E. Mundt, "Government Control of Sources of Information," in *Annals* of the American Academy of Political and Social Science, Communications and Social Action, March 1947, pp. 26-31; Elmer E. Cornwell Jr., "Presidential News: The Expanding Public Image," *Journalism Quarterly*, Summer 1959, pp. 275-83.

[13] See Douglas Cater, *The Fourth Branch of Government* (New York: Random House (Vintage), 1965), pp. 128-41.

be and often is used to represent problems and policy differences among executive agencies that are normally blurred over or ignored in formal testimony or submissions from the White House. On the other hand, the "leak" is increasingly being used as an instrument of policy by the executive. By defining an issue and sensitizing public opinion—to which congressmen are necessarily responsive—it may be employed to orient the Congress in certain directions desired by the executive. Probably the most comprehensive succinct statement of the functions of the "leak" was that prepared for the House in 1964 by the staff of the Subcommittee on Foreign Operations and Government Information of the House Committee on Government Operations.[14]

From the material culled by the staff, it appears that the "not for attribution" technique is used most often for the following purposes:

1. To transmit news to the press when formal channels of communication, such as the presidential press conference, are cut off.

2. To alert the press to the gravity of a situation being overlooked in the news.

3. To permit government officials to talk freely to newsmen. It is often used for this purpose, particularly on foreign affairs and national security matters.

4. To avert press alarm or public hysteria.

5. To test public and congressional reaction to new schemes and projected appointments.

6. To mobilize opinion behind some government project.

7. To advance one particular cause of an official or an agency in the power struggle that goes on within the government itself or among the governments doing business in Washington.

Some of the apparent advantages to public officials in the use of "nonattribution" noted were that it:

1. Gives the official a semi-anonymous voice.

2. Informs press and prevents news stories detrimental to sound policy.

3. Permits the official greater flexibility in taking policy initiative without chancing his own reputation or that of his agency, his party, and the U.S. government.

---

[14] U.S., Congress, House, Committee on Government Operations, *Government News from Anonymous Sources,* Committee Print, 88th Congress, 2d Session, April 1964, pp. 3-4. See also Richard L. Strout, "Government by Leak," *New Republic,* January 21, 1957, pp. 8-10.

4. Serves to measure public and congressional opinion during the malleable period of policy formation.

The subcommittee report also finds serious objections to the "leak":

However, on the part of the press, the Congress, and the public, there are some noteworthy objections to the "not for attribution" technique:

1. The conscientious reporter usually feels compelled to attend briefings at which a top story might be released. Opportunities to question the official and check his statements are minimized by competitive pressure—exerted by other reporters present who will rush to file their stories. He deletes dubious or misleading arguments at the risk of negating his role as a reporter. . . . Competition pressures the conscientious newsman to file all information. What he feels is questionable may be headlined in other papers.

2. The reporter doesn't know whether to believe the official who may be speaking to him as a reporter seeking to use him as an instrument of psychological warfare. . . .

3. Nonattributed stories confuse readers and, by molding public opinion, help generate pressure on Congress to adopt the official point of view.

The "leak" and other personalized sources of information are peculiarly relevant to the congressional function of oversight. As Kofmehl points out with regard to congressional requests for information: "Naturally an agency would not volunteer information on the shortcomings of its proposals. It might disregard or minimize relevant factors that seriously qualified the supporting arguments. And, of course, it would not furnish competitive witnesses from its staff. Similarly, an agency could not be expected to call attention to deficiencies in its administration. . . . Nor would it provide such data in response to ambiguous queries fishing for derogatory material." [15]

Undoubtedly communications between members of Congress and senior persons in the executive on contentious issues convey facts and arguments—the congressional briefings in the White House introduced by President Johnson exemplify this. But interpersonal communications may also convey data on capabilities of either side to reward or punish, the degree to which these capabilities will be employed on any given issue, and the limits of relative bargaining positions. Although the principal emphasis in this paper is on the

---

[15] See Kofmehl, *op. cit.*, p. 157.

factual and analytic information needed for congressional operations, inputs of political and attitudinal information from the executive agencies and the White House are critically important to the Congress' performance.

With regard to legislation, the President possesses a number of informal techniques to influence both the substantive content and eventual passage of a given bill in the executive program. Breakfast meetings with the congressional leadership have become an institution. Presidential aides and often the President himself will make personal or telephone contact with key members of the Congress on important legislation. On occasion "arm-twisting" may be employed, ranging from the obvious positive sanctions of patronage, party preferment, and campaign assistance to negative sanctions such as public obloquy by the Chief Executive from his privileged position vis-a-vis the press, or less obvious sanctions such as effective denial of needed information and support of rival candidates in primaries.

On occasion such communications may be indirect. One member of Congress became aware of White House disapproval when a major newspaper in his state attacked him in editorials that personal inquiry revealed to have been inspired "downtown." It is not inconceivable that political pressure may increasingly be exercised in terms of personality vulnerabilities. Indirect pressure may be conveyed by influential persons (including other members of Congress) known to be close to the administration, or through mass media, or through an "atmosphere" created by a wide variety of informal channels that leaves little doubt in the minds of the politically sensitive about executive wishes or the sanction level that will be employed on a particular issue.[16]

The most effective executive-legislative relationship, of course, is one of mutual confidence and trust in which overt or covert pressure and the resulting tensions and anxieties are at a minimum.[17] In such propitious circumstances, the executive program can be developed in close informal contact with the congressional leadership. Areas of potential conflict are adjusted in an atmosphere of compromise; the legislative outcome is left largely to the internal working of the Congress, with only enough pressure exerted by the executive (often at the suggestion of party leaders in the Congress) to assure

[16] See Lawrence Chamberlain, *The President, Congress, and Legislation* (New York: Columbia University Press, 1946).

[17] See Wilfred E. Binkley, *President and Congress* (3d ed.; New York: Random House (Vintage), 1962), pp. 378-83.

passage of the executive program and avoid emasculation of key measures. Executive proposals are ranked by criteria of urgency and importance, and this information is conveyed informally.[18]

---

[18] For a more detailed survey of many of these channels, see Kofmehl, *op. cit.*, pp. 110-63.

Denial of Access to Information in the Executive

CONGRESSIONAL access to information in the executive and public access to such information present two distinct problems. Mixing them can only create confusion. In the performance of its functions, Congress may legitimately require highly detailed information, that if released to the public (this includes foreign governments) could dangerously weaken the United States, create unnecessary public alarm or misapprehensions, or endanger the good will and international prestige of the United States. On the other hand, some public access to governmental information is required to satisfy the requirements for meaningful popular participation in the governmental process.[19] In the letter of June 9, 1955 authorizing the creation of the Special Subcommittee on Governmental Information (the Moss Subcommittee), William L. Dawson, chairman of the House Committee on Government Operations stated: "An informed public makes the difference between mob rule and democratic government. If the pertinent and necessary information on governmental activities is denied the public, the result is a weakening of the democratic process and the ultimate atrophy of our form of government."

The Moss Subcommittee's hearings and reports have largely been concerned with case by case studies of alleged abuses in executive

---

[19] See U.S., Congress, House, Committee on Government Operations, *Federal Statutes on the Availability of Information,* Committee Print, 86th Congress, 2d Session, March 1960.

withholding of information from the press and Congress.[20] It has been less concerned with the more general problem of providing adequate intelligence to the Congress as a whole. Nonetheless its hearings, questionnaire surveys, and reports, by pinpointing major problem areas and by providing factual data on information policies and activities of executive agencies, are extremely important sources to any student of the overall issue of congressional intelligence.

An analysis of federal information cases during the period 1955-60 made by the Moss Subcommittee indicates the principal interests concerned with current information policies of the executive.[21]

	Cases
Source of Complaint:	
Press	65
Committee of Congress	61
Member of Congress	15
Private individual	13
Federal official	9
Private organization	7
State agency	4
Authority Claimed for Restriction:	
Executive privilege	44
Executive Order 10501	27
5 U.S.C. 22 ("Housekeeping" status)	11
5 U.S.C. 1002 ("Public Information" section of Administrative Procedure Act)	10
18 U.S.C. 1905 ("Trade Secrets" criminal penalty law)	10
Various statutory authorities	32
Various "other" authorities	13
Disposition of Case:	
Restriction removed	95
Restriction continued	68
Removed with limitation	8
Continued with limitation	2

---

[20] See U.S., Congress, House, Committee on Government Operations, *Availability of Information from Federal Departments and Agencies, Index and Bibliography,* Committee Print, 88th Congress, 2d Session, January 1964.

[21] U.S., Congress, House, Committee on Government Operations, *Availability of Information from Federal Departments and Agencies,* House Report No. 2084, 86th Congress, 2d Session, July 2, 1960, p. 36.

Of the 15 cases involving complaints by individual members of Congress, in only four was the restriction continued. Of the 61 cases involving complaints by a committee of Congress, the restriction was continued in 42 cases; of these, 27 involved the Defense Department and in most instances executive privilege was invoked.

Let us consider first the question of access by the public to agency information.

Two laws have provided the principal justification for agency refusal of public access to information: (1) 5 U.S.C. 22 (the "Housekeeping" Statute), (2) Section 3; 5 U.S.C. 1002 (Public Information Section, Administrative Procedures Act). When Congress amended the "Housekeeping" Statute in 1958 to prohibit withholding information, agency claims of authority shifted to the Administrative Procedures Act.[22]

Congressional concern over the executive's practice of withholding information resulted in a proposal in the Senate (S. 1666) to amend section 3 of the Administrative Procedure Act of 1946. It was introduced by Senator Edward V. Long with 21 co-sponsors. Senator Long summarized the contents of the proposal as follows:

. . . the bill which we are introducing today would—

First. Require each agency to publish in the Federal Register (a) descriptions of its organization and places where the public may obtain information, (b) statements of the general course and procedure by which its functions are performed, and (c) substantive rules and statements of general policy.

Second. Make available for inspection and copying all final agency opinions, statements of policy and interpretation for the guidance of the public.

Third. Require an index be kept of opinions, rules, and orders; and deny agencies the right to use an order, opinion, or rule as a precedent unless it has been made available to the party in issue.

Fourth. Require agencies to specify times, places, and procedures for the inspection of their records.

Fifth. Require agencies to make public the individual votes of each member.

The bill provides for these main exceptions: First, where

---

[22] See U.S., Congress, House, *Hearings before a Subcommittee of the Committee on Government Operations, Federal Public Records Law* (Part 2, Appendix and Index), 89th Congress, 1st Session, March 30-31, April 1, 2, 5, 1965. Pages 292-352 provide a tabular analysis of operations under 5 U.S.C. 1002.

there is a statute providing for exemption; second, where a matter relates solely to the internal workings of an agency; and third, where secrecy is vital to the national defense.[23]

Application of the legislation was to rest in the hands of the appropriate district court of the United States which would be empowered to order the production of information deemed improperly withheld and assess the agency the fees of the complainant. The burden of proof in cases of withholding information was to rest with the agency.

On the basis of Senate hearings held on October 28, 29, 30, 31, 1963 and of agency representations, a number of changes were made in the bill by the Committee on the Judiciary.[24] Among the most pertinent criticisms of the bill in its original form was the Civil Aviation Board's comments on the extremely complex indexing and retrieval problems it would involve. A number of agencies desired to continue to restrict data on the negotiation and administration of contracts, personnel matters, internal memoranda, and "company confidential" information obtained from private businesses. The need to protect sources of confidential information was also a major concern. Agriculture and Commerce foresaw opportunities for commodity market speculators, real estate operators, and others to gain economic advantages. General Services Administration was concerned about the use of such data as appraisals. NASA worried about being required to release advance plans to procure, lease, and dispose of materials and real estate.

The State Department objected to the possibility of having to reveal negative aspects of U.S. policy, or indications of differences with allies. It also expressed grave concern at placing ultimate authority in these matters in the hands of the courts, maintaining that the department "is in a better position to determine disclosure than a court." The law presumably would have given the courts access to disputed data and would have permitted the courts indirectly (that is, by requiring the release of information potentially harmful to U.S. interests) to insert itself into the conduct of foreign affairs.

Agencies concerned with financial matters were profoundly disturbed by the potential invasion of privacy, both personal and

---

[23] *Congressional Record,* June 4, 1963.

[24] U.S., Congress, Senate, *Hearings before the Subcommittee on Administrative Practice and Procedure of the Committee on the Judiciary on S. 1666 and S. 1663,* 88th Congress, 1st Session, October 28, 29, 30, and 31, 1963.

corporate. They expressed fears about access to bank records, technical security procedures, private access to customs entries and invoices filed by competitors, publication of the names of holders of government securities in large amounts, disclosure of the nature of Treasury intervention in exchange markets, and access to records of bank examinations.

Treasury also brought up the constitutional question: The Long amendment "is unconstitutional to the extent that it purports to require disclosure to the public of information in the executive branch which the President determines should not be disclosed in the public interest." Treasury objected not to congressional information requests but to the attempt at formalizing the *right* of the public to have access to information in the executive.

It should be noted, however, that it is not necessary to consider problems of "executive privilege" as it relates to the relationships between the executive branch and the Congress. President Kennedy has made clear that this privilege will not be invoked except upon his own personal decision and only in a case of the utmost gravity, where failure to do so would be inconsistent with his constitutional responsibility to the United States.

The problem of executive privilege, as such, is evidently not involved because the issue presented by S. 1666 does not purport to deal with the President's power to withhold from Congress information on good and proper grounds. Rather, S. 1666 presents the issue of whether a private citizen, as distinguished from Congress, may, on the basis of a statute, demand and be entitled to receive information in the hands of the executive branch regardless of the damage which disclosure of such information will do to the United States generally or to private interests of particular citizens; and this, regardless of any legitimate need by the inquirer for the information which he asks.[25]

Certainly on the basis of the limited number of executive agency refusals of information in the period 1955-60, and the proven responsiveness of the executive when pressure was applied, legislation of this breadth hardly seemed required. The incidents recorded did not seem to justify an institutionalized *general public right* of the magnitude proposed—especially since, as the Moss Subcommittee findings showed, it was the Congress and the press rather

---

[25] *Ibid.*, p. 284.

than the public at large that were most often sinned against.[26] Finally, the threat of overload on the executive information-handling capability in the face of already numerous public requests for information should not be overlooked. On the basis of a questionnaire sent to the executive departments and agencies by the Moss Subcommittee, it would appear that information requests to each of the departments from the public average about 50,000 to 75,000 annually, with peak totals of 235,245 at Interior, 350,000 at State, and 2,210,761 at Agriculture. Congressional requests, including referrals, are in the order of 25,000 to 50,000 annually for each department.[27]

One of the more interesting aspects of the Senate bill lay in its provisions requiring agencies to report their internal organization, procedures, policies, and rules in the *Federal Register*. This, in effect, was a demand that the agencies define their "constitutions" and codify their quasi-legislative and quasi-judicial decisions. As such it seems to fit into the general trend recognizing the corporate identity and to some degree the effective autonomy of large social aggregates. Although provisions in this bill on the public's *right* to information may have been somewhat disputable, the "constitutionalization" of federal agencies might well have proved a long step toward social realism in the law.

Bill S. 1666 was passed in the Senate in July 1964 but was not acted on in the House. In February 1965, a public records law to amend 5 U.S.C. 22 was introduced in both houses of the Congress. Both the Senate and the House version (H.R. 5012) contain a court-enforceable requirement that every agency shall "make all its records promptly available to any person." However, certain important exceptions are allowed. The exceptions were originally developed as a result of the Senate's hearings of October 1963 in connection with S. 1666 and were incorporated in the final version of that proposal when it was passed in the Senate in 1964. They include those records which are:

(1) specifically required by Executive order to be kept secret

---

[26] "The reporter is outraged if he experiences difficulty in seeing cabinet members or other political appointees. Even the career civil servant at the upper levels learns to be accessible to the press. . . . his career may well depend on his ability to feed information to reporters during critical policy struggles." Cater, *op. cit.*, p. 6.

[27] I am grateful to the staff of the Foreign Operations and Government Information Subcommittee of the House Committee on Government Operations for access to the raw data produced by this questionnaire.

in the interest of the national defense or foreign policy; (2) related solely to the internal personnel rules and practices of any agency; (3) specifically exempted from disclosure by statute; (4) trade secrets and commercial or financial information obtained from the public and privileged or confidential; (5) interagency or intra-agency memoranda or letters dealing solely with matters of law or policy; (6) personnel and medical files and similar matters the disclosure of which would constitute a clearly unwarranted invasion of personal privacy; (7) investigatory files compiled for law enforcement purposes except to the extent available by law to a private party; and (8) contained in or related to examination, operating, or condition reports prepared by, on behalf of, or for the use of any agency responsible for the regulation or supervision of financial institutions.[28]

Given these exceptions, it is difficult to conceive of any substantive change in executive branch information policies.

Now let us turn to the question of congressional access to executive information. Insofar as the congressional function has gradually diminished in the area of legislative initiative and grown in the area of oversight, extensive information on the details of agency personnel, policies, and activities has become an increasingly important information input to the Congress. This in turn often requires the use of "fishing expeditions" to determine the existence and locus of substantive information relevant to congressional oversight. In May 1954, the Senate Committee on Government Operations asked for information on the discussions during which certain administrative decisions were arrived at. President Eisenhower directed the Secretary of Defense to refuse the information in a letter which was construed by many executive agencies as justifying almost any refusal of information to the Congress.

THE WHITE HOUSE
May 17, 1954

The Honorable the SECRETARY OF DEFENSE

Washington, D. C.

DEAR MR. SECRETARY:

It has long been recognized that to assist the Congress in

---

[28] U.S., Congress, House, *Hearings before a Subcommittee of the Committee on Government Operations, Federal Public Records Law*, Part I, 89th Congress, 1st Session, March 30, 31, April 1, 2, and 5, 1965. Pages 265-76 provide a summary analysis of agency comments on S. 1666.

achieving its legislative purposes every Executive Department or Agency must, upon the request of a Congressional Committee, expeditiously furnish information relating to any matter within the jurisdiction of the Committee, with certain historical exceptions— some of which are pointed out in the attached memorandum from the Attorney General. This Administration has been and will continue to be diligent in following this principle. However, it is essential to the successful working of our system that the persons entrusted with power in any one of the three branches of Government shall not encroach upon the authority confided to the others. The ultimate responsibility for the conduct of the Executive Branch rests with the President.

Within this Constitutional framework each branch should cooperate with each other for the common good. However, throughout our history the President has withheld information whenever he found that what was sought was confidential or its disclosure would be incompatible with the public interest or jeopardize the safety of the Nation.

Because it is essential to efficient and effective administration that employees of the Executive Branch be in a position to be completely candid in advising with each other on official matters, and because it is not in the public interest that any of their conversations or communications, or any documents or reproductions, concerning such advice be disclosed, you will instruct employees of your Department that in all of their appearances before the Subcommittee of the Senate Committee on Government Operations regarding the inquiry now before it they are not to testify to any such conversations or communications or to produce any such documents or reproductions. This principle must be maintained regardless of who would be benefited by such disclosures.

I direct this action so as to maintain the proper separation of powers between the Executive and Legislative Branches of the Government in accordance with my responsibilities and duties under the Constitution. This separation is vital to preclude the exercise of arbitrary power by any branch of the Government.

By this action I am not in any way restricting the testimony of such witnesses as to what occurred regarding any matters where the communication was directly between any of the principles in the controversy within the Executive Branch on the one hand and a member of the Subcommittee or its staff on the other.

Sincerely,
DWIGHT D. EISENHOWER

It is perhaps significant that both President Kennedy and President Johnson have since repudiated the accepted implications of the Eisenhower position, and restricted decisions on executive privilege to their own person. In March 1962, John F. Kennedy wrote to Representative John E. Moss in his capacity as chairman of the House Subcommittee on Government Information:

> As you know, this Administration has gone to great lengths to achieve full cooperation with the Congress in making available to it all appropriate documents, correspondence and information. That is the basic policy of this Administration, and it will continue to be so. Executive privilege can be invoked only by the President and will not be used without specific Presidential approval. Your own interest in assuring the widest public accessibility to governmental information is, of course, well known, and I can assure you this Administration will continue to cooperate with your subcommittee and the entire Congress in achieving this objective.[29]

President Lyndon B. Johnson has given Representative Moss a similar assurance:

> Since assuming the Presidency, I have followed the policy laid down by President Kennedy in his letter to you of March 7, 1962, dealing with this subject. Thus, the claim of "executive privilege" will continue to be made only by the President.
>
> This administration has attempted to cooperate completely with the Congress in making available to it all information possible, and that will continue to be our policy.[30]

In terms of congressional access to information in the executive branch, the most significant barriers are: (1) security classification; (2) appeals to "executive privilege"; (3) use of complex "clearance" [31] procedures, whereby the executive branch agrees to provide requested documents to a congressional committee; (4) what a Moss Subcommittee report calls "simple chaos in filing systems," coupled with an institutional aversion by most agencies to congressional demands for information.[32]

---

[29] Letter of John F. Kennedy to John E. Moss, March 7, 1962.

[30] Letter of Lyndon B. Johnson to John E. Moss, April 2, 1965.

[31] "Clearance," as used here, has nothing to do with security classification.

[32] See U.S., Congress, Senate, Constitutional Rights Subcommittee of the Judiciary Committee, *The Power of the President to Withhold Information from the Congress-Memorandums of the Attorney General,* Committee Print, 86th Congress, 2d Session; *Hearings on Freedom of Information and Secrecy in Government,* 85th Congress, 2d Session, March 6, 1958, April 16, 1958.

1. The basic legislation relevant to the withholding of information "relating to the national defense" is the Espionage Act (Title 18 U.S. Code 793-798). The first nationwide system for government control of security information was introduced by Executive Order 10290, which was issued by President Truman on September 24, 1951. This was the antecedent of President Eisenhower's Executive Order 10501 issued on November 5, 1953 and entitled "Safeguarding Official Information in the Interests of the Defense of the United States." [33] Although subsequently amended in detail, Executive Order 10501 remains in force as the basic ground rule for the classification of information.

In its original form, Executive Order 10501 restricted access to classified information to members of the executive branch requiring it in the course of their official duties. But in 1959 the order was amended to permit the head of an agency to authorize access to such information by "persons outside the executive branch performing functions in connection with historical projects." This presumably permits access to classified data, with executive approval, by properly cleared congressional staff personnel who needed such data in serving a legislative intelligence function. The Moss Subcommittee, however, has raised a number of questions about this Executive Order. Although it provides a uniform classification procedure and restricts, in theory, the right of classification to a limited number of senior officials, the Moss Subcommittee fears its abuse by officials who use classification "to hide errors in judgment, waste, inefficiency, or worse." Moreover, there seems to be no practical way in which executive denial of access to classified information could be challenged effectively by the Congress if it should so wish.

Most agencies of government have the power to classify, and practically speaking, this power is delegated to professional employees, since a document based on a classified document is itself usually classified. It would be difficult to conceive of any official document in the military, foreign policy, or resources area for which an argument could not be made for classification. In some agencies such as the National Security Agency, even the mere fact of classification or the very existence of the document may be classified information. Yet a request assumes knowledge of the existence of information; and unless that knowledge is specific and concrete, such a request

---

[33] U.S., Congress, House, Committee on Government Operations, *Safeguarding Official Information. . . . (The Status of Executive Order 10501)*, House Report No. 456, 87th Congress, 2d Session, September 21, 1962.

may be interpreted, often quite correctly, as an effort to initiate a "fishing expedition." One of the more important informal inputs into the Congress is leaked information on the existence of certain documents or secret decisions. In turn, the President may use the full weight of his investigative resources to discover and neutralize the source of such "leaks."

Classified material is provided to the congressional committees on a "need-to-know" basis. Occasionally, classified information may be presented to an entire house in closed session. Members of Congress are probably no more discreet than most persons, and any generalized legal right of congressional access to classified information might prove hazardous, especially in the area of foreign affairs. Such information might tend to be used to service domestic political concerns. Accordingly, it is largely restricted to a limited number of security-cleared members of Congress and staff, such as those belonging to the armed forces committees and the Joint Committee on Atomic Energy, where access to classified information is necessary for the performance of the authorization, appropriation, and oversight functions. However, in order to assure that security clearances granted by executive agencies may not at some future time be employed as political weapons to exclude members of Congress from sensitive committees on purely political grounds, it might be prudent to establish a Congressional Security Office to engage in joint-clearances with executive investigative agencies, with rights of access to executive files on all members of Congress and staff. This office could also perform a classified document control function on the Hill.[34]

It would be of considerable value to members of the armed forces committees and foreign relations committees to have access at least to the titles of documents relevant to their activities, particularly those documents relating to foreign affairs and intelligence analyses. These committees might do well to try to establish access to CIA's WALNUT system which provides a print out of existing intelligence documentation on specific areas and issues.[35]

Because of the sensitivity and size of government sponsored clandestine operations, some more effective congressional control of

---

[34] See Kofmehl, *op. cit.*, p. 79. "On March 6, 1953, the Senate passed Senate Resolution 16 which provided for a mild form of security check on all Senate employees. . . . Under its terms, full field investigation by the FBI . . . [was] not contemplated nor considered necessary. The resolution provided only for a name check. . . ."

[35] *Time*, September 3, 1965, p. 57.

secret intelligence may well be in order. Information currently available to the Congress permits neither rational legislation nor authorization in an area whose estimated annual budget is in the order of $1 or $2 billion. Congressional oversight is even less possible, despite the evidence that key executive intelligence estimates, major covert intelligence gathering activities, and a number of psychological and politico-military operations have demonstrated inadequacies that came to the Congress' attention only through public media.[36]

However, outside the most sensitive areas of military and foreign affairs, it is open to doubt whether the unified classification procedures established by Executive Order have masked much data relevant to congressional function. They have probably been far more effective in permitting the effective exercise of presidential authority over a congeries of agencies jealous of their prerogatives and not always above using the self-initiated classification procedures in the interagency struggle for prestige, missions, money, and men. Only insofar as the Congress might have a political interest in maintaining the greatest possible agency autonomy, has Executive Order 10501 done it some indirect damage. Committees having legitimate need for classified material largely seem to have been able to gain access to it, albeit with delay; and in turn they make it a practice to seek agency clearance for published hearings and reports based upon such materials.

2. The precedent for both congressional investigation and executive privilege was established during the first years of the Republic, when George Washington invoked the doctrine of privilege in refusing to accede to the House of Representatives' demand to see the correspondence and documents relating to Jay's treaty with Great Britain. The basic position of the contemporary Congress on "executive privilege" is clearly stated in summary fashion in the Moss Subcommittee Report of August 30, 1960, which was unanimously approved and adopted as the report of the full House Committee on Government operations. The relevant portions of the report read as follows:

The proponents of Executive Privilege contend that the executive branch has a constitutional right to make a unilateral deter-

---

36 See U.S., Congress, *Interim Report of the Joint Committee on the Organization of the Congress,* Senate Report No. 426, July 8, 1965, p. 20. See also *Hearings before the Joint Committee on the Organization of the Congress,* 89th Congress, 1st Session, pp. 460-69.

mination as to what information the Congress or its committees are entitled to receive.

The Congress does not, of course, grant that any such right exists. It is recognized that there may be instances when the importance to our foreign relations of limiting access to certain information may outweigh the value to the Congress of receiving it. The subcommittee has on several occasions withdrawn its request for particular documents at the suggestion of the executive branch. Examples of documents in this category are certain memoranda recording high-level discussions between Department of State officials and senior officials of foreign governments.

It should be clearly understood, however, that a voluntary willingness on the subcommittee's part to refrain from pressing for the production of certain information is not the same as recognition of a "privilege" on the part of the executive branch to withhold it.

No court decision has settled the question whether executive officials may refuse to honor a request of a congressional committee for papers, documents, and records. Many court decisions, however, have upheld the power of congressional committees to obtain records and papers in the possession of private individuals, corporations, and associations even though such records might be regarded as of a highly personal nature. It logically follows that the power of Congress to obtain information regarding the public business, the exercise of authority granted by Congress, or the expenditure of funds appropriated by Congress would likewise be upheld in the event of a court test.

The subcommittee, however, does not advocate at this time the forcing of the issue through the issuance of a subpoena and its enforcement through the contempt powers of the House. The subcommittee believes that course should be followed only after all other possible remedies have been exhausted. The unique character of our system of government by checks and balances and separation of powers, so brilliantly conceived by the founders of our Constitution to avoid concentration of power and the tyranny likely to follow from it, requires, if it is to be workable, that the coordinate branches of government treat each other with comity and respect and that they cooperate and compromise their differences, rather than insist upon exercising to the outer limits the power assigned to each. Only thus can a breakdown in our system of tripartite government be avoided. . . .

Although few original documents* are volunteered to the Congress by the executive branch, not many are withheld. Those which are withheld however, can sometimes be crucial. This subcommittee cites, further in this report, two instances in which particular lines of inquiry had to be dropped completely because there was no way to fill, from other sources, the gaps in information occasioned by the denial of significant documents. With these exceptions, however, in most instances, this subcommittee (or any other) can piece together from other sources information which a denied document would more quickly have supplied. . . .

A substantial portion of the time of this subcommittee and its staff goes into the problem of securing clearance of documents or filling gaps through laborious investigation where documents have been withheld. To the extent that the time must thus be spent in needless nonproductive effort, other inquiries must wait. Past experience of this subcommittee suggests that limiting the number and breadth of congressional inquiries may be one of the principal objectives of executive delay.

The great bulk of requested documents are eventually released, but the questionable doctrine of executive privilege results in unwarranted delay. Because of the timing of legislation and the shortness of the sessions of the Congress, delay is frequently tantamount to complete obstruction, preventing the timely exposure and correction of executive branch errors.

The substance of the third agency rule is that, if one agency holds a classified document originated by a second agency, the holder cannot release such document to a third agency (which includes congressional committees) without the consent of the originating agency. Without identifiable authority for so doing, the executive agencies have applied this rule to unclassified documents.

The executive privilege doctrine, incidentally, should not be confused with the problems of "classification" of information important to our national defense or foreign policy. This latter information may sometimes be justifiably withheld from the public at large, but this does not justify withholding it from authorized committees of Congress. . . . If the Congress is impeded from acting through its committees to study the activities

---

* We are not speaking here of self-serving documents prepared especially for the Congress, but of the original documents that repose in executive branch files and form the basis of operations.

of the executive branch, there is no way to identify and resist arbitrary exercise of the executive power. . . .

An atmosphere of denial so thoroughly permeates the executive branch at the present time that a minor official can feel he is behaving as his superiors wish him to, when he withholds documents from the Congress without even advising those superiors; there have been instances in which just this has occurred.

These are not new problems, but they seem to be reaching new heights of absurdity.

This subcommittee is continuing to seek a means by which the

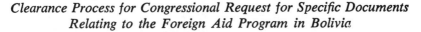

Clearance Process for Congressional Request for Specific Documents Relating to the Foreign Aid Program in Bolivia

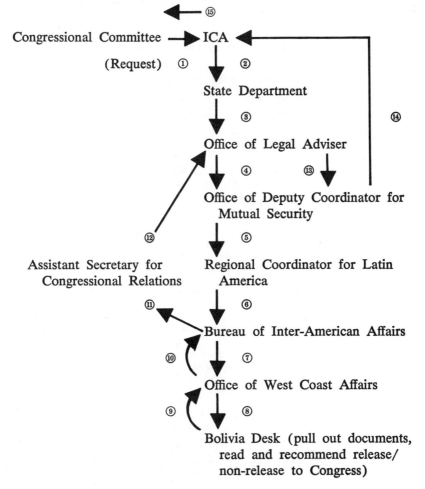

Congress can properly utilize its own legislative powers to overcome this obstruction.[37]

3. Dilatory practices may be employed in "clearance," thus using up congressional research and analytic resources in document procurement. For example, the formal procedures for State Department clearance as of 1960 presented a formidable roadblock.[38] The diagram on page 199 illustrates the lengthy process involved for clearance of a single request for specific documents relating to the foreign aid program in Bolivia.

Since only a relatively small portion of the documents requested normally prove relevant to the committee's interests, it might be well to obtain assent by the head of the agency concerned for direct access to such files by an appropriate committee staff "historical" researcher as provided for in the 1959 amendment to Executive Order 10501.

It should be noted that despite the broad grant of power to the Comptroller General to "have access to and the right to examine books, documents, papers, or records of any . . . department or establishment," the GAO has also experienced frequent frustration in its efforts to get information, especially from the Department of Defense and its three service branches, the Department of State, and the foreign assistance agencies.[39]

---

[37] U.S., Congress, House, Committee on Government Operations, *Executive Branch Practices in Withholding Information from Congressional Committees,* House Report No. 2207, 86th Congress, 2d Session, August 30, 1960, pp. 3-5.

[38] *Ibid.,* pp. 11-14.

[39] *Ibid.,* p. 15, references Senate Document 108, 80th Congress, 2d Session. "Refusals to the General Accounting Office of Access to Records of the Executive Departments and Agencies"; "Examination of Economic and Technical Assistance Programs for the Government of the Republic of China (Taiwan)—International Cooperation Administration—Department of State—Fiscal Years 1955-57, B-133074," August 29, 1958. "Examination of Economic and Technical Assistance Program for Laos—International Cooperation Administration—Department of State—Fiscal Years 1955-57, B-133003," October 8, 1958. "Examination of Economic and Technical Assistance Program for Pakistan—International Cooperation Administration—Department of State—Fiscal Years 1955-57, B-114896," March 31, 1959. "Examination of Economic and Technical Assistance Program for India—International Cooperation Administration, Department of State—Fiscal Years 1955-58, B-114845," September 14, 1959. "Examination of Economic and Technical Assistance Program for Guatemala—International Cooperation Administration, Department of State—Fiscal Years 1955-59, B-114845," March 22, 1960. "Examination of Economic and Technical Assistance Program for Bolivia—International Cooperation Administration—Department of State—Fiscal Years 1954-59, B-133271," May 17, 1960. "Examination of Economic and Technical Assistance Program for Brazil—International Cooperation Administration—Department of State—Fiscal Years 1955-59, B-13383," May 27, 1960.

4. On the basis of cases of withholding information reported by the Moss Subcommittee, executive agencies would appear to be very reserved about showing personnel files, efficiency reports, and internal executive evaluations of governmental programs and projects (which considerably restricts effective large-scale oversight, given the limitations of congressional research and investigative resources). Moreover, executive agencies, especially the State Department, seemingly show few qualms in selecting documents for submission to Congress, and so "screening" information in a manner apt to convey a desired impression.

The instruments available to the Congress to compel (morally or legally) access to information are the resolution, control of appropriations, and the subpoena power. Efforts to employ the subpoena power are probably not feasible politically. The President, if he felt he had the support of the mass media and public opinion, could insist on his constitutional prerogatives; if less sure of his ground, he could simply nullify the issue by repudiating the agency initiative and ordering compliance in the particular case. The same is true of a resolution, although here the Congress as a corporate body is politically vulnerable to a possible massive rallying of party support to the President, defeat of such a resolution and even a successful counter-resolution. A major precedent for such congressional support of the executive exists in Senator Thomas H. Benton's resolution of 1837 which successfully repudiated an 1834 senatorial censure of President Jackson (the original censure had been inspired by Henry Clay in response to Jackson's refusal of information relevant to his decision to withdraw government funds from the Second Bank of the United States).[40]

However, the 1960 report of the Moss Subcommittee concluded: "Utilizing the power of the purse, the Congress can and should provide in authorizing and appropriating legislation, that the continued availability of appropriated funds is contingent upon the furnishing of complete and accurate information relating to the expenditure of such funds to the General Accounting Office and to the appropriate committees of Congress at their request." [41] But if, in practice, such riders were generally attached to appropriations bills, who would

---

[40] Binkley, *op. cit.,* pp. 101-04.

[41] U.S., Congress House, Committee on Government Operations, *Availability of Information from Federal Departments and Agencies,* House Report No. 2083, 86th Congress, 2d Session, July 2, 1960. See pages 179ff for a chronology of the dispute over the "Hardy Amendment" to the Mutual Security Act of 1960.

decide that information was being withheld? Congress as a whole or a committee? And if such a finding were made, what machinery exists to compel cessation of Treasury disbursements? And if such disbursements were terminated, what provision would be made for the provision of the undoubted moral and financial claims of terminated agency employees, contractors, and so forth?

Thus it would seem that the only effective congressional devices for compelling access to information are the force of public opinion, the threat of refusing to authorize *future* agency programs, and a graduated reduction of appropriations. However, the remoteness of the ends-means relationship makes such an approach vulnerable to attack by the President and press, and hence to repudiation by public opinion. Further, the interests behind the various appropriations measures are specific and compelling; an effort to implement an earlier threat, to reduce or refuse appropriations, in the absence of some institutionalized and automatic procedure within the Congress itself, could hardly gain assent in the face of immediate, concrete, and in the main legitimate demands. It might therefore be desirable to consider establishing an institutionalized and automatic procedure for linking denial of information to future appropriations. This would seem as a minimum to involve the following stages:

(1) Report of denial, giving details as to the information requested and the agency and activity involved.

(2) Confirmation of the legitimacy of the request in terms of congressional function, possibly by a Commission of Notables.

The Commission might include nominees of the three branches, and independent members. This Commission would also verify the fact of refusal and the budget item(s) involved.

(3) The Commission would authorize use of the congressional power of subpoena, and set a deadline for the submission of the information requested.

(4) Failure to produce the information requested would result in an automatic notification to the agency concerned and to the Bureau of the Budget that the item(s) involved would not be authorized the following year, and that the agency would be wise to terminate that part of its activity within the current appropriation by June 30 of the on-going fiscal year.

Such an institutional process within the Congress could be created by legislation or by concurrent resolution as a self-enforced internal congressional procedure. Some question might arise as to whether such self-enforced internal decisions could or should be subject to judicial review. The use of a commission mechanism, employing persons of national prestige and presumed objectivity, would create a dignified quasi-judicial character that would blunt accusations of congressional impropriety or irresponsibility in making demands upon the executive or employing the appropriation power as an instrument for enforcing its prerogatives. Moreover, the commission would certainly prove a focus of press attention, since conflict is at the heart of the news. Hence it could serve to direct public attention to congressional functions and prerogatives and their place in the American way of government.

Institutional Devices for Improved Congressional Intelligence

I N the preceding section, particular attention was directed to the problem of improved congressional access to information in the executive departments and agencies as a necessary precondition to the effective exercise of Congress' oversight function in the American governmental system. The problem of congressional intelligence, however, is far broader than this. Effective and independent decision making requires autonomous sources of information and analysis. The Congress today is probably too dependent on executive sources and on the press for the definition of relevant problems, research, analysis, and the development of decisional alternatives. Since the American government is ultimately responsible to the electorate and sensitive to its demands, the Congress therefore might also prudently consider devices to inform the public on its own views of major problems and policy alternatives, so that these may return as effective demands within the political system.

To a large extent, the definition of substantive public problems which members of Congress feel are significant is to be found in the bills they present and the resolutions they propose. A Joint Committee on the Congress might well be set up to abstract and summarize, by the internal use of survey research instruments, the congressional viewpoint of the principal problems facing the American society.[42] This would help to generate public interest and to focus

[42] On May 18, 1965, Representative Rhodes presented a comprehensive statement on the organization and functions of a proposed Joint Committee on the State of the Union which would be responsible for studies directed at:

public attention on a manageable set of national issues defined as an alternative to the presidential perspective. Secondly, it could provide a focus for in-depth studies by congressional and executive staff and independent scholars in the search for alternative solutions to issues defined by the Congress. The definition of problems without an immediate consideration of specific legislative solutions would leave congressional decision making somewhat more open-ended than it is at present. This approach might also encourage a more consensual and systematic definition of major problem areas for committee and subcommittee inquiry.

The generation of a broad spectrum of possible alternative courses of action requires increased academic study and research to supplement current investigative procedures. It also requires an aptitude for social engineering; that is, the devising of institutional structures operationally adapted to the achievement of defined goals. This capability might be developed by establishing a Congressional Institute which could conduct a RAND-type of study activity on a Congress-wide or committee basis, by increasing authorizations for external research and/or by providing a congressional tie-in to a consortium of universities, to mention but a few possibilities. Professional committee staff would be principally responsible for providing a congressional perspective to researchers and for synthesizing the reports on the various institutional alternatives in clear and manageable terms.

The volume of information that must be digested annually in the appropriations process has reached unmanageable proportions. In another essay in this symposium, Professor Wildavsky has suggested introducing into the federal budget a system of "radical incrementalism"—essentially management by exception, in which only substantial deviations from the accepted on-going norm or new items would be examined intensively each year. This approach might be supplemented by taking annually a random sample of budget items,

---

(1) The posture of the federal government vis-à-vis the states and localities, (2) Long-range legislative programs for the Congress, (3) The most healthy level of federal expenditure and tax revenue at any given period of time. Its membership might include the President pro tempore of the Senate, the Speaker of the House, the majority and minority leaders of both houses, the chairman and ranking minority members of both appropriations committees, the Senate Finance Committee and the House Ways and Means Committee plus an additional eight members divided equally between the houses and parties to "carry most of the day-to-day burdens of the committee." U.S., Congress, *Hearings before the Joint Committee on the Organization of the Congress*, 89th Congress, 1st Session, pp. 223-26. See also the testimony of General Thomas A. Lane, June 25, 1965.

(perhaps weighed according to the size of the estimate) for detailed investigation by the appropriate subcommittees of both appropriations committees. Thus over the course of any ten-year period, there would be a very high probability of any given item coming under intense scrutiny.

The appropriations process is a critical area of legislation where long-range *national* planning can be done. Basically what is needed is: (a) projections of prospective tax inputs over given future time spans; this data is easily available and reasonably reliable; (b) projections of existing and proposed agency activities over future time spans, and (c) some means of achieving consensus on ciritcal national needs and the methods required to satisfy them. In terms of an overall national program, projective data might well permit Congress, in cooperation with the executive, to prepare adequately conceived programs to be put into force at a given time in the future. Congressional realism in the area of fiscal control may well reopen the way to true legislative initiative. This possibility is, of course, contingent upon improved input information, improved techniques of analysis, and on the development of internal congressional information-collecting and analytic tools to reduce the number of policy options to a level manageable by parliamentary decision-making techniques.

If the Congress is to retain its essential role and relative strength within the American governmental system, it must consider means to facilitate access to factual knowledge, analytic skills and original ideas, and the development of an organized capability for making institutional inventions, or at least reporting them. Only an institution with an unusual flexibility of organization can satisfy these requirements. The nearest parallel is a university-type of body which has a complete range of disciplines, almost completely horizontal communications channels, and a high degree of freedom for professional staffs as to time budgets and research activities. If the services of such an institution were made available to the Congress, individual members and the committees would have easy informal access on a person-to-person basis to professional students of national problems. And if it was organized as a degree-granting institution, such a congressional facilitiy would have at its disposal large numbers of full-time researchers, at moderate cost, working under the direction of senior professionals who have an *academic* interest in the quality of the work. In addition to counseling and conducting research seminars, each member of the senior staff of the institution could give at least one course of lectures per year in his area of specialization, in order to force him to keep abreast of the professional literature. Relatively easy access to research funds and the opportunity for public service would provide a strong inducement to both professional and student researchers. Moreover, since most of the research would probably be of an unclassified nature and would be published by or under the auspices of distinguished academicians, it would be subject to the critical review of the professions, which would ensure high quality. The institution would, of course, have to be guaranteed essential intellectual autonomy; its members could not be subject to political reprisals for what they write in the course of their work.

This proposal reflects and extends the recommendations of many witnesses who pressed for a Congressional Institute of Scholars [43] before the Joint Committee on the Organization of the Congress. A university-type organization would have the advantages attendant upon establishing a clear corporate identity: continued identification with the professional community, availability of graduate research assistance, independence of thought, high standards of research quality, and an organizational form adapted to the essentially decentralized structure of the Congress itself. Indeed, such an institution could well be chartered by Congress as a National University. However, in terms of tenure appointments, it should probably be kept relatively small and should rely heavily on visiting professors and research associates on leave from their mother institutions. The Armed Forces Staff Colleges have found this an extremely effective device. Leaves should probably be for a minimum period of two years. This would also serve an educational function by acquainting a significant proportion of the academic community, of all disciplines, with the problems of Congress. (A considerable part of that community today has already become acutely aware of the problems of the public administration as a result of action as consultants or contract researchers to federal agencies.) The professional cadre of the institution would require tenure to assure independence, and should therefore be selected with the greatest care to assure the broadest possible professional competencies coupled with the stability of personality, sense of responsibility, and the maturity of judgment (and action) needed for congressional advisers. The institu-

---

[43] See U.S., Congress, Joint Committee on the Organization of the Congress, *Organization of the Congress, Interim Report,* Report No. 426, 89th Congress, 1st Session, July 8, 1965, pp. 15, 28.

tion might also profitably be tied to the various public and private universities in the District of Columbia, and to independent non-profit research groups such as the National Planning Association and The Brookings Institution.

The proposal for a National University under congressional auspices is not meant as a substitute for other, existing and proposed, congressional information facilities. On the contrary, its work should be regarded as supplementing the work of facilities already in existence. I have already discussed the need to expand and strengthen the Legislative Reference Service. As both a national and a congressional facility, the Library of Congress should certainly be given an increased budget to permit purchase by standing order of all books and significant periodicals published annually in the world, plus a corresponding enhancement of staff and physical facilities. The Library could also be made a center for research and development in the area of automated information indexing, storage, and retrieval. There is an increasing need for research in policy documentation systems. These would be of peculiar interest and utility to the Congress.[44]

---

[44] Council on Library Resources, *Automation and the Library of Congress* (Washington: Library of Congress, 1964).

Conclusion

THE objection that much of the research that might be done under congressional auspices would simply duplicate work already being done in the executive branch is not valid. It is true, at the most rudimentary level, present GAO audits, for example, do duplicate agency audits; but they also serve a control function. The same can be said of more sophisticated congressionally-sponsored research and analysis. Secondly, the Congress requires intelligence directed towards its particular functions in the government system. Such data must be available in a manner adapted to Congress' loose organizational structure. Individual members of Congress often have great difficulty in obtaining depth studies which are easily available to the executive. For example, one member's request to the State Department for data on the governmental organization, parties, and key personalities of a group of Latin American states was answered by the provision of short, printed, public relations handouts. But almost any professional employee in an agency concerned with foreign policy could easily have procured the detailed data requested, including the superb analytic synopses of available information found in some national estimates.

Individual congressmen need research and on occasion practical professional assistance (e.g., for office methods studies). However, increases in staff, whether of the committees or of individual members, could easily lead to their bureaucratization and a loss of flexibility and control by their principals. Perhaps each member of Congress should have a research allowance to be expended on qualified individual and institutional consultants. This would seem a highly desirable measure—in addition to the institutional facilities previously discussed—and it would tend to avoid making members into office managers. Abuses, both personal and political, could creep in; but some form of potential control might be introduced, perhaps by submitting the names and qualifications of consultants prior to employment and copies of their reports to a Joint Committee on the Congress.

Another way of helping to improve congressional information would be increased allowances for telecommunications and travel. It has been said that the greatest instrument of research ever devised is the telephone; it permits you to talk to the man who knows. Certainly increased allowances for calls would facilitate members' access to knowledgeable persons in their home state, including faculty of the state universities. And foreign travel does broaden the mind since it permits firsthand access to and impressions of foreign situations and institutions. As regards members of the military and foreign affairs committees, the utility of foreign travel is obvious. But it is equally desirable for members of other committees who might learn much by exposure to other ways of doing the same kinds of things they themselves are responsible for having done. How many members of the legislative committees responsible for Medicare spoke to key figures in the British, Swedish, or Russian National Health programs to find out how they did it, and the problems they met in introducing their programs? How many members of Congress responsible for the Appalachia program have heard about the Italian Cassa per il Mezzogiorno, let alone examined on the spot its organization and methods, successes, and failures? How frequently does one hear the remark: "Oh yes, we tried that particular device twelve years ago. It didn't work and here's why. . . ."

The objection to increased congressional expenditures on the intelligence function are politically cogent. Congress and congressmen make ritual protests of their economy-mindedness, and hence are peculiarly susceptible to charges of waste, duplication, and extravagance. Besides, the Congress itself reflects to a certain extent some of the anti-intellectual sentiments widespread in a society confused by organized complexity. But if knowledge is power, the relative decline of the Congress in the American scheme of government is explicable. Congress' information problem is not primarily one of access to information in the executive. Congress is deluged by information originating in the executive, some relevant, much irrelevant to congressional function, and most of it unintegrated into a larger systemic whole, unanalyzed and unevaluated. There is every indication that, with the exception of requests for data tendentiously serving partisan political objectives, or which could be used to the detriment of individuals (such as investigative files) or of the national security, members of Congress and congressional committees could get the information they need if they had appropriate facilities to define their needs, routinize transmission, and impose appropriate sanctions upon unwarranted refusal of information by the executive.

Thus the problem of congressional access to executive information is only one aspect of the general problem of congressional intelligence; that is the collection, evaluation, analysis, and adequate dissemination of the information required for the effective performance of the functions of the Congress. Members of Congress themselves feel their inadequacy in these respects. The complexity of decision making and the lack of information are the difficulties most frequently cited by members. Yet it must also be pointed out that any overall improvement in congressional intelligence is likely to have profound and unforeseeable consequences not only for relations between Congress and the executive, but for the entire political system. The objective of this paper has been to discuss certain aspects of congressional intelligence with particular reference to factual data and the use of analytic methods. Special attention has therefore been devoted to assessing the availability of information in the executive and to suggesting a variety of institutional devices that might enhance the decision-making capabilities of the Congress. However, analysis of the possible and probable secondary effects of such innovations would certainly be required prior to their introduction.

HEINZ EULAU is Professor of Political Science at Stanford University. He received his Ph.D. from the University of California (Berkeley) in 1941. During the war he was Senior Organizations and Propaganda Analyst in the Special War Policies Unit of the Department of Justice. Professor Eulau has been a Fellow of the Center for Advanced Study in the Behavioral Sciences, 1957-58, and Visiting Legislative Research Professor at the University of California (Berkeley), 1961-62. His books include *Political Behavior,* 1956 (co-author); *Legislative Behavior,* 1959 (co-author); *The Legislative System,* 1962 (co-author); *Class and Party in the Eisenhower Years,* 1962; *The Behavioral Persuasion in Politics,* 1963; *Journeys in Politics,* 1963; *Lawyers in Politics,* 1964 (co-author); and *Political Behavior in America: New Directions,* 1966. He is general editor of the *International Yearbook of Political Behavior Research* and an associate editor of the forthcoming *International Encyclopedia of the Social Sciences.* Professor Eulau is a member of the Council of the American Political Science Association. At the present time he is engaged in a massive interview study of 89 city councils under a grant from the National Science Foundation.

The Committees in a Revitalized Congress

Heinz Eulau

Introduction

CONGRESSIONAL reform is an area where political scientists should fear to tread. For, whatever other virtues political scientists may possess, they do not have at their disposal a knowledge of good or evil, of right or wrong. In fact, even on matters where we can make a claim to knowledge, it is the better part of wisdom to speak with restraint and not to claim too much. But though our knowledge is often fragmentary and even unreliable, we cannot abandon either the critical or the creative functions that our role as politically as well as scientifically responsible observers of and participants in public life calls for—provided we adhere to our own professional standards of appropriate conduct.

One of these standards is that we make as explicit as possible the assumptions, both normative and behavioral, that underlie whatever recommendations we make about public policies. This standard is by no means always adhered to. Yet, behind any proposal for reform of congressional structures, functions, and processes are assumptions about the role of the Congress in the total American governmental system. Unfortunately, only rarely are these assumptions fully articulated. In fact, articulation may sometimes be deliberately avoided, lest it mobilize opposition to a particular proposal, not because of its actual contents so much as because the assumptions behind it seem obnoxious and unacceptable. Avoidance of stating assumptions can therefore on occasion become a strategy of reform. But this cannot be our strategy. As scientists, we have no alternative but to clarify and articulate our assumptions. For our role is primarily to enlighten rather than to persuade.

As one reviews the many recommendations made by members of Congress, interested citizens and organizations, and political scientists concerning reforms of congressional operations, one is struck, first, by the nit-picking character of criticisms of this and that aspect of congressional life—criticisms that are rarely informed by a comprehensive view of the Congress in the American system of checks and balances. Secondly, one is struck by the casual, *ad hoc* character of most of the proposals and by the fact that they do not add up to a coherent program for reform. The purpose of a normative model—such as the model of a vigorous, independent Congress presented in this symposium—is to give direction to particular proposals and to see to it that they constitute a logical, consistent whole.

From the vantage point of our own model, the main feature of the great variety of proposals so far put forward for committee reforms is their limited perspective. At their best, they are oriented to the *contemporary* configuration of power within the Congress or between the Congress and the White House. That the configuration may change in a short time, because of changing personal or party fortunes, is intentionally disregarded. For instance, quite recently we have seen liberal congressmen rise in defense of seniority, a principle of organization that not too long ago was high on the agenda of liberal denunciation. Hence, when viewed in this way, "reform" comes to have a very particular meaning. It comes to mean the creation of temporary devices designed to serve the temporary advantage of partisan groupings, ideological factions, interest-group combinations, or the President. The long-range role of the Congress in the system of balanced powers is ignored, or else the Congress is assigned a secondary role in the scheme of governmental things.

At their worst, proposals for reform are advanced to redress special grievances which are generalized, though we do not know how widely they are held—that a chairman does not schedule bills as they should be scheduled, or that junior committee members are not given a chance to shine at public hearings, or that administrative officials must spend too much time on the Hill. Reform proposals to alleviate these defects, which may indeed occur, are usually so innocuous that they fail to draw blood. That grievances stemming from the human condition can be redressed by structural changes remains largely an act of faith. True, there is always the *possibility* of correcting or at least harnessing human frailties through changes in institutional arrangements. The men who framed the Constitution and thought of the living constitution as one of checks and balances were eminently sensitive, perhaps too sensitive, to the problem of controlling human passions and errors through institutional safe-guards. But one need not be a conservative to recognize that not even the subtlest structural controls can entirely eliminate human folly.

Therefore, it is a modest assumption of this paper that, no matter what proposals for committee reform are made or adopted, there will always be difficulties stemming from the human factor. Whatever system of chairman selection be adopted by a legislative body, for instance, there will always be good and bad presiding officers, and many who are in between. Whatever financial inducements are necessary to attract a presumably competent staff, there will always be good, in-between, and bad staff members. This does not mean that behavior patterns should not be optimized through appropriate structural arrangements. It only means that perfection is not the issue.

It is for just these reasons that framing proposals for reform merely in terms of a normative model is not enough. If the proposals are to be viable, they must also take into account the emergent properties of collective bodies like committees which result from individual and interpersonal behavioral patterns. The congressional structure is not a bloodless mechanism, but a living organism—a system of complex interpersonal and intergroup relations that must be thoroughly understood if proposals derived from the normative model are not to remain altogether utopian. The fact is that we *know* relatively little about the behavioral system that is Congress, at least if by "knowledge" we mean empirically tested propositions as opposed to casual (albeit possibly profound) insights or hunches. This is especially true of the behavioral patterns of congressional committees. We know less about them than about other aspects of congressional behavior and functioning, say the role of the parties or the constituencies. If the few excellent studies of committee structures and functions conducted in the last few years by political scientists tell us anything, it is that the congressional behavioral system as mirrored in the life of the committees and subcommittees is even more complex and manifold than we had hitherto suspected.

Because almost no committee or subcommittee behaves like any other, generalizations about committee behavior are hazardous. Any set of proposals for changes must therefore take this fact as its point of departure. Each committee has its own needs and requirements for effective functioning, its own traditions and norms of behavior, its characteristic tasks and goals, its unique subject matter and relevant skills. If they are to serve any useful purpose, reform proposals must take all these factors into account; and further, reformers must seek to assess how proposed changes would affect committee behavior.

The purpose of the proposals about committees presented in this paper is neither to serve partisan, ideological, or any other advantages, nor to redress familiar grievances. They are derived from a model of Congress that is geared, on the one hand, to the behavioral realities of the present as we know them and, on the other hand, to the developmental context of the future as we hope to shape it. My proposals do not touch, therefore, on every conceivable aspect of committee structures and functions. Rather, they are located in the context of broad, basic problems. They are based on the assumption that the future can be shaped according to man's preferences, that there is nothing inevitable about the future (as there is about the present) if men are prepared to seize their opportunities. Whatever may motivate the other authors represented in this symposium, be they liberal or conservative, my own preference for a strong, independent, representative, responsible, and responsive Congress in the American system does not stem from the conservative's hankering after the past. Rather, it flows from the liberal conviction that, over the long haul, the elected representatives of the people assembled in Congress are at least as qualified to give direction to the American democracy as the President and the federal bureaucracy.

The Problem of Functions:
Manifest and Latent

PROPOSALS for reorganizing congressional committees with a view to strengthening the Congress vis-à-vis the President and the bureaucracy must proceed from a clear view of congressional functions and of committee functions. It is a rather widespread, if simplistic, view that because committees are "creatures" of Congress in the formal sense, they have no functions that can be distinguished from those of the Congress as a whole. This view ignores a number of considerations. In the first place, the functions of Congress cannot be identified independently of the functions of its committees because, for all practical purposes, the work of Congress is done in the committees. Notwithstanding the formal derivation of committees, therefore, identifying the functions of Congress requires prior identification of committee functions.

Second, while it is easy enough to identify those functions which are defined in the Constitution, they do not exhaust the list of functions actually performed by committees in practice. Some of these additional functions are "manifest," like the investigatory function which was inherited, so to speak, from the English Parliament and the early state legislatures. Others, however, may be described as "latent"; these latent functions are difficult to identify and have come to be scrutinized by political scientists only in recent years.

These distinctions are important because changes in congressional structure may have consequences for committee functioning which, from the perspective of one model or another, may be harmful. In turn, changes in committee functions may have important consequences for the position of Congress in the total governmental system. This "structural-functional" view of the congressional process suggests that concrete proposals for committee reform, no matter how picayune they may appear to be, must be appraised in terms of their possible consequences for the total constellation of congressional operations. While this is not the place to do so, it is my strong impression that quite a few proposals recently made would have to be considered detrimental from the standpoint of the model of a strong Congress presented in this symposium.

If possible harmful consequences are to be avoided, perhaps one of the most immediate tasks of the Joint Committee on the Organization of the Congress ought to be to bring into the open, through an appropriate statement, exactly those latent functions that tend to strengthen the Congress as a countervailing power to the President and the bureaucracy. To insist that just the traditional, formal functions of Congress—lawmaking proper, participation in nominations and treaty-making, or investigation—should be strengthened, will not contribute very much to solving the critical problem of congressional-presidential relations. It is my belief that some of the latent functions performed by the committees may be more relevant than the better-known manifest functions. My intent here is to be only suggestive. We shall discuss merely two of the more important latent functions performed by committees—the congressional "veto" and the conflict-resolving function.

Under the Constitution, the veto is a presidential prerogative, introduced precisely because the framers distrusted legislative majorities. The President still has the right to veto and, on proper occasion, he exercises his right. But over the years Congress has gradually come to perform a veto function that was not provided for in the Constitution. Whenever a committee or subcommittee bottles up executive-initiated legislation, votes it down, or refuses to report it out of committee, it is exercising an effective, if latent, veto function. From the perspective of our model, this function is highly desirable, even though it may at times be abused. What James Madison wrote in *The Federalist No. 48* about the legislative department—that it "is everywhere extending the sphere of its activity, and drawing all the power into its impetuous vortex," and that "it is against the enterprising ambition of this department, that the people ought to indulge all their jealousy and exhaust all their precautions" —can be said today of the President and the executive-centered federal bureaucracy. It is testimony to the flexibility of the "living constitution," as against the "parchment barriers" of which Madison spoke elsewhere, that congressional committees have evolved their own veto function. All too often this veto function is denounced as a symptom of congressional ineptness and "hanging back." These denunciations only confirm its effectiveness. For this reason alone, proposals designed to relieve committees of control over legislation should be carefully scrutinized from the point of view of whether they may not jeopardize an important function which is essential in a modern system of checks and balances.

The second latent function I wish to discuss is the conflict-crystallizing and conflict-resolving function that is inherent in the complex congressional committee and subcommittee structure. This function is not always appreciated sufficiently. All too many reform-ers—whether those who would subordinate the Congress to the President, or those whose ideal is a Congress which resembles an efficient business organization—ignore the fact that the Congress is, above all, a broadly representative body, and as such, because it is representative of so many potentially and actually conflicting inter-ests, preeminently a political body. If the conflicts of society that find their way into Congress are not to be resolved by authoritarian means but through mutual accommodation of interests and com-promise, the facilitation of the conflict-resolving function ought to be high on the list of structural requirements. Moreover, it would seem that this function can be better performed by the committees and subcommittees than by the Congress as a whole.

Let us consider only two aspects of the relationship between function and structure in this connection. First, there is the factor of size. It is generally agreed that small committees are more accessible to interests-in-conflict than large groups. From the point of view of those who take a negative stance towards interest-group politics, this fact may appear to be harmful. From the point of view of our model, however, committee accessibility is a strong feature of congressional structuring. For this reason, proposals to combine committees with related jurisdictions may seriously interfere with the functions of conflict resolution. In other words, what is often called the "proliferation" of committees is in fact highly functional from our perspective. And precisely because it is functional, I believe that it will always occur, even if for some reasons the com-mittee superstructure is "simplified."

Second, there is now good evidence to suggest that committees and subcommittees each evolve norms of their own which may be either highly conducive or non-conducive to conflict resolution. In a careful study of the House Appropriations Committee, Professor Richard F. Fenno, Jr., has shown that this committee is faced with basic problems of integration, defined as "the degree to which there is a working together or a meshing together or mutual support among its roles and subgroups"—which are directly relevant to the performance of its manifest functions. In other words, successful integration in this committee has important consequences for its work; for instance, on the acceptability of its recommendations, the reduction of party influence on appropriations decisions, the stability of appropriations procedures, and others.[1]

What these merely suggestive comments add up to is this: there is a high probability that almost any structural change in one sector of congressional life—say, the leadership structure or House-Senate relations—will affect many other sectors; since, if functions are eliminated from one sector, they will probably be performed by another. Before structural change is undertaken, therefore, it is important to identify as many functions as possible so as to assure that the total complex of functions necessary for a vigorous Congress is not undermined by inappropriate structural changes. These considerations will in part guide us in the following sections of this paper. But before I go on, one proposal: Congress should allocate funds for a continuing survey of its structures and functions, to be conducted by a team of disinterested analysts, for the purpose of permitting Congress to reorganize and strengthen itself from session to session rather than from decade to decade or more. What use Congress would make of this continuing survey would be symptomatic of its commitment to remaining a viable institution in our age of executive dominance. But even if the survey should turn out to be more of a *pro forma* operation than a real one, it could serve to alert the Congress to the consistency or inconsistency—from the perspective of a strong legislature—of those piecemeal, incremental changes in structure and functions that are bound to occur over the years.

---

[1] Richard F. Fenno, Jr., "The House Appropriations Committee," *American Political Science Review,* June 1962, pp. 310-24. But, for a negative case of integration, see Charles O. Jones, "The Role of the Congressional Subcommittee," *Midwest Journal of Political Science,* November 1962, pp. 327-44.

The Problem of Jurisdiction:
Conflict and Coordination

EFFORTS to improve the internal organization of Congress necessarily center in what is felt to be a need for the orderly arrangement of the respective jurisdictions of the standing committees. But what criteria should guide this arrangement? Perhaps too much routine, and too little imaginative, thinking has been devoted to answering this question. How else can one explain the general agreement that the organization of the committees along the more or less broad policy lines laid down in the Legislative Reorganization Act of 1946 has worked reasonably well, even though jurisdictional conflicts continue? At least at the present time, there is no widespread demand for reorganization of the standing committee structure as such. Such proposals as are made are largely cast within the "spirit" of the 1946 Act.

The chief argument in favor of the present arrangement is that though almost every committee must deal with several administrative departments or agencies, there is sufficient parallelism between the various congressional and bureaucratic sectors to guarantee efficiency in relations and operations at both ends of Pennsylvania Avenue. The argument is plausible but deceptive. In reality, it is an argument derived from the executive model of the legislature's role in the federal government. If it were really taken seriously, the argument would weaken rather than strengthen the Congress vis-à-vis the bureaucracy.

For the assumption underlying the argument, and implicit in the executive model that strengthening Congress is mainly a matter of achieving greater efficiency through the clarification of committee jurisdictions and the avoidance of jurisdictional conflicts, is the ideal of the public administrator. Needless to say, perhaps, insofar as the quest for efficiency relates to the myriad of routine tasks which the Congress must perform, one can only endorse appropriate efforts (always keeping in mind the possibility that valuable latent functions may be harmed). But what reason is there to believe that efficiency in congressional operations will strengthen the position of Congress as a *policymaking* institution in the total governmental system? Indeed, one might argue that rather than making the Congress more independent of presidential domination, proposals to increase its efficiency will actually make it even more susceptible to executive and administrative pressures and demands. Surely, more efficient reaction to these pressures and demands is not in the best interests of Congress as a strong and independent legislative body.

But the efficiency argument is faulty on another ground as well. It ignores the facts of Washington political life. As a close academic observer of the scene, Professor Richard Neustadt, has pointed out, the actual relationship between Congress and the bureaucracy is just the reverse of what it is often assumed to be: "Both organizationally and in terms of personnel the new bureaucracy is a projection of congressional committee jurisdictions—or, more precisely, since 1946, of standing subcommittee jurisdictions." This, perhaps, overstates the true case, as Neustadt himself acknowledges: "Of course, committee jurisdictions have been influenced, in turn, by organizational developments downtown." [2] In other words, respective congressional and agency structuring appears to be a reciprocal process, and hence tends to make for structural parallelism. Unfortunately, we do not really know whether this parallelism is an advantage or a disadvantage for committee operations vis-à-vis the bureaucracy—say, in regard to their oversight function, for instance. In any case, as Neustadt also suggests, the very rigidity introduced by efforts to attain jurisdictional neatness actually has the adverse effect of depriving committees of their influence on administrative operations: "As a forum for administrative bargaining, our legislative process has its uses in securing and defending fixed positions, not in reaching or applying operational accommodations suited to the job in hand." [3]

---

[2] Richard E. Neustadt, "Politicians and Bureaucrats," in David B. Truman (ed.), *The Congress and America's Future* (Englewood Cliffs, N.J.: Prentice-Hall, 1965), pp. 103-04.

[3] *Ibid.*, p. 108.

If Neustadt is correct, and I believe that he partly is, then, surely, not too much effort should be expended in attempts to clarify and sharply delineate jurisdictions. Such attempts will only impede just those conflict-resolving bargaining processes which an elected legislative body, perhaps better than any other organ of government, is especially capable of performing. Moreover, most modern legislation is usually so complex that it cannot easily and unambiguously be assigned to one or another committee or subcommittee. In other words, setting up neat and sharply separated jurisdictional structures is dysfunctional from the viewpoint of contemporary legislation. It tends to create difficulties where none need to exist. Insistence on defining sharp jurisdictional boundaries between committees, in terms of some purely hypothetical subject matter contributes to legislative confusion because, as Professors William J. Keefe and Morris S. Ogul rightly point out, "policy interrelationships may be missed, emerging policies may begin or come to work at cross-purposes, and committees may wrangle with each other over the custody of measures and activities." [4]

Of course, committee and subcommittee jurisdiction cannot be helter-skelter. As I shall argue later on, committee expertise is an essential requirement for vigorous congressional functioning. But it is only a necessary and not a sufficient condition. The committee structure must remain sufficiently flexible to maximize political bargaining, for which committees are the governmental instruments par excellence. But how can the bargaining process be facilitated so that it has the dual effect of strengthening the hand of Congress in its brushes with the White House and the agencies and of keeping the committee structure as flexible as possible?

It seems to me that proposals for clearly defining committee jurisdictions miss the crucial point that jurisdictional conflicts may be harnessed to maximize congressional bargaining operations. Their proponents tend to look on jurisdictional conflicts as malfunctions that interfere with efficient legislative behavior because they seem to defy organization charts. Hence, they usually call for "coordination" procedures of various sorts—parallel committees in the two houses, interlocking memberships, joint committees, simultaneous bill referrals, intervention by the central leadership, cooperation through staff assistants, exchange of information, and so on. Although such demands do not necessarily imply an assumption that the existing

---

4 William J. Keefe and Morris S. Ogul, *The American Legislative Process, Congress and the States* (Englewood Cliffs, N.J.: Prentice-Hall, 1964), p. 156.

committee structure represents the best of all possible worlds, it appears to be taken for granted that jurisdictional purity, if not possible in fact, is desirable in principle, and that jurisdictional conflicts between committees and subcommittees are to be avoided at all cost.

From the perspective of the model pursued here, however, jurisdictional conflicts can be seen as the first signals that a given piece of legislation may involve a great variety of complex and technical issues whose solution calls for bargaining and also for expertise. The problem involved in resolving these conflicts is not simply one of coordination. Coordination is an administrative, not a political way of doing things. From a political standpoint, and assuming that jurisdictional conflict signalizes a need for political adjustments, structures are not ends in themselves but means. And if the executive agencies pattern themselves after congressional structures, it follows that Congress should experiment with new structures better suited to its own needs than quasi-administrative stopgaps. Instead of becoming embroiled in inter-committee entanglements in the wake of coordinative efforts—entanglements which are usually interpreted as further proof that Congress is an outmoded institution—Congress should be given the opportunity to create new structures as need for them arises. But this requires, above all, that the ongoing committee structure—and there always must be such a structure, if for no other reason than that the bulk of congressional business is routine rather than innovative—should not be frozen to a point where it can no longer respond flexibly to the complexity of public issues.

If, as has been suggested, such new structures are to meet the requirements both for bargaining and for expertise, then clearly conventional notions of coordination, leadership, or authority—geared to hierarchical organizations rather than to collegial bodies like legislatures—are out of place. My proposal is, therefore, that Congress experiment with a new type of committee—a kind of inter-committee committee—composed of members of those committees or subcommittees which claim jurisdiction over a given piece of legislation. This type of committee would meet our two requirements. On the one hand, its members would bring to the new committee the expertise of their standing committees; on the other hand, the bargaining process could go on without being impeded by jurisdictional jealousies. The members of our new committee will not be regarded as delegates from their standing committees and would not be required to report back to the committees from which they are recruited. In other words, the new committee would differ in significant ways from the so-called "select" or "special" committees that are also part of the congressional committee structure. These committees, established for a variety of reasons, do not ordinarily influence congressional decision making; and as they do not have formal power "to report a bill," they are not on an equal footing with the standing committees.[5] By way of contrast, the type of inter-committee committee proposed here would have the power to bring bills to the floor, following whatever procedures are followed by the regular standing committees. It might even happen that this new type of committee becomes a new standing committee—an outcome that would attest to its creativity.

---

[5] See V. Stanley Vardys, "Select Committees of the House of Representatives," *Midwest Journal of Political Science*, August 1962, pp. 247-65.

The Problem of Power:
Autonomy and Integration

A GOOD deal has been said about the so-called usurpation of legislative "power" by the committees of Congress. Interestingly, complaints along this line often come from those who, following the executive model, see in this alleged usurpation an obstacle to strong congressional party government, which, they assume, would support the President's legislative program. But sometimes these complaints also come from those who vaguely feel that the power of the committees in some way undermines the vigor of Congress as a whole vis-à-vis the presidency, because it deprives the Congress (and the House much more than the Senate) of the opportunity to deliberate in an atmosphere that forces the eyes of the nation upon the Hill. Taking the two sets of complaints together, the committee system comes to be blamed for both congressional obstinacy in the face of presidential needs and for congressional weakness.

Textbooks on Congress are generally agreed in their explanations of the power of committees. Committee power is said to be a product of the voluminous business before Congress, the need for specialization and expertise, the close bond between the committees and administrative agencies, the ease of access the committees afford to supportive interest groups, the existence of greater opportunity for bargaining and compromise in small groups, and so on. Whether this power is "good" or "bad" remains a matter of dispute precisely because these explanations are rarely derived from an explicit model of the congressional system.

Let me illustrate the consequences of this instability in criteria. Take, for instance, a hypothetical advocate of the executive model who does not quite know what he is advocating. If he is a member of the majority party, if his party controls both the Congress and the White House, and if he is a strong partisan supporter of the President's program, then he would be likely to deplore committee power, should a committee happen to be composed of a coalition hostile to the presidential program or be chaired by a man who is only reluctantly in favor of it. On the other hand, should a committee happen to be well disposed to the President's program, our hypothetical congressman would be inclined to welcome the committee's power, since it would speed up the process of legislation. Indeed, he might even argue that, given the fact that members cannot inform themselves about all bills as well as they perhaps should, congressmen ought to trust the committee's recommendation and support its bills—in other words, cast a blind vote. It is just such blind voting that worries those who see in committee power a threat to a vigorous, independent Congress.

It is evident that no appraisal of committee power, and certainly no recommendation as to how much power the committees should have, can be built on such opportunistic considerations. No reasonable committee system can be built on the ever-shifting configurations of congressional-presidential and intra-congressional power relations.

But though the actual explanations for committee power may be sound enough, must there necessarily be a conflict over power between the committees and the houses of which they are a part? As far as our model is concerned, we take it for granted that, in the foreseeable future, we cannot expect radical changes in the circumstances that make the committees what they are. However, our model does not assume that power is a zero-sum game, an assumption that seems to underlie the complaints about committee power. The assumption is false because power can be generated out of power, and moreover, it can be distributed—much as wealth can be created out of wealth and distributed. In other words, if one wishes to "restore" the power of the houses of Congress as wholes, one need not necessarily take away from the committees whatever power they may have. Let me illustrate this point and suggest at least one way in which this might be done.

Of the explanations that are offered for committee power, none seems more relevant to the problem than that which attributes committee power to the opportunity they provide for negotiation, bargaining, logrolling, and compromise. This potential, in turn, stems from the fact that, contrary to a common belief, the committees are patently not microcosms of the Congress as a whole—despite the fact that the majority and minority parties are almost proportionately represented on the committees. Congress is not now and is unlikely to be a body in which disciplined majority and minority parties are pitted against each other. Rather, it is a quilt of criss-crossing ideological, regional, and interest-centered coalitions. These coalitions tend to shift from issue to issue. And, moreover, they are not necessarily represented in the committees.

The result of these conditions is that what comes out of a committee need not necessarily coincide with the preferences on an issue that may crystallize in certain coalitions on the floor. To argue, therefore, that the committees have usurped the functions of the houses, because the latter would only be duplicating the work done in committees, if they were to take their lawmaking tasks more seriously, is a spurious argument. If, as the critics complain, the committees have "usurped" the powers that rightly belong to the houses as wholes, the fault does not lie with the committee systems. Rather, it lies with those who view the legislative process as an exercise in "efficiency." There is, admittedly, no easy answer to the problem. But to justify "blind" voting on the floors in the name of efficiency is clearly counter to our model of a vigorous legislative body.

More to the point, therefore, is the committees' ability to perform the latent function of conflict resolution. There is overwhelming logical as well as empirical ground for believing that small groups are more suitable arenas than large collectivities for the negotiations and compromises that must be made in the course of decision making.[6] Not only is a committee more accessible to the interests that have a stake in legislation, but the intimacy of personal relations in the committee setting facilitates the bargaining process. This being so, relations between the committees and the houses as wholes could be enormously improved if each committee were required, in the case of controversial legislation, to issue a report, accepted by proponents of both sides of an issue (and not necessarily party sides), which would inform the houses of those compromises that have been made and the reasons for these compromises. Even if the average congressman does not and often cannot understand the technical aspects of a bill, he can be expected to understand and be highly interested in the political implications of legislative decisions.

---

[6] See Mancur Olson, Jr., *The Logic of Collective Action* (Cambridge, Mass.: Harvard University Press, 1965), pp. 53-65.

Since he is, above all, politically responsible, the least one should guarantee him is a clear statement of the political aspects of what he is going to vote for or against. His vote is a political, not a technical act. The fact is, of course, that he already relies on political advice and not on technical advice before casting his vote. However, my proposal would enable him to appraise a committee's work from the perspective that is most salient to him.

My proposal would also have the effect of restoring the legislative floor to a position of prominence, if not power, especially in the House. Once again, the political principles involved in controversial legislation could be openly and meaningfully debated, instead of being as now smuggled into the statute books. No doubt, passions would be stirred. But such stirring would once more direct the attention of the nation from the White House to the halls of Congress. And the power of the houses would be increased without detriment to the power that the committees must have to go on with their job.

The Problem of Number and Size: Magic Formulas

How many committees each house of the Congress should have, and how large the size of these committees should be, are questions much discussed, but discussed as if they were mattters of magic formula rather than of practical requirements. Too many committees is bad, it has been argued for a variety of reasons (which we need not bother with here); on the other hand, too few committees is bad, it has also been argued on a variety of grounds. Somehow, out of the wisdom which such prejudgments generate, an "ideal" number is contrived; and this number becomes a more or less hard and fast rule for relevant thought on the subject, if thought it can be called. Under the Legislative Reorganization Act of 1946, the number of standing committees was set at 15 in the Senate and 19 in the House of Representatives. Apparently, some magic formula had been satisfied. But the emergence of strong subcommittees in the years since, some of them almost autonomous of the parent committee and powerful in their own right, would seem to belie the effectiveness of trying to organize through magic formula. Organizers are often happy if things look "good" on paper. It satisfies the bosses and silences the critics, they think. But few are fooled, except the organizers themselves. The harm consists in the fact that a *strategem of* organization becomes a *formula for* organization.

Those concerned with making the Congress a viable and vigorous legislative body must beware of this kind of ritualistic thinking. For this is just the kind of thinking that plays into the hands of those who want the Congress to be a mere legitimizing agency for decisions made somewhere in the White House or the administrative departments. It neglects the true needs of the Congress. From the point of view of these needs, the number of committees as such is irrelevant. There may be few committees or many, whatever one may mean by "few" or "many." The criterion for the number of committees should be their usefulness.. By "usefulness" I do not mean "efficiency"—for a committee can be efficient without being useful—but rather its being suited to the particular substantive legislative objectives that Congress periodically faces. As these objectives change in the course of time, the usefulness of particular committees changes. Thus, it is clear that Congress must assess the usefulness of its committees from session to session—if it is to achieve the flexibility in structuring its organizational life which current or prospective developments require. For this reason, all the talk about numbers is largely irrelevant. Above all, one must beware of the assumption that because a given number of committees seems "adequate" at a given time, that number will always be adequate in the future.

It may be desirable to have more committees or fewer committees. It may be desirable to combine committees or partition them. It may be desirable to abolish old committees or create new ones. It may be desirable to elevate a subcommittee into a standing committee. But what is desirable or not depends on an appraisal of usefulness, and usefulness, in turn, due to the nature of the beast that Congress is, can refer only to political and not to administrative criteria. In other words, deciding on the number of committees is necessarily a matter of political bargaining, because politicians are likely to disagree on what is and what is not a useful committee. To turn the job over to business management consultants, as has been proposed, is an admission of congressional impotence. But this impotence is self-imposed and avoidable. I propose, therefore, that there be a biennial review of committee structures, functions, jurisdictions, workloads, and so on, by the Joint Committee on the Organization of the Congress as a permanent body, for the purpose of keeping the committee structure as flexible as possible and adjusting it, as nearly as possible, to the political contingencies of the Congress. This review should be based on the continuing survey of Congress suggested in the first section of this paper.

Magical thinking about the number of committees is even more common in connection with discussions about the size of committees. Though it is not fashionable any more to speak about the size of human groups in terms of "span of control"—long a magic formula of those addicted to models of administrative efficiency—there remains the belief that it is possible and desirable to fix some ideal size of legislative committees and subcommittees. We are told that a committee should not be too large, but that it should also not be too small. This talk barely disguises the assumption that it is possible to fix an optimum committee size, an assumption which the authors of the Legislative Reorganization Act of 1946, for instance, seem partly to have acted upon. Under the Act, all Senate standing committees, with the exception of appropriations, were given 13 members. A more variable quota was used for the House, but there, too, assumptions about optimum size were made. In part, of course, committee size in the Senate was subjected to the principle that, with certain exceptions, no senator should serve on more than two standing committees.

Yet, the important fact is that under the Legislative Reorganization Act *exceptions were* made, apparently on the contrary, though sound, assumption, that some committees need more staffing than others. For instance, Senate Appropriations was given 21 members, House Appropriations 50, House Armed Services 35, House Un-American Activities 9. These exceptions, it would seem, made more sense than the standard formula. The rigid formula has not been observed strictly in practice, but even so hampers full flexibility of numbers and party divisions. If the houses were split along the same party lines and party lines really mattered, the standard formula might serve some purpose as a criterion against which to measure deviations. But the party composition of the houses changes. Moreover, committee places must be found either for freshmen (in the Senate, on "important" committees under the "Johnson Rule" among the Democrats) or for "deserving" senior members of the minority party whose strength has been temporarily reduced as a result of election fortunes. So the numbers game—which is truly a political game—must go on, if only in order to accommodate demands for committee assignments and to make other political games possible. Hence, any rigid formula is dysfunctional, for it hampers rather than facilitates congressional adaptation to the ever changing political complexion of the two houses. It might be argued that fixed committee size—in contrast to the flexible procedure recommended here—promotes stability of membership and therefore promotes an imporant latent function. But though the argument is plausible, there is no evidence to support it. On balance, I favor adaptability over stability in this connection, trusting that committee stability can be achieved in other ways. I would suggest the general practice of having each committee recommend how large it should be:

no one is better qualified to assess a committee's work load better than the committee itself. There is no reason to believe that a committee cannot be enlarged or reduced during the course of a session, as it becomes clear just what its work load will be.

What is needed, clearly, is a continuing appraisal of a committee's workload for the forthcoming sessions. If it can be anticipated that the load of a committee will increase (which, under current conditions, can be gauged from the President's program), then its membership ought to be increased and also the number of its subcommittees, just as a committee's membership should be decreased if its workload is expected to be reduced. This, of course, touches on the problems of seniority and expertise (discussed below) and adjustments in other aspects of congressional life would be necessary. But the proposal would serve the purpose of adapting committee size to the actual work requirements of the Congress; and it would have the further advantage of not impeding the politics of committee composition along party, ideological, or any other lines of cleavage. Once a committee's recommendation is made, the Speaker and Majority Leader in the House can continue their present practice of suggesting the final sizes and political compositions of committees to the whole body for final approval. A similar process is recommended for the Senate.

The Problem of Composition:
Assignment and Seniority

I N the Congress organized according to our model, the assignment of members to the committees would be made to vary
explicitly—rather than implicitly, as is now the case—with the
particular needs of a given committee or subcommittee. Not the
least important source of the tensions now accompanying the assignment process is the discrepancy between members' expectations and
what actually occurs. As Professor Nicholas Masters has shown in
an illuminating study of the assignment process, the number of both
formal and informal criteria used is great, but they are often rather
casually or even arbitrarily used.[7] In other words, in reorganizing
the committee appointment process any mechanical formula would
be sure to fail. Rather, an effort should be made to exploit the
inevitable flexibility of the process in such a way that arbitrariness
will be reduced and functionality optimized. In short, the process
should satisfy both the aspirations of congressmen and the needs of
the committees. In some cases this may be impossible, but as our
model of Congress does not presume an ideal world, our analysis
need not concern itself with inevitable imperfections.

In fact, however, there is reason to believe that our model of
Congress does approximate to real world conditions. The criterion
probably uppermost in a congressman's mind is the question whether
his assignments will maximize his chances of re-election. One must

---

[7] Nicholas A. Masters, "Committee Assignments in the House of Representatives," *American Political Science Review*, June 1961, pp. 345-57.

incline to the view that it is in the interest of our model of a strong Congress and of the effective committee to help members in their electoral battles, since too rapid a turnover of congressmen creates discontinuities which tend to interfere with effective committee operations. But much of this aspect of the assignment process can be left to self-selection, for congressmen are likely to prefer committees whose work either harmonizes with their own personal abilities and experiences or with those constituency interests which they represent. It would be folly, therefore, to legislate into assignment practices a criterion which many believe should be mandatory—namely, that each committee's composition be proportional not only to party strengths in the houses as wholes but also to the variety of sectional, ethnic, or other interests in the two houses. As already pointed out, the conception of the committees as microcosmic replicas of the houses is not desirable as a criterion in assignments, since it would make the legislative process—negotiation, bargaining, and compromise—even more difficult than it is now.

This does not, however, preclude the criterion of balance from being used in connection with assignments to certain committees, especially those which, like the appropriations or ways and means committees, must carry the burden of congressional responsiveness to public demands or needs. The tendency to name to these committees members with seniority—that is, members from relatively safe districts—is understandable but basically undesirable. For, rather than being responsive, these members can afford to be irresponsive—being safe and senior, they can elude the wrath of the electorate. (This is not to say that these members are in fact "irresponsible" from the standpoint of some ethical norm.) But if the wishes of the electorates are to have an effect on congressional actions and decisions, not only should the members of these key committees come from districts where sanctions can be effectively imposed by the public, but the burden of their responsibility should be equitably distributed among the variety of interests that constitute the congressional quilt. In these cases, then, the balance criterion may well be in place. There are, of course, disadvantages, both of a structural and functional kind. Structurally, the tenure of committee members might be shorter and reduce the corps of experienced members available for committee work. As to functions, because shorter-term members are more likely to be subject to local pressures, there might be a tendency toward greater "public spending." Nevertheless, the proposal would aid in making such committees more responsive to public wants and prevent congressional insulation from extra-congressional political life.

Congressmen's personal preferences and committee needs would also seem to coincide in regard to the problem of providing adequate committee expertise. The congressional division of labor and ensuing specialization, one might argue, should not be directly predicated on the need for expertise. A committee should be so composed that it can bring to bear on a piece of legislation the broad views of the generalist rather than of the expert. But this argument is counter to the requirements of our model of Congress. In the latter part of this century the Congress can ill afford the amateurism that characterized the classical nineteenth century legislative assemblies, if it wishes to stand up to the professionalism of the bureaucracy. Congressional committees in the model of a strong Congress require more expert guidance than they have at present—not from professional staffs, but from their own members.

It is, of course, a moot question whether specialization makes for expertise or expertise makes for specialization. No relevant research about the interlocking of congressional expertise and specialization has ever been conducted. However, it is not implausible to assume that as a legislator comes to specialize, he tends to become an expert in his area of specialization. But this in turn presupposes that he has sufficient opportunity to become familiar with the often highly technical aspects of modern legislation. This he cannot do if his committee tenure is of short duration. From this vantage point at least, there is much to be said for retaining seniority as a criterion in guiding committee assignments. But it should also be emphasized that seniority can be regarded as only one criterion among several. Indeed, in some cases the members responsible for assignments ought perhaps deliberately to ignore it—as for instance when a senior member clearly fails to show interest in the work of a committee, or when he is blatantly incapable of comprehending the business before a committee no matter how much claim he may have by virtue of seniority for appointment to a prestigious committee.

Expertise is facilitated, of course, in those committees whose jurisdictional focus is fairly clearly defined, as in the agricultural or judiciary committees. In the case of the former, most members will come from agricultural constituencies having direct interests in the committee's subject matter.[8] In the case of the latter, most members

---

[8] See Charles O. Jones, "Representation in Congress: The Case of the House Agricultural Committee," *American Political Science Review,* June 1961, pp. 358-67.

are likely to come from the legal profession.[9] In our model Congress these circumstances of uniformity of background would be frankly recognized and taken into account in committee assignments. On the other hand, a committee like the House Committee on Education and Labor is severely handicapped by the inevitable heterogeneity of its tasks; and expertise is most difficult to come by, precisely because political considerations necessarily enter the assignment process.[10] In the case of such committees, our model of a strong Congress suggests the need for countervailing measures to reduce partisanship and ideological inflexibility.

---

[9] See Heinz Eulau and John D. Sprague, *Lawyers in Politics: A Study in Professional Convergence* (Indianapolis: The Bobbs-Merrill Company, 1964).

[10] See Richard F. Fenno, Jr., "The House of Representatives and Federal Aid to Education," in Robert L. Peabody and Nelson W. Polsby (eds.), *New Perspectives on the House of Representatives* (Chicago: Rand McNally and Company, 1963), pp. 195-235.

The Problem of Specialization:
What Price Coherence?

JUST as committees are set up to enable Congress to cope with its voluminous business and bring to bear on that business as much expertise as possible, so subcommittees are set up to divide the labor further and maximize detailed attention. In general, there is agreement that the degree of specialization and expertise mobilized through the subcommittee structure serves well the interests of both individual congressmen and the Congress as a whole. The subcommittees provide meaningful employment especially for able and aspiring junior members, permitting them to concentrate their talents on tangible tasks, and giving them a better opportunity than they would otherwise have to prove themselves.

For the Congress and its standing committees, the subcommittee structure serves a myriad of functions, of which specialization and expertise are only a part. Perhaps most important is the communication function. The subcommittee structure links the Congress with the organized interest groups which find in the subcommittees reasonably clearly marked points of access to the legislative process. It facilitates contact, consultation, and coordination with, as well as control of, relevant subdivisions in the federal bureaucracy. Lastly, it facilitates discussion in a face-to-face setting, bargaining, and compromise.

Yet, a number of apprehensions have accompanied what is often alluded to as the "proliferation of subcommittees." Some of these apprehensions are quite well articulated, others are only vaguely felt. But not all of them are equally valid from the perspective of

238

our model of a vigorous, independent Congress. Many are the apprehensions only of those who would make the Congress subordinate to the presidency. In such cases apprehension may express itself in a tendency to translate what should be a functional problem into a structural problem of power and authority. So that instead of asking, "do the subcommittees perform their functions well or not?" the question becomes, "do the subcommittees have too much autonomy vis-à-vis their parent committees or the houses as wholes, and is not congressional power too fragmented?"

The second set of questions provides its own answers because it is invariably predicated on self-answering assumptions. For instance, one assumption seems to be that Congress should somehow develop a "coherent legislative program." One supposes that by this is meant the President's legislative program, since neither the possibility nor the feasibility of a "coherent congressional program" is ever seriously proposed. But even if one were to believe that it is not the President's program that is intended but a genuinely Congress-centered program, the whole assumption of a coherent program is predicated, in turn, on the notion that coherence is attainable only through top-level coordination, supervision, and control. Even if one were to agree that a coherent *congressional* program is desirable, the facts of congressional life suggest that top-level control is most unlikely in the foreseeable future. On the contrary, if a coherent program were to emerge, it would have to result from successful bargaining and compromise between the various congressional decision centers.

But is a coherent program desirable? To answer this question, one must appreciate the unique position which the Congress occupies in the American federal system. In this system, one of the most critical functions of Congress is to represent the diverse interests and tendencies of a pluralistic society. Hence, the very notion of a "coherent program" becomes of doubtful utility, since such a program could probably only be imposed from above. And if it were to be imposed in this manner, it would be clearly in conflict with the representational requirements of a strongly centrifugal system. Whatever programs Congress comes up with, these programs must reflect the great variety of interests and preferences and demands that, like the tributaries of a river system, contribute to the main stream. The main stream has an identity of its own (and given the fact of executive ascendancy over legislation, one really need not worry too much about it). But great care must be taken to ensure that the tributaries do not dry up and deprive the main stream of its vital nurture and sustenance. It is the peculiar function of the sub-committee structure to keep the tributaries open, to see to it that fresh ideas and interests are continuously fed into the main stream. The task of Congress is not to evolve a coherent program, if by such a program is meant a plan promulgated at the top, but to facilitate the emergence of many programs in the crucible of legislation and public policy.

Once it is accepted that a coherent program is not the issue, then the question of subcommittee autonomy becomes largely irrelevant. Quite apart from the fact that the relations between subcommittees, committees, and houses vary a great deal, so that no common pattern can be easily identified, the whole view that sees Congress as a hierarchy of decision centers seems to be mistaken. A hierarchy of sorts there certainly is, but its structure defies the prescriptions of the conventional hierarchical models of organization. The advocates of establishing clear lines of responsibility between the various decision levels in the congressional web of authority-relations often talk as if the lower centers in the hierarchy were children who must be supervised, controlled, and disciplined. Just what it means to "control" a committee or subcommittee is never spelled out. And why, in a collegial body, should a subcommittee be more controlled than the leadership cadre of the houses? The Congress is not an army posts with generals, master sergeants, and privates.

Subcommittees, like any other human group, are subject to human errors and exposed to human dangers. Being small groups, they are characterized by emergent properties that are two-edged: they provide access to interests, but are therefore easily pressured; they develop informal understandings, but their points of view may be therefore parochial; they facilitate easy relations among their members, but are therefore easily manipulated by an aggressive chairman. However, and this is a point all too often overlooked in the complaints about Congress, the subcommittees are composed of congressmen, all elected to their jobs, and all not much better or worse than the American people as a whole. The issue ought not to be the authority or autonomy of these groups vis-à-vis other decision centers in the Congress, but what they make of their power. If a subcommittee, or committee, bottles up legislation for which there is strong support elsewhere in Congress, it certainly misuses its power; if it succeeds in persuading other decision points to accept its labors, its authority is well justified.

The coherence of legislative programs in a collegial body—and we would surely want to keep the Congress collegial rather than make it over into a bureaucratic structure—depends, under modern conditions, on the subcommittees' and committees' reciprocal deference to the authority of expertise.[11] The lesson to be learned, it would seem, is that the subcommittee structure should be so strengthened that each subcommittee can speak with authority in its own domain of expertise, and that the function of bringing about coherence in programs, insofar as this is desirable, can be performed through informal channels of deference and through reciprocity of expertise, rather than through central direction from the top of the congressional hierarchy.

---

[11] For an opposite view, see Clem Miller, *Member of the House* (New York: Charles Scribner's, 1962), p. 51.

The Problem of Control:
Who Shall Rule?

N O ASPECT of committee operations occasions more criticism
than what is usually referred to as the "committee oligarchy,"
which, invariably, is seen to be composed of "dictatorial
chairmen." This criticism is mainly made by advocates of the executive model because they see the committee oligarchy, so-called, as
the main obstacle to strong House leadership, anchored in a
disciplined two-party system. And they propose centralized authority
as the only effective remedy for what are felt to be the evil ways
of the committee oligarchy. What should be said here about both
diagnosis and cure can be said very simply and briefly. First, the
diagnosis is inadequate; it is usually based on the insufficient evidence of a few cases of improper chairman behavior, for the behavior of congressional chairmen has never been systematically investigated. Second, the prescribed cure does not follow from the
diagnosis but rather from the underlying premises. Internal committee democracy would seem to be at least as feasible a remedy
as centralized House leadership.

The existence of the committee oligarchy is often inferred more
from the formal privileges of chairmen than from their actual behavior. That the chairmen possess a good deal of formal authority
cannot be denied; but whether or not they make use of it in an
authoritarian manner is another matter. Until chairman behavior is
inspected more thoroughly than it usually is, a good case can also
be made out for the opposite argument. My own admittedly casual,
at-a-distance observations are that chairmen differ a great deal in

242

their ways of running their committees, and that they are by no means inevitably the oligarchs which they are made out to be. Moreover, committee and subcommittee chairmen are not invariably or necessarily the real leaders of committees; there are many important and influential committee members who are not chairmen. All of this is not to deny the presence of some chairmen who may be called oligarchs; it is to assert that the existence of a general committee oligarchy cannot be confirmed.[12]

But if we accept, for argument's sake, that under present arrangements the chairman is *potentially* an oligarch, and if we assume that oligarchial control is undesirable, we may ask what changes in the procedures are necessary to bring about a change in the substance of committee operations. Invariably, the first item that comes to mind is the practice of selecting chairmen according to seniority. The succession of the member of the majority party who has served longest on a committee is seen as the first cause of the chairman's power, for it makes it virtually impossible to depose and replace him. But does it follow that the chairman chosen on this basis is necessarily an oligarch? Clearly not. For one thing, it is much too simple to assume that the chairman will always ride roughshod over his committee. If he is a leader, then like any leader who wishes to retain his position, the chairman must ultimately have the backing of his committee and especially of his subcommittee chairmen. He may have at his disposal certain sanctions, but, given the congressional culture of mutual accommodation, he is more likely to attain his goals through persuasion and negotiation. In short, while it may be difficult to replace the chairman because of the seniority tradition, one must not underestimate the "countervailing power" that committee members have at their disposal.

What, then, of the seniority procedure itself? Is it the best way to select committee chairmen who will be leaders? Our answer must be generally negative. Seniority does not guarantee ability and competence; moreover, the procedure favors one-party areas and sectional interests, and it tends to make for political irresponsibility, to mention only a few items in a large catalogue of familiar complaints. Nevertheless, the practice is as lustily supported as it is attacked. Seniority, its defenders say, makes for committee stability and continuity, and it avoids the competition for office and resultant strife that

---

12 This appraisal agrees, I think, with the observations of Richard F. Fenno, Jr., "The Internal Distribution of Influence: The House," in Truman, *op. cit.,* pp. 55-56.

would enormously harm the atmosphere of good will and conviviality that is so essential to political relations in a collegial legislature; precisely because seniority is an impersonal criterion, it assures friendly relations and harmony within Congress.

The trouble with this argument (or should we say folklore?) is that it cannot be really disproved, for to disprove it one would have to have numerous cases of chairman selection where seniority was not the tradition. What evidence there is for the presumably harmony-creating consequences of seniority comes largely from the testimony of individual congressmen or from journalistic observers of Congress.[13] In state legislatures the question of seniority also has some influence on the selection of committee chairmen and on committee appointments, but in general plays a much less important role than in Congress, and practices vary considerably from state to state. Moreover, as far as I know, no study has ever been made of the effects of varying practices with respect to legislative harmony or disharmony.[14] My inclination is to be rather skeptical of the beneficial effects of the seniority procedure. I see no reason to believe that some form of electoral procedure, for instance—and many varieties of such a procedure have been proposed—would create such turmoil as to prevent the committees from doing their work.

After all, congressmen encounter many conflict situations in other arenas of congressional life and manage to live with each other reasonably well. As masters of bargaining and compromise, as elected politicians who must face the possibility of defeat at the polls in primaries or general elections, congressmen often find themselves in situations which make severe demands on their personal sensitivities. And, in fact, the bitter struggles that have often been waged for positions of party leadership in Congress[15] or over the composition and power of the House Rules Committee,[16] do not suggest that any detrimental consequences would inevitably follow from the competitive struggles for chairmanships if the seniority practice were abandoned.

[13] The one article devoted to the subject reports these impressions but does not really cope with the problem. See George Goodwin, Jr., "The Seniority System in Congress," *American Political Science Review,* June 1959, pp. 412-36.

[14] For a comparative study of chairman behavior in four states—California, New Jersey, Ohio, and Tennessee—see John C. Wahlke, Heinz Eulau, William Buchanan, and LeRoy C. Ferguson, *The Legislative System* (New York: John Wiley & Sons, 1962), pp. 170-92.

[15] See, for instance, Nelson W. Polsby, "Two Strategies of Influence: Choosing a Majority Leader, 1962," in Peabody and Polsby, *op. cit.,* pp. 129-64.

[16] See Robert L. Peabody, "The Enlarged Rules Committee," in Peabody and Polsby, *op cit.,* pp. 129-64.

Nor do I find much more convincing the argument that seniority guarantees the kind of experience and expertise so necessary to committee functioning. The argument is not necessarily false, for senior men may in fact have acquired much experience and relevant knowledge as a result of long service. What is wrong with the argument is that it rules out by presumption the possibility that junior men, even though less experienced, can be good committee chairmen. Moreover, the whole concept of the seniority practice seems to violate the spirit of American culture with its stress on equality of opportunity. By establishing norms that are opposed to the surrounding cultural forms, Congress isolates itself from one of the mainsprings of vitality in the American culture.

It is exactly this anomaly which is responsible for producing the kind of tensions between congressional behavior and expectations that often lie at the bottom of criticisms of Congress. Like other vital organizations in the American culture, and notably the bureaucracy where merit is an important criterion for advancement, Congress should similarly reward those members who have earned it through their achievements. Bringing into the limelight of publicity its best talent in the shortest possible time would therefore strengthen the Congress vis-à-vis the bureaucracy where talent and merit perhaps contribute more heavily to advancement. And it is with those at the top of the bureaucracy with whom committee chairmen must deal. If the bureaucrats often seem to have the advantage over their congressional counterparts, Congress need only blame itself.

However, most proposals that have been so far put forward as alternatives to the seniority system do not measure up to the requirement that the most talented members be brought to the top of the committees. Electoral processes, whether within a committee, the majority party, or the houses as wholes, do not assure its fulfillment, for elections are just as likely to result in promoting the most popular as in rewarding the most talented and gifted. Arbitrary rotation of the chairmanship among all majority party members is likely to produce even worse results than those criticized by the opponents of seniority. Appointment of those who are considered by the majority leader as being most capable is undesirable from the point of view of our model, for it would make for centralized authority sensitive to presidential pressures.

My own proposal is a radical one: abolish the chairmanships as now constituted with their familiar rights and privileges! Instead, let the housekeeping functions and the administrative work of the committees and subcommittees be handled by a "presiding officer" assisted by a competent head of staff. If this were done, we would expect that the legislative, investigative, and oversight work of the committee, and especially the work on major legislation, would fall into the hands of those who take on the responsibility of seeing to it that the work is done. In other words, the proposal would allow the committee to evolve a "natural" leadership team. This may sound utopian, but it is not. In the first place, as I have pointed out already, most committees already have such "natural" leaders who give the committee its orientation and direction. Second, precisely because the committees are in fact "little legislatures" (though not micro-replicas) whose decisions are influential in determining final legislative outcomes, abolition of the permanent chairman would increase the collegiality of Congress and give each member of Congress an opportunity to count for more than he does now. It might even serve to attract more capable people to seek a seat in the Congress.

But how to select the "presiding officer"? I would suggest this: nobody is as qualified to know about and assess the skills and competences of committee members as committee members themselves. From this it follows, clearly, that the "presiding officer" should be selected by his peers—his colleagues on the committee. And I am prepared to retract some of the negative appraisal of seniority that I expressed earlier. That is, I would say that while the present seniority system does not possess the virtues it is so often alleged to possess, it may possess *some* virtue. And one of these virtues, certainly, is the possibility that long tenure does enable certain members to acquire skills and abilities less likely to be possessed by more recent members. For this reason, I would have the presiding officer elected from among the three ranking members of the majority party, on the assumption that at least one among the top ranking members is better qualified than the rest of all the members.

Finally, I am inclined to believe that in any case the more senior members of a committee (and not just the presiding officer or leading minority member alone) have a greater need for staff assistance than the more junior members. Having been around longer, their workload, arising out of the cumulative net of connections with fellow members of Congress, with interest groups, constituents, and with departmental agencies, is likely to be heavier. I would propose, therefore, that in the assignment of staff the senior committee members, of both the majority and the minority party, be given appropriate staff help, such as is necessary and feasible.

(By way of a side remark or, rather, a side question: why should the more senior members of Congress not receive higher salaries than more recent members, as is the case in the rest of government? Just as additional staff would be a help to senior congressmen, so higher salaries would go a long way, it seems to me, in offsetting some of the pressure for becoming a committee or subcommittee chairman which currently exists under the present seniority system of succession.)

The Problem of Assistance:
The Need for Nonpartisanship

THE objection will be raised that this proposal for the abolition of chairmanships and reliance on staff for conducting the routine business of the committees will create a congressional bureaucracy with too much independence and undue influence over committee decisions and the shaping of public policies. I do not wish to minimize the weight of this objection. But I feel that if the goal of a vigorous and independent Congress is to be realized, Congress must take a chance and not be too much concerned about the possible ill effects of staff bureaucratization before they have occurred.

In fact, I do not believe that whatever ill effects may occur will be so widespread and disastrous that they cannot be remedied. Just as, at present, the internal life of different committees, the role of committee chairmen, and the power and prestige of the committees in the houses vary considerably, so we can expect that under the presiding officer and staff assistance plan the relations between staff and committee will also vary a great deal. Whether the responsible policy officials or the hired administrative officials are dominant in an organization always depends upon the kind of persons who occupy given positions and the kind of interpersonal relations that develop between them. The multiplicity of possible patterns is great. To mention just one example from another arena of government where policy officials and administrative officers confront each other, take the relationships between city councils and city managers in the hundreds of American cities which have this arrangement (and

248

which seems appropriate here because it involves small groups). Whatever the formal features of the relationship, we know that city councils and city managers meet each other in manifold ways— ranging from submission of one to the other to close cooperation, from manager withdrawal in policy matters to active initiation, and so on. I would expect that the congressional committee staff patterns under my schema would resemble such informal patterns.

From an organizational viewpoint, the possibility of genuinely complementary relationships between committees and their staffs opens up new possibilities for invigorating congressional life. Where a committee fails to produce "natural leadership" from among its members, a competent and aggressive staff can do a great deal to offset committee sluggishness. Where a committee is saddled with apparently unending routine tasks, a reliable and intelligent staff can perform many of these tasks. The staff schema will thus free the committee members for the kind of creative and innovative thinking that should be done by the committees.

The trouble with most proposals for additional staff assistance for committees is that they are predicated on the assumption that the committee structure will remain pretty much what it is. Hence, while there is usually a demand for a larger and more competent staff, and while there is even a quest for methods of integrating staff operations more fully into legislative policymaking, the benefits to be derived from merely augmenting staff assistance remain doubtful. As so sensitive and experienced an observer of Congress as Professor Bertram M. Gross has noted, increased staff assistance does not automatically strengthen the Congress vis-à-vis the executive agencies, and it does not automatically lighten the workload of congressmen.[17] In my own proposal, on the other hand, the increased staff assistance would be used in a directed manner for specific purposes. For under this proposal, congressmen would themselves do things now assigned to the staff, and the staff would do things now done by congressmen. This, it might be objected, would make the individual committee member even more anonymous than he now is and even less of a symbolic force. Perhaps. But I do not believe that the proposal would undermine the prestige of the Congress as a whole. In fact, it might strengthen it, because committee members would be doing more significant things than they do now.

In the first place, much routine committee work now absorbing a

---

[17] Bertram M. Gross, *The Legislative Struggle* (New York: McGraw-Hill, 1953), pp. 421-22.

good deal of the members' or chairmen's time—scheduling, investigation, hearings, markup, and so on—would be done by the staff, as would much of the liaison work with and the oversight of the executive agencies. The collecting, sorting, and analyzing of data and the preparation of studies and committee reports would also be staff matters in this division of labor. On the other hand, the really creative aspects of committee work, now often delegated to the staff, would revert to where they properly belong, to the committee members. Somehow the notion has developed that staffs are more competent, more expert, and even perhaps more intelligent than the average congressman. Then it is said that the task of identifying problems and suggesting policy alternatives should be preeminently a staff rather than a political function. This, it seems to me, is false. If the staffs are enlarged, as most proposals suggest they should be, and more fully integrated into the work of the committees (so that committee and staff become a team in the best sense of the word), it should be possible for the committee members to develop that broader perspective on problems, issues, and policies which a vigorous and innovative legislative body requires.

The proposal would also tend to remove some of the nit-picking criticisms that are often made of how at present staffs are used (or misused) by the committees. In a collegial committee without a permanent chairman, no staff member could become the "property" of any one member. Committee staff could no longer be used to do the chairman's case work. Moreover, because staffs would be less concerned with the policy aspects of legislation, the whole debate over whether staff members should be picked on the basis of partisan, bipartisan, or nonpartisan criteria would subside. Our model, of course, suggests the need for a politically neutral and nonpartisan staff, equally available to majority and minority party members. This objective would be attainable because the selection of staff personnel would no longer be the prerogative of a chairman or presiding officer, but would be handled by a congressional personnel office. Since a nonpartisan staff would be unaffected by shifts in the committee's majority control, it would contribute stability and continuity to routine committee work. Finally, the cooperation between the staff directors of various committees would be less encumbered by partisan considerations and would become more task- than strategy-oriented.

The debate over whether staffs should or should not be partisan, and over whether the minority party should have staff personnel of its own, has usually proceeded on the assumption that lines of cleavage in committees mostly follow party lines. They may in fact often do so, but the few solid studies made of congressional committees suggest that splits along other than party lines are also frequent. And if such non-party splits occur, with majorities and minorities emerging along ideological, regional, urban-rural, or sundry interest lines, how can these majorities and minorities have the staffs they need if the staff members are recruited along party lines? As with so many proposals for the various aspects of congressional reorganization, the demand for separate majority and minority party staffs is based on the wishful belief that Congress ought always to divide more closely along party lines, in order to facilitate what has been called "more responsible party government." But this is undesirable from our perspective, since it spells executive ascendancy over the Congress.

The Problem of Intelligence:
Scarcity or Abundance?

PROPOSALS for giving congressional committees more staff assistance are not infrequently justified in terms of the committees' lack of adequate data necessary for intelligent decision and their inevitable (but presumably undesirable) reliance for information on the administrative agencies. As is so often the case, if an alleged shortcoming is repeated enough times, first by those who claim to feel it directly, then by those to whom they complain (in this case by congressmen to each other and to the press), and then by those whose job it is to study the problem (i.e., by political scientists), the shortcoming tends to assume a reality which comes to be defined more in subjective than in objective terms. The general problem of the amount and kind of information needed by congressmen in order to do their work is being discussed elsewhere in this symposium. As far as committees are concerned, my own impression is that the problem has been exaggerated or, to put it better, that the accent has been usually placed on the wrong aspect of the problem. The problem, it seems to me, is not one of scarcity, but of an abundance of information, most of which remains unassimilated and undigested.

As one peruses the hundreds and thousands of committee hearings and committee reports on every conceivable topic of public interest, one is appalled by the huge bulk of information that comes to congressional attention. In any case, whether abundance or scarcity prevails, I am not aware of any scientific study ever having been attempted to test either allegation. Of course, all this is not to say that committees should not have at their disposal all the background material and immediate data necessary for arriving at a considered judgment. But to say this is largely platitudinous. For all the information that comes in, from whatever source—the administrative agencies, interest groups, disinterested scholars, or the Congress' own Legislative Reference Service—is of no avail if it is not collated and digested.

I find it rather interesting that congressmen simultaneously complain about lack of information and about their inability to keep up with the information they do receive. It would seem to follow, then, that congressmen do not receive the right kind of information. But what is the right kind of information? Here, I think, one must be rather hard-nosed. Whether one likes it or not, whether congressmen like it or not, the fact is that "objective" information, so-called, has only marginal utility in committee work. For congressmen, being human, act like humans: they take positions first and seek to back them up with data and rationalizations later on.[18] This being so, what congressmen in committee need is information that supports their positions and seems to confirm the rationality of their actions.

Having made this perhaps startling statement, I would like to retract somewhat and elucidate the point. It must be viewed in the context of my general emphasis on the fact that individual congressmen are different from each other, and that the various committees are also different from each other. Therefore, while I think it is correct to say that most people most of the time seek information to reinforce their own predetermined positions, there are, of course, exceptions. And certainly there are well-known exceptions where congressmen have genuinely sought very specific information about highly complex economic and technical matters, about matters of vital interest to their constituencies, and about departmental operations, on which they had open minds, or were at least ambivalent. It is for these congressmen, in particular, that the Congress should provide the necessary means, discussed elsewhere in this symposium, to satisfy their thirst for factual knowledge, in order to facilitate their efforts at diagnosis and prognosis of problems.

Some of the criticisms that have been leveled against committee hearings as information-gathering devices seem to miss the main point. For instance, the fact that hearings sometimes assume the

---

[18] For congressmen's confessions on this point, see Charles L. Clapp, *The Congressman—His Work as He Sees It* (Garden City, N. Y.: Doubleday & Company, 1964), p. 303.

character of a court of law with its adversary system of seeking the truth is often criticized. Actually, hearing the pros and contras on particular issues is probably more useful to a committee member than lengthy reports from administrative agencies, interest groups, or scholars which pretend to objectivity. Available evidence indicates that committee hearings reach their high points of usefulness if and when committee members themselves participate in the hearings in a variety of active roles, notably those of protagonist and antagonist.[19]

Insofar as hearings are the main avenue by which committee members inform themselves, their various functions should be clearly differentiated. My concern here is not with those functions of hearings, whether legislative or investigative, which Professor David B. Truman has identified as "propagandistic" and "safety-valve" functions.[20] Rather, my concern is with the communication function of hearings. Two types of hearings can be distinguished—those designed to produce technical information and those designed to produce political information. It has been argued that if the purpose is purely technical, experts from the agencies or interest groups should be invited to testify, and no others. But experts and technicians are often notoriously unable to communicate their knowledge, and to place restrictions on the kind of witnesses who should testify strikes me as altogether useless. Moreover, more often than not, we have the spectacle of experts—all equally well-trained and well-informed— testifying on opposite sides of a question. The committee member exposed to this spectacle is more likely to discount expert testimony altogether than to be impressed by it. Similarly, the sheer repetition of much expert testimony stifles rather than excites the member's interest. There is good reason to believe that committee members prefer succinct resumés of arguments pro and con on a bill by those who can speak with the authority of a department or organization behind them.

Proposals to make legislative committee meetings and hearings resemble fact-finding procedures, such as those which have been developed in investigative or oversight situations, are ill-conceived. They ignore the fact that Congress is above all a political body—that its vitality and maintenance as an independent branch of the government depend on its successful performance of its political func-

---

[19] See the study of the Senate Committee on Banking and Currency by Ralph K. Huitt, "The Congressional Committee: A Case Study," *American Political Science Review*, June 1954, pp. 340-65.

[20] David B. Truman, *The Governmental Process* (New York: A. A. Knopf, 1951), p. 372.

tions. Congress needs help in keeping informed; but the information must be adapted to the most relevant needs of congressmen and committees—in other words, political needs. Hearings, other impressions notwithstanding, are the most effective devices for committees to inform themselves in a *political* context. This is not to say that committee hearings should not be improved. Certainly, many of the criticisms that have been made—the badgering of witnesses beyond what a fair adversary system would permit, the tendency to limit the scope of hearings, insufficient planning, hearing the same witnesses over and over again, preventing junior members from playing an active role, and others—should be remedied. But to reduce hearings to a kind of directors' meeting that benignly and passively listens to experts, bureaucrats, technicians, engineers, and so on, is counter to our model of the Congress as a strong, independent legislative and representational body.

Conclusion

IT HAS BEEN my purpose in this paper to review, from the perspective of a model that envisages a strong and independent Congress in a governmental system of checks and balances, a number of problems faced by congressional committees; to analyze, from the same perspective, just what is problematic about these problems; to evaluate and criticize, again in terms of the model, some of the assumptions and proposals for committee reforms made by advocates of other models; and to present, on the basis of our model, certain propositions and recommendations about committee behavior under varying conditions. It has not been my intention to exhaust all possibilities, but rather to be suggestive. The important point to be made, in conclusion, is that, hopefully, the propositions and recommendations that were made here are in accord with the basic assumptions of a model for a strong and independent Congress. Even if they are so outrageous as to remain unrealized, it is my expectation that they can and will serve as criteria against which to assess changes that may occur in the congressional committee system, regardless of whether they are purposefully instituted or spontaneously created in the course of events.

DR. JAMES A. ROBINSON is Professor of Political Science at The Ohio State University. A former Congressional Fellow of the American Political Science Association, he is co-author of *National and International Decision Making* (1961) and author of *Congress and Foreign Policy Making* (1962), and *The House Rules Committee* (1963), as well as numerous articles and chapters in both scholarly and popular publications. His studies of policy- and decision-making processes have emphasized the close relation between the ways in which decisions are made and their content and effects.

In addition to his academic research, Dr. Robinson has been a consultant to various business, governmental, political, and private organizations. Some of the recommendations in this paper were first presented in his testimony before the Joint Committee on the Organization of the Congress in June 1965.

Decision Making in Congress

James A. Robinson

Introduction*

AMONG the primary responsibilities of Congress is to check and balance effectively the other two branches of the nation's government. Two major theories prescribe ways of guaranteeing checks and balances between Congress and the executive.[1] The first theory, which stems from the Constitution itself, assumes the need for independence—even for some competition—between the legislative and executive branches.[2] The second theory is the newer doctrine of party responsibility, which has developed since

---

* Perhaps a few personal remarks may be conveyed by means of a footnote. I am not a frustrated victim of a Senate filibuster; I do not have a pet bill pigeonholed in the House Rules Committee; I am not suffering from a Discharge Petition signed by a majority of the members of the House. Although I am a "liberal Democrat," my purpose in contributing to this symposium on Congress, like that of my fellow participants, arises out of my occupation as a political scientist. Because of the continuing improvement in the caliber of political analysis, political scientists can now adopt a professional attitude that differs from their citizen attitudes. As private citizens, we speak from personal concerns; as political scientists, we speak from the perspective of the specialized knowledge that we possess, and can demonstrate, about the subject under discussion. Our responsibility is, therefore, to report objectively the knowledge that we have accumulated about Congress and its implications for congressional reorganizations. The burden of my essay is to emphasize the need for finding legislative procedures that will better inform Congress and provide it with a more coherent view of the relations among public policies.

[1] James A. Robinson, *The House Rules Committee* (Indianapolis: Bobbs-Merrill, 1963), pp. 110-11. Permission to re-use some of this material was granted by the publisher.
[2] Charles S. Hyneman, *Bureaucracy in a Democracy* (New York: Harper, 1950), pp. 38-74.

259

the adoption of the Constitution to fulfill the need for a continuous and open opposition to the government.[3]

The first theory postulates a bargaining process in which congressional leaders check and balance and control the leaders of the executive; the second theory postulates a polyarchal process in which the electorate controls and checks *both* congressional and executive leaders through the responsible parties.[4] The theory of legislative independence conceives of Congress as a bipartisan body in which the leaders of the two parties align themselves to form a check on the executive. In contrast, the theory of party responsibility, by seeking to promote party competition as the chief means for checking the government (that is, the President plus the majority party in Congress), cuts across the constitutional division of power. Hence, whereas legislative independence stresses the importance of Congress as a governing institution, party responsibility emphasizes the political parties as vital checks on government.[5]

Adherence to the theory of legislative independence is the major theme of the articles contributed to this symposium. The doctrine of party responsibility, on the other hand, because it envisions a leadership centered upon the presidency, embodies the "executive model" of government—to which the majority of contemporary political scientists now subscribe. During recent years the responsible party system has shown signs of taking root on a nationwide scale. The Democratic and Republican National Committees, for example, are contributing to some nationalization of politics;[6] so also are the high costs of campaigns and of coverage in the national media of communication.[7] It is now possible for a Salinger from Virginia

---

[3] Austin Ranney, *The Doctrine of Responsible Party Government* (Urbana: University of Illinois Press, 1954, 1962); James McGregor Burns, *Deadlock of Democracy* (Englewood Cliffs, N.J.: Prentice-Hall, 1963).

[4] Robert A. Dahl and C. E. Lindblom, *Politics, Economics and Welfare* (New York: Harper, 1954).

[5] Samuel P. Huntington asserts that "party responsibility" reforms would strengthen Congress rather than the presidency, just the opposite of the intended effects. This is an intriguing interpretation, one I have not seen advanced elsewhere. Regrettably, Huntington's essay did not elaborate the argument in any detail. "Congressional Responses to the Twentieth Century," in David B. Truman (ed.), *The Congress and America's Future* (Englewood Cliffs, N.J.: Prentice-Hall, 1965), p. 27.

[6] Cornelius P. Cotter and Bernard C. Hennessy, *Politics Without Power* (New York: Atherton, 1964).

[7] Alexander Heard, *The Costs of Democracy* (Chapel Hill: University of North Carolina Press, 1960).

to run for the Senate in California, and for a Kennedy from Massachusetts to be elected in New York. In 1965 the House Democratic caucus actually disciplined two members who did not support the 1964 presidential ticket.

Nevertheless, the essentially decentralized character of the American party system remains an obstacle to its further development. "Responsible parties" on a national scale are still a long way from actuality. And so, by extension, is political party government—at least, after the example of the British system, which is usually regarded as the prototype of what political party government should be like. For the present, therefore, it is clear that the traditional concept of legislative independence continues to be the relevant theory on which to base an evaluation of Congress' capacity to check and balance the executive.

Essential to the larger objective of the check-and-balance mechanism is the operation of Congress as a constructive or positive instrument of national policy. Congress can, of course, always check the executive and judiciary by negative acts; that is, by merely amending or legitimating their decisions. However, we naturally expect Congress also to balance the other two branches by proposing its own original, creative solutions to both old and new problems. Thus, any appraisal of the effectiveness of Congress must necessarily include an assessment of its effectiveness in contributing major decisions of government policy.

The Decline of Congress
in National Policymaking

THE historical record of Congress' effectiveness as a check-and-balance instrument and as a creative mechanism in making public policy is eminently clear. Much as we may regret to acknowledge it, political scientists agree that congressional power has been steadily declining relative to the power of the executive.[8]

A survey of the relative importance of Congress and the presidency as initiators of legislation between 1880 and 1945 can be extrapolated in graph form from Lawrence Chamberlain's study of 90 bills enacted during that period. (See figure p. 264.) The major trends are clearly discernible. Prior to 1900, Congress was the primary initiator. Then, beginning with the presidency of Theodore Roosevelt in 1905, its initiative declined sharply. A gradual in-

---

[8] Lawrence Chamberlain, *The President, Congress, and Legislation* (New York: Columbia University Press, 1946); David B. Truman, *The Congressional Party* (New York: Wiley, 1959), pp. 1-7; Samuel P. Huntington, "Congressional Responses to the Twentieth Century," in Truman, *The Congress and America's Future, op. cit.,* pp. 5-31.

With respect to foreign policy, see James A. Robinson, *Congress and Foreign Policy Making* (Homewood, Ill.: Dorsey, 1962), pp. 1-69.

With respect to atomic energy, see Harold P. Green and Alan Rosenthal, *Government of the Atom* (New York: Atherton, 1963), pp. 21-25.

With respect to defense and military policies, see Raymond H. Dawson, "Congressional Innovation and Intervention in Defense Policy: Legislative Authorization of Weapons Systems," and Lewis Anthony Dexter, "Congressmen and the Making of Military Policy," both in Robert L. Peabody and Nelson W. Polsby (eds.), *New Perspectives on The House of Representatives* (Chicago: Rand McNally, 1963), pp. 273-304, 305-24.

crease in the initiative occurred until 1925, another high peak of congressional initiation. In 1930 Congress' activity dropped off again and remained relatively low until the end of the period. By contrast, the presidency was inactive as an initiator of legislation through 1930; its role took a strong upturn during the early 1930s, slackening off by the end of the decade. Corresponding with the decline of Congress and the emergence of the presidency respectively as an initiator of legislation during the thirties is an overlapping trend of an increase in joint initiation by Congress and the presidency that persisted into the forties. An extension of Chamberlain's study from 1945 to 1965 would show that this collaboration has now yielded to virtually exclusive initiation by the executive.

The decline in congressional power has been especially acute with respect to its innovative or creative contributions to public policy. Needless to say, individual congressmen and particular committees have frequently introduced new legislation over the opposition or the neutrality of the executive. Such events, however, are exceptions to the rule; [9] and the rule is aptly summarized in the shopworn phrase "the executive proposes and Congress disposes." Today legislation usually is drafted in the executive branch and is introduced by committee chairmen or other members in Congress. (The House Ways and Means Committee, in drafting tax legislation on the basis of executive recommendations rather than working from an executive draft, constitutes a rare exception.) [10] Moreover, it is not uncommon for administration personnel to attend executive sessions of congressional committees when the committees' final decisions on the form and text of a bill are taken. Nor is it considered inappropriate for a committee to clear a report with the relevant executive agency before printing and circulating it to the rest of Congress.

Not only are the technical drafts of legislation usually prepared in the executive branch, but the strategic agenda of both House and Senate is largely determined by the President's State of the Union Message and his special messages throughout the year. To be sure, temporary factors in Congress may affect niceties of actual timing; for purely tactical considerations, for instance, the Rules Committee may prefer to consider one bill before another, or the leadership

---

[9] James A. Robinson, *The Monroney Resolution: Congressional Initiative in Foreign Policy Making* (New York: Holt, 1959).

[10] Everett Cataldo, *The House Ways and Means Committee*. Ph.D. dissertation (The Ohio State University, 1965).

ORIGINS OF LEGISLATION—CONGRESS AND THE PRESIDENCY

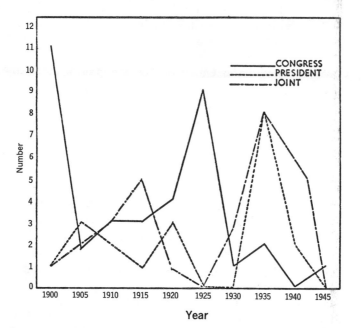

Source: Lawrence Chamberlain, *The President, Congress, and Legislation* (New York: Columbia University Press, 1946).

Reproduced from James A. Robinson, *Congress and Foreign Policy Making* (Homewood, Ill.: Dorsey, 1962), p. 9, with permission of the publisher.

may decide to call up a bill out of order.[11] Even in such tactical decisions, however, White House congressional liaison officials collaborate with the majority leaders and the whips in scheduling bills and producing compromises between the different interests represented in the legislature.

How does one explain the decline of congressional initiative in policymaking? Why is it that most of the initiative for dealing with public problems now emanates from the executive?

Much of the decline must be attributed to the profound change in the requirements of public policymaking, and to the failure of Congress to alter its organization to cope with the new demands made upon it. Public problems have grown both more numerous

---

[11] Robinson, *The House Rules Committee, op. cit.,* pp. 1-42.

and more complicated. However commonplace this observation may be, its implications are staggering. In his widely praised address on economic myths at Yale University in 1962, the late President Kennedy recalled that during the first century of the Republic legislators dealt with only a few perennial problems. Speaking of nineteenth-century statesmen, he said: "They and their contemporaries spent entire careers in grappling with a few dramatic issues on which the nation was sharply divided—issues that often occupied attention for a generation at a time: The National Bank, the disposal of the public lands, nullification or union, freedom or slavery, gold or silver." In our time, however, the agenda of Congress is not so stable. New problems arise constantly, and the agenda of one Congress is usually quite different from that of the next.

As problems proliferate, the amount of information required as a basis for making policy decisions also radically increases. In consequence, no legislator today can be an expert on more than a few policy issues. Effective and influential legislators who are successful in obtaining passage of their bills are those who carve out for themselves a particular subject on which they become expert. (The same is true in the state legislatures, where most congressmen acquire their first political and parliamentary experience.)[12] Each committee and subcommittee of Congress always has some members who are specialists in the field concerned, as well as a few senior members possessing long records of relevant experience.

Arriving at creative decisions on public problems demands something more than knowledge of the particular subject in hand. What is primarily required is combining bits and pieces of information on many different subjects, or relating what is known about one aspect of a problem to what is known about relevant aspects of other problems. Inventive problem solving requires, in a word, *integrative*

---

[12] Donald R. Matthews, *United States Senators and Their World* (Chapel Hill: University of North Carolina Press, 1960), pp. 92-117; Charles L. Clapp, *The Congressman: His Work as He Sees It* (Washington, D. C.: The Brookings Institution, 1963), pp. 23-24.

John C. Wahlke, Heinz Eulau, William Buchanan, and LeRoy Ferguson, *The Legislative System: Explorations in Legislative Behavior* (New York: Wiley, 1962), pp. 193-215; James David Barber, *The Lawmakers: Recruitment and Adaptation to Legislative Life* (New Haven: Yale University Press, 1965), p. 209.

Malcolm Jewell, *The State Legislature* (New York: Random House, 1963); William J. Keefe and Morris S. Ogul, *The American Legislative Process: Congress and the States* (Englewood Cliffs, N.J.: Prentice-Hall, 1964), pp. 482-87.

solutions.[13] The decentralized character of Congress, however, does not lend itself to the ready integration of specialized knowledge—indeed, some of its subcommittees are so autonomous that their decisions are rarely reviewed, much less reversed, by their parent committees.[14] Moreover, the knowledge of a few individual experts is an insufficient foundation for public policy decisions; for most of its necessary basic data, Congress is in fact heavily dependent upon executive sources of information.

Because it is organized more or less bureaucratically, the executive branch is, by contrast, in a much better position not only to absorb and comprehend vast amounts of data, but also to marshal the information in the manner required by its leadership for policymaking.[15] The Bureaus of the Census and of Labor Statistics, and other intelligence agencies of the executive, regularly gather huge numbers of facts on innumerable subjects. Many of these data are made public. But only the President, through the centralized agencies like the Bureau of the Budget, has the means at his disposal to receive and to use information so that he can arrive at a picture that resembles an integrated view of the demands the country faces. It is well known that before any proposals of an executive agency can be submitted to Congress, they must be cleared by the Bureau of the Budget, where they are evaluated in relation to the President's program.[16]

The need for the integration of knowledge in policymaking (and the consequent superiority of the executive in this respect) becomes very clear once we have in mind a model of the process of policymaking. The model used here describes the process in terms of seven major kinds of activity that are performed in the making of any decision.[17] The first of these activities is *intelligence gathering*, which includes both collecting information that suggests a problem for

---

[13] Consult the work of Herbert A. Simon and his colleagues on decision making and problem solving. For example, "The Decision Maker as Innovator," in Sidney Mailick (ed.), *Concepts and Issues in Administrative Behavior* (Englewood Cliffs, N. J.: Prentice-Hall, 1962), pp. 66-69; and James G. March and Herbert A. Simon, *Organizations* (New York: Wiley, 1958), pp. 173-210.

[14] Richard F. Fenno, Jr., "The Appropriations Committee as a Political System," in Peabody and Polsby, *op. cit.,* pp. 79-108.

[15] See Kenneth Janda's essay in this series.

[16] Richard E. Neustadt, "Presidency and Legislation: The Growth of Central Clearance," *American Political Science Review,* 48, 1954, pp. 641-71; "Presidency and Legislation: Planning the President's Program," *ibid.,* 49, 1955, pp. 980-1021.

[17] Harold D. Lasswell, *The Decision Process* (College Park, Md.: Bureau of Governmental Research, 1956).

attention and assembling the data necessary for the formulation of alternative solutions. The second activity is the *promotion* of one or more possible alternatives. The third phase is the *prescription* or enactment of one among the several alternative solutions proposed. The fourth is the *invocation* of the adopted solution; and the fifth is its *application* in specific situations by executive or enforcement officers. The sixth stage of the decision process is the *appraisal* of the effectiveness of the prescribed solution, and the seventh is the *termination* of the original policy adopted. The last two stages present an opportunity to reevaluate the policy and to consider whether new problems which might require new decisions, have arisen since or as a result of its enactment. And then the whole process may begin again.

To assess the weight of the influence that Congress exercises within the total government policymaking process, it is necessary to identify which of these stages are normally performed by legislatures rather than by executives. The main responsibilities of legislatures pertain to the intelligence-gathering, promotional, prescriptive, and appraisal phases of the decision-making process. In fact, however, Congress is probably less influential in each of these four phases than it was, say, 50 years ago. And this is particularly true, of course, in the sphere of intelligence gathering.

It is not known what Congress' primary sources of information were at the beginning of this century, but as already noted it is clear that today its primary source is the executive branch. Indeed, Congress has no independent information sources. To be sure, its committees hear interest-group representatives, and some individual congressmen consult academic scholars or experts from research institutions. But its own research arm, the Legislative Reference Service, relies upon executive agency publications for information; most of the data in reports and studies for the legislative committees are from, and most of the bibliographic references are to, these sources. Such powerful and esteemed committees as the House Appropriations Committee borrow executive employees, including F.B.I. men, to investigate executive proposals and performance. Executive witnesses usually testify first at hearings on any bill or resolution. And anyone who has observed committee hearings must have noted the difference in the attendance of congressmen when a cabinet Secretary or the Joint Chiefs of Staff testify and when private or non-governmental groups testify.

Many people have commented on the "information revolution"

of the twentieth century.[18] The effects of this revolution are in turn revolutionizing the nature of governmental policymaking. Although executive decision making has not yet been successfully reduced to highly rational, computational techniques (even by Secretary McNamara's "Whiz Kids"), it is now possible to compare various proposed means to achieve given ends much more precisely than 50 years ago.[19] As a result, the guesswork and intuition usually required to supplement inadequate information about a problem have been appreciably reduced. But it is the executive branch, not Congress, that has taken advantage of the new information techniques; and in so doing, it has gained the advantage over Congress throughout the entire policymaking process.

Because of the proliferation of problems, intelligence gathering and analysis has become the central element in policymaking: on its successful accomplishment depends the success of the other phases of the process—especially the generation and promotion of alternative solutions. Because of its superior information resources, the executive branch is in a preferred position to identify problems and to formulate possible solutions for them. This is the reason that it can organize the agenda of the government's overall policy program, including even the timetable of the legislative branch. And indeed one notes Congress' own complete acceptance of executive superiority in this regard. Increasingly congressmen, including their leaders, expect the executive to assume initiative both in proposing problems for attention and in finding solutions for them. Democrats, for example, complained that Dwight D. Eisenhower was not a "strong President" who gave "leadership" to the legislature. The tendency of Congress to look to the executive for leadership is now endemic throughout all fields of government policymaking (although, of course, it is particularly acute in the field of foreign affairs, where the executive has always had a constitutional advantage that the information revolution has only enhanced). Thus Congress' role is steadily becoming less and less one of initiating policy alternatives and more and more that of modifying, negating, or legitimating proposals that originate in the executive.

Congress suffers, then, from a severe information disadvantage

---

[18] E.g., Kenneth Boulding, "Decision-Making in the Modern World," in Lyman Bryson (ed.), *An Outline of Man's Knowledge of the Modern World* (New York: McGraw-Hill, 1960), pp. 418-42.

[19] On the application of new decision-making techniques to military policy, see Charles J. Hitch, *Decision-Making for Defense* (Berkeley: University of California Press, 1965).

compared to the executive, and as a consequence it is frustrated in obtaining a comprehensive analysis of public policies so that it can estimate the effects of one program on others. We need to consider ways to offset or to overcome these handicaps. In inventing legislative reforms, and in assessing their significance, it is useful to do so for each of the major stages or phases of the governmental decision procss in which Congress participates: namely, for the *intelligence, promotional, prescriptive*, and *appraisal* stages. Our consideration of possible changes in legislative organization as regards decision making, therefore, concentrates on these four stages.

Information and Policy:
Improving Facilities
For Intelligence Gathering

ONGRESS needs two kinds of information: that which applies
to current matters demanding immediate attention, and that
which applies to issues likely to emerge in the future. It
is a common weakness of organizations, both large and small, to
concentrate on problems at hand and to take little thought of the
morrow. Moreover, organizational decision makers typically adhere
to the obverse of Benjamin Franklin's advice; namely, they never
do today what they can do tomorrow. Nevertheless, the consequences of today's actions, or inactions, often determine tomorrow's
possibilities of maneuver and decision. It is useful, therefore, for
bodies like Congress to organize themselves in ways that anticipate
the future, or at least some aspects of it, and to prepare for problems lying beyond the horizon.

Measures to improve the flow of intelligence to Congress would
undoubtedly help both in making current decisions and in planning
for future ones, though care should be taken not to overload the
organization with more information than it can process effectively.

Considerations of staffing

The first recommendation that must occur to anyone, whether he
be a congressman or an observer, is to increase staff available to
individual members and to committees. Few members of the House
of Representatives have professional staffs because the daily de-

mands of answering mail, caring for constituents' Washington problems, and managing ordinary office duties exhaust most of the financial resources. By the time a congressman hires a sufficient number of secretaries, receptionists, robot typewriter operators, and authorities on the politics and problems of his district, he has few dollars available for employing a legislative assistant who can help him with his committee work and other policy interests. And not only is there a severe dollar limitation for representatives, but there is also an acute shortage of space. Despite the recent opening of a new building, quarters remain cramped, and it is not uncommon to find that in a busy office the congressman no longer has any privacy, because he has given over part of his own room to an assistant. The disappointments associated with the construction of the Rayburn Building may make some members chary of voting for more House office space. But if more legislative assistants are to be added to the staffs of representatives, then the Rayburn Building will need to be followed by more buildings named in honor of former Speakers or other distinguished members.

Senators are handicapped less seriously. Their smaller number, their more adequate quarters, and their larger budgets provide for some legislative assistance as well as for the familiar battery of secretarial and clerical help. Senators can assign their legislative assistants first to one policy problem and then to another. If these overburdened people are not equally prepared to deal with all possible issues, at least they give the senator a personal and private adviser not available in most House offices. To say that senators have the advantage over representatives is not, however, to deny that senators also need and deserve supplementary assistance. Their statewide constituencies require more extensive concern than the smaller House districts.

Congress should, therefore, allocate a larger budget and more space facilities to both senators and representatives so as to enable them to augment their personal staffs. And it should take the necessary measures now rather than introduce them piecemeal over the next few years.

The rationale for providing members with policy advisers on their individual staffs is that at present most congressmen, especially House members, are dependent upon their own experience and wisdom. They have no immediate, confidential counsel to help with the vast array of issues that confront them. To be sure, on issues before their respective committees, advice and assistance may be obtained from the committees' staff. But, on other issues, the members may be without counsel. Moreover, their need for counsel and assistance intensifies as the amount of information required to handle public problems increases.

It is a commonplace, however, to say that Congress should have more staff. The subject deserves to be discussed with more explicit reference to the kind of personnel required. Congressmen and their committees need assistants whose qualifications complement their own strengths and weaknesses. Legislators are typically lawyers or businessmen, with a few farmers, physicians, and teachers.[20] Scientists, whose occupational specialties are increasingly relevant to national policy, are rarely elected. Thus, Congress does not possess expertise on atomic energy, chemical warfare, biological evolution, pollution, water desalinization, public opinion surveying, and information retrieval equal to its expertise in law, taxation, investments, agriculture, and banking. What is primarily required, therefore, is staff who can furnish Congress with the scientific and technical knowledge that the elected politician seldom brings with him to Washington.

While inventing ways to augment intelligent resources, one should not overlook the fact that some members of Congress are reluctant to increase the size of the committee staffs. My impression is that opposition in the House to augmenting the number of legislative assistants comes more from "conservative" members than from "liberals." Part of this opposition stems from the fact that conservatives assume, and probably rightly, that with more policy advisers more new proposals will be promoted and government activity will extend further into various domains of public policy.

A partial answer to this bias against increasing intelligence facilities is to suggest that conservatives themselves need help in constructing their alternatives to liberal proposals. The recent efforts of Representatives Gerald Ford, Melvin Laird, and others to develop the Republican alternatives to Democratic programs attest to the value of increasing the scholarly competence of the staff of the minority leader.[21] Even if the Republican leaders have not so far been successful in defeating Democratic proposals, they have at least sharp-

---

[20] Donald R. Matthews, *The Social Backgrounds of Political Decision-Makers* (New York: Random House, 1954), pp. 28-32; also see Heinz Eulau and John D. Sprague, *Lawyers in Politics: A Study in Professional Convergence* (Indianapolis: Bobbs-Merrill, 1964).

[21] Charles O. Jones, *Party and Policy-Making: The House Republican Policy Committee* (New Brunswick, N. J.: Rutgers University Press, 1964).

ened and clarified alternatives and have given a constructive character to the minority party's positions.

The controversy over minority staffing is not surprising in view of a congressman's natural ambitions for power. Information is a source of power, and the majority understandably wishes to restrict the minority's chances to acquire power, even though it knows that it may itself some day be the minority. Undoubtedly, a sense of fairness has mitigated the demand for power in certain committee majorities, and some of them have been much fairer to the minorities than others.

It is not fairness, however, that constitutes the most compelling argument for providing minorities with a staff almost equal in numbers to that of the majority. The best argument is that the improved performance of the minority members helps to strengthen the legislative way of life. If the majority party becomes increasingly aligned with the executive branch (as is not impossible and is certainly in accord with the hopes of the "party responsibility" and "executive force" schools), then we must look to the minority to check the majority and in so doing to provide the necessary legislative counterbalance to executive power. Hence, generous allocations of minority staffings are essential to the normative theory of Congress that this symposium articulates.

Changes in the Legislative Reference Service

Any discussion of staffing inevitably turns to the justly famous Legislative Reference Service in the Library of Congress. The LRS has at its disposal the world's greatest library facilities, yet these advantages together with its close proximity to the Halls of Congress have not made it an outstanding research organization. To be sure, a few distinguished scholars reside on its staff, men who have contributed to their scholarly and scientific disciplines as well as to the intelligence of Congress. On the whole, however, LRS has not been as useful or as esteemed among congressmen as one might expect.

The difficulties of organization currently confronting the Legislative Reference Service are several. To begin with, "the organizational norm" seems to be that the Service has 535 bosses. One effect of this is that some of its scholars are reluctant to commit themselves on controversial matters, which in turn compromises the documents prepared by the Service and gives them a pallid style and an unimaginative content. The norm undoubtedly also enters into the recruitment of personnel, and inhibits the employment of "political types" whose special scholarly competences might be of extraordinary help to the legislative body. Partly as a result of its anonymous and non-political character, the Service has failed to develop close ties with more than a handful of congressmen. Hence, it is often asked for information much too late for it to do the intensive job for which it is certainly equipped. Nothing more than "off the top of the head" documents can be expected if the LRS is called upon to prepare these the night before a bill comes up for vote.

An effective way to offset these failings would be to politicize the service by giving it a separate Democratic party division and a Republican party division. Each party would then be entitled to appropriate a number of qualified LRS researchers for its own exclusive use. Both groups of researchers would be authorized and requested to prepare materials on issues that they anticipate will arise without awaiting a formal request from a member of Congress. They certainly should not feel any compulsion to pull their punches but should frankly assist the parties in their partisan arguments.

Another failing of the Service is that it is less helpful on scientific matters than on other kinds of issues. Yet, as is now widely acknowledged, science is of increasing importance to Congress, as to the whole society. Matters of atomic energy, weapons technology, health, and space exploration—all these and other aspects of the information explosion are giving rise to legislative issues on which Congress needs much more specialized assistance than is typically available in LRS.

It is clear, then, that the Service's scientific personnel needs to be appreciably increased. Recent developments are encouraging, but it is too early to evaluate the creation of the new office of technology. In testimony before the Joint Committee on the Organization of the Congress, I recommended that the Library award a number of non-renewable fellowships of approximately three years' duration to young scientists, and equip them with laboratory and other research facilities. This was meant as an effort to attract promising scientists without depriving them of their professional accoutrement. Professor Duncan MacRae of the University of Chicago suggested to me a less costly variation on this idea, that the Service award fellowships not to young scientists but to retired ones. Men who have completed their laboratory, field, or experimental work and are now in their years of reflection presumably would not need the extensive equipment and other supplementary facilities required by their younger colleagues. The fellows, whether young or old, would, of course, be available to members of the House and Senate on the same basis as advisers and researchers in other divisions of the Legislative Reference Service.

A substantial number of congressmen take periodic surveys of the opinions and attitudes of their constituents on current issues.[22] The most common form of congressional survey is a mail questionnaire. Some members send mimeographed sets of questions to every constituent whose name they can find in voter registration books, city and county directories, telephone listings, and their own correspondence files. Others "sample" these sources by polling every fifth or tenth name. Many congressmen take great pains in wording the questions and in drawing a sample, in a conscientious effort to obtain a valid and reliable profile of their constituents' policy preferences. Others, however, use polls, especially questionnaires, simply as one more means of placing their own names before the voters, and have little concern for actually informing themselves about the views of their districts.

No one can, or should, prescribe for what purpose congressmen question their constituents. This depends on the "role" that a congressman adopts for himself. Members assume different kinds of roles,[23] and the particular role taken determines the way in which a member relates to his district, and therefore how seriously interested he is in having trustworthy polls.

Among those members who actually want to know what their constituents think, few are trained to construct samples and design questionnaires. Their administrative assistants usually have only a rudimentary knowledge of surveys, and few members can afford to hire private consulting and opinion survey experts. Congress should authorize the Legislative Reference Service to make available two or three technical specialists in the use of survey methods and in the interpretation of survey results. Members of Congress, of course, will decide whether and when and about what issues they want to send questionnaires to their constituents, but they should be able to obtain expert assistance in selecting samples, wording questions, and analyzing results.

Other information sources

The proposals so far discussed apply principally to furnishing congressmen with resources for dealing more effectively with current

---

[22] James A. Robinson, "The Social Scientist and Congress," in Roger Fisher (ed.), *International Conflict and Behavioral Science* (New York: Basic Books, 1964), pp. 267-68.

[23] Raymond Bauer, Ithiel de Sola Pool, and Lewis Anthony Dexter, *American Business and Public Policy* (New York: Atherton, 1963).

problems on its daily agenda. Several measures can also be introduced to improve Congress' facility for long-term planning.

One of the easiest and least expensive ways of enlarging legislative perspectives on the world is foreign travel.[24] Regrettably, congressional trips abroad have frequently been pejoratively dubbed as "junketeering," even, by such scholarly and usually sympathetic organs as *Congressional Quarterly*. If arguments are needed or precedents required to justify foreign travel for legislators, they are readily at hand. It is not uncommon in the commercial worlds of business and finance to send top level officials abroad to enhance their understanding of current markets and of future opportunities. Similarly, in the Foreign Service, officials are regularly rotated between various overseas assignments for many reasons, among them the belief that experience in different climes and places broadens the perspectives of Foreign Service officers and prevents their becoming victims of the ideology or interests of particular locales.

Because the United States possesses bales of local currency, resulting from our foreign aid programs and Public Law 480, congressmen could travel extensively at virtually no new expense. These local currencies, which are partly under U.S. authority, can pay the travel and local living expenses for most of the trips that congressmen would take. For reasons that need not concern us here, these moneys are not being used now, and as they exceed any sum that is ever likely to be spent, they should be put to a constructive use such as this. When local currencies are unavailable, Congress ought not to be reluctant to provide the requisite dollar appropriations.

Currently a congressman's foreign travel is usually arranged for him by the legislative liaison office of the Department of State, and transportation is often provided by the Department of Defense in Air Force planes. This places congressmen in the debt of executive departments and at the mercy of the perspectives of their executive hosts while abroad. Congress ought not to be dependent for its travel facilities upon the agencies that it intends to check and balance. Instead it should establish its own travel office, and use Air Force accommodations only as a last resort. Because the government subsidizes airlines, congressmen could justifiably travel at reduced

---

[24] Ithiel de Sola Pool, "Effects of Cross-National Contact on National and International Images," in Herbert C. Kelman (ed.), *International Behavior* (New York: Holt, Rinehart and Winston, 1965), pp. 108-29; Bruce M. Russett, "International Communication and Legislative Behavior: The Senate and the House of Commons," *Journal of Conflict Resolutions*, 6, 1962, pp. 219-307.

fare, just as executive personnel presently travel at less than full fare on subsidized railroads.

Another useful measure would be to provide each member with an annual allowance budget of, say, $1,000 for the purchase of books, reports, and other published materials. Although the Government Printing Office makes available to Congress virtually unlimited copies of its many publications, and Congress can readily command many of the other materials published in the executive branch, members have no funds allocated to them for the purchase of non-governmental publications. A congressman can quickly requisition an annotated copy of the Constitution published by the Government Printing Office, but he must pay out of his pocket for privately and commercially published volumes and reports of interest to him. To be sure, these can be borrowed from the Library of Congress, if they are not in great demand, but personal copies cannot be obtained.

From time to time a few committees have commissioned non-governmental consultants to prepare reports for them. For example, the Senate Foreign Relations Committee twice engaged experts from universities and other research institutions to study special topics. Other committees have also on occasion commissioned outside research assistance. Congress' use of outside assistance, however, is paltry compared to that of the executive branch. The Air Force has long retained the RAND Corporation, not so much to advise it on immediate problems as to anticipate future concerns of the defense establishment. In addition, the executive departments have the financial resources to engage consultants from outside the government on a *per diem* basis. Virtually no such resources are available to Congress. It would be worth experimenting with a provision that any member of Congress could call on the expertise of non-governmental bodies at rates commensurate with private consultation fees. The experiment would determine the extent of demand, and give individual congressmen the opportunity to learn whether this sort of arrangement facilitates their work.

Another possibility for enlarging the opportunities for Congress to obtain outside counsel is the public commission. The President frequently appoints commissions to investigate and recommend on such matters as civil rights, health, crime, smoking, sex discrimination, etc. No reason exists to inhibit Congress from establishing similar commissions, which would report either to particular committees or directly to the Speaker and the Vice President.

Promotion of Policy:
Improving Capacities
For Evaluating Alternatives

ONE of the consequences of the proliferation of information is the generation of alternatives for dealing with problems. Integrating information and evaluating alternative solutions constitute the second phase of the decision activity in public policy-making. Congress, however, usually does not integrate its specialized knowledge very well, and it seldom promotes new and creative alternatives. In this section I shall review several possible measures that might help Congress to overcome its difficulties in these respects.

One proposal that has received considerable support is the creation of a National Security Committee that would combine consideration of foreign policy and defense policy,[25] which has been endorsed by the National Policy Machinery subcommittee under the chairmanship of Senator Henry Jackson. A National Security Committee could take one of two forms. It might be a non-legislative committee that would include the leaders of the present committees on Armed Services, Foreign Relations, and Foreign Affairs plus the elected floor leaders in the two houses. Or, alternatively, it might replace the present committees. In either case, its purpose would be to provide

---

[25] An early recommendation to this effect was made by Harold D. Lasswell, *National Security and Individual Freedom* (New York: McGraw-Hill, 1950), pp. 106-08. More recently, a Brookings Institution report also advocated it: *United States Foreign Policy Compilation of Studies,* prepared under the direction of Committee on Foreign Relations, U.S., Congress, Senate, 87th Congress, 1st Session, March 15, 1961, pp. 791-989.

foreign and defense specialists in the House and Senate with opportunities to combine and integrate foreign and military policies.

Because military and foreign issues intersect, it would seem eminently reasonable that they be considered in relation to each other. Nevertheless, my own view is that the idea of establishing a new committee in foreign and defense affairs should be approached with circumspection. To begin with, the form of the committee will, to a large extent, determine the likelihood of its achieving its purpose. For example, if it is to be conceived of as an additional committee whose work would merely supplement that of the present committees on Foreign Relations, Foreign Affairs, and Armed Services, then it will probably not be successful. Senators and representatives frequently complain that their full schedules do not permit them to attend all their present committee meetings. If attendance on a new committee is added to their current duties, they will be forced to neglect other assignments. Moreover, if this committee is primarily a discussion committee and not a legislative committee, members would understandably ignore its activities.

If, on the other hand, the National Security Committee were to stand in lieu of the present committees, it would not impose additional demands on committee attendance. More importantly, it would then be an active legislative committee, not just a talking one. Members who serve on it would, therefore, soon come to have a much more integrated and comprehensive view of foreign and military policies than they now possess. However, a committee that combined the jurisdictions of the existing Senate and House Committees on Foreign Relations and Armed Services probably would not contain all the members who presently serve on these committees. If some members were "bumped" from their current assignment on either the foreign or defense committees, the total number of senators and representatives closely acquainted with the details of these issues would thus be appreciably reduced.

This is a possible outcome that cannot be considered desirable. One of its consequences would be to undermine legislative-executive consensus on foreign and military policies. In my studies of Congress and foreign policymaking, I have found that, in the aggregate, members who are satisfied with their information and contacts with the Department of State are more sympathetic with its policies. Satisfaction with information partly depends upon the availability of channels for the exchange of information between the executive and Congress. If these channels are closed to a number of members, I would expect legislative-executive consensus on foreign policy to decline. Second, because exchange of information is particularly important in maintaining bipartisan congressional support for foreign policy, I personally would view such a consequence with misgivings. Members of the President's party in Congress have the pull of party to encourage them to support the administration's decisions. But bipartisan support requires the sharing of information with members of the minority who especially would be affected by a reduction in the number of members concerned with foreign and military issues if the present committees were replaced by a new committee. Thus, a National Security Committee could achieve a successful integration of the congressional viewpoint on external affairs only at the expense of bipartisanship in foreign policy. If I am right in this prediction, we will have to choose whether we want more integrative policies and a little less bipartisanship in Congress or less integrative policy and more bipartisanship.[26]

Policies other than those pertaining to foreign relations and national defense also fall within the jurisdiction of more than one committee and need to be better integrated than is presently the case. Fortunately, the Joint Committee on the Organization of the Congress is considering the problem of the overlap, and also the serious gaps affecting fiscal and monetary policies that have been left by the diverse work of the Banking Committee, the revenue committees (Finance in the Senate, Ways and Means in the House), and the Joint Committee on the Economic Report.

Another example of hit-or-miss, unintegrated policymaking concerns education. The Department of Defense, through its research and development programs, probably puts more money into universities than does the Office of Education. In addition, the Department of Agriculture, the National Science Foundation, the National Institutes of Health, and other agencies spend funds and make policies for research and teaching. Federal aid to education has been introduced through the back door and without much attempt by Congress to relate these disparate and sometimes conflicting efforts to each other. Now that the President has given the Secretary of State a veto over federally sponsored research in foreign countries, still another executive department is making decisions about research programs in educational and other knowledge-producing institutions. Nor are government policy decisions the only ones to affect education; the philanthropic foundations through their vast funds have a pro-

---

[26] Robinson, *Congress and Foreign Policy Making, op. cit.,* pp. 182-90; 199-201.

found influence on the nature of educational programs. Yet neither the House nor the Senate education groups has shown any interest in foundation actions; and a series of special and select committees have investigated philanthropies without touching on their educational policies.[27]

One sphere in which a semblance of policy integration exists is in decisions about the national budget, that is, in the appropriations committees. In many instances, members of a subcommittee of the Senate Appropriations Committee are also members of the corresponding legislative committee; and the parent committee itself holds frequent sessions, particularly with regard to the annual foreign aid appropriation. However, it is the House Appropriations Committee that is preeminent in most money matters, and it unfortunately shows few of the signs of integrative policy appraisal exhibited by its Senate counterpart. It is an "exclusive" committee, and none of its members serve on legislative committees; moreover, its subcommittees are highly specialized and each subcommittee, out of concern for its own autonomy, zealously respects the other subcommittees' independence.

Some of these divisive tendencies cannot be overcome easily. They might, however, be attacked indirectly. The annual budget, for instance, need not be regarded as sacrosanct. If anything, it is an anachronism. It became a convention when forecasting capacities were less sophisticated than they are now. If Congress would require the executive to submit a two-year budget instead, it could take greater care in examining government estimates and appraising the relation between proposed expenditures and expected policy results.[28]

One method of integrating the diverse work of all the congressional committees is to centralize the party leaderships in both houses. The Legislative Reorganization Act of 1946 originally provided for the establishment of both policy and steering committees under party leadership, but these have not developed as the Committee on Reorganization hoped. The House eliminated policy committees from the Act, although House Republicans have since created a relatively active policy committee. The Senate later established its own. Leaders often regard these committees as threats to their preeminence, whereas in fact they could be used to strengthen personal

---

[27] John Lankford, *Congress and the Foundations in the Twentieth Century* (River Falls: Wisconsin State University, 1964).

[28] More explicit budget reforms are contained in Aaron Wildavsky's essay in this series.

as well as party leadership.[29]

An example of what can and should be done was established by the experience of Lyndon Johnson when he was Senate Majority Leader in the late 1950s. Johnson assembled a staff of approximately 50 professional people. He was able to do this because he chaired numerous committees and had multifarious responsibilities assigned to him. He drew on professional staff from his office as a senator from Texas, from his office as Majority Leader, from his office as head of the majority policy committee, from his office as the chairman of the Subcommittee on Preparedness, and from still other offices. The Senate provided him with this help not because he was Majority Leader, but because of his separate responsibilities. With the aid of this staff, to which he distributed assignments not on the basis of the source of their salary but on the basis of his daily requirements, he gave unusual leadership to the Senate. It was probably the nearest thing to centralized leadership ever seen in Congress.[30] Unfortunately Johnson's methods have not been continued by his successor, nor has his example been emulated in the House of Representatives. It is precisely this style of leadership, however, that makes it possible for senators to act as members of the Senate and representatives to act as members of the House of Representatives. For such leadership contributes to a comprehensive view of policy and to the integration of decisions throughout the different committees. The lesson is clear: to achieve more leadership of this caliber, the leaders must be assigned more staff.

As far as the House is concerned, the history of Congress surely demonstrates that as much as the House opposes autocratic leadership (witness the House's "overthrow" of Speaker Cannon), it also demands strong leadership. And as Congressman Kenneth Hechler has shown (in his description of the period when Speaker Cannon was dethroned), the case against Cannon was founded not so much on procedural grounds as on the fact that members did not like the policies he advocated.[31] Had Cannon been a more progressive leader, it is doubtful whether he would have been stripped of his power to appoint the Rules Committee and dominate the agenda of the House.

[29] Jones, *op. cit.*

[30] Ralph K. Huitt, "Democratic Party Leadership in the Senate," *American Political Science Review,* 55, 1961, pp. 333-44; Robinson, *Congress and Foreign Policy Making, op. cit.,* pp. 194-96, 214-16.

[31] *Insurgency: Personalities and Politics of the Taft Era* (New York: Columbia University Press, 1941), pp. 31, 38; also see William R. Gwinn, *Uncle Joe Cannon: Archfoe of Insurgency* (New York: Bookman Associates, 1958).

In recent years we have witnessed a partial restoration to the Speaker of some of the formal powers that he once held. The checks and limitations now put on the House Rules Committee provide an instance of this. In themselves, however, they do not arm the leadership with the necessary means to integrate actions of the various committees.

An effective way of forcing on the party leaders the responsibility for integrating the work of committees and introducing some "rational" order for taking up committee work would be to remove all decisions concerning the agenda of the House from the jurisdiction of the Rules Committee. The party leadership would have to assume responsibility for determining when bills will be debated by the House and in what order. The Majority Leader would move the adoption of a special order. In the Senate the leaders already perform this function by asking unanimous consent; and if 100 men can set their agenda by unanimous consent, surely the House of Representatives can at least operate under majority rule.[32]

The centralization of party leadership in both houses carries one risk to the maintenance of legislative independence. If the Speaker or Minority Leader should be too much "the President's man," the congressional point of view would be tempered. However, a number of institutional safeguards exist, and are likely to continue, that insure an autonomous legislative leadership. Among these are the partial separation of congressional and presidential elections, which helps to insulate members from dependence on the President for re-election. (Should House terms be lengthened to four years and scheduled between presidential elections, this insulation would be further strengthened. But if terms were scheduled simultaneously with presidential elections, it would be destroyed except for a few senators and some representatives from safe, one-party areas.) This means that the congressional party leaders must bargain with relatively independent committee chairmen and other influential individual congressmen as well as with the President. In any case, the risk entailed in strengthening House and Senate leaders is nothing compared to the dangers of weakening them; if the Speaker and Majority Leader are without staff, they will depend increasingly upon the White House Congressional Liaison Office, as Speaker John McCormack and Majority Leader Carl Albert have done.

[32] Robinson, *The House Rules Committee, op cit.,* pp. 123-27.

Prescription of Policy:
Improving Procedures for
Selecting and Voting Alternatives

THE prescription stage of the decision process refers to the procedures by which decision makers select one alternative from among those that are available. I shall begin by discussing the pros and cons of introducing a system of electrical voting into Congress, a proposal that has been enthusiastically viewed in many quarters.

Electrical voting is used in several state legislatures and foreign parliaments. It promises certain conveniences for congressmen. For instance, a member could vote by remote control if for any reason he could not be in the chamber. And this in turn, besides reducing the time previously consumed in calling the roll, would permit committees to meet or individual members to work in their offices while the vote proceeds. The 20-minute round trips between offices and chamber could thus be dispensed with entirely.[33]

Convenience and timesaving are, however, only two criteria by which to evaluate the proposal. It is at least as pertinent to ask what are its implications for a legislative model of government, as opposed to an executive model. The effects doubtless depend in part on the rules governing its use and the occasions or circumstances in which it is employed.

I confess to a long-standing fear of electrical voting, an appre-

---

[33] Kenneth Janda describes details of machine voting in his essay in this series.

284

hension that stems from a tour of the Louisiana State Capitol when I was a high school senior. Not only are votes displayed in the legislative chambers, the boards are also in view in the Governor's office. They were installed there by Huey Long, and if a member cast his vote contrary to the wish of Governor Long, word went out to liaison officials on the floor to have the legislator "correct" it. The possibility of having a voting board in the White House or anywhere outside either the House or Senate is hardly consistent with the ideal of an independent Congress.

It is not unlikely, however, that such a duplicate board might be placed in the offices of the Speaker and the Minority Leader. (Because the Senate is smaller, the necessity or temptation for the leaders to have their own boards might not be so great.) Whether this would increase the power of the leadership over individual House members is not clear. At present on crucial roll calls, the leaders may obtain switches from members who are willing to go along with the leadership if their vote will make the difference, but who would prefer to take another position. Electrical voting might make leadership control more efficient, although less circumspect.

The ambiguity embodied in current practices may mean less efficient (i.e., successful) control for leaders, but it also means easier compromises, accommodation, give and take. Politicians usually are thought to be less rigid in their opinions privately than publicly.[34] The more formalized and public procedure becomes, the fewer possibilities exist for resolving conflicts of interests between a large number of parties.

One of the problems with electrical voting is to decide upon the length of time the boards are to remain open. Under present procedures, the presiding officer has some personal discretion about when to announce the end of the vote and can, by long counts or short, influence close votes. Although these occasions are rare, they are dramatic and important. Among the most famous instances was Speaker Sam Rayburn's timing of the announcement of the end of the vote on the extension of the Selective Service Act in 1941. Had Mr. Rayburn closed the vote either sooner or later than he did, his bare winning coalition for extension of the Act might easily have

---

[34] *The Private Papers of Senator Vandenberg* (Boston: Houghton-Mifflin, 1952), p. xx; Dean Acheson, *A Citizen Looks at Congress* (New York: Harper, 1956), pp. 70-71; Jack Sawyer and Harold Quetzkow "Bargaining and Negotiation in International Relations," in Kelman (ed.), *op. cit.*, pp. 491-92.

lost. He always regarded his judgment of that day as his most important parliamentary decision.

Before Congress adopts this procedure, the consequences of which are hardly foreseeable, I would recommend that a survey be taken of the experience of the state legislatures. Alternatively, or in addition, the House or Senate might experiment with using such electrical voting for one session, and then reconsider whether it wants to use it permanently.

Perhaps the most notable characteristic of the prescription stage of decision making as practiced within Congress is that it is easier to defeat a bill than to pass one. This is, of course, a feature of any institution that takes decisions by recorded votes and according to complicated parliamentary procedures.[35] Proponents of a particular piece of legislation must win at every stage of the prescription process; opponents need only defeat the proposal at any one of a number of crucial choice points, and the bill is dead. Thus, for the affirmative side of any legislative struggle, victory must be won and re-won, but for the negative side success may be had at almost any stage in the act of prescription. In Congress, the opposition's stronghold may be a subcommittee or perhaps a full committee. Then the bill must clear the Rules Committee, if it is a House bill; or it must be scheduled by the Majority Policy Committee if it is a Senate bill. Even after a bill is reported out of committee or approved by one of the scheduling committees, the leadership must call it up for debate. And, in the Senate at least, a bill that is debated is not necessarily guaranteed a vote. Even in the act of voting, however, amendments and motions can create further obstacles that successful passage must hurdle.

These innumerable legislative hurdles confer an advantage on those who would oppose congressional initiatives in offering and selecting alternative solutions to public problems. John Stuart Mill would have justified this parliamentary condition on the ground that the business of a legislature is as much to prevent the passing of bad laws as it is to pass good laws. Nevertheless, it is hard to justify a legislative process that contains a built-in and perpetual bias in favor of negative action. In equalizing the opportunities for initiative in Congress, one does not have to take the converse position that legislative proposals ought to be allowed to pass simply

---

[35] Duncan Black, *The Theory of Committees and Elections* (Cambridge: Cambridge University Press, 1958), pp. 230, 232; Kenneth J. Arrow, *Social Choice and Individual Values* (New York: Wiley, 1963), p. 95. Robert Bendiner, *Obstacle Course on Capitol Hill* (New York: McGraw-Hill, 1964), pp. 15-31; Robinson, *The House Rules Committee, op. cit.*, pp. 10-16.

because they are regarded as innovative.

It is this consideration, as much as any other, that argues for relaxing certain of the restrictive procedural rules now governing the House and the Senate. In the House the diminution of negative power is already underway, with the recent reforms in the Rules Committee—that is, its removal from participation in decisions on conference reports by the House. Complete removal of the Rules Committee from agenda-setting decisions in the House would further equalize the forces of initiative and opposition. Another helpful measure would be to reduce the number of signatures required on House petitions to discharge committees. During the era of the New Deal, when there were large Democratic majorities in the House, the number was raised from 145 to 218, in order to strengthen the hand of the President.[36] It was assumed that the Roosevelt Administration could control enough members of its own party to prevent untimely (from its point of view) bills from being brought to the floor by determined anti-administration coalitions.

In the Senate there has already been some relaxation in the size of the majority required to vote cloture, and further restrictions on the possibilities of filibustering probably should be taken. Although in recent years Senate filibusters have been broken with relative ease, they still give significant advantage to an entrenched minority opposition, especially during the closing days and weeks of a long and exhausting session. One possibility, in the way of a partial reform, is to relax the discharge and the cloture restrictions during the last six months of the calendar year. This would overcome the end-of-session advantage that at present normally accrues to the opposition in legislative struggles.

I wish to conclude this section with a proposal that calls for research first and action later. I refer to the need for a special study of certain House and Senate rules, especially those governing voting on amendments. Parliamentary procedure has long been a favorite topic among lawyers, politicians, and mathematicians. Lewis Carroll, author of *Alice in Wonderland,* applied mathematics to various voting schemes in an effort to develop fair and rational procedures. Recently a few political scientists, with the necessary training in modern mathematics, have begun examining parliamentary procedure from new perspectives. As a result, occasional "irrational procedures" or "intransitivities" in voting rules have been uncovered. One such

---

[36] Floyd M. Riddick, *Congressional Procedure* (Boston: Chapman and Grimes, 1941), pp. 271-300.

discovery was a House rule that permits no more than four motions to amend a clause in a bill or resolution.[37] The rules are now such that there may be one less vote than there are amendments. Consequently, it is possible for an amendment to be adopted that is not the majority's first preference. Although precisely the same situation does not occur in the Senate, the rules committees of both houses should undertake an examination of their respective rules of procedure to see whether similar anomalies exist that should be eliminated.

---

[37] William H. Riker, "The Paradox of Voting and Congressional Rules for Voting on Amendments," *American Political Science Review,* 52, 1958, pp. 349-66; also see the same author's "Voting and the Summation of Preferences: An Interpretative Bibliographical Review of Selected Developments During the Last Decade," in *ibid.,* 55, 1961, pp. 900-11.

Appraisal of Policy: Improving Capacity for Reviewing Effects of Policy and Policymaking Procedures

THE appraisal stage of the decision process is the evaluation of the relationship between the intentions of a policy and its actual effects. In addition, appraisal also entails the continuing monitoring of the effectiveness of the decision process itself. Therefore, we should also take into account the congressional function of "oversight" and supervision of the administrative process in the executive branch.

Congress is not only a lawmaking institution; it also contributes to temporary resolution of conflicts and is responsible for legitimating executive decisions. As more and more legislation becomes "administrative law," and Congress faces the inevitable decline of its lawmaking power, it ought seriously to consider taking on new activities with respect to other basic political functions.[38] One way in which Congress might enhance its role in the total governmental enterprise is by increasing its appraisal activities.

To be sure, the various executive agencies are required to make periodic reports to Congress on their work and with reference to particular laws. Nevertheless, the great volume of these reports have become *pro forma*. In the absence of complaints from interest groups, these reports are unlikely to receive much attention in either the

---

[38] Huntington, *loc. cit.*

House or Senate. Debates and speeches in both houses have long constituted occasions for individuals or small groups of legislators to air their views on important public problems. The "special orders" in the House make provision for members to speak at the end of the day, but attendance is invariably small. Visitors to the Senate gallery are often struck by the disparity between the number of senators who listen to a "major" address and the attention it receives in the next morning's newspapers. Consequently, few of these debates are really debates, that is, exchanges of points of view between contending interests.

I think it would be useful for both the House and the Senate to *experiment* with a parliamentary procedure, not unlike that used in certain other national legislatures, whereby a resolution would be offered for debate but without any legal consequence, not even so much as a joint or concurrent resolution. Subjects of the debate would be confined to a topic or a series of topics that the leaderships of the two parties agreed to be of national scope and importance. Such debates might then provide occasions for reviews of the administration of particular public policies, or appraisals of problems on which Congress contemplates eventual legislation.

In this connection, we should mention the familiar proposal for a "question period" modeled after that of the House of Commons. A number of difficulties obviously stand in the way of successfully implementing such a procedure. First, no secretary of any department is responsible to Congress but solely to the President. Second, possible competition between the House and Senate for the attendance of a cabinet official might lead to unfortunate consequences. Third, the question period would serve no useful purpose, in view of the elaborate system of committees that supervise and maintain oversight over the various governmental departments, agencies, and bureaus.

Much more important than calling upon the secretaries or other executives to answer questions is creative thought-provoking debate among senators and representatives. These debates could highlight issues that the executive prefers not to raise, and provide for the executive explicit guidelines on the intent of Congress. At present, the intent of Congress is often solely that of a committee, as expressed in a committee report. Such reports may or may not be carefully examined by other members of Congress, but they surely do not express a corporate view of the House or of the Senate. On the other hand, debates in which a reasonable number of members participate ought to go far toward establishing something like a congressional point of view.

Investigating committees, whether standing committees or special or select ones, are likely to become increasingly important. Given the change in the balance of power between Congress and the executive, they are an obvious means for Congress to increase its participation in the appraisal of national policy. I would emphasize that certain rules of procedure that are widely regarded as fair and legitimate ought to be introduced by Congress for the conduct of its investigation. Both the House and Senate have been shamed into gradually reforming their investigative proceedings as a result of a good deal of public criticism of both houses, following the spate of investigations during the 1950s. The rules that most need to be applied pertain to the rights of witnesses, both private and public. The guidelines for the development of these rules might be the extension to legislative inquiries of the "due process" concept that governs judicial inquiry.

In addition to appraising policies and their administration, Congress is also charged with assessing the organization and decision process of the executive branch. This is one of the matters on which Congress retains some of its former power vis-à-vis the executive.[39] Studies and recommendations such as those made by the Jackson Subcommittee on National Policy Machinery exercise considerable influence on the way in which policy is made by the executive. Although the relationship is not one-to-one, we assume that the process of making policy affects the substance of policy. If Congress would take advantage of this special influence over the executive, it would make gradual improvements in the policymaking machinery throughout the government. To help it perform this task, Congress could avail itself of a large body of extant research and of the services of social scientists skilled in the necessary organization theory and techniques.

To give just one example of what I have in mind, consider the problem of executive planning. It is a common lament among the executive departments that their personnel lack time to plan, to see the forest instead of the trees. Congressmen often echo this lament as they review executive decisions and see the consequences of failures to look ahead and to consider the long-range implication of short-term decisions. Why should Congress not, then, raise its

---

[39] Robinson, "The Social Scientist and Congress," *loc. cit.*, pp. 269-70; Robinson, *Congress and Foreign Policy Making, op. cit.*, pp. 105-06, 114-15.

objectives from the criticism of day-to-day decisions, on which it often has little information, and concentrate on finding organizational devices to encourage the executive to plan ahead in such a way as to represent the kind of values Congress favors? The simplicity of the question cannot be matched by any simple answer. It does suggest, however, an opportunity for Congress to be at once innovative and constructive instead of merely reactive and critical. Moreover it would give Congress the chance to be influential where its strength is greatest, in overseeing the organization of the executive.

Conclusion

WHAT if Congress doesn't reform? If no changes are made in the status quo, we can expect a continuation in the decline of Congress as an effective check-and-balance instrument and in its innovative role in policymaking. If anything, the present trend is likely to become still more pronounced.

The best support for this prediction is supplied by the experience of governments in other countries. In no nation is the legislature as powerful as it is in the United States. The "Mother of Parliaments" is now grey and dependent upon the ministries. In France the National Assembly has yielded its power to the leadership of de Gaulle. In what are referred to as "the developing nations" one-party systems have been established; even where the semblance of parliamentary machinery is maintained, the center of actual decision making is a single-party dictatorship under the Head of State.[40] And in countries in which the tenure of the executive is short and unstable, the cause of the turnover is seldom a powerful legislature.[41]

The conditions that account for this almost universal decline in the power of the legislative branch of government are everywhere the same: the increasing number of problems combined with the ever growing complexity of the information required to deal with them. Moreover, these conditions may be expected to intensify in the

---

[40] Arthur S. Banks and Robert B. Texter, *A Cross-Polity Survey* (Cambridge: MIT Press, 1963), pp. 97-101, 110-11.

[41] Bruce M. Russett and Hayward R. Alker, Jr., Karl W. Deutsch, and Harold D. Lasswell, *World Handbook of Political and Social Indicators* (New Haven: Yale University Press, 1964), pp. 103-04.

293

future: we cannot anticipate fewer public problems or that information will become any less complex. Hence, unless new ways of strengthening parliamentary competence can be invented and implemented, the outlook for the survival of independent legislatures is pessimistic.

In 1939, the President's Commission on Administrative Management declared, "The President needs help!" and his office was strengthened. In 1966, Congress needs help, and that institution can and must be strengthened. Changes are likely to be incremental rather than sweeping, but that is characteristic of democratic decision making.[42] If Congress will act now, however, the House and the Senate can renew their historic contributions to the check-and-balance system and to creative policymaking.

---

[42] C. E. Lindblom, *The Intelligence of Democracy* (New York: Free Press, 1965).

EDWARD DE GRAZIA, Washington attorney and writer, holds A.B. and J.D. degrees from the University of Chicago, and is a member of the American Bar Association and the Federal Bar Association. He has contributed to *Law and Contemporary Problems, Columbia Law Review, George Washington Law Review, Evergreen Review, New Republic, New York Times Book Review,* and others. He has served with the office of Director General of UNESCO in Paris and consulted with the Agency for International Development and The President's Interagency Committee on Youth. He is research associate to Georgetown University Law Center's Institute on Criminal Law and Procedure and associate Fellow of The Institute for Policy Studies, Washington, D. C.

CONGRESSIONAL LIAISON
An Inquiry Into Its Meaning For Congress

Edward de Grazia

Introduction

A FUNDAMENTAL inhibition is preventing congressmen today from approaching the question of their liaison with the executive branch of government in such a way as to maximize their influence over the administration of the programs which they enact into law. This inhibition seems to stem largely from the mistaken belief that the constitutional doctrine of the separation of powers precludes their participation in, as opposed to review of, the executive branch's administration of the laws.

The system of the separation of powers in government seems to have been instituted by the Founding Fathers so that the legislative and executive arms would constantly check and balance each other. Underlying its institution was the classic fear that without a check-and-balance mechanism one arm would naturally come to dominate the other and the people would be exposed to the excesses either of unrestrained legislative rule or of unrestrained executive rule. It is no doubt chiefly because "separation" seems so far to have successfully warded off these twin evils that the doctrine today is regarded with a respect amounting to awe.

Awe of constitutional doctrine has perhaps led contemporary congressmen to overlook the fact that the Constitution itself contains no provision that actually precludes Congress from participating in the administration of the laws. At the time of the Convention, the concept of administration as we know it, did not exist. The President was assigned "the executive power" and instructed to "take Care that the Laws be faithfully executed." The Congress was given "all legislative powers" and the power "to make all laws . . . for carrying into execution" its powers as well as the powers of "the Government of the United States," and of "any Department or Officer thereof." The (substantive) executive power vested in the President was a whittled-down version of the King's power, as described by Blackstone, while his mandate that the laws be faithfully executed was designed to insure that he *enforced* the laws, and did not dispense with any, as had been the custom of certain of the English Kings. The terms "administration" and "execution" are not synonymous, although historical changes and loose constitutional interpretations have tended to blur the distinctions. The original meaning of the term "execute" is also suggested in the provision empowering the Congress to call "forth the Militia to execute the Laws of the Union." If administration is conceived to include rule-making, regulation, and enforcement functions, the Constitution seems to have intended to assign the first and second of these to Congress and the third to the President. Madison and Hamilton, in *The Federalist Papers,* were under no illusion concerning the honest import of the "separation of powers" doctrine, which they traced to Montesquieu: "There can be no liberty where the legislative and executive powers are united in the same person, or body of magistrates, or, if the power of judging be not separated from the legislative and executive powers." But this "did not mean that these departments ought to have no *partial agency* in, or no *control over,* the acts of each other." It was only "where the *whole* power of one department is exercised by the same hands which possess the *whole* power of another department, [that] the fundamental principles of a free constitution are subverted."

To make explicit a basic premise of this paper, Congress has as much right to participate in the administration of the laws as it has in their formulation. Indeed, it has the right to participate in each stage of the life of a law or program—before, during, and after its enactment. Under the terms of the Constitution, it takes the Congress and the President together to enact a law that launches a program of administration; but either, to the exclusion of the other as well as together, can formulate the law which determines the program, administer the law, review the law's wisdom or effectiveness, compose the law's reform or amendment, or let it wither away.

Thus the congressional role with respect to the business of administration is in no way legally confined, as is often supposed, to the work of reviewing *post facto* the activities of the executive departments. Such *post facto* review is what is generally meant by "oversight," the term presently favored by political scientists and congressmen alike, to describe the congressional task in administration. But as Cornelius Cotter points out in his comprehensive study of the subject,[1] historically "oversight" has always meant more than mere review.

A second premise should now also be made clear: Respect for the constitutional doctrine of the separation of powers does not entail Congress placing undue self-restraint upon the exercise of traditional and legitimate prerogatives concerning the administration of the laws it has helped to pass, and the oversight of the agencies it has helped to create. Excessive self-restraint of this kind might work towards upsetting the balance of powers and tip the scales irretrievably in favor of the executive arms. This is a possibility which is particularly to be guarded against today. For if Congress has been inhibited by regard for constitutional doctrine from participating in the business of administration, the executive branch for its part has shown little sign of being deterred by a similar regard from participating in the process of legislation. On the contrary, observers are agreed that a growing proportion of programs now being enacted into law has its origin not in Congress but in the executive, and that this trend is likely to become more pronounced in the future.[2]

In such circumstances, it seems all the more essential for it to be widely appreciated that Congress has a legitimate, even an indispensable, function to perform in the administration of the nation's laws and programs. Oversight of the executive is not only the right of Congress, it is also a duty enjoined upon it by the nature of the administrative process itself. Administration is neither a simple nor

---

[1] Cornelius P. Cotter's contribution to this symposium, "Legislative Oversight," shows that with respect to administration the congressional role can range from "direct legislative conduct of the business of government" to *post facto* legislative review of the conduct of administrative agencies.

[2] For an elaboration of this point see the contributions to this symposium by Cornelius P. Cotter, James A. Robinson, Lewis Anthony Dexter, and Alfred de Grazia. Elsewhere consult: Daniel Berman, *In Congress Assembled* (New York: Macmillan, 1964); Donald C. Blaisdell, *American Democracy Under Pressure* (New York: Ronald Press, 1957); Bertram M. Gross, *The Legislative Struggle* (New York: McGraw-Hill, 1953).

an automatic business. It is packed with opportunities and demands for exercises of discretion, on the part of the agency and administrative personnel involved, which should be made politically accountable as far as possible.[3] And the greater the degree of authority given to the agency under the terms of the law enacting a particular program, the greater is the duty of Congress to participate in and supervise the agency's decisions.

It is in the context of this understanding of the role of Congress in relation to the work of the executive branch that the matter of congressional liaison with the executive branch should be viewed. If their potentialities are properly appreciated, channels of liaison between Congress and the White House, the departments, the bureaus, offices, agencies, and even the independent regulatory commissions, could be used as an instrument for recovering congressional ascendancy over legislation and for extending congressional influence in administration. This, however, would require a basic revision of the prevailing somewhat negative attitude of Congress towards the idea of liaison in general, and in particular towards the idea of direct inter-branch "lobbying."

In keeping with, and arising out of, their concern not to bridge the constitutional separation of the government branches, congressmen tend to regard inter-branch lobbying activity with suspicion. Not surprisingly, perhaps, most of their concern to date has been with the amount of open executive branch lobbying of Congress. The agency anti-lobbying law,[4] which was enacted in 1919, for instance, seems to have been chiefly directed at prohibiting executive personnel from trying to influence congressmen by direct communication. A few examples of the type of action "caught" by congressmen, if not by the statute will illustrate the nature of congressional preoccupations in this regard.

When Health, Education, and Welfare Secretary Anthony Celebrezze wired all congressmen to support an administration bill on aid for institutions of higher education, he was roundly denounced from the Hill.[5] While Nathan Strauss was Administrator of the U. S. Housing Authority, he and members of his staff were sharply criticized for "gumshoeing about the Capitol and offices of Congressmen,"

---

[3] See Blaisdell, *op cit.*, 25 1ff.

[4] *Lobbying with Appropriated Moneys* (18 U.S. Code, Section 1913). One reason why prosecutions of executive personnel are so rare doubtless involves the fact that a department of the executive branch, the Justice Department, has charge of the initiation of prosecutions! The text of the law is set out *infra*, n. 61.

[5] See Berman, *op. cit.*, p. 88.

seeking support for passage of the housing bill.[6] When, in 1963, the secretaries of Defense and State sent co-signed letters to House members urging adoption of the foreign aid bill, Representative Gross of Iowa urged that they be prosecuted under the law.[7] Congressman Smith of Ohio, in 1940, charged that every bureaucrat should be put in jail for lobbying to put his schemes through Congress.[8] In fact, the agency anti-lobbying law, if rigorously enforced, could do just that.

No law exists of course to restrain congressmen from communicating with or "lobbying" the executive branch. Nevertheless, the idea of systematic reverse lobbying seems to be regarded with some disapproval. Robert Ramspeck, representative from Georgia, once called for a constitutional amendment which would "entirely prohibit a member of Congress or a senator from contacting the executive branch of government except in regard to legislation." [9] And in 1945, The Committee on Congress of the American Political Science Association proposed that Congress should abolish its "errand-boy" functions,[10] that is, the present practice whereby members contact the executive on behalf of constituents and others concerning appointments to government posts and cases before government agencies.

In opposition to such views, this paper recommends that direct inter-branch liaison activities, including those which amount to lobbying, should not be abolished but augmented; and, further, that Congress itself should participate much more energetically in these activities than heretofore.[11]

Inter-branch liaison channels are generally regarded, by legislators and administrators alike, as being primarily a means for the executive lobbying of Congress. But from the point of view of Congress, certainly liaison could be much more validly conceived as a network of two-way avenues through which the two branches of government can communicate with each other, for the purpose of exerting a reciprocal influence upon their respective decision-making processes.

[6] See V. O. Key, Jr., *Politics, Parties, and Pressure Groups* (New York: Crowell, 1964), pp. 192ff.

[7] This incident is reported in Abraham Holtzmann's forthcoming work on congressional liaison, to be published by Rand McNally.

[8] Key, *op. cit.*

[9] See Gross, *op. cit.*, pp. 135-41.

[10] *Ibid.*

[11] Kenneth G. Olson's contribution herein on "The Service Function of the U.S. Congress," also urges the importance to sound government today of more efficient congressional service and case work. And see Paul H. Douglas, *Ethics In Government* (Cambridge: Harvard University Press, 1952).

Liaison should above all be regarded as a condition of *mutual* access, with the objective of enhancing the legitimate functions of both branches.

Thus conceived and pursued, it is unlikely that liaison would work to undermine the independence or the power of either branch. On the contrary, it might tend to redress the balance which today is inclining in favor of the executive. If individual congressmen, committee members and leaders, together with their staffs, would increase their direct contacts, their liaison with officials of the various executive offices and departments, the role of Congress in planning, formulating, overseeing, and revising legislation would be systematically enhanced. Liaison would become a principal means, rivaling committee inquiry, whereby Congress could gather information about and exert influence upon the executive's administration of the laws.

In developing its channels of liaison with the bureaucracy, Congress should especially concentrate on applying its new information and increased influence in the executive to servicing the needs of its constituents. A major reason why the executive has been able in recent years to gather power at the expense of Congress is the superior ability of its agencies to develop effective liaison with and "service" the greater public, in particular the various private interest groups who form the agencies' respective "clienteles." Largely as a result of this increased bureaucratic-public contact, the impression has been steadily gaining ground that congressmen can no longer satisfactorily represent the people's interests. To regain full status and function as the representative of the people's interests, therefore, the congressman will have to offer more efficient services to his constituents than he is able to do now. Since his inability to provide effective constituent services stems from his present inadequate knowledge of, and means of influence over, the administrative processes of the various executive agencies, the need for greater access to the proceedings and personnel of the executive branch seems clear. And just as the development of liaison channels with the executive would enable congressmen to offer improved service to their constituents, so the undertaking of more constituent casework would enlarge their role in representative government.

The overall proposal contained in this paper, then, is that congressmen should adopt a more positive attitude toward the idea of liaison and develop more effective techniques of liaison both with the executive branch and with the public. In so doing they will simultaneously increase their capacity to oversee the administration and to represent their constituents, thus forging an instrument for achieving strengthened legislative government.

In what follows, it is proposed first to examine the nature of the congressional liaison system established by the executive, and then to survey in greater detail the use which Congress is currently making of the channels composing the system. The remaining sections contain a discussion of three areas in which Congress could with advantage develop liaison activity. The first section examines the potential of liaison as a principal means of enhancing oversight of the executive. Treated as a separate subject is the development of liaison so as to gain a measure of control over the regulatory commissions, the quasi-judicial segments of the bureaucracy that are outside the executive branch apparatus and have tended to acquire autonomous or non-politically accountable power, partly due to their special status, and a consequential development of "exclusive" liaison with their clienteles. The significance of liaison in the area of constituent services and the desirability of using it to strengthen the representational capacities of congressmen, is explored in the final section. Recommendations as to practical ways in which Congress might advantageously develop liaison in each area are presented in the pertinent section.

Liaison Viewed From the White House

WHEN examined from an executive force perspective, channels of liaison with Congress are, first and foremost, a good means of influencing or lobbying Congress, to secure passage of bills in the form wanted by the executive. Secondarily, they are means for obtaining the benefit of congressional views, "know-how," and political intelligence in the fashioning or amending of the laws.

However, in these respects the aims of the President must be distinguished from those of the numerous departments, bureaus, and agencies within the executive branch. To some extent, the conduct of liaison with Congress when directed from the White House necessarily involves a tightening of presidential control throughout the executive branch. As Donald Blaisdell points out:

> The federal bureaucracy is not subservient to the President, it is neither homogeneous in composition nor unified in purpose . . . it is not insulated from external forces but is tied in criss-cross relations to private individuals and groups and to Congress.[12]

Hence the President will have neither perfect knowledge of nor control over the operations of the branch of government which he heads. But since the time of Eisenhower, at least, the presidency has increasingly sought to organize congressional liaison so as to achieve the twin objectives of enhancing control over the bureaucracy at the same time as it extends its influence over Congress.

Much of the new force that is now discernible within the presi-

---

[12] *Op. cit.*, p. 183.

dency (and executive branch as a whole) seems to have been gathered by a successful harnessing of the liaison activities of the mammoth federal bureaucracy with Congress to the White House staff Office for Congressional Affairs and the Bureau of the Budget (whose director is the only presidential appointee not subject to congressional approval). The origins of the Office for Congressional Affairs go back to the Eisenhower Administration. Its chief function today is systematically to clear and coordinate certain executive branch relations with Congress—especially (as will be explored in some detail hereafter) legislative priorities and assistance to congressmen.

The main liaison functions of the Bureau of the Budget are the preparing and proposing to Congress of a single budget to finance all executive branch and regulatory commission operations, and the coordinating and clearing of all departmental, bureau, agency, and even regulatory commission presentations (except those of the oldest, the Interstate Commerce Commission) to the Congress concerning proposed new legislation, changes in existing legislation, and views on existing and proposed legislation. It would seem useful to say a word about the origins of these functions.

Prior to 1921, when the Bureau of the Budget was created in the Treasury Department, the various agencies and departments of the executive branch each went to the Congress with their own budget proposals, not knowing or caring about the budgets being asked by others. Prior to 1939 when the Bureau was transferred to the new "Executive Office of the President," they were, moreover, relatively free to communicate directly to Congress their own views on the desirability of proposed changes in the laws under which they functioned and with which they were most concerned. Today, however, the Bureau maintains surveillance over the legislative proposals and comments of every department and agency, as well as over their actual programs and their individual budgets. As one Bureau director expressed the relationship between budgetary and program supervision: ". . . the major determinant in any budget is whether a given activity should be conducted at all . . . ." [13]

Until about ten years ago, most executive branch liaison with Congress was carried on at sub-departmental levels, that is, at the level of the bureau head rather than of the secretary department head. This fact was brought to official notice in 1949 when the Hoover

---

[13] Frederick J. Lawton, as quoted in Blaisdell, op. cit., p. 176. For the history of BOB, see U.S. Government Manual (1964-65), pp. 55-57. Berman, op. cit., pp. 76ff; Holtzmann, op. cit.

Commission Task Force on Departmental Management pointed out
that bureau chiefs had built closer connections with the congressional
committees than had the secretaries and suggested that the latters'
authorities were impaired as a result. By 1955 the Post Office Department and the Departments of State, Commerce, Defense, and
Health, Education, and Welfare each had special departmental-level
congressional liaison staff; by 1963, all departments had special
departmental-level liaison staff.[14]

Today no cabinet officer dares to ignore the job of congressional
relations, and most departments expend sizable sums to equip themselves with effective congressional liaison offices. The Department
of the Army, for instance, has a liaison staff of 90 devoting (in fiscal
year 1963) an estimated total of 81,280 man-hours to liaison, at a
combined salary cost of $380,000. The Department of State has a
liaison staff of 30 whose combined salary costs $350,000 and who
devote 141,800 man-hours to liaison work (in fiscal year 1963).
Less important agencies will have comparatively modest staffs, but
no agency or bureau is without its congressional liaison personnel.

The congressional liaison officers in the various executive agencies
and departments, besides reporting to their own directors, also report
directly to the White House via the President's Special Assistant for
Congressional Affairs. Under the present practice, every Monday
noon, each department and agency provides him with a written
report of the department's dealings with Congress during the preceding week, and the projection for the current week. These reports
are immediately reviewed and an analysis is given to the President
for his Monday night reading, along with a suggested agenda for use
in his Tuesday morning meetings with congressional leaders. In addition, the heads of the congressional liaison offices in the departments
and agencies are called to periodic meetings at the White House to
discuss "mutual legislative problems," with emphasis constantly on
the President's program.

The efforts of the White House to increase control of bureaucratic liaison with Congress are understandable when we remember
that to the extent that the bureaucracy relates to Congress (or private
interest groups) with respect to its budgetary and legislative requests,
free of presidential supervision or control, to that extent are the

---

[14] The developments are traced by Holtzmann, *op. cit.* Raw data on size
and expenditures of departmental staffs are found in the files of the chairman,
Subcommittee on Foreign Operations and Government Information, House
Committee on Government Operations.

possibilities weakened of the President fully implementing his own program. The situation has been commented upon by a number of observers:

> Many a bureaucrat maintains his position because of the support of one or more members of Congress who occupy influential positions. Sometimes this support is based upon the backing of private organizations to whom the executive official in question has demonstrated a friendly and cooperative attitude.[15]

> Not always do all units within a department maintain an undivided loyalty to the cabinet member at the head and to his superior, the Chief Executive.[16]

> The average unit of the bureaucracy is far more deeply committed to its own particular program than to the program of the Administration as a whole. Accordingly, an agency whose pet project has been turned down by the Budget Bureau and the White House is seldom inclined to accept this verdict as final. If it has influential friends in Congress, it may be in an excellent position to challenge the President's decision.[17]

If Congress also disagrees, "the agency may still be able to achieve its ends by collaborating directly with its clientele interest groups."

> Agency clientele will be mobilized to apply pressure in the proper places. The Department of Commerce will find it easy to obtain the cooperation of business organizations; the Department of Labor will enlist the unions; and the Department of Agriculture will be assisted by the farmers' organizations.[18]

The clientele, of course, can try to change the President's plans, by working upon Congress.

> Every executive agency lobbies for expanded functions and increased funds. When the departmental estimates are assembled by the Budget Bureau and are presented to the President for his review and decision the influence of the citizen groups may again be actively exerted. After the estimates are submitted to Congress, the groups continue to exert influence actively, openly and covertly.[19]

The attempt to frustrate autonomous bureaucratic liaison with

---

[15] Gross, *op. cit.,* p. 135.
[16] Blaisdell, *op. cit.,* p. 38.
[17] Berman, *op. cit.,* p. 80.
[18] *Ibid.*
[19] Blaisdell, *op. cit.,* p. 177.

Congress and to replace it with an effective system of liaison responsive to the President is reflected in these words of Lawrence O'Brien,
while he was serving as President Johnson's Special Assistant for
Congressional Affairs:

> So by establishing this team and working very, very closely
> with these people in the departments and agencies, it gave us
> additional manpower, and it insured that our activities would be
> properly channeled for maximum results, and we would not have
> cross-wires and individuals going off in separate directions and
> working with the congress.[20]

And, just as the liaison of the bureaucratic agencies with Congress
when uncontrolled by the President could frustrate his policies, so
may liaison when controlled by him be used to promote his program.
Again, Lawrence O'Brien:

> For example, we would anticipate that the Secretary of Agri-
> culture would have a great interest in our education program,
> although it does not come under his activities in his department.
> Nevertheless, he has friends and associates on the Hill, and he
> would be an advocate of our educational legislation whenever an
> opportunity presented itself.[21]

Of course, the Secretary of Agriculture's "friends and associates on
the Hill" may be likely to lend more weight to the Secretary's views
on education if he has already lent some weight, or evidenced a willingness in the future to lend some weight, to the views of those Hill
friends and associates on agricultural matters—such as the hiring,
promotion, and firing of personnel within the department, and the
opening of departmental doors to inquiries concerning the problems
and desires of important constituents.

Recognition of the importance to the presidency of congressional
liaison has reached the stage where President Johnson has repeatedly
told his Cabinet that "next to the Cabinet officer himself" the congressional liaison man is "the most important position in the
Department." [22]

Presidential control of the channels of congressional liaison is by no
means absolute. Even today many departments preserve, in the office
of legislative "presentation" and perhaps more notably in the offices
of their general counsels, important separate functional liaison chan-

---

[20] Transcript of interview prepared for National Education Television
Network, July 7 and 14, 1965.

[21] *Ibid.*

[22] *Ibid.;* see also *White House Press Release,* November 19, 1964.

nels with the Congress concerning legislation. And it is not yet clear whether the less formal links from the executive branch to Congress, established when the bureaucracies dealt with Congress at the bureau rather than departmental level, have been entirely disbanded with the move to control liaison at the departmental level and coordinate the overall liaison effort in the White House. From the standpoint of Congress, of course, it is desirable that access be maintained into as many different levels of the bureaucracy as possible.

Liaison Viewed From Capitol Hill

ALTHOUGH, as Abraham Holtzmann's forthcoming comprehensive work on congressional liaison will document, Congress has not in general resisted the President's attempts to establish a centralized system of congressional liaison, it has on two notable occasions refused cooperation. The House Appropriations Committee declined to accept the new "official" channels in lieu of their traditional liaison channels with departmental budget officers. Express requests from Secretary of Defense McNamara and Secretary of Labor Goldberg that departmental liaison staff be used by the committees were rejected. The reason given by a House committee member was the desire "to protect the working divisions when this point of view is different from the Secretary's." [23] Another executive defeat was received in 1962 when the Department of State's Congressional Relations Office initiated a policy to "coordinate" *all* relations between officials of State and Capitol Hill. Although framed as though its main motive were to provide better service to Congress, it was construed by congressmen as a general effort on the part of the executive to monitor all channels of inter-branch communication and close off their unofficial sources of information within the bureaucracy. Objections from the Hill were sufficiently strong to persuade the department to discontinue the attempt almost as soon as it was begun.

Lawrence O'Brien's theory on the reasons for the otherwise generally positive responsiveness of Congress to the new system of liaison deserves note:

---

[23] Holtzmann, *op. cit.*

Now they talk about arm twisting and all that sort of thing . . .
the fact of the matter is that what we have by way of strength,
if we do have anything, in promoting the program, is the attitude
of the average member of Congress toward President Johnson,
that there is a good feeling on the Hill, if you will, toward the
President. There is a realization of his massive problems, there is
an attitude of general acceptance of his basic proposals in the
legislative area, and therefore we find the doors are open to us.
The members are interested in hearing our views, we are equally
interested in having their views, and their views are extremely
important.[24]

In fact, the executive attitude towards liaison gets mirrored in
the Congress. Members see, in the White House Office for Congressional Affairs, ways of satisfying legitimate executive branch
needs: the President's need "to promote his program," the need of
department heads to account "politically" for their programs, the
need of the executive branch "to lobby Congress" because of the
latter's "complex and difficult nature." As one congressman put it
to Abraham Holtzmann:

We expect and welcome White House legislative liaison men
O'Brien and Manatos to tell us what they feel is important in the
legislative field. They know the priorities; we can't read through
all (the executive) messages and know what the priorities are.[25]

Dissent can arise whenever the White House liaison activities become too "obvious" or "crude" and whenever threats, rather than
favors and services, are tendered. It also arises, as shall subsequently
be explored, when executive officials go "over the heads" of Congress
directly to the public.

Once when asked about the nature of the "hundreds of calls"
that must come to him from members of Congress, the President's
Special Assistant on Congressional Affairs referred to the special
White House tours and other prestige-lending favors, and to services
that could be performed for the important constituents of friendly
congressmen. He concluded his reply with the following remarks:

This is a rather massive government, many departments and
agencies and sub-divisions, and we find at times *we can encourage quicker action, and earlier decision,* or perhaps *we can
express the Presidential view directly to his constituents.* It would

---

[24] *Op. cit.*
[25] Holtzmann, *op. cit.*

indicate what *his close relationship is to the White House*. . . .
(We) are constantly aware of the need and the right of the
Congressman *to receive reasonable service* from the Executive
Branch. After all, most of those fellows give us great service,
because they support the program, and again—always recogniz-
ing they're elected to office (emphasis supplied).[26]

The "hundreds" of calls which the White House Office for Congressional Affairs receives from members must be viewed in the
context of: the 47,000 inquiries from individual congressmen received in one recent year at the Department of State, plus 1,200
inquiries from congressional committees on pending legislation; the
204,600 queries by individual congressmen, received at the Department of the Air Force, plus 22,700 requests by congressional committees concerning pending legislation; and the hundreds of thousands
of other calls received annually by other departments and bureaucratic agencies. The "independent" regulatory agencies, for instance,
received over 2,000 inquiries each during the year in question from
individual congressmen, plus from 50 to 1,500 requests concerning
pending legislation from congressional committees.[27]

James Robinson's study [28] of the State Department's congressional
liaison operations disclosed two classes of information being sought
in this area by congressmen—information relating to constituents'
requests and information relating to executive foreign policy. Seventy-
five percent of the Congress communicated, either directly or indirectly through their staffs, at least weekly with the department.
Most of the communications concerned problems of their constituents.
But, however trivial or unrelated to policy many of these problems
may have seemed, Robinson found that it was often by these means
that the interest of individual congressmen in foreign policy developed.
For in some cases, what begins as a small inquiry of limited scope
develops into a major policy question. As a result, the State Department operates on assumptions similar to those of the White House
Office for Congressional Affairs, as described by Mr. O'Brien in the
words just quoted. Robinson puts the point as follows:

> The more satisfactorily it handles constituent-initiated re-
> quests, the more likely it is to obtain the support of members on

---

[26] *Op. cit.*

[27] Data in the files of the chairman, Subcommittee on Foreign Operations and
Government Information, House Committee on Government Operations.

[28] James Robinson, *Congress and Foreign Policy Making* (Homewood, Ill.:
Dorsey Press, 1962).

policy matters . . . non-policy good will is transferred to and reinforces policy relations, and regardless of the content of a Member's request, the Department is anxious to oblige.[29]

Throughout the executive branch congressmen seek and are provided with policy information specifically requested by individual constituents or for use in general explanations of government programs to constituents. Some offices of congressional liaison are assiduous in furnishing congressmen with documentation explaining their programs, tailored to the congressman's institutional needs. In a related connection congressmen can obtain executive agency help for speech making. Publicity in local newspapers concerning helpful congressmen may also be arranged by some departments. A valued service performed by most, if not all, departments and agencies is to advise the interested congressman of an awaited decision or action as soon as it occurs, and before the information reaches the constituent through other channels. A closer look at the activities of the congressional liaison office belonging to an important agency which was once well-known for the hostility shown it by congressmen provides an insight into the developing pattern.[30]

The Agency for International Development's Congressional Liaison Office was given the responsibility to provide assistance to members of Congress and their staffs on matters pertaining to foreign aid, "so that one call could be made to AID on any aspect of the Agency's operations and a quick and responsive reply would be received, along with whatever assistance might be required." Its staff presently numbers 11, and is headed by a senior grade officer who is a political scientist with a broad Capitol Hill background.

The staff acknowledges all congressional mail and follows up on each inquiry "to make sure that the Member gets the information he needs as promptly as possible." With the exception of a limited amount of correspondence signed by the Administrator or Deputy Administrator of AID, all AID correspondence with Congress is signed by the Director of Congressional Liaison Office. The staff also furnishes information or services requested by members of Congress by telephone. These requests relate to all areas of the world where AID has programs and all aspects of those programs. The staff arranges interviews and conferences requested by members of Congress and committee staff members with AID officials and with

---

[29] *Ibid.*

[30] The information on AID was provided by William Gibbons, Director, Congressional Relations, Agency for International Development.

foreign representatives or technicians engaged in AID-sponsored programs. They themselves receive members of Congress, or their constituents, in order to explain AID's programs, objectives, and accomplishments, to arrange job interviews, or to help constituents who are interested in doing business with AID or investing abroad. When requested, the staff assists members of Congress and staffs with arrangements for congressional study missions abroad.

In addition the congressional liaison staff is responsible both for the distribution of all congressional bills, reports, and hearings relevant to the AID executive staff in Washington and the missions abroad, and for the coordination of agency comments in response to such reports, surveys, and investigations. Finally, in order to keep the agency personnel in Washington and overseas "fully informed about all statements of Congressional opinion on foreign aid, as well as action on AID legislation," the congressional liaison staff prepares a daily summary of pertinent items in the *Congressional Record*.

A sampling which represented probably 75 percent of the total, was made of matters handled in the AID Congressional Liaison Office during a single week. The sampling revealed 168 telephone calls from members of Congress and their staffs on such matters as: a company in Wisconsin wanting to bid on planes; a constituent wanting an appointment on a project in Guatemala; a company in North Dakota wanting a contract; a firm protesting an AID contract award to an Oregon firm; another inquiry on behalf of the Oregon firm; the faculty at Roberts College in Turkey complaining about AID clearance requirements; the population problem; Vietnam; housing guaranties; an OAS conference; aid to Yugoslavia; AID-financed procurements in the United States; balance of payments and gold flow; Cooley loans; and employment interest of constituents. During that week there were also 84 requests from members of Congress for information; the appropriate materials were assembled and sent out by the Congressional Liaison staff. Calls or visits were made by the staff to 71 senators and congressmen for the purpose of assisting them, at their request, with various AID questions and problems. Approximately 75 letters were sent during that week to members of Congress in response to mail or telephone requests.

The major subjects of congressional inquiry and liaison with AID are personnel, constituency business, and program or policy problems. On policy, the Congressional Liaison Office seeks to interpret and fill the need of congressmen to explain the AID programs to their constituents, through speeches and public statements. The office also tries to arouse the interest of congressmen in the importance of foreign aid. Those congressmen who "believe" in foreign aid are given assistance in building support for the AID programs among their constituents. The office seeks to furnish these services on an individual basis, where possible, and on as broad a base as possible; it functions upon the belief that if more congressmen took the initiative in applying for the assistance available to them and to their constituents, the success of the AID programs would undoubtedly be enhanced. In addition to the normal types of contact, the Congressional Liaison Office prepares programs for coffee discussions which take place almost every week with six members of the House Foreign Affairs Committee (three Republicans and three Democrats); lunches are also arranged on occasion with the "foreign affairs committee" of The Democratic Study Group.

Abraham Holtzmann's forthcoming book [31] indicates that in general members of Congress value their relations with the liaison officers within the executive branch, and view their functions as legitimate. There were even a few complaints among the congressmen Holtzmann interviewed of being "insufficiently lobbied." In sum, liaison with key members of the executive branch appears to give the congressman (1) direct access to those who make executive policy—high-ranking officials in the secretaries' offices; (2) a "point of view" concerning departmental administration; (3) information about policy questions, to fill what sometimes seems "a vacuum"; and (4) perhaps most importantly, assistance in the meeting of constituent needs.

---

[31] *Op. cit.*

Liaison as a Means for Heightening
Congressional Oversight of the Bureaucracy

A LINK between the achievement of satisfactory White House-Congress relations and the placement of executive branch personnel was acknowledged in the original title of Mr. O'Brien's office under President Kennedy: "Special Assistant to the President for Congressional Relations and Personnel." [32] News analyst Edward P. Morgan reported in March of 1962 that O'Brien had "trained Cabinet and agency liaison officers to alert him on their prospects, problems—and potential vacancies." O'Brien's office was also understood to have set up an exhaustive card index of up-to-date information about each congressman's whims, needs, and interests—and his voting record. This intelligence, of course, was and is put to use in the President's attempts to win the congressional support necessary to implement his legislative program. It ought not to be surprising if Mr. O'Brien's operations have, on occasion, to be painted by observers in Machiavellian tones:

> Only when sweet reasonableness produced no results did (O'Brien's) men resort to threats and strong-arm methods. The most extreme sanction they could impose was to eliminate a Congressman from consideration when patronage jobs were available and when favors were requested at the White House. A blacklisted member would be "dead" as far as the White House was concerned. He would find every office in the Executive

---

[32] The personnel function, it may be noted, has now been transferred to a different White House office.

316

Branch ignoring his requests for services whether substantial or petty.[33]

Actually, the "punishment" which the President, through his White House Office for Congressional Affairs, may be able to administer to an uncooperative congressman, if properly regarded, carries clues for strengthening congressional oversight of administration. The task now is for congressmen to resist whatever domination may be implied by the system of coordinated liaison established under presidential control, and seek instead to shape the system to their own vital purposes.

In 1961, there were an estimated 36,000 jobs bearing annual combined salaries totaling $50 million, classed as dispensable by patronage. Judgeships, U.S. Marshal posts, postmasters and customs collectors, the legislative branch posts of the Public Printer in the Government Printing Office and the Librarian of Congress, and seats on the regulatory commissions are included.[34] Not classed as patronage jobs, but of comparable significance to the presidency are the many posts throughout the higher levels of the bureaucracy which get filled, vacated, and refilled on the basis of recommendations coming from the Hill via the White House. As Robinson observed, patronage can be dispensed by the President, to establish credit with an individual legislator either for some unspecified future purpose, or to secure some particular present legislative objective.[35]

It is, of course, mistaken to view the practice of appointing to executive posts officials recommended by congressmen as a necessary evil. At best, the practice can and does infuse into the executive branch gifted and experienced personnel, many with invaluable Hill experience whose credentials may be otherwise undiscoverable to the administration. Moreover, from the point of view of Congress, they constitute a corps of individuals whose ties to the Congress can be used to assist congressional participation in administration and to counterbalance those elements contributing to the build-up of autonomy within the bureaucracy. Among the reasons why the Presi-

---

[33] Berman, *op. cit.*, p. 84. See also William Chapman's article "LBJ's Way: Tears, Not Arm-Twists" in *The Washington Post*, October 17, 1965, p. E-1, for these words from a freshman congressman whose vote was wanted on a House Rules Committee discharge petition: "The White House liaison people came and talked to me. Then some contributors to my campaign back home called me up. Then my party chairman back home called to remind me that Home Rule for Washington was part of our Democratic platform. . . . It wasn't any accident. They've got a file on me over there a mile long."

[34] See Berman, *op. cit.*, p. 88.

[35] *Op. cit.*, pp. 123-24.

dent will want to have some, possibly all, of his agencies and departments sprinkled, if not larded, with congressional favorites, is his need for congressional assistance in controlling problematical segments of the bureaucracy. In the case of the Department of Defense, for example, some commentators have expressed a fear of the existence of a military autocracy which promotes its vested interests in many ways. Its members "intervene in the formation of policy, press both the Bureau of the Budget and the President for funds necessary to carry out and support the programs they help to make, and direct this pressure to Congress." [36]

The appointment to key positions within "problem" departments or bureaus of persons loyal to members of Congress as well as persons dedicated to the President helps counteract such autonomous powers. Reliable congressional liaison with the White House is a prerequisite to the finding and filling of such critical staff positions within the bureaucracy. It is important, in this connection, however, to determine to what extent the congressional and White House senior grade appointees get "sinecured" by the bureaucracy or are able to fulfill their key assignments.

Cooperation with the President in the area of personnel appointments is one way to enhance congressional participation in administration, but other forms of contact with the agencies are needed if Congress' proper role in the governmental process is to be regained. For example, increased direct liaison between Congress and the bureaucracy might help repair the deficiency in political accountability frequently said to exist in departments like those of the Army, Navy, and Air Force. But this would not be enough. Here, the main need for Congress would seem to be to counteract the inordinate degree of direct "liaison" which has steadily grown up between the departments and their clientele and interest groups. Overly long tolerated executive-defined and enforced security and secrecy regulations have further weakened congressional oversight of and control over the nation's military and defense programs. To counteract this subservience, and having in view that each of the three Pentagon military Departments already maintain offices of "congressional liaison" on Capitol Hill, consideration ought to be given to establishing *within the Pentagon* congressional offices of "executive liaison," whose personnel have

---

[36] See Blaisdell, *op. cit.,* pp. 183ff; B. M. Sapin and R. C. Snyder, *The Role of the Military in American Foreign Policy* (New York: Free Press of Glencoe, 1954); Edward L. Katzenbach, Jr., "How Congress Strains at Gnats, Then Swallows Military Budgets," *The Reporter,* July 20, 1954, p. 2

been cleared *by Congress* for access to classified data of the most sensitive categories. They might perhaps be part of or attached to the staff of the armed services committees or the military subcommittees of the government operations committees. Alternatively they might perhaps be attached to a new joint committee of Congress charged with matters affecting congressional relations with the other branches of government. Reference points for such administrative innovations might be Alfred de Grazia's proposal for establishing "Congressional Tribunes" within departments and agencies,[37] and George Galloway's recommendation of the appointment within the agencies of congressional "boards of visitors" with full access to the agencies' personnel and activities. Under the latter's proposal, the congressional "visitor" would:

> . . . become especially informed by observation and experience concerning (the agency's) programs and problems. He would become a special champion of the public interest in relation to the work of that agency. . . . Among his colleagues in Congress he would become a recognized and trusted authority concerning conditions in the agency, mediating between them, adjusting disputes, clarifying issues, and developing cooperative attitudes and arrangements.[38]

Or, as shortly will be discussed, introduction of an American-style Ombudsman system may be in order.

Having clearance for access to classified data and armed with some investigative rights, possibly linked in some way to the departments' own offices of congressional liaison, *or replacing them,*[39] such "executive liaison" staff or congressional Ombudsmen could convey

[37] Alfred de Grazia, *Republic in Crisis* (New York: Federal Legal Publications, 1965), pp. 238ff.

[38] *Legislative Process in Congress* (New York: Crowell, 1953), p. 458.

[39] In this connection, Congress might itself wish to examine, within the context of the desirable organization of the executive branch, the position of the congressional relations officers within their departments and bureaus, to determine: (a) the extent to which the congressional liaison officers should participate in the deliberations and decisions of highest policy importance to their departments and agencies; and (b) the degree to which some of the legislative liaison functions, still largely performed within departmental and agency offices of the general counsels, might be brought within the operational scope of the new liaison offices. There is a sense in which good congressional liaison officers, within the executive branch, sometimes find themselves "in the middle," as the two branches compete and cooperate with each other in endeavoring to accomplish the sound administration of law and program. Without bidding such officers any disloyalty, members of Congress should feel free to tax them to the utmost to defend or amend their agency's policy actions.

informed opinions to Congress as to viable areas for changes in the military departments' critical operations.

Measures of this kind applied selectively to or throughout the executive branch for the purpose of making Congress more effective in the administration of the laws seem more promising than certain other types of proposals involving greater inter-branch liaison and communication. One such type of proposal, for instance, would invite executive participation in the floor debates of Congress. Non-voting seats on the floor of the House would be available to the heads of executive departments to "provide members of congress with a first-hand opportunity to learn about executive operations" and "prevent department heads from neglecting congressional opinion and require them always to be prepared to defend their operations before Congress." [40] Despite the formal attractiveness of the idea, and its relevance to a parliamentary system of government, any move in this direction would seem unlikely to provide Congress with significantly greater insight into, oversight of, or participation in, the administration of laws and policies by the executive branch.

A proposal made by Kefauver and Levin in 1947 would provide quarters on Capitol Hill "for liaison staff for each Federal department and major agency." [41] This comes closer to present political and administrative realities; in effect, it would expand across the executive board the existing practice of the Departments of the Army, Navy, and Air Force in maintaining congressional liaison staff offices on Capitol Hill.

But, from the standpoint of Congress it is the reverse of this process—the placing of congressional "Tribunes," "Advisers," "Ombudsmen," or "Boards of Visitors" physically within critical administrative departments and agencies—which would seem most conducive to enhancing congressional oversight; and it would be particularly valuable, if, as Galloway proposed, they "would have full access to (the agency's) personnel and activities and would become especially informed by observation and experience concerning its programs and problems." [42]

Other proposals for strengthening congressional oversight would require administrators to give Congress more complete and regular

---

[40] Robert Heller, *Strengthening The Congress* (Washington, D. C.: National Planning Association, 1945), p. 27.

[41] Estes Kefauver and Jack Levin, *A Twentieth Century Congress* (New York: Duell, Sloan & Pearce, 1947), p. 149.

[42] *Op. cit.*

reports on their activities.[43] From the standpoint of improving over-sight, there is little doubt that the regularization and deepening of agency reporting would theoretically aid the Congress; but as has been often remarked, the standing committees are already too heavily burdened with their legislative duties, and too restricted by their limited staff, to keep a close, continuous watch upon even those parts of the executive branch whose activities are within their jurisdiction.[44] Unless the government operations committees or other organs of the Congress could find new systematic means to digest additional information concerning executive branch administration, the implementation of such proposals will not strengthen but further burden congressional oversight of administration.[45]

---

[43] Roland Young, *This Is Congress* (New York: Knopf, 1943), p. 255.

[44] See George Galloway, "The Operation of the Legislative Reorganization Act of 1946," *American Political Science Review*, March 1951, pp. 59-60.

[45] Consult Kenneth Janda's "Information Systems For Congress" and Charles R. Dechert's "Availability of Information for Congressional Operations" in this series of papers.

Liaison as a Means of Increasing Congressional Control of the Regulatory Commissions

A N area where increased liaison between the Congress and the bureaucracy could have a particularly salutary effect, is with the regulatory commissions.

The new centralized system of congressional liaison has developed almost exclusively within the ambit of the normal executive departments and bureaus of State, Defense, Agriculture, Health, Education, and Welfare, etc. It has not effectively been introduced into so-called quasi-judicial agencies like the Federal Communications Commission, Federal Trade Commission, Civil Aeronautics Board, and Interstate Commerce Commission. Inasmuch as neither the President nor Congress has been able effectively to bring them to political account, there are compelling reasons to consider extending the system to cover these so-called "independent" agencies as well.

Since congressmen are rarely experts in the complex fields with which the regulatory commissions deal, their inability to penetrate the quasi-judicial curtain surrounding their administration might be diagnosed as a traditional case of impotence through lack of information, and no further questions asked. But more questions should be asked when a presidential appointee to the chairmanship, the highest post of such a commission, can lament:

Elected officials and political appointees in high office often find that they are only nominally in charge of a bureaucracy so firmly entrenched that it is all but impossible to do more than slightly deflect the previously prescribed line of march. "The way things always have been done" becomes a substitute for a creative recognition of new problems. "Whatever is, is right," bit by bit, becomes "an adequate surrogate for social theory." The rule-book of governmental bureaucracy fastens the chilling tentacle of precedent upon the ironclad base of the law. Occasionally, under stress and urgency and lionheartedness, the tentacle may be ripped asunder, in business or education or even in government; but whereas business or education can now proceed without the dead tentacle of the past, government is still held by the ironclad grip of the law which vested interests refuse to disengage.[46]

As Newton N. Minow went on to observe, for all their importance to the economic welfare of the country, the regulatory agencies are in fact responsible neither to the executive nor the legislative branch. This independence was intended to be curtailed by the judiciary, through the process of judicial review of administrative adjudicatory and rule-making actions. The supervision of agency action by the judicial branch is now generally recognized as unsubstantial and incomplete. The efficacy of judicial "oversight" of commission action is suggested by a recent remark of Minow's, in 1964: "Once, while testifying in Congress, I was asked about a specific case, and upon checking I discovered that it had begun when I was in the Army in India in World War II. It is still pending." [47]

Congress' own feelings of frustration, with respect to the maintenance of effective oversight of the regulatory commissions are just as strong; they were expressed in this way by one committee member:

Even when we (on the Committee) suspect something's not right (in the agencies) what can we do about it? It would take forever to really get into the thing. First we'd get a long run-around in and out of the Statute. There's always some little provision that nobody knew was there, except the bureaucrat who pulls it out of the hat. . . . Before we finish they have us thinking it's all because of the terrible law we wrote and nothing at all to do with how they treated it.[48]

Another member put this problem more simply:

The (regulatory) agencies' work is pretty technical. Most of us just don't know enough about it to even begin to ask intelligent questions.[49]

---

[46] Newton N. Minow, in "The Mazes of Modern Government," *An Occasional Paper on the Role of the Political Process in the Free Society* (Center For The Study of Democratic Institutions, 1964).

[47] *Ibid.*

[48] In Seymour Scher, "Conditions For Legislative Control," *Journal of Politics,* August 1963, pp. 526, 533ff.

[49] *Ibid.*

The sometimes deliberate discouragement of the congressman, of course, not only minimizes his oversight function but precludes his effective participation in the formulation of new policies and laws.

Nor is the formal committee investigating apparatus readily able to break the "independent" bureaucracy's lock on expertise and knowledge. Another member asserts:

> Getting involved with those agencies can be a trap. We start out with what is a good case of hanky-panky and by the time we finish clearing away the smokescreen they (the agency) send up, the point's lost. Before one hearing we sent a couple of our staff people over to the agency to go through their files of decisions and intra-agency memoranda. They were snowed under. It would take an army of staff men a year to begin to make sense out of what's going on over there.[50]

When in addition to such handicaps congressmen wishing to intervene in the agencies' administration of a program also have to cope with judicial norms of the type alluded to by Minow, the restraints upon the congressional oversight function become formidable.

The traditional juridical point of view shielding the regulatory commissions' administration from traditional forms of oversight was expressed by the Committee on Administrative Law of the New York City Bar Association, in 1950, in this way:

> Legislative committees ought not try to influence the decisions of pending cases, issues before an agency, or the manner in which a particular case is being handled—"a precept not universally respected in practice." Nor should decided cases be criticized with a view to influencing an agency to reverse a previous ruling or to limit a trend in agency decisions, except when a committee is genuinely considering amending a statute.[51]

These few succinct caveats, if slavishly honored or rigorously enforced, could end the possibility of effective congressional oversight of the administration of the regulatory commissions. It is, of course, the exception which leaves Congress the legal and ethical room needed to employ institutional techniques like committee hearings, to discover and seek to repair regulatory agency maladministration. Congressmen will intervene and even block regulatory agency rule-making processes which they consider to be outside the bounds of

---

[50] *Ibid.*

[51] In Seymour Scher, "Congressional Committee Members as Independent Agency Overseers: A Case Study," *American Political Science Review,* December 1960, pp. 911, 913.

the authority vested in the agency, by introducing legislation, or holding hearings dealing with the subject matter involved. Although this technique of oversight is not often used to intervene where "cases of adjudication" are in process, there appears to be no legal objection to such use,[52] while the objection of "unfairness" raised by the agencies seems merely to reflect the judicial norm.

In view of the overriding right and power of Congress to legislate, and to investigate in order to legislate, juridical precepts of this kind should not preclude congressional oversight of rule-making proceedings, nor cases of adjudication, at any proper time. The inhibitions seem to involve inappropriate extensions of the ethics of the courtroom into the commissioner's office; and one reason why congressmen intervene less than they might probably has to do with their traditional respect for legal norms and the large number of members who are lawyers. The flesh of lawyers is educated to crawl at the idea of "off the record" and "ex parte" communications with a judge, by a party or anyone else "interested" in a pending case. But the transplanting of the precept of judicial isolation into the soil of regulatory administrative proceedings—where the President, the Congress, and of course the greater public, are usually directly "interested" in, and affected by the outcome—may have done more harm than good.

For example, in rate-making proceedings, where a rate increase will directly affect consumers, perhaps even exclude some from the market, a rule which prohibits them, their President, and their congressmen from communicating with, and having their views taken into account by the commission involved, seems to mock, not satisfy, notions of due process. Such rules serve further to insulate the regulatory commissions' operations, and render them responsible in fact to the utilities, "common carriers," and other industrial conglomerates, which they are supposed to regulate, and virtually unaccountable to the public in whose interest the regulation theoretically takes place. Typically, the commission is legally restrained from considering consumers' views—except via cumbersome and costly methods of formal intervention which, moreover, often fail to admit the relevancy of the consumers' interest.

In addition, many cases of adjudication by commissions are really

---

[52] However, the FCC recently adopted rules further to discourage congressional and other "ex parte" influence upon its proceedings. A party to a proceeding who "directly or indirectly" makes or "encourages or solicits others to make" any "unauthorized ex parte communications" "may be disqualified" from the proceeding. *FCC Docket No. 15381.* ("In the matter of Rules governing ex parte communications in hearing proceedings.") *Report and Order,* July 21, 1965.

semi-planned pieces of legislation. To preclude public and congressional intervention in such cases simply results in leaving the formulation and enactment of such "little laws" entirely to the commission and its clientele. This has less to do with due process for litigants than with private lawmaking by industrial conglomerates.

Nowhere else in the broad range of the federal executive has the governmental conduct created misgivings of the kind raised by the operations of these independent, "quasi-judicial" bodies.[53] Their very structure is now called under question. The fault lies in the absence of political accountability and excessive insulation of the decision-making officials within the organizations, from all but their clientele. A way to reform and political responsibility may therefore consist in opening commission doors to the broadly interested public, especially through their representatives in the Congress, as distinct from the commissions' familiar clientele. For the real problem with the "independent" agencies, of course, has been that they are not very independent of their clientele.

> The organized and unorganized interests with privileged access to the Chief Executive and the regular departments are usually fairly apparent; but it is never clear which interests initially will have such access to a new agency that is expected to act with some of the detachment of a court. Experience indicates, however, that the regulated groups will have more cohesion than those demanding regulation, that they can therefore keep close track of the work of the commission, and that consequently little will be done by a commission beyond what is acceptable to the regulated groups. Even when groups have sought regulation, such as the licensing of occupations, the commission has been regarded as the most appropriate form for their purposes because it assures privileged access for the initiating group.[54]

[53] See, for example: James A. Landis, *Report on the Regulatory Agencies to the President-Elect* (Washington, D. C.: Government Printing Office, 1960); Bernard Schwartz, *The Professor And The Commissions* (New York: Knopf, 1959); Marver H. Bernstein, *Regulating Business by Independent Commission* (Princeton, N. J.: Princeton University Press, 1955), pp. 130ff.

[54] Pendleton Herring, *Public Administration and The Public Interest* (New York: McGraw-Hill, 1936), p. 213; see also Harmon Zeigler, *Interest Groups In American Society* (Englewood Cliffs, N. J.: Prentice-Hall, 1964), pp. 280ff; David Truman, *The Governmental Process* (New York: Knopf, 1951), pp. 416ff; Pendleton Herring, *Presidential Leadership* (New York: Farrar and Rinehart, 1940), pp. 115-16 suggests: "The existence of independent commissions, while sometimes inconvenient to presidential power, may yet relieve the chief excutive of a greater burden of political power than any one man can carry."

It is thus that agencies like the ICC, FCC, AEC, and CAB have sometimes come to be characterized as "captive" agencies. Precisely because the decision-making officials are overprotected from external, public influence, they are underprotected against the pressures of the industries they are intended to regulate, and tend to succumb to institutional captivity.

A Commission formally independent of the Chief Executive and expected to assume the detachment of a judicial body is more likely to be primarily accessible to organized elements among the regulated than is an agency in the executive branch. It can less easily command the resources of the Presidency for defending its policies; and it is less readily accessible to some of the interests that reach the Chief Executive.[55]

Although congressional committee investigative process can, subject to the limitations arising from lack of expertise, legitimately intervene in the processes of the regulatory agencies, effective oversight or participation by Congress requires more than occasional full-scale investigation. Needed, here perhaps even more than elsewhere, are channels by which congressmen can constantly raise questions and get answers, concerning cases, rules, and policies on all matters attended to by the agency officials. If the answers are not satisfactory to Congress, the law governing the agency can be amended accordingly. But when questions cannot be asked, the ground cannot be laid for improvement of administration through changes in the law. In short, Congress' access into the executive, afforded by informal and formal channels of liaison, should be extended to the independent regulatory commissions.[56]

In view of the special criticism that has gathered round the

---

[55] David Truman, *op. cit.*, p. 420; see also Scher, *Journal of Politics, op. cit.*, pp. 526ff.

[56] There is some evidence that some congressmen have not been intimidated by the application of juridical norms to regulatory proceedings. In one of the few important published studies of congressional relations with regulatory agencies, Seymour Scher concluded that:

"For the Committee member there was no abstract meaning in the term 'proper' when used to describe the relationship between the independent commission and the Committee. Anything was proper that served to bring the agency, in its handling of cases in the regional offices or in its own orders, into accord with the members' view of how the agency should act. . . . Formal norms intended to restrict the Congressman in checking the adjudicatory activity of an independent commission are not, in practice, observed by him. The committee member recognizes no limitations on his behavior by virtue of the agency's judicial functions. He may or may not see a distinction between using his committee status as a weapon against an executive bureau operations of the regulatory commission it would seem indicated for Congress to reexamine the basic question of the "independence" of these commissions, and their relationship to the President and to the legislative branch whose "creature" or "arm" they were originally designed to be. As has been shown, prevailing juridical norms are restraining the exercise even of normal congressional oversight of these agencies.

Apart from budgetary supervision, at present the President's control over the commissions seems mainly to concern his right to name the chairmen and influence the latters' powers over "housekeeping" operations, meetings, and the establishment of agenda. The ICC declines even to permit the Bureau of the Budget to coordinate its legislative proposals and comments.[57] Newton Minow has proposed severing the commissions' judicial functions and placing their administrative functions under presidential control. It may be, on the other hand, that some new institutional form of access by the Congress to the commission's basic processes could be established. In this connection the Congress' experience with existing liaison offices in executive departments (such as the Department of State) which have adjudicatory or "quasi-judicial" functions (such as passport and visa operations), should be studied in greater detail. Sooner or later, some more creditable system must replace the caricature of the judicial process which haunts regulatory commission operation, and for which the Congress is itself partly to blame:

---

with largely service functions and against a quasi-judicial regulatory agency. If he recognizes the distinction in words, he acts as though none exists. Agency orders, equally with agency rules, are fair subjects for his attention. Whether the adjudicatory determination by the agency is in process or has been completed makes no noticeable difference to him." (Scher, *American Political Science Review, op. cit.,* pp. 911, 919).

Senator Everett Dirksen made a long statement in the wake of congressional disclosures of "off-the-record" contacts between regulatory agency commissioners and their clientele, of which the following is an extract:

"These people get lost down here in this baffling, bewildering labyrinthine Government. Even we Senators get lost in it. I sometimes wonder what the average citizen would do if he didn't have the opportunity to come down here and talk with us and see what his rights are, and where he has to go, and whether we can't do a little something for him. . . . I went beyond the trial examiner; I didn't even bother with him, he is just an intermediary, I went where the decision is to be made. The Commissioners I talked to would have a vote. If it is a five-man commission and I get three votes on that commission for my constituent, everything is hunky-dorey. So I went right to the point where the decision is made." (Quoted in Scher, *Journal of Politics, op. cit.,* p. 536.)

[57] Information received from Wilfred Rommel, Director, Office of Legislative Reference, Bureau of the Budget. Also see Herring's provocative remark, *op. cit.*

The job that Congress gave the Commission was somewhat comparable to asking the Board of the Metropolitan Opera Association to decide, after public hearing and with a reasoned opinion, whether the public interest, convenience, or necessity would be better served by having the prima donna role on the opening night sung by Tebaldi or by an up-and-coming American soprano who might prove herself the Tebaldi of tomorrow, or. . . .[58]

David Truman more soberly observed:

The more undefined and unprecise the policy determinations reached by the legislature in passing a statute, the more certainly will the activities of an enforcing Commission have to reflect a *modus operandi* worked out with the regulated groups.[59]

Some legal commentators suggest that maybe the commissions should be obliged to adopt investigative and rule-making proceedings, with maximum public participation, in lieu of adjudicatory proceedings. It is quite possible that all adjudicative operations of these commissions could be made over into rule-making functions and that these could be broadly opened up to oversight by Congress or control by the President, and be made accountable in such form to the public. If Congress were to assume a new responsibility toward the commissions, some type of consumer "Ombudsman" would probably need to be created to provide properly representative institutional channels for public liaison.

---

[58] Judge Henry Friendly, as quoted by Newton N. Minow, *op. cit.*
[59] *Op. cit.*, p. 419.

Liaison as a Means of Improving
Representational Capacity of Congress

ACCESS to the bureaucracy is a key to effective oversight. Access for an hour to the correct official within an agency can be more useful to a congressman, and more conducive to participation in administration, than a bale of official files or a week of investigative hearings. Increased means of access not only facilitate oversight, they can also help congressmen broaden and strengthen their services to their constituents, their ultimate source of rightful power.

Roger H. Davidson has pointed out [60] that the strength of the legislature has traditionally rested on its control, if not its outright monopoly, of the vital channels of communication with the constituencies and those interests making demands on the instruments of government. He, and other contributors to this symposium, are calling attention to the way in which, because of the proliferating relations between the executive branch and private interest groups, a species of executive "representation" is threatening to overpower congressional representation of the constituents. Yet, as has been recognized by Abraham Holtzmann and other students of congressional-executive relations, the Congress especially resents, as an intrusion on its prerogatives, bureaucratic appeals to the public "over Congress' head." Inasmuch as the bureaucratic channels of communication, or liaison, with the interest groups are the chief means by which this new mode of executive representation is being pursued, some way should be found for Congress to open up similar liaison

---

[60] See his contribution to this series of papers, "Congress and the Executive: The Race For Representation."

channels of its own so as to develop countervailing congressional representation of the various interest groups.

Before considering methods by which this objective might be achieved it is perhaps necessary to point out the shortcomings of a negative proposal that has received some general support: namely that Congress should seek to curtail executive-clientele liaison via the agency anti-lobbying law.

There are certain types of public and private agency-clientele liaison which because they can result in pressures upon Congress might be considered to violate the agency anti-lobbying law, or be otherwise contrary to sound public policy. An example of the former type, hotly criticized in Congress at the time, was Secretary of Agriculture Brannon's visiting St. Paul, Minnesota, and other cities in 1950 and delivering talks on the problems of farmers and the purposes of his "Brannon Plan." An example of the latter type might be the head of a defense contracting company visiting Washington to discuss with the office of the Secretary of Defense a new military requirement of interest to his company, and the defense budget. Both types of contact can strengthen executive representation at the expense of congressional representation. But can either type wisely be curtailed by invoking or expanding the anti-lobbying law?

Public addresses, speeches, conferences by heads and other senior officials of executive departments, although paid for out of public funds cannot, it seems to me, wisely be restrained—even when they are designed specifically to promote an executive program and indirectly to influence Congress, and may thereby involve technical violations of the existing anti-agency lobbying law.[61] As a repre-

---

[61] The text of the law, *Lobbying with Appropriated Moneys* (18 U.S. Code, Section 1913), follows:

"No part of the money appropriated by any enactment of Congress shall, in the absence of express authorization by Congress, be used directly or indirectly to pay for any personal service, advertisement, telegram, telephones, letter, printed or written matter, or other device, intended or designed to influence in any manner a Member of Congress, to favor or oppose, by vote or otherwise, any legislation or appropriation by Congress, whether before or after the introduction of any bill or resolution proposing such legislation or appropriation; but this shall not prevent officers or employees of the United States or of its departments or agencies from communicating to Members of Congress on the request of any Member or to Congress through the proper official channels, requests for legislation or appropriations which they deem necessary for the efficient conduct of the public business.

"Whoever, being an officer or employee of the United States or of any department or agency thereof, violates or attempts to violate this section, shall be fined not more than $500 or imprisoned not more than one year, or both; and after notice and hearing by the superior officer vested with the power of removing him, shall be removed from office or employment. . . ."

sentative of the Bureau of the Budget's Division of Legislative Reference suggested to the House Select Committee on Lobbying Activities:

It has been the practice of Presidents for as far back as I can remember, to make specific assignments of given subjects to members of the Cabinet or to other agency heads, and say, Here is something I advocate. It's up to you, Mr. So-and-So, to marshal all the support you can for this particular measure.[62]

A simple antidote to excessive executive speech-making is increased congressional speech-making. Thoroughly adequate provision could be made at the staff level of Congress, for furnishing members with the means, including expertise, for making counter-administration policy speeches, during debates and in "St. Paul" as well.

Private meetings, conferences, and discussions with special interest-group representatives on particular matters pending in the departments and agencies may inadvertently or intentionally result in an indirect lobbying of Congress through the interest groups concerned. However, as it stands now, the agency anti-lobbying law cannot restrain the kind of indirect lobbying that may be involved here; nor would any amendment of the existing law—short of forbidding all communications between agency officials and private interest groups about pending matters that are not made a matter of public record—have the intended effect.

There is a more positive and practicable way in which Congress might seek to counteract such agency-clientele liaison activities: By offering inducements to encourage constituents to refer their problems vis-à-vis the bureaucracy to their elected representatives.

Constituents with bureaucratic problems today can go direct to the agency concerned, or hire a lawyer, or ask their congressman to speak on their behalf. Asking their congressman will avail them only to the extent that he has the means to inquire and intervene on their behalf. These means range from a letter to the agency to repeatedly summoning the agency's head to meetings on the Hill to defend the agency point of view, with threats of burdensome formal committee investigation, or bad reports to appropriations committee colleagues, lurking in the background. If the member has the requisite power,

---

[62] U.S., Congress, House, *Hearings Before the House Select Committee of Lobbying Activities Pursuant to H. Res. 298,* 81st Congress, 2d Session, 1950, Part 10, "Legislative Activities of Executive Agencies," p. 15. To some extent the problem can be dealt with in the program and appropriations authorizations given each department and agency.

the agency will be forced to give the problem the consideration it may deserve.

Congressmen should therefore seek to develop methods of systematically increasing their ability to service the needs of their constituents at every level of the bureaucracy. In this respect, they should not hesitate to utilize to the full the contacts and expertise made available to them by the congressional liaison offices of the various departments, agencies, and bureaus.

But of course the simplest way to induce persons to refer their questions and problems with the bureaucracy to their elected representatives, in preference to the agencies themselves or to lawyers, is for Congress to enlarge its members' own individual staffs available for case work, provide members of Congress with special funds for the retention of outside assistance, including legal assistance, and make it plain to constituents that they are in a position to provide them with more (free) services and to present cases effectively to the bureaucracy.[63]

A complementary measure to increase congressional and cut back bureaucratic representation of, and liaison with, constituent interest groups would be to forbid any agency or department from denying any request for a service, benefit, grant, award, contract, loan, etc., without notifying the applicant's congressman in advance. Agency officials would then probably tend to clear intended denials informally with the congressman's office before taking an actual decision, thereby involving congressmen directly in the administrative process.

The necessity for congressmen to inquire and intervene with the executive branch in regard to particular cases and problems of interest to constituents can scarcely be questioned. As has been indicated, if properly developed, case and service work would provide Congress with important means and motives for oversight, and with a mode for participating in administration. At present, however, this activity tends to be informal and is often subject to the criticism that it is too selective and involves too much special pleading. Priority consideration should be given to the possibility of institutionalizing the service function, and elevating it to the level of a formal, comprehensive duty of the congressman.

The results could hardly be other than deeper and broader congressional oversight of agency administration, with a corresponding decrease in bureaucratic force and instances of political unaccount-

---

[63] For a detailed account of the staff requirements needed to undertake case work effectively, see Kenneth Olson, *op. cit.*

ability. Essentially, members of Congress and their staffs would be undertaking to represent directly their constituents—including the agencies' existing clientele and interest groups—before the agencies and departments of the executive branch.

Pendleton Herring once predicted that:

> The congressman more and more will . . . come to serve as a mediator between his constituency and the operations of government within it. He is in a strategic position to observe how governmental functions actually impinge upon his constituents. He is in a position to advise his constituents how to receive maximum benefits from what the government stands ready to give them and how to make their views felt about desirable fields for governmental action. He is in a position to discover areas where governmental activity should be withdrawn or modified.[64]

A strengthening of the ability of congressmen to service their constituents' needs in relation to the bureaucracy would underwrite the essential "mediating" function of congressmen. This would be accomplished, in effect, by members of Congress increasing direct liaison with the great bureaucracy on the one hand and with their individual constituents on the other.

In the end, the augmentation and strengthening of the mediating functions of congressmen, with the bureaucracies, *on behalf of their own constituents,* should give rise to a congressional corps of persons with loyalties and duties akin to those of the Ombudsmen of Sweden, Denmark, Norway, and New Zealand. As is rather well known, these legislative agents or commissioners investigate citizens' complaints of bureaucratic abuse and although they properly do not have any punitive powers nor the power to amend administrative decisions, they have vital powers to investigate and to form and issue opinions. Recently, proposals for the establishment of comparable offices have been made in England, Canada, Australia, Ireland, and Holland, and also in New York, Illinois, Connecticut, and California. West Germany is reported to have adopted an Ombudsman system for military affairs.[65]

Congressman Henry S. Reuss' proposal for the creation of an Administrative Counsel of the Congress, a concept reported on and supported by Kenneth Olson [66] and others, should be considered in

---

[64] *The Politics of Democracy* (New York: Rinehart, 1940), p. 383.

[65] See Donald C. Rowat, *The Ombudsman: Citizens Defender* (Toronto: University of Toronto Press, 1965).

[66] *Op. cit.*

relation to the Ombudsman experience. It seems desirable, however, that the image be recast in the more positive terms of the Ombudsman's function, and away from the rather negative conception of the office as a means of taking "some of the load" of citizens' complaints off congressmen's shoulders, leaving them more time for legislative matters.

When Congress comes to realize that doing constituent case work and solving citizens' complaints are essential aspects of the governmental process and incomparable methods of overseeing administration, which in no way threaten the constitutional checks and balances, Congress will be able to discern and reach for a new, more creative role. To the degree that Congress imaginatively develops plainly needed new institutional means for the public to obtain satisfaction from the vast and remote bureaucracies, and yet retain control over those means, will Congress' role in the classic American experiment in republican government be revitalized and rewarded. Hopefully in the offing is an historic marriage of the sometimes despised but nevertheless essential case-work function of the congressman with the sometimes annoying but generally healing work of the Ombudsman.

KENNETH G. OLSON is a Washington consultant to federal government agencies, business firms, and private organizations. Currently he is writing a book, "Congress and Military Policy," as part of The Study of Congress sponsored by the American Political Science Association. He is Associate Professorial Lecturer in Political Science at The George Washington University. Educated at Minnesota and Harvard, he has taught American government and politics at both universities and at Smith and Mount Holyoke Colleges. His experience includes newspaper reporting, speech writing, and active duty for three and a half years as a U.S. Naval intelligence officer. His writings include contributions to scholarly publications as well as to popular periodicals. He has had legislative and political campaign experience on the staffs of Vice President Lyndon B. Johnson, Senator Hubert H. Humphrey, and Congressman Charles E. Bennett.

The Service Function of the United States Congress

Kenneth G. Olson

T HE GLORY—and the problem—of the United States Congress is its thoroughly human admixture of brilliant vision and momentary blindness, of reason and prejudice, of stubborn obstinacy and prudent adaptability. These qualities, built into the very organization of Congress, permit it to perform some governing functions exceedingly well and others not so well. Yet the overriding significance of the congressional mode of governing is clear. It was well stated by Emerson when he wrote, "A Congress is a standing insurrection, and escapes the violence of accumulated grievances." [1]

Congress offers a hearing to every American who has a request, complaint, inquiry, fear about, or panacea for almost any matter, public or private. It does not always have solutions or answers, but it does have the patience to listen and to react. Thus, while Congress at its best serves as a creative instrument for governing the American people, at minimum it acts as a kind of safety valve for citizens whose frustrations and anxieties might otherwise find destructive outlets.

This paper examines the nature and significance of the voluminous set of personal demands and requests which citizens increasingly press upon their congressmen. I shall use the term "service function" to describe this welter of congressional activities which are seemingly unconnected with the function of legislating, a melange of duties described by one former member in this way:

> A Congressman has become an expanded messenger boy, an employment agency, getter-out of the Navy, Army, and Marines, a wardheeler, a wound healer, trouble shooter, law explainer, bill finder, issue translator, resolution interpreter, controversy-

---

[1] Ralph Waldo Emerson, quoted in Stephen K. Bailey and Howard D. Samuel, *Congress at Work* (New York: Henry Holt, 1952), p. 1.

oil-pourer, glad hand extender, business promoter, veterans affairs adjuster, ex-serviceman's champion, watchdog for the underdog, sympathizer for the upperdog, kisser of babies, recoverer of lost baggage, soberer of delegates, adjuster for traffic violations and voters straying into the toils of the law, binderup of broken hearts, financial wet nurse, a good Samaritan, contributor to good causes, cornerstone layer, public building and and bridge dedicator and ship christener.[2]

An individual complaint or a request for a favor may itself be trivial, except to the aggrieved or hopeful citizen and his family. Responding to it may tax the energy and ingenuity of an overworked member of Congress and his staff. No single request left unheeded is likely to rock the Republic. But the provision of millions of such minuscule services, in their totality, amount to a major function of modern American government. How well these services are performed goes a long way in determining the confidence of citizens in their representatives.

The basic contention of this paper is that the service function, far from being merely a time-consuming diversion from the essential legislative duties of members, is central to all of the work of the Congress.

Looking at it very broadly, Congress plays three major roles in the American system of governing. It is a *representative* body, expressing the needs and wishes of the American people. It is a *deliberative* body, passing judgment upon proposals for legislation made by its members and by others. And it is a *supervisory* body, exercising surveillance over the activities of the other branches of government, and serving, in a sense, as a check and balance upon them.

What is here called the "service function" is part of its role in representing the American people. But how that function is carried out also has an important bearing upon the quality of congressional deliberation and supervision. Close contact between a member and his constituents, resulting from their incessant demands upon him, helps to shape his deliberative decisions on how to vote on pending proposals and, moreover, sometimes leads directly to new legislation.

Similarly, responding to constituents' complaints and problems provides a recurring opportunity for a member to scrutinize the work of the executive and judicial branches and, indeed, of state

---

[2] Luther Patrick, "What Is a Congressman?" reprinted in *Congressional Record,* May 13, 1963, p. A2978.

and local governments as well. Characteristically, this scrutiny takes the form of interfering in federal administrative processes on specific issues of complaint. Sometimes such interference goes beyond the individual issue concerned and results in systematic changes in administrative procedures. Occasionally it leads to corrective legislation. In any event, the mere threat of congressional intervention helps insure that the federal bureaucracy will anticipate problems before they arise and will not neglect its duties. Thus, the exercise of the service function infuses new life into the theory of Congress as a check upon the other branches of government and as a kind of balance-wheel within the entire system of government.

My purpose in examining the service function of Congress is to call attention to the fact that members urgently need additional help in order to discharge this function more effectively. Improvement in the service function, in turn, will heighten the capability of Congress to carry out its deliberative and supervisory responsibilities.

In line with this reasoning, a number of specific organizational innovations and reforms are commended below to the Joint Committee on the Organization of the Congress. If put into practice, these changes would have the effect of enabling the Congress better to meet its obligations under the Constitution.

Service in Theory and Practice

THE CONSTITUTION does not make explicit that members of Congress shall be servants of their constituents. But the simple logic of the requirement that members are to be locally nominated and locally elected ensures that they will serve—or else take the electoral risks of not doing so.

The total number of citizens actively doing special pleading for themselves may be small, perhaps only a fraction of a House district containing half a million persons or of a state many times larger than that. But as long as "the world's greatest publicity organ is still the human mouth," [3] this active minority of citizens can play a critical role out of all proportion to its numbers.

Consider the calculations of a senator from a large eastern state: "During the last year and a half, I have done favors for about 3,000 persons. When you consider the word-of-mouth spread, this amounts to a substantial number of voters." [4] Over a six-year term at this rate, favors for 12,000 persons could have the multiplier effect of informing 50,000 to 100,000 constituents about the senator's diligence.

Are citizens upon whom such largesse is bestowed appreciative? Political folklore has it, of course, that dispensing a single patronage job creates "one ingrate and twenty enemies." But even if true, this is a comment on the expectations of persons deeply involved in politics, where favor demand always outruns supply. Citizens on the margin of politics, with their occasional requests and blurred view

---

[3] Phrase of a senator's assistant quoted in Donald R. Matthews, *U. S. Senators and Their World* (Chapel Hill: University of North Carolina Press, 1960), p. 226.

[4] *Ibid.*

340

of how to obtain results, apparently feel very different. One administrative assistant to a southern senator indicated their reactions in the following way:

> When we get a positive action of some significance in our case work, we add the man's name and address plus a report on what we have done for him to our card file of friends. The last time _____ ran for re-election, we sent this file down to his campaign manager. His manager then wrote a personal letter to every person on that list, informing him that _____ was facing opposition in the primary and would he help out. The response was amazing—75 to 80 per cent must have volunteered to help.[5]

From a purely political viewpoint, however, deciding when to do favors and when not to can be a tricky business. One farm-born and reared congressman, who believes that he gets his "biggest assist from people I have been able to help on *little* things," has told about the nuisance to his constituents of walking long distances to rural mailboxes:

> I was helpful in getting inserted in post office regulations a provision that there be extensions granted for farmers in certain instances. A survey indicated I had 3,000 farmers in my district who had to go over half a mile for mail so I started a campaign. By the last election I had gotten 1,300 extensions. They think of me every time they go get that mail.[6]

The congressman added that he had "assisted with some Small Business Administration appointments and got myself in terrible trouble."

The net conclusion is that helping enough constituents can provide that decisive margin of good will, votes, campaign funds, and assistance, which enables a member to remain in Congress and play his additional roles of legislator and overseer. This was the advice given by a former senator to a group of freshman House Democrats recently: "First join the Tuesday to Thursday Club. Be a statesman later."

However much some citizens—and a few legislators—may look askance at the political nature of the service function in practice, that function is based upon what can be called the principle of

---

[5] *Ibid.*, p. 226n.

[6] Charles Clapp, *The Congressman* (Washington, D. C.: The Brookings Institution, 1963), p. 83.

voluntary reciprocity. The *quid pro quo* works both ways in politics, and modern theories of democratic representation are built upon that premise.

But the service function has not arisen solely out of the exigencies of democratic, representative politics. It is sanctified by the belief of most legislators that citizens *need* and *deserve* a response to their legitimate requests. Witness one member of the House:

> Most people who write me have valid problems and feel that only their representatives can help them get action. Now sometimes they are wrong in sending things to us or in thinking their case has merit, but they are sincere, and I think it is one of the functions of a congressman to do what he can for them. It really doesn't irritate or bother me.[7]

Similarly, Congressman Gerald Ford, at an orientation session for freshman House members in 1963, counseled them "to determine at the outset whether cases are a chore or an opportunity." He amplified his point, saying, "We try to make our office the human link between a vast Federal Government and the individual at home. If your office becomes this human link I think you will render excellent service to your constituents." [8]

Many members undoubtedly agree with Mr. Ford, but some probably turn political necessity into civic virtue and rationalize their devotion to the service function. A congressman lacking seniority, expertise, and a network of relationships with other members may choose to throw his energies into the work of helping constituents; for here at least some results of his efforts are immediately apparent in contrast with his efforts in legislative work where he finds he has little influence.

But in the main, it has to be recognized that it is primarily the localized system of nominations and elections which forces a member to pay heed to the service function. In most constituencies, the basic electoral practice is that every man runs essentially by himself for his own election. A candidate must be a political entrepreneur who builds a personal organization out of whatever resources are available to him, from among family, friends, business associates, party workers, and union or other organizational officials. If he is to have a career in Congress, he must solve the persistent and recurring problems of obtaining campaign funds and assistance.

---

[7] Quoted in Clapp, *op. cit.*, p. 76.

[8] Congressional Quarterly Service, *Transcript of Seminars for New Members of the 88th Congress, January 14-21, 1963*, Washington, D. C., p. 7.

Quite as important, between campaigns he must have sources of help and information in his district.

The member competes for these scarce local resources with others: with local party leaders, for example, who may differ with him on matters of patronage allocation or even in basic ideological orientation; or with local or state officeholders who have the twin advantages of being in the district while the member is away and of being able to distribute far more tangible rewards to their supporters. When it comes to "gut-politics," from the local viewpoint, a member of Congress is a bit of a luxury, unless he can prove otherwise.

So, under most circumstances, it is this highly competitive nature of American political life, the essential isolation of the representative in Washington, and the risks of his losing his investment of time, money, and personal sacrifice which impel a member to throw himself with unremitting energy into the task of building a personal following among his constituents.

Indeed, most members have a generally positive attitude toward the service function. For example, 80 House members were asked recently by a group of Dartmouth College professors whether "an important part of a Congressman's job should be to go to bat for constituents in their dealings with executive agencies." More than three-quarters of them (78 percent) agreed or tended to agree that such casework is important. Only one-fifth flatly disagreed.[9]

However they handle the service function and however much they may privately begrudge the effort involved, most members of Congress—even those who dedicate most of their time to legislative work—believe that it is one of the best ways to achieve personal job security.[10]

The burden of constituent services

How heavy a working load do constituent requests place upon a member of Congress and his staff? Charles Clapp asked this question of a number of House members and concluded that many spend a major portion of their time on such non-legislative matters. Some said they devoted 90 or even 98 percent of their personal working hours to dealing with these requests. Another said that he had

---

[9] Material prepared by Roger Davidson, David Kovenock, and Michael O'Leary. See U. S., Congress, Joint Committee on the Organization of the Congress, *Hearings Pursuant to S. Con. Res. 2*, 89th Congress, 1st Session, Washington, D. C., 1965, p. 775. (Hereinafter cited as "JCOC, *Hearings*.")

[10] Senator Joseph S. Clark has an illuminating discussion of his own views of the service function in *Congress: The Sapless Branch* (New York: Harper & Row, 1964), pp. 56-67.

reduced the burden upon himself from "105 percent" to 10 percent once he was able to delegate most of it to a staff which now handles nothing but constituency problems.[11]

Whether the service function is the single most time-consuming activity of congressmen depends upon whether one is measuring the personal labors of a member or the work-load of his staff. In the Dartmouth College survey already referred to, the 80 House members being interviewed were asked to describe the job of the congressman as they interpreted it. While 77 percent of them mentioned legislation and committee work as "the major time-consuming activity," only 16 percent so described casework and constituent errand-running. However, more than half of the members who did not mention casework as the "major time-consuming activity" stated that it is an important secondary one.[12] And the chances are good that an analysis of the total time expended by members and their staffs on all congressional work would find casework the leading activity. In the Dartmouth study, for example, more than half of the sample cited casework as one of the most burdensome problems confronting them.[13]

The burden upon the member of the Senate is potentially even heavier, given his larger constituency. Yet most senators have lightened it—to meet more diverse committee responsibilities—by a greater delegation of constituent work to larger staffs, by using more highly automated mail-handling systems, and by the exercise of personal self-restraint. Senator Clark, for instance, believes that his colleagues are more able to insulate themselves from constituency pressure than are members of the House.[14] Some, however, are quite unwilling to do so, fearing that they "will get out of touch" if they delegate the service function to others.

For senators, the sheer handling of constituent mail is the most time-consuming part of the service functions. Its volume in the office of a senator from a state with a large population can be staggering. Senator Thomas Kuchel of California says his daily mail runs to 1,000 to 2,000 letters from constituents, occasionally mounting to 6,000 pieces.[15] Senator Hugh Scott of Pennsylvania receives 500 to 600 letters a day, with a record of about 2,000, while his senior colleague, Senator Clark, calculates his own mail totals for a year

---

[11] Clapp, *op. cit.*, pp. 53-55.
[12] JCOC, *Hearings*, p. 775.
[13] *Ibid.*, p. 776.
[14] *Op. cit.*, p. 56.
[15] JCOC, *Hearings*, p. 326.

as running to 110,000 letters and postcards, together with 15,000 pieces of bulk mail, such as periodicals, reports, and brochures.[16] Senators from less populated states receive much less, but Senator Gale McGee of Wyoming points out that the bulk of his mail actually comes from outside his own state. He believes that "the concept is emerging more and more that a Senator is a Senator of all of the United States and not of just one state." [17] Hubert H. Humphrey, when a senator, complained that there were days when he had to run a kind of miniature post office in his own suite. One staff member would spend "all day long just opening the mail—not answering it—just opening it, just sorting it." [18]

The mail load in a House office, of course, is much lighter, averaging perhaps 50 to 100 letters a day, but overwhelming in its aggregate for the whole House—such as in 1962 when nearly 23,000,000 pieces of incoming mail were handled.[19]

Mail, telephone calls, and visits from constituents—both to Washington and to district offices—are rapidly increasing in volume, from all present indications. This is partly a by-product of America's population growth, of course. Congressman Ray Madden of Indiana, for example, relates how his Gary district's population has nearly doubled since he arrived in Congress in 1943, with that much more pressure of demand for services.[20] Increasing electoral competition in many congressional districts also increases the number of services performed. Some southern members from two-party districts, for instance, find their constituency contacts increasing, but this is probably due as much to their own anxious cultivation of new voters as it is to heightened political awareness in their districts. Other developments help explain the growing burden of services. A more highly educated population than ever before is placing greater demands upon congressmen, while the heightened affluence of many families encourages them to call long distance and to travel to Washington.

But the key factor in the burgeoning of constituent requests is undoubtedly the vast increase of federal programs affecting the ordinary citizen. One Washington newsman put it in a phrase: "As the federal government continues to expand its functions, the

[16] *Ibid.,* p. 299; Clark, *op. cit.,* p. 56.

[17] JCOC, *Hearings,* p. 337.

[18] Quoted in Daniel Berman, *In Congress Assembled* (New York: Macmillan, 1964), p. 55.

[19] Clapp, *op. cit.,* p. 69n; Berman, *op. cit.,* p. 54.

[20] JCOC, *Hearings,* p. 265.

congressman finds himself more and more a pleader of special problems and a prisoner of the mailbox." [21]

A large proportion of a congressman's mail concerns the problems of citizens in their dealings with the Social Security Administration, the military services, the Veterans Administration, the immigration authorities, the Internal Revenue Service, and other agencies close to the daily lives of individuals. And with the recent passage of legislation providing for medical care for the aged, there is already apprehension on Capitol Hill about the vast new workload expected in mediating between senior constituents and the Department of Health, Education, and Welfare, over "medicare" rights.

Yet many congressmen even seek additional ways to stimulate constituent requests, however much they and their staffs may complain about the resulting deluge. Some send polls or questionnaires to persons on their mailing lists to elicit views on pending issues, as well as to advertise the congressman's name and his concern for his constituents' opinions. Some members send bulk mailings. (One engaged extra clerical help for three weeks, for example, to inform every relevant businessman in his district on "how to do business" with the National Aeronautics and Space Administration, thereby soliciting new problems for himself.) Others use their Washington newsletters to invite even more correspondence by calling upon constituents to write to them on any occasion.

"One way or another," says Congressman Peter Frelinghuysen of New Jersey, "we like . . . to encourage mail from back home. For no matter how close you live, no matter how close you keep in touch with your district, there tends to be something of a vacuum between the people that you represent and you as their legislator, their representative in Congress." [22]

This restless urge to keep in touch, believes Senator Clark, is "compounded by the widely held belief that legislative work is not particularly noticed or appreciated by the constituents, and that it does less to help the Congressman get re-elected than 'bringing home the bacon'—providing service to constituents—and good public relations." [23]

Indeed, one political scientist, who has interviewed many members about their legislative interests, found that they often give only

---

[21] William Broom of Ridder Publications, quoted in Clem Miller, *Member of the House* (New York: Charles Scribner's Sons, 1962), p. 64.

[22] Congressional Quarterly Service, *op. cit.,* p. 10.

[23] *Op. cit.,* p. 66.

"marginal attention" to many of the supposedly "key issues" before the Congress. Many members, he found, deny feeling pressures from constituents on these issues probably because *"real* pressure— e.g., those things which constituents really press on—is likely to be on matters of patronage, jobs, passports, immigration visas, etc., and a Congressman often spends a good deal of time on such matters." [24]

Members' attitudes toward the service function, it seems clear, can inflate the significance of the function beyond reasonable bounds —or even beyond reasonable expectation of being able to perform it. Picture the plight of Congressman William Ayres of Ohio as a freshman in 1951, newly arrived in Washington after a campaign in which he promised "to do more" for his district. He "soon found that his position as a Congressman did not open doors or cut red tape automatically." He had few agency contacts to approach. The large tire and rubber-goods firms in his Akron district snubbed him, for each "had its own offices in Washington, staffed by professional expediters who knew their way around the maze of executive agencies better than Ayres." [25]

To perform the service function at all thus requires not only adequate *resources* but also *access* to agencies and persons who can render assistance. For what specific purposes is this assistance needed?

The types and volume of services requested

Performing the service functions for constituents can involve a member in a vast array of activities, some of them capable of accomplishment within congressional precincts, some necessitating his interference in the work of the agencies, and others potentially requiring contact with persons and organizations outside the federal government.

Constituent requests can be broken down into the following rough classification:

1. *Legislative matters:* Many constituents request the views or voting intentions of a member on pending legislation. These make up the largest volume of requests, but many can be answered by mechanically-prepared form letters.

2. *Cases:* A large number of constituent requests ask for, or neces-

---

[24] Lewis A. Dexter, "Marginal Attention, Pressure Politics, Political Campaigning, and Political Realities," *International Review of History and Political Science* (Meerut, India), I, 1963-64, pp. 115-23, at 118.

[25] Bailey and Samuel, *op. cit.,* p. 114.

sitate, the interference of a member in federal agency proceedings to investigate a complaint, speed agency action, obtain special treatment, or develop information. Some members draw the line at "procedural interference," simply asking an agency for information or expressing their interest in a case. Others, on special occasions or as a matter of policy, will apply pressure to obtain action favorable to a constituent, sometimes even acting as counsel to the constituent in agency proceedings.

3. *Publication requests:* A sizable number of requests are made for congressional or federal agency publications. While easily managed, the task of fulfilling these demands is onerous mostly because of the volume. In one year, for example, the Department of Agriculture alone supplied 4,721,413 copies of publications to members for distribution to their constituents.[26]

4. *District projects:* A small number of complex "group projects" are usually pending in a member's office. Sometimes his help has been solicited by individual constituents or by local governmental units and organizations within his district. At other times the project may have been initiated by the member himself, but it nonetheless requires protracted consultation with constituents and negotiation with agencies. Examples of district projects are public works projects, area redevelopment and urban renewal projects, community action programs, rivers and harbors developments, and the like. Occasionally a member will stake his congressional career on obtaining a major public project for his constituents. On other occasions members will wage concerted fights to prevent agency transfer of defense or veterans activities out of their districts. The rivalry among House and Senate members to announce defense contract awards to firms in their districts is an indication of the significance most of them place upon projects of this kind.

5. *Employment, appointments, and patronage:* Every member receives a sizable number of requests for information about federal employment and how to apply for it. Some are more specific and ask for the member's active help or endorsement. Many members devote additional time to interviewing young men for appointments to the service academies, although others have developed competitive examination systems whereby appointment goes automatically to top scorers. While the number, and kind, of patronage positions which a member has at his disposal to offer his constituents is severely limited—some district postmasterships, rural mail carriers,

---

[26] Clapp, *op. cit.,* p. 77.

census workers, and minor Capitol Hill appointments—the time expended in filling them can be considerable. And the exercise of "senatorial courtesy" over certain presidential appointments may require lengthy negotiations.

Constituents sometimes seem to expect "miracles" from members on employment matters. Charles Clapp makes this point about their over-expectations:

> Fearful of the results of disclosing inability to achieve the goals sought by the constituent, the congressman and his staff devote large amounts of time needed for other activities in seeking results. If results are achieved, they often come only after strenuous congressional effort. The constituent is less grateful than the legislator thinks he should be, partly because he overestimates his representative's power in such matters.[27]

6. *Unusual requests:* Constituents often ask a member for assistance on matters well beyond the bounds of normal federal government activity. One wealthy but politically inactive married couple, making plans for an extensive trip to Europe, requested their representative to make all of their transportation and hotel arrangements and elicit social invitations from American embassies in foreign cities along their route. (The member complied.) Requests for United States flags which have flown briefly over the U.S. Capitol are no longer considered unusual (since procedures have been developed for their distribution), but requests for historical souvenirs, autographs of celebrities, collections of rock specimens, and the like, still are.

7. *Washington visits:* Easily overlooked is the time-consuming task of making arrangements for Washington visits by home district families, organizations, and high school graduating classes. These visits not only involve arranging transportation, accommodations, tours of the White House and other public buildings, but also scheduling the member—and often some of his colleagues—for special meetings, luncheons, and photograph-taking sessions. While members from districts near Washington may have heavier constituent traffic, those from distant districts find their constituents usually stay longer and expect more service.

It is very difficult to obtain accurate information about the number of all these various requests or the time members and staff devote to each, or of the relative importance they may attach to them.

---

[27] *Ibid.*, p. 103.

A very crude way to estimate the service work-load requirements is to analyze the types of incoming and outgoing mail of any member. Kenneth E. Gray, Legislative Assistant to Senator Paul H. Douglas of Illinois, has made a systematic attempt to identify the volume and types of mail received and answered in the Senator's office during a single more or less typical week when Congress is in session. (It may be noted that whereas most offices experience their largest volume of "legislative" mail during a session, usually at times of great press attention to the more dramatic legislative issues, case mail comes in a uniform flow every week of the year.) Gray's findings are set out in Tables 1 and 2.

Gray found, as Table 1 shows, that more than four-fifths of the Senator's incoming mail, comprising letters, cards, and telegrams, was legislative in character, much of it answerable by robotyped form replies. That week, nearly half of the legislative mail hap-

TABLE 1: One Week's Receipt of Mail in a U.S. Senator's Office [a]

	Letters, postcards, and telegrams received	
	No.	%
1. Legislative mail	2,953	81.2
2. Case mail	284	7.8
3. Agency business, no action required	16	.4
4. Screened mail (to staff members)	77	2.1
5. Miscellaneous	303	8.3
Total	3,633	99.8 [b]

[a] Count taken in the Washington office of Senator Paul H. Douglas of Illinois for the week of March 19-25, 1958. Includes mail forwarded from his Chicago office.

[b] Does not equal 100 because of rounding.

Source: Table adapted from Kenneth E. Gray, "Congressional Interference in Administration," prepared for delivery at the 1962 Annual Meeting of the American Political Science Association, September 1962, Appendix 1, p. 4.

pened to be on a single issue, and was part of an organized campaign to influence the Senator's vote on an "anti-billboard" amendment to the Federal Highways Construction Act.[28] Although case mail amounted to only 7.8 percent of the total influx, the 280 letters represented problems far more complex than their mere number

[28] Kenneth E. Gray, "Congressional Interference in Administration," prepared for delivery at the 1962 Annual Meeting of the American Political Science Association, September 1962, Appendix 1, p. 3.

would indicate. Screened mail to staff members and miscellaneous mail also contained some constituent requests.

During the same legislative week, as set out in Table 2, Senator Douglas and his staff dispatched 2,320 pieces of mail from his office, although almost two-thirds were standardized form replies. There

TABLE 2: One Week's Output of Mail from a U.S. Senator's Office[a]

	Letters and telegrams sent	
	No.	%
1. Individually prepared & typed		
Replies to legislative mail	276	30.9
Case mail: to constituents	243	27.2
Case mail: to agencies	86	9.6
Information and publications	99	11.1
Miscellaneous	188	21.0
	892	99.8[b]
2. Form legislative mail	1,428	------
Total Outgoing Mail	2,320	

[a] Count taken in the Washington office of Senator Paul H. Douglas of Illinois for the week of March 19-25, 1958. Count excludes mail on service academy appointments, machine-addressed press releases, mimeographed material, and certain other materials.

[b] Does not equal 100 because of rounding.

Source: Table adapted from Kenneth E. Gray, *op. cit.,* Appendix 1, p. 5.

remained 892 letters to prepare individually, of which more than a third were straight casework, involving replies either to constituents or to agencies. These often required additional telephoning. Other replies concerned other types of constituent requests, for legislative information, publications, jobs, and speaking engagements.

If these rates are correct, it can be estimated that on case mail alone, Senator Douglas would receive nearly 15,000 letters in a single year and would send out nearly 21,000 letters in connection with them. Moreover, Gray estimates that since 1958, the year he made his analysis, the overall volume of the Senator's mail has increased at least 20 percent.[29]

Case mail, to repeat, embraces the most complex of constituents' requests; that received by Senator Douglas in the week studied covered problems ranging across the whole gamut of federal agencies.

[29] *Ibid.,* Appendix 1, p. 2.

Table 3 contains a breakdown of the types of cases involved, showing the number of letters on each type received from constituents and agencies respectively. The breakdown reveals sizable

TABLE 3: Volume and Types of Case Mail Received in One Week in a U.S. Senator's Office

	Number of letters	
	From constituents	From agencies
Illinois projects (public works, urban renewal)	29	6
Federal welfare programs	20	8
Veterans programs	17	6
Civil Service claims & problems	9	10
Post Office personnel & operations	7	4
Military—personnel	28	17
Military—non-personnel	3	5
Immigration	20	14
Miscellaneous agency problems	24	23
Federal employment	6	4
Complaints about federal agencies	9	1
Complaints about non-governmental groups	10	1
Totals	182	99

Source: Table adapted from Kenneth E. Gray, *op. cit.*, Appendix 1, p. 9.

mail volume on several subjects, such as public works projects for Illinois, federal welfare programs, military personnel, immigration, and veterans programs. The multiplicity of subjects and agencies covered by the mail underscores a belief held in many congressional offices that a bewildering variety of expertise is needed to cope with casework.

Senator Douglas, to be sure, represents a populous state, with a significant number of foreign-born constituents who could be expected to raise an unusual number of requests about immigration matters. How does his service work compare with that of a House member?

Gray analyzed the casework burden of a midwestern congressman for the year 1957, when the member was in his fourth term and served on the Committee on Appropriations. Casework was presumably vital to this member, since his elections had been close, one of them by less than a 700-vote margin.

The volume and character of this member's entire casework load for the year is set out in Table 4, which shows that a total of 386 separate cases were handled for individual constituents and another 61 for groups, organizations, and governments within the district, making a grand total of 447 cases. As the compilation reveals,

Table 4: The Volume and Character of One Congressman's Casework During the Year 1957

	No.	%
Individual cases		
Personnel matters (civilian)	62	16.1
Personnel matters (military)	63	16.3
Veterans benefits	98	25.4
Social Security, Old Age and Survivors Insurance, and Unemployment Compensation	49	12.7
Immigration	15	3.9
Federal agency programs	58	15.0
Special service requests	41	10.6
Total	386	100.0
Group cases		
Requests for general information	6	9.8
Requests for specific information	10	16.4
Complaints	12	19.7
Requests to expedite or promote	33	54.1
Total	61	100.0

Source: Table adapted from Kenneth E. Gray, *op. cit.*, pp. 13-15.

personnel matters and veterans benefits bulked largest among individual problems. Gray reports that about 10 percent of all individual cases were pressed beyond routine handling. The member's efforts involved contact with more than 64 major offices and bureaus within the 12 executive departments and the office of the Secretary of Defense, together with 13 independent agencies.[30]

Taking an overview of the casework burdens in the senatorial and congressional offices just analyzed, two tentative conclusions emerge.

A House member may have a relatively heavier case load than a senator. Gray calculated that the senatorial office he studied received one new case per week for each 87,000 constituents, whereas

---

[30] *Ibid.*, pp. 12-16.

the representative's office received one for each 48,570.[31] While a senator represents more voters altogether, his staff is also larger. The much lower request rate for the senator suggests that the existence of two senators for each state almost halves the potential case work for each of them. If a senatorial office is ill-prepared to handle its casework, a House office can be expected to be almost doubly hard-pressed.

The other point which emerges is the tremendous variety of problems arising in casework, ranging across the work of the entire complex of federal agencies. Obviously the longer a member and his staff have worked in Washington, the more able they are to develop and maintain personal contacts in dozens of offices, bureaus, and independent agencies. Here, too, a senator may have an advantage over a representative. One would expect greater effectiveness and efficiency from a senatorial staff in dealing with so many contact points, because its larger size both embraces a wider variety of fields of expertise and insures a higher output of work.

Thus, while all members of Congress carry sizable service burdens, contributing to the feeling that it is "beyond effective legislative control" and that "the limits of capacity have been reached," [32] House members seem to be at a relatively greater disadvantage. Perhaps that is what Congressman John Moss of California had in mind when he said, "Sometimes we treat ourselves like poor relations. . . . You will find that the other body is in many respects far more generous with themselves than the House is. We have no control over that." [33]

In a more optimistic vein, Congressman Michael J. Kirwan of Ohio, in his capacity as chairman of the House Democratic Campaign Committee, wrote recently:

> No Congressman who gets elected and who minds his business should ever be beaten. Everything is there for him to use if he'll only keep his nose to the grindstone and use what is offered.[34]

If the service function is basic to congressional longevity, what resources are available to the member who "minds his business"? Indeed, are they sufficient?

---

[31] *Ibid.*, p. 12.

[32] A House member quoted in George B. Galloway, *History of the House of Representatives* (New York: Thomas Y. Crowell, 1961), p. 126.

[33] Congressional Quarterly Service, *op. cit.*, p. 4.

[34] *How to Succeed in Politics* (New York: Macfadden Books, 1964), p. 20.

The Need for Assistance to Members

THE BURDEN of services for constituents has been considered so heavy by some observers of the Congress that extreme remedies have been advanced. One member has formulated it this way: "It is too bad we don't have two members of Congress for each district, with one having the responsibility for handling constituent requests, the other being free to study legislation and to legislate." [35] Such an idea assumes the former to be a chore and the latter a calling, and that the two duties are unrelated to each other.

The point that has to be reiterated is that the service function is founded upon political necessity and cannot be evaded or delegated. What is more, the service function, properly performed, can make the member a better and more creative legislator and can help the entire Congress discharge its collective responsibility of supervising the federal bureaucracy. The need of a member to be re-elected and the need of the Congress to operate effectively as a collegial body are complementary, not contradictory, objectives. Proposed changes and reforms in the congressional system must foster both objectives if they are to be meaningful.

The staffing problem in the Senate

However much personal attention a member gives to his service and deliberative responsibilities, most of the more routine and mechanical work must be delegated to staff assistants. Widespread disagreement prevails among members, however, over the proper number and types of assistants to be employed and the size of the clerk-hire allowances that should be available.

---

[35] Clapp, *op. cit.,* p. 55.

In the Senate today, personal staffs range from six to eight assistants to more than 30, with the typical office employing 13 to 15, authorizations being determined by the size of the state population being represented. Usually a senator's office is managed by an administrative assistant, supported by a corps of secretaries and caseworkers handling mail and services, while a legislative assistant and press assistant help the senator on his legislative and public relations work. Usually one or two assistants maintain offices within the home state.

Some of the service burden can be shifted as a senator gains the prerogatives of committee or subcommittee chairmanship and is able to name committee staff assistants loyal to him. Although committee staff assistants only occasionally concentrate on a chairman's constituent problems, they can take on a variety of duties which leave his personal staff freer to perform services.

Usually, therefore, complaints about inadequate staff provision come from the more junior senators from larger states who have not yet gained extra perquisites and who tend to be the most anxious about re-election. Some dig into their own pockets to hire extra staff. Others are warmly receptive to paid speaking engagements, earmarking their *honoraria* for staff expenses. One senator paid for a full one-fourth of all his staff salaries by this method for several years.

Some senators want more staff help; [36] others are contented. Senator Clifford P. Case of New Jersey fears that the demand potentially is insatiable: "Everyone wants his job to be done ideally, you could expand the staff indefinitely. I think there is a point where we ought to make a conscious decision that this will not get any bigger." [37]

Work undoubtedly can expand to absorb the energies of whatever staff is assigned to it, in the best Parkinsonian sense, yet there is one brute fact which sets a limit to the size of senatorial staffs: the lack of office space. Even with the New Senate Office Building, accommodations for members and their staffs—particularly for junior members—are small and often less than adequate. Senior members, not surprisingly, are reluctant to give up their private studies and committee rooms. And given recent costs and problems

---

[36] Senator Ralph W. Yarborough of Texas has testified before the Joint Committee on the Organization of the Congress on the need for additional personal staff. See JCOC, *Summary of Hearings*, June 24, 1965 (mimeographed).

[37] JCOC, *Hearings*, p. 376.

in office building construction, the Senate is unlikely to build more.

There is also an administrative limitation to the expansion of staffs: the limited span of control which a senator or his chief assistant can exercise effectively over the multifarious operations. A frequent, but only privately voiced, complaint of many Senate staff employees is that they rarely have the chance to talk with their senator. Many caseworkers feel they are tied to a production line and are given little policy or political guidance.

Given the factors of limited space, staff control, money, the essential insolubility of the problem, and the relative contentment of many senators, two proposals may be worth consideration which would have the *effect* of increasing personal staff without actually doing it.

Present senatorial office operations can be made more effective by improving the quality of personal staff assistants themselves. This objective would be enormously advanced by creation of an Office of Personnel under the joint management of the Congress which would serve members of both bodies.

Such an office could be a source of highly qualified personnel, professional, caseworker, and secretarial, able to provide full-time, part-time, or short-term employees quickly in response to member requests. The office could also maintain a roster of expert consultants available to members and committees to meet the often-expressed need to avoid undue dependence upon federal agency or private pressure group sources of expertise.[38] Moreover, it would serve members in giving them a central point to which to refer constituents seeking Capitol Hill employment.

While the rationale for such an office has been presented admirably by several members to the Joint Committee on the Organization of the Congress, one further point should be made here:[39] There is no reason why an Office of Personnel should interfere in any way with the personal or political prerogatives of members. The office would be available to any member who wished to use it, but no member would be compelled to do so.

The chances are that an aggressive Office of Personnel could help recruit more highly trained and readily available administrative and

[38] See especially the testimony of Congressman John Brademas of Indiana, JCOC, *Hearings,* pp. 586-602; and also of Congressmen Chet Holifield of California, *ibid.,* p. 200, and Benjamin S. Rosenthal of New York, *ibid.,* pp. 66-67.

[39] Congressman Rosenthal of New York presented detailed testimony on this idea to the Joint Committee. See JCOC, *Hearings,* pp. 66-72 *passim,* and also the ideas of Congressman Samuel Stratton of New York, *ibid.,* p. 554.

professional talent than is now normally within the personal acquaint-ance of many members. Upon request, it could carry out the "executive search" techniques now used by many private firms and organizations. If desired, it could give routine typing and shorthand tests to job applicants to help insure that standards of secretarial competence were met. It could query professional organizations, universities, and foundations for names of professionals interested in congressional consulting work.

A second suggestion for improving the effectiveness of staff assistants, especially for their work on constituent services, is to organize a regular program of orientation sessions for members and staffs, at which federal agency legislative liaison representatives and congressional committee staff directors would discuss agency organi-zation, case procedures, and legislative problems. These sessions should be sponsored by the leadership of both houses and be directed primarily at freshman members and their staffs. They might well be held during December, prior to the opening of Con-gress. They could bring together the excellent work already being done in this sphere by the American Political Science Association, the Democratic Study Group, and some of the agencies themselves, only they should concentrate on casework procedures rather than on policy matters and parliamentary procedures.

However, beyond these two innovations—an Office of Personnel and formal orientation sessions— there are legitimate staff problems which cannot be solved *without* the addition of new personnel.

In the Senate, multi-committee memberships, always several in number and sometimes totaling as many as eight subcommittees, place a most serious burden on a senator. Any senator, facing several simultaneous committee meetings on the same morning, must try to find assistants to sit in for him at important meetings he cannot attend. His legislative assistant, of course, can help. His admin-istrative assistant is often sent. And the more senior the senator, the more likely he will be able to call upon a committee staff assist-ant to help him.

But for all senators, except committee chairmen and ranking minority members, there remains an urgent need for more legislative help. The need is compounded for minority senators who have more subcommittee responsibilities and less claim upon committee staff.

Senators Scott and Kuchel have both proposed ways of providing such help; the former calling for a special legislative assistant for each senator to handle his committee obligations, and the latter suggesting a separate assistant for each committee assignment.[40]

But however the specific assignments are allocated, provision should be made for at least additional part-time committee staff assistance for each senator, made responsible to the senator instead of to the committee. Such an assistant could also help on constituency problems falling within the committee's general area of jurisdiction.

The side effect of this arrangement would be to release more of the senator's administrative assistant's time for constituency problems and supervising caseworkers. Simultaneously, it would help a senator solve one of the most pressing of his problems: how to participate effectively in more than one place at a time.

The staffing problem in the House

In the House, where each member has one primary committee responsibility, and only occasionally two, the problem of keeping abreast of his legislative work is much less acute. This is said with full knowledge that occasionally House subcommittee meetings conflict, but this is more an exception than a rule. Therefore a member is far more able to concentrate on one area of legislative work and be his own committee expert.

Two activities, however, interfere with his role as specialist. One is the press of other legislation, ready for debate and voting, for which he does not have the services of a specially-designated legislative assistant, as do senators. The other is the service function, for which he does not have an administrative assistant.

Members of the House are circumscribed by many self-imposed limitations on their personal-staff hiring practices. Clerk-hire allowances, amounting to approximately $50,000, may be divided among no more than ten assistants at a time, unless the member has more than 500,000 persons in his district, in which case an extra assistant, and an increased salary allowance are authorized.[41] Other inflexible rules hem in the congressman. Part-time employees are counted as full-time for purposes of the limitation. An extravagantly complex schedule of base salaries with raises has to be used, and a ceiling limits the pay for a member's chief assistant.

In practice, a member can, of course, create a highly organized staff within these limitations. For example, Congressman John

---

[40] *Ibid.,* pp. 299-300, 325.

[41] Approval of House Resolution 416 on June 16, 1965, authorizes each member to employ one student intern for two and a half months each summer at total compensation of $750. The arrangement does not affect the statutory clerk-hire allowance and the intern is not counted under the regular ceiling number.

Tunney of California, who reports a heavy burden of service requests from his rapidly growing Riverside district, has organized a staff of ten as follows:

Administrative Assistant: handles purely administrative matters.

Legislative Assistant: legislation, press, and utility work.

Senior Secretary: casework.

Assistant Secretary: casework.

Personal Secretary: handles personal correspondence.

Secretary: runs robotype machines, puts out newsletters, etc.

Two Part-Time Assistants: college girls who do miscellaneous clerical work.

Two District Secretaries: each runs a district office.

Nevertheless, despite this staff of ten, Mr. Tunney believes he needs more assistance.[42]

The fact is, however, that most representatives do not use their full staff authorizations. In 1963, when the staff ceiling was nine or ten assistants, depending upon district population, Clapp found that 17 members had only three employees each and that nearly half of the members had six or fewer.[43] The distribution for the entire House was:

Size of staff	Number of members
10	12
9	67
8	90
7	85
6	71
5	57
4	36
3	17
	435

Thus, many members obviously can build more effective and more sizable staffs within present statutory limitations. The quality of the staff also could be improved by drawing upon the proposed Office of Personnel, as discussed above, and by insisting that assistants participate in orientation sessions of the kind described.

One modest reform can be suggested to alleviate the most pressing problem in many House offices, however. The Congress should authorize each representative to name an administrative assistant with salary, status, and responsibilities similar to his counterpart in the

---

[42] JCOC, *Hearings*, pp. 372ff.

[43] *Op. cit.*, p. 60n.

Senate. Many House members now designate a chief assistant in this way, but salary ceilings often prevent their hiring a person equal to the responsibilities of the job. A modest increment to the present overall clerk-hire allowance for each member, together with a higher salary ceiling to apply only to the administrative assistant, would make possible at least one professional assistant on each member's staff.

Overwhelming support for this reform already exists in the House. In a recent interview survey of a sample of House members, 79 percent of them said they favored the idea, while only 18 percent opposed it. Indeed, among a list of 32 projected reform ideas, the creation of the office of administrative assistant was the most popular of all.[44]

Since the same limitations of office space, staff control, and money, together with the insatiability of some members' demands, apply to the House as to the Senate, this single reform seems the most that can reasonably be proposed at present. It would not revolutionize handling of the service function in the House, but it could mean much more capably directed staffs for its members.

The member's office and its resources

The House and Senate provide their members with office space in Washington and, if desired, in their home districts. To operate the offices, a full panoply of allowances is furnished to pay for stationery, air mail and special delivery stamps, telegrams and telephone calls, office equipment, and other sundries.[45] The franking privilege, ice, and, for some, mineral water, are provided free. In general, the Senate is more liberal with its member allowances than is the House.[46]

For many House members, these allowances and services are inadequate. For others, some of whom cultivate their districts or their public relations more aggressively, they are not enough. Some House members do not spend their annual $2,400 stationery allowance. Others pay an additional $1,000 or $2,000 out-of-pocket when they consume unusual quantities of supplies. Two of the most pressing office problems in the House—the increasing need for long-distance

---

[44] JCOC, *Hearings*, p. 761.

[45] Details for the House can be found in *Information for Representatives-Elect to the Eighty-Ninth Congress*, prepared by the Clerk of the House. No similar publication exists for the Senate. Details may be obtained by verbal request from the Senate Disbursing Office.

[46] See the Legislative Branch Appropriations Act for 1966 (P.L. 89-90) and the discussion in *Congressional Quarterly Weekly Report*, July 30, 1965, p. 1506.

telephone calling and the rising costs of rented office space in the districts—have been somewhat alleviated by recent legislation.[47]

What remains, however, is the general question of how to help a member make the most effective use of all these resources. A legislator does not necessarily know how to organize an office properly, nor can he always give it adequate supervision. Provision for House members to hire administrative assistants would be helpful, of course, but one further suggestion seems appropriate.

An Office of Management Adviser should be established to serve those members of the House—and the Senate as well—who wish to seek its advice on how to organize their office work for more effective and efficient service.

Such an office could employ several professional management consultants to provide, *when requested,* advice on setting up an office budget and records system, files for case materials, office layout, work systems, use of office machines and photocopying, and divisions of functions between Washington and district offices.

This idea, which already has some enthusiastic support from members who have talked with private management consultants, would be most helpful to freshman members.[48] But it has applicability to every member who finds that the deluge of constituent demands is about to overwhelm both staff and office.

The problem of travel

"Mending fences" back home in the district is not only important as a reminder to voters about who represents them. It probably is a necessity. Many senators shudder at memories of what happened to Senator Robert LaFollette, Jr., when he chose to stay in Washington to shepherd the LaFollette-Monroney Reorganization Act through Congress in 1946, instead of spending his time in Wisconsin preparing for a primary contest. One result was congressional reorganization. Another was LaFollette's defeat by Joseph R. McCarthy.

With lengthier legislative sessions, it grows more difficult for members to spend substantial periods of time in the district. One group of exceptions, of course, are those members living close enough to Washington to belong to the "Tuesday-to-Thursday Club." As jet speeds shorten travel time, the club enlarges its membership and at

---

[47] H.R. 10139, which became law (P.L. 89-131) on August 21, 1965, increases the number of long-distance telephone calls reimbursed. H.R. 10014, which became law (P.L. 89-211) on September 29, 1965, increases district office rental allowances.

[48] See the discussion with Congressman Benjamin S. Rosenthal in JCOC, *Hearings,* p. 65.

least one Rocky Mountain State and several California members are virtually candidate members. Others, with family responsibilities in Washington and insufficient funds to travel often, live in fear because of their prolonged absences from the district. One representative from the southwest, just before Christmas-time adjournment in 1963, was deeply worried because he had been able to spend only 14 days that year in his district.

Travel allowances differ between the two houses of Congress. In July 1965, the Senate increased the number of reimbursable district-to-Washington round trips for its members to six a year and also raised Senate staff assistants' mileage payments by two extra round trips a year in those senatorial offices representing state populations of ten million persons or more.[49] The staff assistants' travel allowance for all other states remains at four round trips a year.

House members until recently were paid for three round trips a year between their homes and Washington, one of them at a rate of 20 cents a mile (on which savings can be set aside for additional travel) and the other two for actual transportation expenses. In the face of the Senate travel increases contained in the Legislative Branch Appropriations Act passed in 1965, the House successfully sought similar privileges by special legislation. Congress has now approved two additional round trips for House members each year (raising the total to five) and the option (of interest to members living near Washington) of substituting a $300 lump sum payment for the two extra trips. Two round trips to the district each year were also authorized for a House member's staff.[50]

Given the widespread belief among members that travel home during a session is essential, how realistic is an allowance for five or even six trips?

Almost all members travel much more than that. One New Jersey representative calculated that he spent $2,000 out-of-pocket for some 30-odd weekend trips home during 1964. A Massachusetts representative that year journeyed to his district 39 times. Three trips were reimbursed by the House, six by district organizations before which he had speaking engagements, and 30 were paid out-of-pocket at a cost equal to one-sixth of his gross salary.

Costs increase vastly for western members, even though travel time may be less than to New England. Senator Gale McGee of Wyoming

[49] Legislative Branch Appropriations Act for 1966, P.L. 89-90, approved July 27, 1965.

[50] P.L. 89-147. On the restrictions surrounding official travel for House members, see *Congressional Record*, August 16, 1965, p. 19686.

reports that he traveled to his home state 86 times during the six years of his first term. Eighteen were official trips, but the other 68 were paid for by himself or as part of speech-making expenses.[51] Many western members decry the need to "sing for their supper" in order to get home. Others feel that the high cost of travel forces some members from distant places to accept too readily airline tickets donated in the form of campaign contributions. Members from Hawaii and Alaska simply do not get home very often.

Those members from distant states whose electoral hold on their districts is tenuous are in the worst position. One midwestern senator, appointed to fill a vacancy late in 1964 and facing a 1966 election for a full term, has journeyed to his home state every weekend except two since his arrival in Washington. At present, as shown in Table 5, there are 24 Democrats and 14 Republicans from west of the Mississippi River who won their House seats in 1964 by margins of less than 55 percent. One of them, who journeys to a far western state

Table 5: Number and Location of "Marginal" House Seats

Distribution of Democratic and Republican House Seats Won in 1964 by Less than 55 Percent of the Vote

	East	West	Total
	of the Mississippi River		
Democrats	37	24	61
Republicans	35	14	49
Total	72	38	110

nearly every weekend at great expense, calls the three-trip allowance "ridiculous." But travel costs are high, too, for the 72 House members from marginal seats east of the Mississippi, for the closer to home Washington is the more often they are expected to visit it.

As with other expense allowances, it is difficult to set an equitable amount for travel. Moreover, the difficulty is compounded by the frequent need for a member's chief assistants to journey to the district on office business, particularly on service projects for local governments and organizations.

Judging by need, and by expressions of a willingness to compromise, it seems warranted to suggest that members be reimbursed officially for up to 12 round trips to their district annually and that they further be reimbursed for up to 12 round trips to the district for

---

[51] JCOC, *Hearings*, p. 337.

staff members whom they authorize to travel on official business.[52]

The alternative to official reimbursement for most members who live at any distance is reliance for their expenses upon others—such as wealthy contributors, party committees, or private organizations—a situation which does not promote legislative independence.

A word should be added on foreign travel. The American press has contributed to a widespread public belief that all congressional travel abroad is "junketeering." Some members feel so vulnerable about such criticism that they refuse to make foreign trips, even on official business. Foreign travel, however, is vital for every member, regardless of committee assignment. He must make decisions nearly every day, which ought to be based upon a working knowledge of international relations. Congress should, therefore, do what it can to rectify public misunderstanding. One approach would be to prohibit all official trips for "lame-duck" or retiring members, thus eliminating a major reason for public criticism. Another would be to bring certain counterpart funds under the stringent control of the Congress, with stricter reporting and accounting requirements.

Assistance from party organizations

For many years the Democratic and Republican campaign committees for the House and Senate have provided a variety of forms of assistance to members, ranging from raising campaign funds for them to helping them with constituent problems. Although practices have varied, the emphasis of the Democratic committees in recent years has been upon providing personal assistance and research, while the Republican committees have stressed help on publicity and public relations. But with only small staffs and limited funds at their disposal, all of the campaign committees have been forced to set priorities. For this reason their help is usually earmarked for those members with the greatest need who are also potentially re-electable. As a result, the committees have concentrated on assisting incumbents of the more marginal House and Senate seats, numbering no more than a quarter of all members at any time.

Other party resources, however, are available to all. In the House, the Majority and Minority Rooms serve as staff auxiliaries on a modest-cost basis. Their personnel can themselves relieve a member's office of clerical chores like mimeographing and photocopying and

---

[52] On the need for member and staff travel funds generally, see testimony in *ibid.*, p. 261 (Congressman Thomas Ashley of Ohio); p. 326 (Senator Thomas Kuchel of California); pp. 408, 410, 416 (Congressman James Kee of West Virginia); and p. 426 (Congressman Claude Pepper of Florida).

mailing newsletters and Christmas cards, or they can sometimes suggest sources of clerical help. These activities are calculated to help the party faithful be re-elected and therefore fit loosely into the category of aids to the better performance of the service function.

In recent months the Democratic National Committee has undertaken an ambitious plan to assist 71 freshman Democrats in the House in a number of ways. The Committee has assigned some of its experienced employees to help freshman members with their public relations and research work. The Committee also has offered members many new contacts with federal agency officials, thereby presumably opening new administrative channels through which constituent requests can be transmitted by members to the agencies. One member from Hawaii, for example, reportedly is drawing upon these new agency acquaintances to try to create a joint federal agency liaison office in Honolulu. Other freshmen apparently have pressed for new federal projects to be undertaken in their districts. Members also have been given useful detailed data about federal expenditures benefiting their constituents.[53]

This Democratic National Committee scheme undoubtedly helps many freshman Democrats perform the service function much better since they are given systematic and cordial access to the vast resources of the administration. It is really not a new idea, though, but only a much expanded extension of the work which each Capitol Hill campaign committee has always tried to perform whenever its partisans have controlled the administration. In this case, however, the full prestige and backing of the White House seem to have been committed because of President Johnson's determination to preserve the legislative support of the congressmen involved.

From the viewpoint of an independent Congress, however, one criticism should be leveled at the plan: while it strengthens their hand in their own districts, it results in an increased direct dependence of freshman members upon the executive branch. How much, if any, freedom of legislative action is actually lost remains a moot question. Yet the same plan, if it were effectively organized under control of the House leadership and the Democratic Congressional Campaign Committee, would preserve all of its advantages for members without laying them open to executive pressures.

Additional aspects of the service function

Certain service activities of the Congress—such as work on pri-

---

[53] *Washington Post,* September 19, 1965; *Washington Evening Star,* July 2, 1965.

vate bills and patronage—have been criticized recently by individual members on the ground that they are too onerous or too "political" and should therefore be reformed or discontinued. Part of the reasoning is that these activities now distract members and their staffs from more crucial work. Reform or discontinuance, it is envisioned, would release time, energy, and other resources for better perfomance of the service function.

These proposals, everything considered, have little merit. Many of the service activities criticized are of as much direct benefit to constituents as other types of casework. From the viewpoint of the reasoning set forth in this paper, namely, that constituent services of all types are politically necessary and legislatively vital for members, the reform proposals can only diminish the effectiveness of congressmen. Some of these more contentious aspects of the service function, however, deserve a brief discussion at this point.

Private bills. The Legislative Reorganization Act of 1946 created administrative procedures to handle the vast bulk of private claims and immigration matters which previously had required legislative attention. The small number which remain, to be sure, can be burdensome to members who introduce them on behalf of constituents. Yet private bills offer a remedy, a chance for equitable treatment, which may be vital to the lives and livelihoods of the constituents. Moreover, some of them give sponsoring members an insight into the functioning of immigration laws which otherwise would receive far less scrutiny. With the use of partisan official objectors to screen these bills on the private calendar, few members spend any appreciable time on them. For these reasons it seems desirable to retain the present private bill procedures.[54]

Patronage. Some members deplore pressures put upon them by candidates for postmasterships, rural letter-carrier jobs, and the roughly 1,400 Capitol positions filled by personal patronage methods. Senator William S. Proxmire of Wisconsin reported that his staff received more than 5,000 letters, calls, and visits in 1961 and 1962 on postmastership appointments alone, and suggested that they be placed entirely on a merit basis.[55] Minority party members, on the other hand, often criticize the small share of patronage jobs which they control, running, in one estimate, to only 2.5 percent of the

[54] See the criticism of Congressman Ashley and Senator Kuchel, JCOC, *Hearings,* pp. 268, 326. Senator Kuchel reports that he tries to transfer private bill requests to members of the House from California.

[55] "Congressional Reform," *Congressional Quarterly Special Report,* June 7, 1963, p. 896.

available positions on Capitol Hill.[56] The individual prerogative to exercise patronage should be retained as a way of benefiting deserving constituents. Creation of an Office of Personnel would enable members who prefer not to exercise their prerogative to delegate their responsibility to a personnel officer who would choose the most qualified available candidate. The present option of members in connection with service academy appointments—to choose with or without competitive merit examinations—should also be retained.

Announcement of agency awards and contracts. The present practice, followed by the Department of Defense and certain other agencies, of giving majority party members advance notice of contract awards in their states and districts, enabling those members to make advance announcements, should be retained as a majority party perquisite. The criticism that the practice takes too much of a member's staff time is implausible.[57]

* * * * *

To be sure, each of these aspects of the service function—private bills, patronage, and contract announcements—can be time-consuming and occasionally troublesome for some members. And members of the minority party understandably feel discriminated against by their lack of control over the perquisites of patronage and contract announcements.

The overriding principle, however, is the importance of constructing and maintaining lines of communication between a member and his constituents, both for his sake and for theirs. Alteration of present procedures would weaken these lines and dissipate a part, however small, of each member's influence.

---

[56] Testimony of Congressman Joel Broyhill of Virginia, JCOC, *Summary of Hearings,* August 12, 1965 (mimeographed); *Washington Post,* August 13, 1965.

[57] See testimony of Senator Jacob Javits of New York, JCOC, *Hearings,* pp. 496, 503.

The Service Function, Legislation, and Administrative Supervision

ERVICING constituent requests, especially those involving case-work, forces members of Congress and their staffs to evaluate hundreds of thousands of individual administrative decisions and actions over a period of time. Usually they go along with bureaucratic decisions in disputed cases, even though constituents customarily are given the initial benefit of doubt. But, as Paul H. Appleby has so aptly pointed out, the nature of the American system of government makes any low-level administrative action potentially susceptible of being elevated by the Congress to the level of a policy issue.[58] It is this power of Congress to politicize seemingly routine, administrative decisions that provides major opportunities for members to relate the service function to their supervisory and deliberative responsibilities.

Some members believe that the service function operates in this way already. One House member, discussing the matter with colleagues, argued:

> You should not underestimate the value of constituent work on the legislative process. Don't you get a lot of your ideas about needed changes in the laws from the problems of your constituents? In processing a problem before the VA or a draft problem you gain your best insight as to how laws operate, and you discover where they might be changed.[59]

---

[58] *Policy and Administration* (University, Ala.; University of Alabama Press, 1949), pp. 10-12.

[59] Clapp, *op. cit.*, p. 79.

Another member thinks highly of citizen watchfulness as an aid to congressional oversight of federal agencies:

> I would emphasize that the best watchdogs we have are not the committees but our constituents who in their letters bring to our attention things which require looking into. We get plenty of warnings of real significance in our mail which are extremely helpful in assisting us to carry out our responsibilities.[60]

From the standpoint of making more effective legislative use of the information obtained from case problems, however, many obstacles stand in the way. Members are often too pressed for time to dig into a case beyond the level necessary to get a favorable result for his constituent. In one such instance a House member commented, "I will not have time to follow that up. I will get the guy's contract and I will forget it. Obviously some bureaucrat just overstepped his authority. This happens every day."[61] Indeed, the probability that some agency officers consistently act beyond their authority—let it "happen every day"—suggests the need for some effective method of ascertaining when patterns of administrative malfunctioning or malfeasance exist and when cases arise out of simple error.

The difficulty of discovering the root causes of poor administration is compounded by the fact that most casework is handled by staff assistants, with members often giving only cursory supervision. Congressional knowledge of recurring problems arising within a given agency, therefore, is difficult to coordinate because of the many individuals involved. Hence, it is usually an accident—or a particularly flagrant abuse—that leads to a full-scale investigation and the necessary remedial legislation.

Interference in administration on behalf of constituents is essentially a task for individual members. Kenneth E. Gray reports, after careful study of the matter, that congressional committees rarely perform this function except for committee members, and then usually only for those of greatest seniority.[62] As a result, most committees have little knowledge of the great majority of case problems arising in the agencies within their legislative jurisdiction.

A greater degree of systematic supervision was expected to result from the Legislative Reorganization Act of 1946. "It was the intention of the authors," according to George B. Galloway of the Legislative Reference Service, ". . . that the oversight committees would

---

[60] *Ibid.,* p. 80.

[61] *Ibid.,* p. 79.

[62] Gray, *op. cit.,* p. 2.

serve as a 'clearing house' to which members would refer all such constituent complaints and inquiries and which would bring them to the attention of the agencies concerned." [63] Gray concludes that this practice has been encouraged only by the Government Information Subcommittee of the House Committee on Government Operations and then solely on "tough cases" involving denial of information by agency officials.[64]

So far as oversight is concerned, then, much of the potential value of casework is lost by the "shotgun" effect of having 535 members and several thousand staff employees serve as overseers. Can a modicum of systematization be created out of such chaos?

The office of Administrative Counsel

There is, I believe, great potential value in the idea of an Office of Administrative Counsel for the Congress. Congressman Henry S. Reuss of Wisconsin has proposed on many occasions that such an office be established to assist those members who wish to use it in the processing of constituent cases involving federal agencies.[65]

Most critical discussion by members of his proposal suggests that they have a basic misunderstanding of it, perhaps exacerbated by their reluctance to take it seriously because it has been labeled the "Ombudsman" idea (owing to its resemblance to a governing technique of that name used in Finland, Denmark, Norway, and New Zealand).[66]

Mr. Reuss proposes in a pending bill, H.R. 4273, that an Administrative Counsel's office of perhaps ten to 20 subject-matter specialists be created to:

> . . . review the case of any person who alleges that he believes that he has been subjected to any improper penalty, or that he has been denied any right or benefit to which he is entitled under the laws of the United States, or that the determination or award of any such right or benefit has been unreasonably delayed, as a result of any action or failure to act on the part of any officer or employee of the United States.

---

[63] *The Legislative Process in Congress* (New York: Thomas Y. Crowell, 1953), p. 416, quoted in *ibid.*, p. 2.

[64] *Ibid.*, p. 2n.

[65] See JCOC, *Hearings,* pp. 79-100, and *Congressional Record,* February 11, 1963, pp. 2078-84.

[66] Apparent misunderstanding of the Reuss proposal is visible in the discussion of Senator Scott and Congressman James Cleveland of New Hampshire, JCOC, *Hearings,* pp. 304-05, 350-51, 364. In the countries mentioned, citizens may appeal to an Ombudsman for administrative remedy, bypassing the legislature.

While one can argue the potential merit of the idea from the viewpoint of citizens' rights and attack the proposal on its potential abuses, two major benefits might accrue to the Congress from its adoption.

First, the Office of Administrative Counsel could lift some of the burden of the service function from any member who chose to use it to handle the more mechanical aspects of investigation into a case. H.R. 4273 envisions an entirely voluntary agency, prohibited from accepting any case complaints directly from citizens and permitted to process cases only when these are specifically referred to it by members. All contact with a constituent would therefore be conducted by a member; all credit for success could be taken by a member; and all blame for an unsuccessful case could be shifted to the administrative counsel.

In effect, the Office of Administrative Counsel would become an adjunct to a member's staff and it would help lighten the load in a far more expert way than the addition of extra caseworkers in a member's office.

Second, a major benefit would result from the fact that the Reuss proposal embodies techniques whereby the administrative counsel could systematize much of the knowledge gained by individual members from casework and report it to the congressional committees for the purposes of assisting them in their work of agency supervision and remedial legislation. Congressman Reuss writes:

> A single defective law or administrative procedure may be the cause of hundreds of difficulties between citizens and the Federal bureaucracy. But with the complaints being funneled into 535 separate congressional offices it may not be recognized that a vast amount of casework has a single source. The Administrative Counsel, on the other hand, would gain a unique insight into the cause of citizens' complaints and could easily spot the sources of recurring problems. In his reports to Congress, he could recommend steps to eliminate part of the growing volume of casework at its sources. Thus, . . . the Administrative Counsel would be an important factor in improving administration and tightening up any loose or defective statutes.[67]

The potential promise of this idea and the difficulties of achieving its objectives by other means suggest the wisdom of experimentation.

It is, therefore, proposed that an Office of Administrative Counsel be established along lines set out in H.R. 4273 as a mechanism to

---

[67] Prepared statement of Representative Henry S. Reuss of Wisconsin, reprinted in JCOC, *Hearings,* pp. 80-84.

assist the entire Congress in discharging its service, legislative, and supervisory responsibilities.

There are, of course, important mechanical details to work out to insure that the Office of Administrative Counsel would serve its specific purposes. For instance, the office should not interfere with the prerogatives of members and it ought not to become partisan. Questions remain about staff size and the types of experts who ought to be employed. Decisions on the structure and organization of the office, however, can be easily negotiated, once the basic desirability of this innovation is recognized.

A concluding note

Pessimism about the viability of legislative arrangements for governing people is as old as legislatures themselves. In some quarters today, the fact that legislative power is increasingly co-mingled with executive power in the United States has led to the *prescription* that Congress ought to redefine its functions away from legislation. One proponent of this view, Samuel Huntington, has argued:

> If Congress can generate the leadership and the will to make the drastic changes required to reverse [current] trends . . . it could still resume a positive role in the legislative process. If this is impossible, an alternative path is to abandon the legislative effort and to focus upon those functions of constituent service and bureaucratic control which [prevailing trends] . . . enable it to play in the national government.[68]

Without discussing the merits of the argument about the alleged decline of Congress, it is worth saying that most critics agree that Congress is an institution which plays a supremely important brokerage role in linking citizens to the federal bureaucracy. In this belief they concur with the staunchest defenders of Congress who see the same service functions as vital.

Critics, such as Professor Huntington, however, are able to perceive a dichotomy between legislation on the one hand and a combination of the service function and congressional oversight on the other, which I believe is a falsification of reality.

A fundamental assumption in this paper has been that a major source of the total knowledge required by the federal government in order to govern effectively resides in the constant press of con-

---

[68] "Congressional Responses to the Twentieth Century," in David Truman (ed.), *The Congress and America's Future* (Englewood Cliffs, N. J.: Prentice-Hall, Inc., 1965), pp. 5-31.

stituent requests upon members of Congress. That knowledge is essentially indivisible; it can be used for remedial legislation as well as for stimulating administrative changes within the bureaucracy. Knowledge of a constituent's problem can lead to a single, specific solution, or it can be the germ of a creative legislative idea ultimately affecting millions of persons as it is made the law of the land. Certainly, however, such knowledge is a necessary—if not a sufficient—condition of creative legislation.

Democratic government thrives as it transforms the needs and wishes of citizens into effective public policies and programs. Able performance by Congress of the service function is a major method of ascertaining these needs and wishes. What remains for the Congress is to improve the methods by which the resulting knowledge is transformed into policy decisions and their subsequent administration. The reforms in the execution of the service function and in the use of its results, as set out in this paper, hopefully will contribute to that crucial objective.

ROGER H. DAVIDSON is an Assistant Professor of Government at Dartmouth College. He has served as co-director of an extensive survey of the role perceptions of members of the U.S. House of Representatives, a study sponsored by the Dartmouth Public Affairs Center. He is the author of several articles on legislative behavior, and is co-author of two forthcoming books—*The Politics of Congressional Reform,* and *On Capitol Hill: Studies in Legislative Politics.* An honor graduate of the University of Colorado (1958), he received his doctorate from Columbia University in 1963. During the 1965-66 academic year, he has been a Guest Scholar at The Brookings Institution in Washington, D. C.

Congress and the Executive: The Race for Representation

Roger H. Davidson

Introduction

THE competitive tensions between Congress and the executive establishment, it has been said, are only the side manifestations of a far larger war over the future of America.[1] These two institutions embody major rival value systems in our society which are competing for popular allegiance. To be sure, mutual suspicions and recurrent open warfare have always characterized relations between the White House and Capitol Hill—a fact which would no doubt please the framers of the Constitution. But the past two generations have witnessed dramatic developments which have considerably sharpened the sense of conflict. Political scientists have lost no time in chronicling these developments, and even the general public has seemed at times fascinated by the contest. Indeed, the popular press often appears to consider congressional-executive relations as a gigantic tournament at which no spectator should be without his program.

Yet despite all the attention that has been lavished on the subject, the commentators—whether academic or journalistic—have often misidentified the battlefields on which this war is being fought. Most observers have rightly remarked on the decline of the classic preeminence of Congress in legislation, and the concurrent rise of its more passive oversight function. This finding has formed the context for lengthy debates, often from a prescriptive point of view, over the distribution of formal powers between the two branches. Should there be a presidential "item veto"? Should there be "legislative vetoes"? How much oversight should Congress engage in? Should it be general-

---

[1] Clinton Rossiter, *The American Presidency* (New York: New American Library, 1956), pp. 150-51.

ized and detached, or specific and "meddlesome"? Such discussions have their utility, but often as not they mistake what are actually side skirmishes for the real battle.

It is the thesis of this paper that this conflict between Congress and the executive can best be understood as a test of the representational capacities of these two institutions. The strength of the popular assembly theoretically rests upon its control, if not its outright monopoly, of the vital channels of communication with those interests making demands on the instruments of government. In describing the eclipse of the presidency during the Monroe Administration, for instance, Justice Joseph Story observed that "the House of Representatives has absorbed all the popular feelings and all the effective power of the country." The presidency was subsequently rescued from its debilitated condition, in the nineteenth century by the periodic emergence of "strong Presidents," and more recently by the aggregation of more permanent legislative and administrative prerogatives. The critical question for the contemporary Congress is its capability for "absorbing the popular feelings." The viability of legislative institutions rests in large part upon their continued ability to function as representative instruments; and if this power is yielded to alternative institutions within the political system, the traditional rationale of legislative power is undermined.

Representation:
Concepts and Indicators

EPRESENTATION, broadly speaking, is the embodiment of the particular and general wills of the community in the processes of political decision making. One student of representation has described it as "a condition which exists when the characteristics and acts of one vested with public functions are in accord with the desires of one or more persons to whom the functions have objective or subjective importance." [2] As we shall see, the mechanisms and manifestations of representation are various; but the broadest possible representation of societal interests is usually taken as the norm for democratic politics. As Mosca wrote, "the only demand that is important, and possible, to make of a political system is that all social values shall have a part in it, and that it shall find a place for all who possess any of the qualities which determine what prestige and what influence an individual, or a class, is to have." [3] Thus, the inclusiveness of representation may be accepted as a criterion of performance both for political systems and for political institutions.

What are the mechanisms of representation, and what are its indicators? Analytically, the test of representation is whether, in public policymaking, the demands or interests of every relevant and definable public have been effectively articulated. These publics may be geographic, occupational, professional, organizational, and so

---

[2] Alfred de Grazia, *Public and Republic* (New York: Alfred A. Knopf, 1951), p. 4.

[3] Gaetano Mosca, *The Ruling Class,* trans. Hannah D. Kahn (ed), Arthur Livingston (New York: McGraw-Hill, 1939), p. 258.

379

forth. The policymaker may represent them through actual membership or through intermittent contact—for example, the unwritten rule that legislators should reside in the district from which they are elected, and the frequent hearings which legislators are constrained to give to constituent groups. By such means, the viewpoints of relevant publics are transferred overtly into the policymaker's field of vision. For elected officials, this communication is reinforced by the periodic ritual of the campaign, with its ultimate sanction of defeat for the politician who strays too far from the interests of his constituents. In addition, there are "virtual" means of representation, in which no discernible communication has taken place between the policymaker and his publics. In such cases, the policymaker "takes into account" a particular viewpoint, perhaps by anticipating the responses of constituents even in the absence of overt cues. The traditional view of the politician as a "broker" implies that what he contributes to the decision-making process is a tactile sense of the strains and tolerances of the political environment.

A number of techniques have been employed with some success to probe the representative capacities of individual political decision makers. For instance, an audit may be taken of their social backgrounds and formal associations, under the assumption that these cumulative experiences constitute an important frame of reference for decisions.[4] Alternatively, the formal constituencies, such as legislative districts or bureaucratic clienteles, may be catalogued with a view to identifying convergences between their presumed "interests" and the public choices of decision makers.[5] These techniques rest on inferences drawn from the relationships between demographic characteristics and patterns of decisions. Somewhat more adjacent to the choices themselves the the decision maker's attitudinal and behavioral patterns, which can be uncovered through sophisticated research methods. One approach is through a comprehensive audit of communications cues received by the decision maker.[6] Another is to conduct interviews in order to extrapolate the decision maker's role perceptions—that is, his normative views of what interests he should take into account in

---

[4] See, for example, Donald R. Matthews, *The Social Background of Political Decision-Makers* (Garden City, N. Y.: Doubleday, 1955).

[5] One example is Julius Turner, *Party and Constituency: Pressures on Congress* (Baltimore: Johns Hopkins Press, 1952).

[6] See David M. Kovenock, "A Communications Audit of Members of the U. S. House of Representatives" (paper presented to the 1964 meeting of the American Political Science Association, Chicago, Ill., September 8-12, 1964).

making choices.[7] Through a combination of such techniques it may be possible to discern the policymaker's "state of mind" in relation to his various constituencies, both actual and potential. Such indicators constitute the "premises" on which decisions may rest.

The individual decision maker need not be assumed as the only point of reference, however: decision-making systems may also be said to be representative in the aggregate. Thus, we can say that Congress, or the presidency, or the bureaucracy typically represent certain foci of interests when they process decisions. Of course, one can be content merely to add up the constituency forces presumed to be operating upon all the individual actors in a decisional system; but here the sum is greater than its parts. Hence the leading question is whether, taken as a whole, the system allows for the possibility that all relevant interests can be heard at some point between the inception and the implementation of a policy.[8] Moreover, if certain interests are underrepresented in one arena in the system, can they be compensated for in the operations of another arena? The methods employed to probe these questions would certainly include aggregative use of data gathered concerning individual decision makers, as well as conventional descriptive tools for analyzing decision-making processes. Survey techniques may additionally be employed to suggest the subjective "satisfaction levels" of the constituencies deemed relevant.

This distinction between micro- and macro-representation is of considerable conceptual significance. In the former case, we are dealing with a psychological predisposition to act caused by the convergence of constituent forces upon an individual political actor. In the latter, we are discussing those properties of a system (or subsystem) taken as a whole, which render it effective in the articulation and combination of various interests and cause it to be an object of satisfaction among those interests.[9] The interaction of these two factors should not be minimized: indeed, an institution's representational capacities are directly related to its propensity to recruit personnel who are receptive to cues from a multiplicity of constituencies.

---

[7] John Wahlke, Heinz Eulau, James Buchanan, and Leroy Ferguson, *The Legislative System* (New York: John Wiley, 1962).

[8] Robert A. Dahl, *A Preface to Democratic Theory* (Chicago: University of Chicago Press, 1956), pp. 132-33.

[9] It should be clear from this discussion that these two types of "representativeness" overlap the two "representative" functions proposed by Almond and Coleman: articulation and aggregation of interests. See Gabriel Almond and James Coleman, *The Politics of the Developing Areas* (Princeton: Princeton University Press, 1960), pp. 33-45.

With these definitions in mind, we shall attempt to compare the respective representative capacities of Congress and the executive establishment. The term "executive establishment" may have sinister connotations which are unintended. By this shorthand term, we mean to refer to two sets of institutions within the executive branch: on the one hand, the President and the "executive agencies" (including the White House Office, Bureau of the Budget, Council of Economic Advisers, etc.); and on the other hand, the bureaus and agencies staffed by career civil servants. (Presidentially appointed executives are in this scheme marginal men, owing dual allegiance to the President and to their adopted agencies.) What types of "representative men" are recruited into the legislative and executive branches? And, taken as a whole, how do these two systems perform as representatives of relevant interests in American society? As has been noted previously, our assumption is that the effectiveness of either system rests substantially upon its ability to make critical contributions to the representative character of our democratic polity.

Competing Historical Claims

DEMOCRATIC theorists of the seventeenth and eighteenth centuries gave to the legislature a paramount place in their scheme of things. The attention that was devoted to the representative assembly stemmed from the need, in the initial phase of the democratic revolution, to justify the claims of the legislature against the Crown as the fundamental voice of the commonwealth. Thus, John Locke characterized the legislative power in sweeping terms as "that which has a right to direct how the force of the commonwealth shall be employed for preserving the community and the members of it." [10] Like the monarch, the parliament of course was subject to the metes and bounds of the underlying social contract, which formed the enabling act for society's political institutions. But it was the intimate relationship of the representative assembly to the sovereign electorate, no matter how narrowly the latter was defined in practice, which rendered the legislature "not only the supreme power of the commonwealth, but sacred and unalterable in the hands where the community have once placed it." [11]

On this side of the Atlantic, the role of the colonial assemblies in articulating popular will in opposition to the Crown-appointed governors originally worked to reinforce belief in the primacy of the legislature as the legitimate representative of the people. Experience with the Continental Congress, however, later induced the framers of the

---

[10] John Locke, *Second Treatise on Civil Government* (London: J. M. Dent & Sons, 1924), p. 190.

[11] *Ibid.*, pp. 183-84.

American Constitution to temper the traditional democratic enthusiasm for legislatures. On the one hand, the framers took note of the
inability of the Continental Congress to wage war or conduct diplo-
macy; on the other, they argued that legislatures would be particularly
liable to tyrannize over other institutions in a republican form of
government. As sober an observer as James Madison criticized the
drafters of the earlier state constitutions for overindulging legislatures,
concluding that "the legislative department is everywhere extending
the sphere of its activity and drawing all power into its impetuous
vortex." [12] Alexander Hamilton and James Wilson were even more
harsh in their judgment of legislatures.

The product of the framers' deliberations is familiar to every school
child: a governmental system marked by a connecting or blending of
powers, so that each branch would exercise certain controls over the
other. The legislature was divided, so that the popular house would
be offset by an indirectly elected house controlled by the state legislatures. Though not elected popularly, the executive also had representative possibilities. As Gouverneur Morris expressed it, "the executive ought to be so constituted as to be the great protector of the
Mass of the people." [13] Thus, Article II contains a breathtaking list
of executive prerogatives, including a potentially significant role for
the President in the legislative process. [14]

The constitutional formula of blended powers produced a pre-
carious balance of forces which has sometimes resulted in alternating
periods of executive or legislative hegemony. Enlargement of the
franchise in the first half of the nineteenth century seemed to reinforce
the legislature's claims as the prime representative of the people—
Justice Story's observation, referred to earlier, was echoed by many
observers throughout the century. On the other hand, the periodic
appearance of strong Presidents was typically accompanied by assertion of the democratic features of that office. In foreign and military
affairs, of course, the President has always claimed to represent the
national interest and to be the guardian of "the peace of the United
States." During the stormiest period of the Civil War, when it was
questionable whether a public referendum would have supported him,
Lincoln appeared to conceive his constituency as being no less than

---

[12] Max Beloff (ed.), *Federalist 48* (Oxford: Basil Blackwell, 1948), p. 253.

[13] Max Farrand, *Records of the Federal Convention of 1787* (New Haven:
Yale University Press, 1937), II, p. 52.

[14] See Charles C. Thach, *Creation of the Presidency, 1775-1789* (Baltimore:
Johns Hopkins University Press, 1922).

the Constitution itself.[15] By 1888 James Bryce could observe that the nation regarded the presidency as "a direct representative and embodiment of its majesty." [16] House Speaker Joseph Cannon said of President McKinley that he kept his ear so close to the ground that he got it full of grasshoppers. Theodore Roosevelt viewed the President as a "steward of the people." And long before his own elevation to the office, Woodrow Wilson sensed its representative potentialities: "His is the only national voice in affairs. . . . He is the representative of no constituency, but of the whole people." [17] But it was the journalist-scholar, Henry Jones Ford, whose vision first took in the full representative nature of the office: behind the historical variability of the presidency, he wrote, stands the essence of the elected kingship, the oldest political institution of the race.[18]

The representative character of the modern presidency has been widely commented upon, and particularly by Presidents themselves. It took the 36th President, however, to invoke the Pedernales River as a source of constituent inspiration. In a remarkable passage from his 1965 State of the Union Message, President Johnson declared: "A President does not shape a new and personal vision of America. He collects it from the scattered hopes of the American past." [19]

The advantages of the presidency over the legislature as a representative symbol are not hard to fathom. Legislatures are complex and hard to identify with for people who like their heroes embodied in human form.[20] Moreover, the particularism of locally based legislators seems today inadequate for an age of nationalized political issues. As Senator Joseph Clark of Pennsylvania, a spokesman for the "national" wing of the Democratic party, remarked.

    . . . Congress is filled with the plea that "what's best for Podunk is best for America," while the Executive looks at

---

[15] Edward S. Corwin, *The President: Office and Powers* (4th ed.; New York: New York University Press, 1957), pp. 23-24.

[16] James Bryce, *The American Commonwealth* (New York: Macmillan, 1888), I, p. 278.

[17] Woodrow Wilson, *Constitutional Government in the United States* (New York: Columbia University Press, 1908), p. 83. In general, see Corwin, *op. cit.,* Chapter 1 and *passim.*

[18] Henry Jones Ford, *The Rise and Growth of American Politics* (New York: Macmillan, 1898), pp. 279-93.

[19] January 4, 1965. Reprinted in *Congressional Quarterly Weekly Report,* January 8, 1965, p. 53.

[20] The subject of popular attitudes toward Congress will be explored in detail in Roger H. Davidson, Michael K. O'Leary, and David M. Kovenock, *The Politics of Congressional Reform* (to be published 1966), Chapter 2.

his constituency and replies that "what's best for the nation helps Podunk." [21]

Behind such observations lies a resentment of the disproportionate weight which many American legislative assemblies give to rural, underpopulated, and one-party areas. Although the Supreme Court's recent series of reapportionment decisions promises radical readjustments in this balance of power, the persistence of such anomalies is a concrete policy motivation for those who are advocates of the Executive-as-Representative.

Nor is the presidency the only institution in competition with Congress in representing the people. The non-elective federal bureaucracy also has significant and long-standing claims as a representative instrument. The Federalists themselves, of course, made no pretense of creating a representative public service: in their view, government was *for* but not necessarily *by* the people, and was to be conducted by persons of superior education, ability, and training. Consequently, the Federalist administrative apparatus represented primarily what Adams had called "the rich, the wise, and the well-born." As Leonard D. White explained:

> [The Federalists] believed that only by a good public service could the interests of the mercantile classes be properly served; and to these interests they were well attuned. The country, as well as the merchants, was well served by its officials. [22]

The public service under the Jeffersonians was no more egalitarian: Jefferson believed that the "natural aristocracy" of men of talent and virtue was a providential gift, and from 1801 to 1829 the public service continued to be dominated by "gentlemen" selected on the basis of ability and character. [23] It was during the age of Jackson that there emerged a genuine "democratic" theory of administration. Jackson rather perversely contended that all citizens were equally qualified to implement the affairs of state; and the nefarious results of his "rotation in office" are well known. Nevertheless, his democratization of the public service was a genuine and a lasting achievement. As White concluded:

---

[21] Joseph S. Clark, *Congress: The Sapless Branch* (New York: Harper & Row, 1964), p. 20.

[22] Leonard D. White, *The Federalists* (New York: Macmillan, 1948), p. 514.

[23] Leonard D. White, *The Jeffersonians* (New York: Macmillan, 1952), pp. 548-50.

It brought endless sources of vitality into the body administrative directly from the body politic, granting all the confusion and waste that were finally to be corrected by more orderly and systematic methods, themselves democratic in character. The relationship between the people and their administrative system was not again to suggest preference to the well-born and the well-to-do.[24]

A modern scholar has asserted that the bureaucracy "is itself a medium for registering the diverse wills that make up the people's will and for transmitting them into responsible proposals for public policy."[25]

---

[24] Leonard D. White, *The Jacksonians* (New York: Macmillan, 1954), p. 566.

[25] Norton Long, "Bureaucracy and Constitutionalism," *American Political Science Review,* September 1952, p. 810.

Who Represents Whom?

The congressman

S
UCH are the respective historical claims of Congress and the executive establishment to represent the interests of the nation. In light of the legislature's traditional claim as a principal performer of representative functions in democratic systems, it is a matter of no little concern that Congress has recently fallen under mounting criticism for its alleged failure to perform these functions adequately. The challenges to congressional prerogatives are predicated in part upon the increased ability of the executive establishment, in Justice Story's words, to "absorb the popular feelings" of the nation. Indeed, Samuel Huntington has argued vigorously that the key to Congress' decline in influence is its growing isolation from the vortex of American life. "Congress has lost power," he writes, "because it has . . . defects as a representative body." [26] It is well to consider this argument; for, if true, it is perhaps the most serious indictment against contemporary legislative institutions.

Democratic theorists have never put much weight on Aristotle's observation that elections were essentially oligarchic affairs, but it is nonetheless true that elected officials are not recruited equally from all the various social, economic, educational, and occupational strata of society. The vicissitudes of an extended public career foreclose this occupational possibility to many Americans. The occupational

---

[26] Samuel Huntington, "Congressional Responses to the Twentieth Century," in David B. Truman (ed.), *The Congress and America's Future* (Englewood Cliffs, N. J.: Prentice-Hall, 1965), p. 16.

distribution of members of the 89th Congress (shown in Table 1) is fairly typical for recent Congresses. Aside from previous experience in public office (which includes 43.7 percent of the members), the occupations most frequently represented by legislators are law and business, with farming, teaching, and journalism far behind. Persons in these occupations typically enjoy what is termed "role dispensability," because they can move readily in and out of their jobs without jeopardizing their careers.[27] Moreover, the so-called "verbalizing professions" are considerably overrepresented—those who, like lawyers, businessmen, teachers, and writers, presumably possess skills

TABLE 1: Occupations in the 89th Congress

Occupations	Number [a]	Percentage
Agriculture	50	4.7
Business-banking	147	13.7
Civil service-politics	465	43.7
Journalism	36	3.3
Law	305	28.6
Teaching	46	4.4
Engineering	7	b
Medicine	4	b
Minister	2	b
Labor leader	2	b
Machinist	1	b
TOTAL	1065	100.0

[a] Numbers total more than 535 because members typically listed more than one occupation.

[b] = less than 0.5 percent.

Source: *Congressional Quarterly Weekly Report,* January 3, 1965, p. 26.

and resources especially appropriate for embarking on a public career. Needless to say, these resources include the benefits of education, which legislators possess in abundance: no less than 84 percent of the senators serving between 1947 and 1957 had at least some college

---

[27] For a discussion of this occupational characteristic, see Joseph Schlesinger, "Lawyers and Politics: A Clarified View," *Midwest Journal of Political Science,* May 1957, pp. 26-39. Andrew Hacker has purported to see sinister consequences in the predominance of lawyers in Congress. His argument rests on the presumed correlation between legal background and "conservatism." It would appear, however, that the variable is more regional than occupational: that is, southerners (at least in the Democratic party) tend more often to be lawyers, and southerners are more "conservative" by most indices. Hence, lawyers "look" conservative; but the correlation is spurious. See his "Are There Too Many Lawyers in Congress?" *New York Times Magazine,* January 5, 1964, pp. 14ff.

training, compared with 14 percent in the population as a whole (of adult males over 25).[28]

Nor are congressmen and senators particularly typical of the general populace in terms of their social origins. If we were to enumerate the occupations of congressmen's fathers in an attempt to ascertain social mobility, our list would look very much like Table 1. Professional, proprietary, and farming occupations would be strongly overrepresented, while laborers of all kinds would be underrepresented.[29] Additionally, congressmen are more likely to be drawn from rural or small-town backgrounds than are members of other elite groups, such as business executives and federal political executives.[30] This perhaps accounts for the seeming "parochialism" of legislators when viewed in comparison with more "cosmopolitan" elite groups. Reinforcing this tendency is the political fact that most legislators continuously identify themselves with their home states or districts. A crude test of this attribute is geographic mobility, and Huntington has shown ingeniously that legislators move, if at all, very early in their lifetimes and then not very far.[31] Only 19 percent of legislators have made interregional moves during their lives, compared with 75 percent of bureaucrats and 73 percent of political executives. (Those legislators who are geographically mobile are concentrated in areas, such as the west coast and the border states, which have been the focus of major population shifts during the past generation.)

Meanwhile, the congressional career itself has grown somewhat more insulated from other occupations. The tenure of the average congressman or senator is now significantly longer than in the nineteenth century; it seems that once elected, the incumbent can now usually anticipate the continued indulgence of his constituents as a reward for good behavior.[32] The enforced turnover of electoral defeat is nonetheless an ever-present threat for many legislators; and some

---

[28] Donald R. Matthews, *U. S. Senators and Their World* (Chapel Hill: University of North Carolina, 1960), p. 26.

[29] *Ibid.,* p. 20.

[30] See, for example, Matthews, *op. cit.,* pp. 14-17; Andrew Hacker, "The Elected and the Anointed," *American Political Science Review,* September 1961, pp. 540ff; W. Lloyd Warner, *et al., The American Federal Executive* (New Haven: Yale University Press, 1963), pp. 56-58; and W. Lloyd Warner and James C. Abegglen, *Occupational Mobility in American Business and Industry* (Minneapolis: University of Minnesota Press, 1955), p. 38.

[31] Huntington, *loc. cit.,* p. 13.

[32] On this general topic, see *Congressional Quarterly Weekly Report,* December 7, 1962, pp. 2225-30; and H. Douglas Price, "The Electoral Arena," in Truman, *op. cit.,* pp. 42-45.

congressional elections result in particularly large exchanges of seats (e.g., 1958 and 1964). But the last two decades have witnessed a general trend toward stability of congressional tenure. In the House, moreover, turnover tends to occur in that minority of districts where there exists lively two-party competition. In part as an outgrowth of this heightened "security," the legislator is less likely to transfer laterally to or from positions in other elite groups—for example, administrative or business leadership positions.[33] More than his predecessors, the legislator of the 1960s tends to be a political professional whose election has capped a long period of apprenticeship in public life at the state or local level. In the wake of these developments, the congressional *career* has undoubtedly emerged as a more meaningful and attractive vocational alternative than in the past. While these factors have operated to lend the congressional career greater distinctiveness, they have at the same time heightened the congressman's insularity from the general public.

These findings demonstrate beyond doubt that legislators, at least at the national level, are not a representative cross section of American life. As already noted, for example, they are likely to overrepresent certain occupational, educational, and social groupings; and they are apt to be "locally" rather than "nationally" oriented. Moreover, the growth of the congressional career as a distinctive vocational pattern has tended to supersede the civics-class image of the legislator who, like Cincinnatus, was chosen by his neighbors as the "best man among us for the job." Congressmen and senators are political specialists, many of whom have made the decision to pursue a political career early in their life. However, the factors we have so far discussed are little more than demographic indicators, and it should not automatically be assumed that legislators so recruited are incapable of performing representative functions. To cast further light on this question, we must turn to attitudinal indicators surrounding the legislator's conceptions of his roles and functions.

Role perceptions are here defined as those prescriptive elements which the legislator identifies with his job. If one were to ask a congressman to draw up a job description, how would he characterize his tasks? We stress what the congressman thinks he *ought* to do in his job, since it is this attitude which draws him psychologically in certain directions as he performs his duties.[34] A legislator's total role

---

[33] See Dean E. Mann, "The Selection of Federal Political Executives," *American Political Science Review,* March 1964, p. 97.

[34] John Wahlke, *et al., op. cit.,* pp. 7-17.

perceptions comprise many elements—ranging from generalized conceptions of the purpose of the job, to specialized views of his relationships with specific "others." Rather than exploring the total dimensions of this concept, our purpose will be the narrower one of identifying and describing the representative aspects of the legislator's role perceptions.

The notion of representation looms quite large in legislators' assessment of their tasks and of the environment in which they must work. In a survey of 116 members of the House of Representatives during the 88th Congress, the author and his colleagues attempted to probe the role perceptions of congressmen.[35] In general, the interview responses were congruent with the previously mentioned role typologies developed in 1962 by Wahlke and his associates; and those categories will be utilized here. Of central concern is the legislator's "purposive role"—his substantive conception of the ultimate aim of his activities, of "the where-from and what-for of legislative action." [36] Nearly 85 percent of the members interviewed mentioned some element of the "Tribune" role—that is, the legislator as discoverer, reflector, or advocate of popular needs and wants. Another 19 percent expressed the classical brokerage role of the politician—as balancing various geographic and policy interests. Other roles which were articulated bear less directly on what we have termed the representative functions. Among these are orienta-

TABLE 2: Distribution of Purposive Roles in the House of Representatives

Role	Percentage [a]
Tribune	84.3
Inventor	29.6
Broker	19.1
Ritualist	68.7
Opportunist	7.0

[a] Percentages total more than 100 because each respondent held an average of 2.1 role orientations.

---

[35] The 116 members interviewed represent a stratified random sample of total House membership. The breakdown is: general sample, 87; leader over-sample, 23; top-leader over-sample, 6. The original sample was 132 members, and the completion rate was 88 percent. For a report based on an earlier sub-sample of 80 members, see Michael K. O'Leary (ed.), *Congressional Reorganization: Problems and Prospects* (Hanover, N. H.: Dartmouth Public Affairs Center, 1964), esp. pp. 12-15.

[36] Wahlke, *et al., op. cit.,* pp. 12, 242.

tions which stress policy innovation ("Inventors"); formal aspects of legislation, investigation, and committee work ("Ritualists"); and campaigning and gaining re-election ("Opportunists"). The proportion of respondents expressing each role orientation is set forth in Table 2. Recent literature on legislative behavior has tended to lay emphasis on those cues which originate internally within the institution; and the relative frequency of the "Ritualist" conception suggests that this emphasis is well founded. Nevertheless, external constituency cues, however defined or interpreted, seem to form the most pervasive element of the member's substantive conception of his tasks.

Styles of representation, however, differ markedly. At the crux of the member's orientation as a representative is the question of whether he sees himself as following his own conscience or knowledge in making choices, or whether he views himself as following "instructions," either actual or implied, from his constituencies. Unfortunately, the point of departure for this distinction has traditionally been Edmund Burke's assertion that a legislator should act as a trustee for the national interest rather than the receptacle for localized pressures.[37] Needless to say, what came to be referred to as the "Burkean conception" was abhorrent to majoritarian theorists, who saw the legislature precisely as "a congress of ambassadors from different . . . interests." [38] In fact, the contemporary congressman typically shifts between the "Trustee" and "Delegate" orientation, depending on the nature of the issue, its relevance to the constituency, and even on the particular constituency being represented.

The distribution of representative role orientations in the House is shown in Table 3. Though many respondents articulated one or the other of the two orientations, fully 50 percent articulated *both* roles (i.e., "Politico"). And in a surprising number of cases, the responses included sophisticated explanations of the manner in which one role may be played off against the other. Fortunately for the congressman, the issues upon which his constituents speak with a clear voice are limited; and in most cases he must find other cues and premises upon which to act.[39] As would be expected, the pure "Trustees" were

---

[37] Edmund Burke, "Speech to the Electors of Bristol," November 3, 1774. See the discussion of this point in Wahlke, *et al., op. cit.,* pp. 268ff.

[38] For example, James Mill, *An Essay on Representative Government* (New York: Haffner edition, 1948).

[39] For a superb discussion of the relationship of constituency attitudes and legislative actions, see Warren Miller and Donald Stokes, "Constituency Influence in Congress," *American Political Science Review,* March 1963, pp. 45-56.

concentrated among southerners, members from rural (or in any case uncomplicated) constituencies, and those with relatively high seniority; "Delegates" were found disproportionately from competitive or marginal districts.

TABLE 3: Distribution of Representational Roles in the House of Representatives

Role Orientation	Percentage
Trustee	27.6
Delegate	19.9
Politico	50.0
Unclassified	2.5
TOTAL	100.0

Quite another question is the *focus* of representation—that is, the particular constituency being referred to. Quite apart from his prescribed style of representation (following conscience or knowledge as the criterion for decision making), Burke believed that the legislator was the representative of the *national* interest. The local basis of representation in most legislative assemblies renders the Burkean ideal of the legislator as trustee of the national interest a difficult one to follow in all instances. The results reported in Table 4 tend to underscore the impression of the diversity of foci for constituency-

TABLE 4: Distribution of Area Roles in the House of Representatives

Role Orientation	Percentage
District only	16.3
District primary, national secondary	19.0
District-national equal	28.4
National primary, district secondary	28.4
National only	1.8
Non-geographic	4.3
Unclassified	1.8
TOTAL	100.0

oriented behavior. Of particular interest were the few members who expressed a non-geographic role focus—for example, the northern urban Negro who saw himself as the representative of "Negroes everywhere," or the southern rural member who looked out after "all the dairy farmers." No doubt these functional constituencies also underlie the committee specialization inherent in the "Ritualist" role, and perhaps in the "national" focus generally.

Thus, while the social background data emphasize the severe limitations upon the "representative" character of congressmen, our findings concerning legislators' role orientations (here only superficially set forth) suggest a rather different conclusion. While the congressman may not be demographically representative of the American public, he is apparently sensitized to the interplay of demands originating from diverse publics. The realities of electoral politics may yield a certain parochialism, but many congressmen indicate no little sophistication in describing the boundaries of the influence of local constituencies upon their decision making. And even their seeming parochialism may be said to contribute to the traditional representational strength of the legislature as a repository of minority viewpoints. However, there are certain "qualitative" and non-geographic constituencies that the present electoral system leaves Congress less prepared to articulate. And it is precisely this focus of representation which the bureaucracy expresses in great measure.

The civil servant

The bureaucrat, no less than the politician, suffers from an unflattering public image, in part because of his alleged insulation from "the people." Confined to his office and hedged about with routine, the civil servant is perceived to operate in a vacuum, with little sensitivity to the needs and demands of flesh-and-blood human beings. Like most popular myths, this view of the civil servant has serious flaws.

In many respects, the civil service represents the American people more comprehensively than does Congress. Taken from top to bottom, the civil service roster (a total of 2,467,385 persons in mid-1965 [40]) is probably broadly representative of middle- and lower-middle-class Americans; persons from virtually all educational levels are represented, and occupations range from dishwashers and mail carriers to engineers and executives. However, we have chosen to direct our attention to the higher civil service, which has been the subject of several important studies during the past few years.[41]

---

[40] Civil Service Commission figures (May 31, 1965).

[41] Material in this section is drawn from Warner, *et al., op. cit.*; David T. Stanley, *The Higher Federal Service* (Washington: The Brookings Institution, 1964); and Franklin P. Kilpatrick, Milton Cummings, and M. Kent Jennings, *The Image of the Federal Service* and *Source Book* (Washington: The Brookings Institution, 1964).

Civil servants at these levels (approximately GS-15 to GS-18) are more likely to possess considerable discretionary or policymaking authority.

The median age of the higher civil servant is approximately 50 (which compares with 57.7 for the Senate and 50.6 for the House in the 89th Congress), though because of retirement civil servants are less likely than legislators to be superannuated: only about 1 percent are over age 65.[42] Educationally, the higher civil servant would appear to be the equal of congressmen—83 percent with some college experience in one sample, compared to 84 percent of post-World War II senators. Graduate disciplines in the arts and sciences are overrepresented in the civil service: 9.1 percent of the civil servants had doctorates. And rather fewer members of the high-level bureaucracy have no college experience at all—only 3.8 percent compared with 15 percent of Matthews' senators.[43]

A wide range of occupations is represented in the federal service, as a consequence of the diversity of tasks performed by the bureaucracy. And significantly enough, the most frequently listed occupations in the federal service are precisely those skills which are rarely found among legislators: engineering, 17.5 percent of the sample; general administration, 17 percent; and physical sciences, mathematics, and statistics, 13 percent. A comparison of selected occupational categories in Congress and the higher civil service is shown in Table 5. The comparability of the figures is difficult to assess, given the specialized nature of many government jobs outside of the natural sciences.

TABLE 5: Distribution of Selected Occupations in Congress and the Higher Civil Service

Occupation	89th Congress[a]	Civil Service[b]
Agriculture	9.3%	3.6%
Business-Industry	27.5	2.9
Education	8.6	1.1
Law	57.0	7.0
"Public information"	6.7	0.9
Engineering	1.3	17.5
Physical sciences	0.7	18.7

[a] Re-calculated from Table 1 on basis of percentages of total membership.
[b] Stanley, op. cit., p. 137.

[42] Stanley, op. cit., p. 25.
[43] Ibid., p. 32.

A somewhat better comparison would be provided by referring to the prior occupations of civil servants, but unfortunately these figures are difficult to compare, given the relative length and stability of the civil service career. In one sample of civil servants, however, the major prior occupations were: business and industry, 31 percent; education, 13 percent; and students, 24 percent.[44] These figures would seem to refute the common assumption that civil servants have little experience in the "outside world" of private business and industry.

One possible defect of the civil service in performing representational functions is the relative absence of lateral recruitment into the higher levels of the service. Although total accessions and separations in the entire federal civil service are quite high—about 20 percent each year—the higher civil servant is likely to be a veteran of from 10 to 20 years working for Uncle Sam. And once recruited, he tends to stay in the same agency and occupational field. In one study, no less than 69 percent of the respondents reported that their present jobs were in the same occupational group as when they entered the public service.[45] The author of a 1964 Brookings Institution survey gives the following capsule portrait of the higher civil servant:

> The typical federal civil servant . . . is a man of 50, working in Washington. He is a college graduate. He started in grade GS-9. He has 23 years of continuous federal service, and he took 20 of those years to reach his present grade. He has had a relatively stable career, working in no more than one or two occupational fields. He has also been employed in only one or two departments or agencies.[46]

Though civil servants are drawn from a wider range of occupations, their career patterns display more stability than those of the elected politician.

As with congressmen, these crude indicators are of limited usefulness in suggesting the psychological responsiveness of bureaucrats to external demands. And studies of attitudes among bureaucrats, unfortunately, do not permit exact comparisons with the data on legislators' role perceptions. Reasoning from the characteristics already identified, however, one would expect civil servants to give primary allegiance to their dual constituencies of agency and pro-

---

[44] *Ibid.*

[45] *Ibid.*, p. 32.

[46] *Ibid.*, p. 22.

fession. To a considerable extent, this appears to be the case.[47] Professionals in the public service often appear little different from their colleagues in industry or the academic world. They are trained in the same methods, engage in similar research, digest the same professional journals, and attend the same professional meetings. Yet at the same time they show greater dependency upon their institutional home base, the department or agency. In addition to normal organizational loyalties, there are the important attractions of internal advancement and the federal retirement system. Also required of civil servants is the "psychological capacity to function within large, complex organizations"[48]—a quality which outsiders may interpret as deferential and timid behavior. Compared with his associates outside the public service, the bureaucrat probably exhibits less independence and entrepreneurial disposition.

The civil servant perceives his relationship to the general public in terms of a generalized code of neutrality and public service. In part to compensate for his perceived lack of power and prestige, the civil servant frequently regards himself as part of a public-spirited elite:

> We are professionals; we perform our work with integrity.
>
> I have always linked myself with people who like the arts and sciences. For the most part these are government people.[49]

By the same token, he tends to regard the "people outside" as "materialistic, less educated, and less intelligent; 'they sell their souls.' Because of this, their views count for little." [50] There is something curiously platonic about the role perceptions of civil servants as presented by Warner and his associates: a mixture of self-denial and self-glorification, of elitism and insularity.

We have explored the representative characteristics of bureaucrats as individuals. The processes of selection in the federal civil service are more routinized than the complicated electoral ordeal for legislators; but those who reach the higher levels represent an educated elite no less than the members of Congress. In the breadth of professional representation, however, the civil service has the advantage over

---

[47] See Warner, *et al., op cit.,* Chaps 13-14; Kilpatrick, *et al., op. cit.*
[48] Warner, *et al., op. cit.,* p. 248.
[49] *Ibid.,* p. 229.
[50] *Ibid.,* p. 230.

Congress, which clearly is defective in its representation of the sciences, the professions (except for law), and the learned institutions.[51] The attitudes fostered by the career civil service, however, are not congenial to the development of representational roles as articulated by congressmen. Rather than the precise representational role perceptions, generated no doubt by ever-present constituent consultation and the threat of electoral defeat, the civil servant sees his job as broadly embodying the general "public interest." His ties to external constituencies, when they are articulated, are with his professional calling.

---

[51] For a rather broader assertion than I think the facts warrant, see Long, *op. cit.,* p. 813.

Systemic Representation

IF the individual legislator finds himself unprepared to speak
for technical and non-geographic constituencies, the congressional
decision-making system as a whole necessarily encounters the
same problem writ large. In classical theory, the representative assembly was conceived as a superior gatherer of information precisely
because it could draw together the interested parties, assess their
demands, and give them priorities. "The laws should be framed
by the Legislature," observed Abraham Baldwin of Georgia in criticizing the wide latitude given Hamilton by the Treasury Act of 1792:

> . . . Both modes of originating laws have been tried;
> but that system which originated in the House . . . had
> set well on the feelings of the people, whose interests and
> wishes, joys and sorrows, must be better known to their
> Representatives than it is possible for any Executive officer
> to be acquainted with, in so extensive a country.[52]

The functions which we would today call "articulation" and "aggregation" of interests were thought to be almost coterminous with the
task of lawmaking itself. And the representative assembly was
deemed best suited to perform these functions because of its superior
vantage point as consultant of the interests of "so extensive a
country."

It may be said that Congress carried out these functions with
striking independence until fairly recent times. The pattern varied

---

[52] *Annals of Congress,* III, November 20, 1792, p. 705.

of course with issues and with Presidents; and executive personnel were frequently consulted (as often as not on congressional initiative) on technical points. Still, the legislature's monopoly of representative functions went unchallenged in most political conflicts. The classical occasions for the exercise of full congressional prerogatives were the periodic revisions in tariff schedules, so graphically described by E. E. Schattschneider.[53] Many producer interests were forcefully represented on this issue by their elected officials, and their voices were supplemented by trade association spokesmen invited to present testimony. In many cases, the producers were given free rein in shaping tariff schedules for their own commodities; at other times, the legislators could play off conflicting interests in drafting compromise sections. Not all producers enjoyed equal advantages in such bargaining; but the tariff issue, no matter how entangled it became, was one to which geographic representatives were especially sensitized, and Congress retained relatively tight hold on tariffs until the 1930s.[54] The arena of conflict shifted toward the executive with the introduction of reciprocal trade agreements; and the Trade Expansion Act of 1962 signaled the end of the era of congressional initiative in tariff legislation.[55]

In the twentieth century, Congress has found itself confronted by a mounting body of decisions which are "legislative in nature yet executive in locus." This is particularly true in the fields of national security and foreign affairs, where the President's preeminence arises from his constitutional roles as commander-in-chief and "the nation's sole organ in foreign affairs." Additionally, however, the contemporary Congress suffers a representational disadvantage in these fields. It lacks not only the technical expertise, but also the ability to bring the interests together. Relevant interests—foreign constituencies, developers of weapons systems, the military services themselves—find their most useful spokesmen within the executive branch. Effective decisions are typically reached within the executive, with Congress reduced to the role of lobbyist and appellate court. As Huntington has observed, "No congressional

---

[53] *Politics, Pressures, and the Tariff* (Englewood Cliffs, N. J.: Prentice-Hall, 1935).

[54] Lawrence Chamberlain, *The President, Congress, and Legislation* (New York: Columbia University Press, 1946).

[55] P.L. 87-794. For a perceptive study, see Raymond Bauer, Ithiel de Sola Pool, and Lewis A. Dexter, *American Business and Public Policy* (New York: Atherton Press, 1963).

body gets more than a partial view of the interests involved. . . ." [56]

Congress has usually been able to influence decision making at the perimeters, and has been especially active in such bread-and-butter decisions as the location of military installations. But with the advent of strong civilian control in the Department of Defense, even these "marginal" decisions have become less tractable to congressional involvement. Even knowledgeable senators, determined to discipline Secretary Robert McNamara and armed with an impressive case, found it impossible to reverse the administration's contract award in the controversial TFX issue. Foreign affairs, too, have become increasingly the prerogative of the executive branch. Congress has of course conducted great foreign policy debates, often with strong constituency and ethnic overtones. But the prevailing philosophy of legislators today seems to be that expressed by Senator J. William Fulbright of Akansas, chairman of the Senate Foreign Relations Committee and no amateur in international relations. Congress is poorly equipped to participate in "short-term policies and . . . day to day operations," but perhaps it can cooperate by representations on "longer-range, more basic questions" and by initiating alternatives "on the periphery." [57] Fulbright's own record indicates that this role need not be an inactive one.

The energy of the executive establishment in performing representative functions has broadened from these fields to embrace in the 1960s practically the entire range of domestic policymaking as well. This development underlays the growth and institutionalization of "the President's program" as the agenda for Congress. [58] A full two generations ago Henry Lee McBain observed that the President had emerged as "Chief Legislator," but it was not until the post-World War II decades that this role became institutionalized. Until then, the presidential program seems to have been a relatively casual affair, with the President lending his prestige to a handful of bills among the legislative proposals floating around Washington. But as this paper is being written, President Johnson has already begun to cast

[56] Samuel Huntington, *The Common Defense* (New York: Columbia University Press, 1961), p. 131.

[57] For an exposition of the Fulbright viewpoint, see James Robinson, *Congress and Foreign Policy Making* (Homewood, Ill.: Dorsey Press, 1962), pp. 13 and 212-14.

[58] See Richard Neustadt's two articles, "Presidency and Legislation," *American Political Science Review*, September 1954, pp. 641-71; and December 1955, pp. 980-1021.

his net for proposals to be included in "packages" for future Congresses, a suggestion that the development of this practice has not yet reached its conclusion. Presidential initiation of legislation is an especially critical inroad on the traditional representative functions of Congress. It implies that competing interests are resolved, or aggregated, among the executive agencies "downtown" rather than in the halls of Congress. To the contestants in the political struggles, this means that the processes of representation and conciliation must be effected even before executive proposals are sent to Capitol Hill. Two brief case histories will serve to suggest the dimensions of this development, and its effects upon the representative functions of Congress and the executive.

The Communications Satellite Act of 1962 was notable not only as a thoroughly "executive" piece of legislation, but also as a controversy in which spokesmen for .every relevant interest were located within the executive. The controversy is remembered today chiefly for the spectacular (and unsuccessful) filibuster in July and August of 1962 by Senate liberals who charged that the vast public expenditures which assured the feasibility of a communications satellite system were being "given away" to the semi-private Communications Satellite Corporation. In fact, the structure of the communications satellite enterprise had been worked out during the previous year by executive agencies. Although several hearings were held on Capitol Hill, the impetus for the legislation had come almost entirely from "downtown." Once the use of satellites to ease the world's crowded intercontinental communications facilities became an imminent possibility, the National Aeronautics and Space Administration began to be concerned about its authority to enter into contracts for the launching of privately developed satellites—mainly those developed by the Radio Corporation of America, American Telephone and Telegraph Company, and Hughes Aircraft. At the same time, the Federal Communications Commission inaugurated studies of regulatory problems involved in such ventures. Finally, the State Department wanted the United States to have an adequately functioning system to present to an international conference scheduled for 1963.

The conflict which developed within the administration during 1961 went beyond the interplay of technical constituencies. Influenced by its ties to existing communications firms, the FCC was won over to the idea of a private corporation composed of existing carriers. Such a plan would give clear advantages to AT&T, which handles 80 percent of all overseas electronic communications. Other carriers were wary, as were equipment and "hardware" manufacturers frozen out of the scheme. NASA wanted other carriers to be included, but it was the Justice Department which finally stepped in to point out the proposal's antitrust implications. Along with the National Aeronautics and Space Council, Justice Department lawyers evolved a unique formula for a quasi-public firm to manage the system, and the bill sent to Congress by President Kennedy was modified only in details. However, the bill failed to satisfy the Capitol Hill advocates of public ownership—a small band of Senate liberals who reacted by staging a filibuster which stalled other bills on the President's agenda. But the filibuster was in the nature of a last-minute appeal to what turned out to be an indifferent public opinion. When the expected public outcry failed to materialize, and when a bipartisan coalition succeeded in invoking cloture, passage of the administration measure was assured.

The Economic Opportunity Act of 1964 was an even more spectacular exercise in executive representation. A memorandum written in the summer of 1963 by an economics professor temporarily working for the Council of Economic Advisers first attracted the attention of Council Chairman Walter Heller. Further studies were asked for, and by fall a small task force was drawing in proposals from various executive departments. President Johnson showed interest in developing a package of anti-poverty programs, and in February 1964 he appointed R. Sargent Shriver, administrator of the Peace Corps, to lead the "war on poverty." After Shriver's appointment a second wave of consultations on the programs got underway. The subsequent drafting of the Economic Opportunity Act by Shriver's task force must surely rank among the most fascinating legislative histories of recent times. For a period of five weeks, in and out of the fifth and eleventh floors of an office building in Washington came a stream of persons from private and public life—professors, social workers, Ford Foundation officials, business executives, writers, mayors, churchmen, and bureaucrats. Government departments and agencies were canvassed for proposals, and several bills already before Congress were recalled. Shriver and his closest associates accepted, rejected, and compromised; once or twice conflicts were referred to the President for resolution.

The resulting package was a series of programs designed to assist that fifth of the nation's population falling below the poverty level. The entire proposal was referred to Congress on a Friday, hearings were begun the next Tuesday, and the bill was ratified with only minor alterations. The programs themselves involved new linkages between the federal government and community agencies which promised to alter the structure of American federalism.

These two major enactments, involving disparate subjects, illustrate the full representative potentialities of the executive system. It is not that Congress played no role in these measures—though its contribution was manifested most notably in the form of executive behavior designed to anticipate the reactions of legislators. What makes these two cases instructive is the executive's monopoly of the traditional "representative" functions of interest articulation and aggregation. In both cases, private interests found spokesmen within the federal agencies. The executive system also resolved the conflicting demands through preparation of the authorizing legislation— NASA and the Justice Department for the Communications Satellite Act, and the Shriver task force for the Economic Opportunity Act. In neither case did the interests most directly involved see fit to make meaningful appeals to Congress.

In neither instance did the President publicly exploit the representative characteristics of the process, though this practice is not unknown. After his election in 1960, President-elect Kennedy appointed a series of public task forces to make recommendations for his future legislative program. Many did little more than to resurrect Democratic proposals that had been dormant during the Eisenhower years; but in any event their primary purpose was to lend legitimacy to the Kennedy program. President Johnson has also employed task forces or advisory groups to recommend domestic and foreign policy measures or to legitimize politically hazardous actions.

Of course, the representative process does not end with enactment of legislation, for executive agencies are in a position to cultivate clienteles for their activities. Oftentimes programs actually give birth to organizations centered around the newly created clienteles. The creation of the National Association of Small Business Investors within a year of the passage of the Small Business Investment Act of 1958 is a conspicuous example. The relationships between the American Farm Bureau Federation and the county extension services have been documented;[59] and perhaps the most influential farm organization, the National Rural Electric Cooperative Association (NRECA), is essentially a clientele group for the Rural Electrification Administra-

---

[59] See, for example, Charles M. Hardin, *The Politics of Agriculture* (Glencoe: Free Press, 1952); and Grant McConnell, *The Decline of Agrarian Democracy* (Berkeley: University of California Press, 1953).

tion. In some cases agencies may even be "captured" by their clienteles.[60]

Consultation between agencies and their publics is facilitated through field activities. This phenomenon is as old as the Republic itself: in 1801, all but about 150 of the 3,000 federal employees were located in the field.[61] Currently about nine of every ten federal employees are stationed outside Washington.[62] "One of the principal advantages of administrative decentralization," wrote David Truman in his study of the Agriculture Department's Chicago field office, is that:

> . . . it brings the government into more intimate contact with the governed, with the result that it can adjust administrative policy and practice to local peculiarities and can continually win the consent of those affected by declaration of national policy. The field offices . . . can narrow the gulf between the citizen and the bureaucracy and, hence, can contribute in large measure to the over-all efficiency of the latter.[63]

Agency field operations are marked by formal consultations and pressures applied by local groups. Perhaps more typical, however, is representation by osmosis. Although formally commissioned "as emissaries sent to live among the local populace and represent the agency to the people," field personnel may "become so identified with the communities in which they reside that they become community delegates to headquarters rather than the reverse." [64]

Another consultative device is the public advisory committee— "a group of individual experts, usually serving without compensation, formed for the purpose of consulting with and advising department or agency officials with respect to problems presented to it for con-

---

[60] On the subject of the regulatory commissions, see Marver Bernstein, *Regulating Business by Independent Commission* (Princeton, N. J.: Princeton University Press, 1955).

[61] White, *The Federalists, op. cit.*, p. 256.

[62] As of May 1965, 246,142 of the 2,467,385 federal employees were located in Washington. This contrasts with the higher civil servants (discussed above), about two-thirds of whom were located in headquarters offices.

[63] David B. Truman, *Administrative Decentralization* (Chicago: University of Chicago Press, 1940), p. 170.

[64] Herbert Kaufman, *The Forest Ranger* (Baltimore: Johns Hopkins Press, 1960), pp. 75ff.

sideration." [65] Created either by statute or administrative action (sometimes with congressional insistence), these groups apparently range in activities from perfunctory review to active participation in policymaking. Often these groups are little more than executive committees of the program's clientele interests which are called to Washington periodically to hear *pro forma* reports on the agency's activities. The extent to which such groups influence policy by communicating the views of relevant interests is unfortunately not known. (One of the best known advisory groups is the Business Council, a large group of executives from the "business establishment" which meets periodically to discuss business-government relations and the state of the economy, and which retains loose ties with the Department of Commerce.[66]) Whatever their influence, these groups are quite numerous. The current issue of the *U. S. Government Organization Manual* lists some 32 advisory boards, committees, and councils. In 1956, however, one official estimated that there were some 5,126 advisory groups then in existence, of which 4,182 were Department of Agriculture committees.[67]

Linkages between federal agencies and their publics are becoming more numerous and varied. The poverty program, discussed earlier, has generated unique ties between the Office of Economic Opportunity and community organizations. Sometimes existing local, state, and even federal government units have been entirely bypassed, with contracts for local programs going to "umbrella-type" civic organizations supported by welfare, religious, and community associations. In Hartford, Connecticut, for example, OEO contracted with the "Community Renewal Team of Greater Hartford" for more than half a million dollars in community action programs. The "Renewal Team" is actually an alliance of ten public and private agencies, among them the local health service, board of education, and housing authority, as well as such groups as the Visiting Nurses Association and the Catholic Diocesan Bureau of Social Service.[68] At the national level, OEO claims endorsements from hundreds of private groups and has created a National Advisory Council, a Business Leadership

---

[65] U. S., Congress, House, Committee on Government Operations, *Employment and Utilization of Experts and Consultants,* House Report 2894, 84th Congress, 2d Session, July 25, 1956, p. 5.

[66] See Hobart Rowen, "America's Most Powerful Club," *Harper's,* September 1960, pp. 132ff.

[67] House Report 2894, *op. cit.,* p. 132.

[68] Office of Economic Opportunity, *Congressional Presentation,* 2 vols. (Washington: Office of Economic Opportunity, April 1965), I, pp. 48-49.

Advisory Council, a Labor Advisory Council, and a national group called "Citizens Crusade Against Poverty." Still another organization, the National Association for Community Development, has emerged among local community action program officials administering funds under Title II of the Economic Opportunity Act. OEO has encouraged participation by the impoverished themselves in local program planning—no easy objective considering the size and resources of this clientele; and has taken pains to publicize the minority group representation among its civil service staff (18.3 percent versus 13.2 percent for all federal agencies).[69]

The executive branch has thus come to exercise representative functions by establishing channels of communication with relevant publics at almost every stage of the policymaking process, from inception to implementation. Its increasingly frequent performance of the politician's traditional roles of articulation and "brokerage" among the diverse publics has profound consequences for the functioning of Congress. As Arthur Bentley foresaw in 1908:

> If the group interests work out a fair and satisfying adjustment through the legislature, then the executive sinks in prominence . . . when the adjustment is not perfected in the legislature, then the executive rises in strength to do the work . . . the growth of executive discretion is therefore a phase of the group process. . . .[70]

Where effective communications with the electorate lead to the executive branch, Congress is in danger of becoming an onlooker (and in some cases a court of appeals) in the processes of political bargaining. Yet the specialized relations between agencies and clienteles do not add up to a representative system; and within the executive, only the President and his personal agents can interpose broadly political priorities upon these tight bargaining arrangements. The President needs help, and Congress should be in a position to give it to him. The political specialist is sorely needed to police the "sub-governments" which have grown up around specialized constituencies. Hence, the revitalization of Congress' representative functions is essential not only to shore up its own institutional position, but to reassert democratic controls upon the decision-making system itself.

---

[69] *Ibid.*, II, Appendix A.

[70] Arthur F. Bentley, *The Process of Government* (Chicago: University of Chicago Press, 1908), p. 359.

Strengthening the Representative Capacities of Congress

THE electoral system guarantees only that members of the national legislature will be selected from distinct geographic areas. With the apparent nationalization of political issues, the need for geographic representation is less crucial than it once was. Yet for many purposes—and especially on bread-and-butter issues surrounding "economic development"—individual localities sorely need political agents in Washington. Some have begun to hire lobbyists for this purpose. Although localities are increasingly forming functional linkages with bureaucratic agencies that dispense specialized services, they will continue to find that congressmen can often lend valuable political weight to demands for geographic dispersion of federal activities.

Provision for House districts of relatively equal population is useful in perfecting the present geographical mode of representation.[71] Recent political history demonstrates clearly that interests which are under-represented in legislative assemblies will gravitate toward alternative power-points within the political system—often with consequences at variance with the model of legislative functioning explored in this symposium. It is not necessary to construe the "equal protection" clause as demanding that every legislative district be as close as possible to the electoral tipping-point. The full variety of interests can effectively be embodied in the legislature when some districts are

---

[71] Wesberry v. Sanders, 376 U. S. 1 (1964). A subsequent House-passed bill would provide congressionally set standards for apportionment by specifying deviations of no more than 15 percent above or below the state average.

homogeneous and semi-competitive, and others heterogeneous and highly competitive.

The recruitment process also assures that legislators will carry a set of attitudes orienting them to the feelings, interests, and even prejudices of localized publics. Contrary to the contentions of many who write on this subject, sensitivity to local demands is not in itself deplorable. Indeed, every effort should be made to formalize and broaden the members' communications with their states and districts.

One innovation which would assist legislators in their representative tasks would be a moderate formalization of the congressional schedule to provide for planned, periodic recesses. In addition to alleviating the personal inconveniences which accompany the present uncertainties of the annual schedule, these recesses would enable members to spend substantial amounts of time in their home political bases.[72] This step could easily be taken through an informal agreement between the parties' leaders at the beginning of each session. Unlimited allowances for travel to and from the member's state or district would also be a small price to pay for the resulting increment in representational effectiveness.

Some members are already scheduling series of constituent meetings on specified topics, and this practice should be encouraged and extended. Alternatively, bipartisan teams of legislators might undertake lecture and discussion tours to various communities throughout the country, covering a wide range of topics. Or funds could be made available to permit legislators to convene public advisory groups in their states or districts. Whether general or specialized, such groups would meet with the member at frequent intervals to discuss mutual problems and interests. These suggestions indicate what might be attempted, although in any event the specific forms should remain flexible to fit legislators' individual styles of operation. Such innovations would not only supplement existing channels of communication, but would in their own way help to enhance prestige and public understanding of congressional institutions.

Every effort must be made, moreover, to provide legislators with current and sophisticated information concerning their formal constituencies. Congress should direct the Bureau of the Census to make periodic reports on demographic trends upon request. (Such reports

---

[72] No less than 16 members testified in favor of the several variations of this idea. See U. S., Congress, Joint Committee on the Organization of the Congress, *Interim Report,* Senate Report 426, 89th Congress, 1st session, 1965, p. 17. (Referred to hereinafter as JCOC *Interim Report.*)

could be made available to certified opposition candidates prior to the campaigns.) In addition, members desiring to employ survey research techniques upon issues in their constituencies should be able to draw upon competent professional advice.

We have seen that congressmen themselves place different interpretations on the representative role, and upon the relative weight to be given localized demands.[73] The widest possible diversity in role orientations among legislators, and within the individual legislator's consciousness, is undoubtedly desirable. It is in dealing with non-geographic constituencies, as we have seen that congressmen, and Congress as a whole, encounter the most serious challenges to their representative functions.

How can legislators be kept sensitive to forces which may be only imperfectly reflected in geographic constituencies? Subject matter specialization through the standing committee system has been effectively used to supplement geographic representation; and the efficiency and vitality of the committees is a primary instrument of congressional survival. Committee assignments should not be made merely on the basis of pre-existing constituent interest in the committee's subject matter. Otherwise unrepresented viewpoints should be stimulated, especially on so-called "interest" and "pork" committees, so that these groups do not become cabals of those most intimately affected by the subject matter.[74] Those Brooklyn congressmen who occasionally find themselves waiting out their "sentence" on the House Agriculture Committee should be urged to remain there in order to articulate consumer interests. In view of the emphasis laid on producer concerns at many points in the political process, such broad representation will surely remain difficult to enforce. But every means of enhancing the committees' effectiveness as bargaining arenas should nonetheless be explored.

As our dynamic society produces new complexities in the congressional environment, a modest increase in the number of standing committees might be contemplated. A committee on urban affairs and housing and a committee on education are two immediate possibilities. Congress' responsiveness to new problem areas need not be hampered by a compulsive resistance to committee "proliferation."

---

[73] On this subject generally, see also Lewis A. Dexter, "The Representative and his District," *Human Organization*, December 1957, pp. 2-13.

[74] See Charles O. Jones, "Representation in Congress: The Case of the House Agriculture Committee," *American Political Science Review*, June 1961, pp. 358-67.

It is anomalous in the year 1965 to find political scientists still attempting to impose extreme bureaucratic neatness upon the committee system.[75]

Fortunately, many individual congressmen and senators find additional rows to hoe, often quite apart from their committee assignments. Arising more or less spontaneously from the legislator's own background or interests, these specializations may provide the member with unique expertise and publicity; and, more importantly for our own inquiry, they give specific publics some voice on Capitol Hill. Devices should be found to encourage this tendency. Perhaps *ad hoc* congressional task forces could be created to study and interpret topics handled only tangentially by the standing committees. These groups might gain added weight from detailed, *ad hoc* mandates, though they could be put on a standing basis to handle recurrent problems. In any event, the task forces would range widely in their subject matter areas, commissioning research, holding seminars, and making trips into the field when appropriate.

This proposal is similar to a research-oriented suggestion presented to the Joint Committee on the Organization of the Congress. The suggestion was that "anytime a group of members wish to pursue a particular study, the Congress itself should provide them with the facilities to do so." [76] The stylized practice of "taking testimony" from scheduled witnesses, while appropriate in many cases, should not preclude more imaginative techniques of gathering information. Delicate problems of scheduling are involved, for the last thing that most individual members need is the burden of "another committee." Some limitation on the number of standing committee assignments given each member might be a feasible prerequisite, as would the practice of granting leave from committee work without loss in seniority privileges. Regularizing the annual congressional schedule might also facilitate the development of these specialized work groups.

Legislators must remain conversant with at least a few of the qualitative professional constituencies which bear on complex decision making. There are no simple or automatic ways to ensure the

---

[75] See, for example, the summary of James K. Pollock's remarks in JCOC, *Interim Report,* p. 21.

[76] Testimony of George E. Agree, executive director, National Committee for an Effective Congress (unofficial transcript, August 9, 1965). He further explained: "This would not be very expensive. And it would be relatively easy to ensure that such study enterprises did not conflict with or disrupt current legislative processes, and that public funds involved would not be misused for strictly partisan or frivolous purposes."

adequacy of congressional expertise. Devices might be fashioned which would counteract the advantages of certain professions in the recruitment of legislators; but there is no evidence that they would be either desirable or effective. Sabbaticals could be granted to allow legislators to pursue definite study programs, and a Congressional Institute of Scholars could be created.[77] Many of the improvements in information-gathering discussed in other papers in this series might well commend themselves additionally for what they can contribute to the representative capacities of our national legislature. A Congress which is estranged from the learned and scientific professions is indeed estranged from contemporary decision-making premises.

In the final analysis, however, what counts is not only Congress' ability to speak for technical constituencies, but also its ability to bring these constituencies together before the bar of politics. The rhetoric of the specialist will help, but it is not sufficient. The legislator's indispensable contribution to policymaking is his delicate feel for the political system of which he is a part. He need not, even if he could, merely add his voice to the Babel of technical language now being spoken by experts within decision-making arenas. His special expertise lies in his ability to inject the unique data of politics into this process, in order to render policy outcomes tolerable as well as rational.

---

[77] JCOC, *Interim Report*, p. 15.

KENNETH JANDA received his undergraduate degree in 1957 from Illinois State University and his Ph.D. in government in 1961 from Indiana University. Since 1961, he has been Assistant Professor of Political Science at Northwestern University.

A contributor to the *International Encyclopedia of the Social Sciences,* Mr. Janda is the author of *Data Processing: Applications to Political Research* (Evanston: Northwestern University Press, 1965); and the editor of the *Cumulative Index to the American Political Science Review, Volumes 1-57; 1906-1963* (Evanston: Northwestern University Press, 1964); the *Index* was prepared on a computer with the key-word-in-context (KWIC) indexing technique and was cited by the American Library Association as an Outstanding Reference Book of 1964.

Dr. Janda's major substantive interests are in voting behavior, the legislative process, and political parties. He is currently engaged in a major comparative study of political parties throughout the world, which will employ a variety of information retrieval and data processing techniques.

Dr. Janda is on the Editorial Board of the *Midwest Journal of Political Science* and is a Council Member of the Inter-University Consortium for Political Research.

Information Systems for Congress

Kenneth Janda

S TUDENTS of government generally agree that the legislative branches of modern governments have gradually lost power relative to the power of executive authorities. This phenomenon has been referred to variously as the "parliamentary crisis," [1] the "atrophy of the legislature," [2] and the "decline of the legislature." [3] Although some students hold that Congress constitutes an exception to this generalization, [4] most detect the same trend in the United States. Indeed this very symposium of recommendations for revitalizing Congress is an acknowledgment of it.

Congress' loss of power is manifested in three important governmental functions traditionally reserved to the legislature: initiating legislation, evaluating legislative proposals, and overseeing the execution of legislation. In recent decades, Congress has abdicated to the President its initiative in preparing a legislative program, has faltered in thoroughly evaluating proposals submitted by the President, and has been unable to exercise effective direction and control over the administration of legislation in which Congress has aquiesced.

Some students of government are not alarmed by the diminution of congressional power. [5] They favor what has been termed an "executive force" model of government, which would ascribe even greater power to the President and relegate Congress to the role of

---

[1] David B. Truman (ed.), *The Congress and America's Future* (Englewood Cliffs, N.J.: Prentice-Hall, 1965), p. 1.

[2] William J. Keefe and Morris S. Ogul, *The American Legislative Process: Congress and the States* (Englewood Cliffs, N.J.: Prentice-Hall, 1965), p. 483.

[3] K. C. Wheare, *Legislatures* (New York: Oxford University Press, 1963), p. 221.

[4] *Ibid.*, p. 223; Ernest S. Griffith, *Congress: Its Contemporary Role* (New York: New York University Press, 1961), p. 88.

[5] See, for example, James MacGregor Burns, *The Deadlock of Democracy* (Englewood Cliffs, N.J.: Prentice-Hall, 1963).

notarizing the President's legislative demands. Other students, including the authors of these essays, do not favor a governmental system in which Congress sits as a corporate notary public and are consequently alarmed by the present imbalance of power between the two branches. Their position is inspired by the belief that democratic government functions neither long nor well in the absence of a strong and independent representative legislature.[6]

As an alternative to government by executive force, this symposium creates a model of government by legislative force wherein Congress functions as a vital, independent authority which boldly initiates legislative proposals, thoroughly evaluates proposals presented to it, and effectively oversees the administration of enacted legislation. The recommendations in these papers are calculated to redirect the flow of power away from the presidency and back toward Congress. They do this by identifying the major obstacles to government by legislative force and by suggesting ways to remove or circumvent those obstacles.

Most of these recommendations are of two types: proposals for reform and proposals for reorganization. Broadly speaking, proposals for reform are designed to make Congress more representative of popular demands within the country and to facilitate expression of majority sentiment within Congress. Proposals for reorganization concentrate on improving the structural and procedural aspects of the legislative process.

The symposium contains many far-reaching proposals for reform and reorganization designed to strengthen Congress. The recommendations in this paper, however, cannot strictly be classified either under "reform" or "reorganization." They are better described as proposals for *retooling* Congress. This paper advocates the development of automated information processing systems to help Congress surmount one of the biggest obstacles to government by legislative force—the lack of information and knowledge by legislators faced with increasingly complex problems and decisions. My concern and recommendations focus exclusively upon the information problem confronting Congress.

---

[6] This philosophy forms the central theme of Charles S. Hyneman, *Bureaucracy in a Democracy* (New York: Harper, 1950), especially pp. 10-17 and 77-79.

The Information Problem for Congress

STUDENTS of the legislative process have identified the information problem as a major factor in the decline of modern legislatures. Griffith, for example, fixes the need for information in "problems inherent in the complexity and magnitude of the legislative output itself."[7] Woll also notes that "legislation today, in regulatory and nonregulatory fields alike, requires specialized information on the part of policy makers before it can be conceptualized, drafted, and implemented."[8] The legislature's need for information to conduct the business of modern government has not gone completely unfulfilled; it has been satisfied largely by the executive. As Keefe and Ogul have observed, "The problems of modern government now have become so technical and complex that the legislature has found it increasingly necessary to defer to the executive for answers and recommendations."[9]

The concentration of information resources in the executive branch has had several consequences for legislative-executive relations. One of these, Robinson concludes, "is an increasing inclination to rely on the executive for the presentation of proposals to deal with problems. Congress' role, then, becomes less and less one of the initiation of policy alternatives and more and more the modifier, negator, or legitimator of proposals which originate in the executive."[10] Not only does Congress lose initiative in creating a legislative program,

---

[7] Griffith, op. cit., p. 72.

[8] Peter Woll, American Bureaucracy (New York: W. W. Norton, 1963), p. 130.

[9] Keefe and Ogul, op. cit., p. 483.

[10] James A. Robinson, Congress and Foreign Policy Making (Homewood, Ill.: Dorsey Press, 1962), p. 8.

but lack of information also prevents Congress from adequately evaluating the proposals it receives from the executive. As Woll states, "To a considerable extent, when the administrative branch can control the channels of information to Congress it can control the policies supported by that body." [11]

As a consequence of these developments in legislative-executive relations, the very function of legislatures in the total governmental structure has altered over time. Harris' recent book, *Congressional Control of Administration,* begins, "Control of administration is one of the most important functions of legislative bodies in all modern democracies." [12] A recent survey of the structures and functions of parliamentary institutions in 41 countries concludes with an even starker recognition:

> . . . the legislative function is no longer the preserve of Parliament. The initiative in legislative and financial matters has to some extent slipped out of its grasp; the practice of delegating powers has made for the curtailment of its role in the realm of law. But concurrently, the prerogatives of Parliament have shifted in the direction of control of government activity. The Government initiates and directs; Parliament controls, approves, disapproves and, now and then, inspires.[13]

But how well equipped are legislatures to play this new role?/ Again the information problem is present—this time frustrating the legislature's direction and control of the executive.

The executive branch is perhaps the legislature's main source of information.[14] As Robinson reports:

> For reasons which are not altogether clear, bureaucracies associated with executive offices have more efficiently collected and processed information than have legislatures. Not only is Congress unprepared to obtain independent information about the world through its own resources, but it must rely on data collected by the executive.[15]

---

[11] Woll, *op. cit.,* p. 131.

[12] Joseph P. Harris, *Congressional Control of Administration* (Washington: The Brookings Institution, 1964), p. 1.

[13] Inter-Parliamentary Union, *Parliaments* (London: Cassell and Company, 1961), p. 298.

[14] Charles L. Clapp, *The Congressman* (Washington: The Brookings Institution, 1963), pp. 115-18.

[15] Robinson, *op. cit.,* p. 192.

Dahl and Lindblom state in general terms the consequence of a situation which finds the governed possessing more information than the governors:

> Because the hierarchy originates much of the information its nominal superiors require in order to act intelligently, and because the superiors are usually less expert on any particular subject than some of their nominal subordinates, it is often possible for the hierarchy to manipulate communications in order to control their nominal superiors.[16]

Later on the same page, they continue:

> In these situations the saving element is the existence of a plurality of competing and conflicting hierarchies that provide alternative sources of information to those who need to make decisions.

What "alternative sources" of information are available to Congress, and are they adequate to support a vital, independent legislative force in government? Some authors have implied that they are adequate by singling out Congress as one of the few legislatures in the world that has held its own with the executive.[17] Griffith, in fact, asserts: "Congress has mastered, or has provided itself with the tools to master, the problem of assuring itself of an unbiased, competent source of expert information and analysis which is its very own."[18] The tools of which Griffith speaks are Congress' professional staffs:

> . . . the enlargement and strengthening of the staffs of Congress have in fact been a major factor in arresting and probably reversing a trend that had set in in the United States as well as in every other industrialized nation. This is the trend in the direction of the ascendancy or even the virtually complete dominance of the bureaucracy over the legislative branch through the former's near-monopoly of the facts and the technical and specialized competence on the basis of which decisions are ultimately made.[19]

Notwithstanding the fact that staff aids have helped Congress considerably with its information problem, few writers are as sanguine

---

[16] Robert A. Dahl and Charles E. Lindblom, *Politics, Economics, and Welfare* (New York: Harper and Row, 1953), pp. 260-61.

[17] See footnote 4.

[18] Griffith, *op. cit.*, p. 88.

[19] *Ibid.*

as Griffith in evaluating their contribution. The collective judgment seems closer to that of Woll, who writes:

> Although Congress has made strenuous efforts to fulfill its constitutional responsibilities, neither its committees nor its staff aids are any match for the administrative branch with respect to knowledge and information in particular areas of legislation. Much of the staff employed by Congress comes directly from the administrative branch, in which initial competence was acquired in an atmosphere where the points of view of the agencies predominated.[20]

Keefe and Ogul concur: "No matter how hard the legislature tries to inform itself (and Congress tries very hard indeed), its store of information and its access to necessary knowledge are rarely if ever as developed as that of the executive authority." [21]

One test to determine whether Congress has adequate access to information for fulfilling its governmental function is to examine congressmen's attitudes toward obstacles confronting them in performing their job. Unfortunately there have been little reliable data available on this point. But a recent study by Dartmouth's Public Affairs Center has provided the answer at least for the House of Representatives.[22]

Findings for a random sample of 80 representatives interviewed during the summer and fall of 1963 indicate that congressmen do not feel that they have adequate control of information. Each respondent was asked to "name any problems which prevented him from carrying out the role he would like to play in the House and all problems which he saw as preventing the House from operating as he thought it should." [23] The responses were grouped into 14 categories; the percentages of all respondents mentioning something in each category are given in Table 1.

---

[20] Woll, *op. cit.*, p. 131.

[21] Keefe and Ogul, *op. cit.*, p. 483.

[22] This study is reported in Michael O'Leary (ed.), *Congressional Reorganization: Problems and Prospects—A Conference Report* (Hanover, N. H.: Public Affairs Center, Dartmouth College, 1964).

[23] *Ibid.*, p. 22. According to personal communication from Roger Davidson, one of the researchers, the exact wording of the questions was as follows:

"Now, what are the most pressing problems you face in trying to do your job as Congressman—what are the things that hinder you in your tasks?" and "What are the most pressing problems which prevent Congress from doing what you think it ought to do?"

Answers given to both these individual and institutional foci were lumped together in Table 1.

TABLE 1: General Categories of "Problems" Articulated by Eighty Members of the House of Representatives [a]

Type of problem	Percent mentioning
1. Committee system, seniority system and Rules Committee	27
2. Scheduling and general procedure	43
3. Member pay, office allowance, staffing	26
4. Diffusion of leadership and "failure" of incumbent leadership	23
5. Caliber of individual members	29
6. Problems arising from present operation of separation of powers	50
7. Problems of House-Senate comity	12
8. Public lack of understanding of Congress and failure in communicating with constituents	45
9. Service for constituents	58
10. Electoral system and electoral vulnerability of Members; campaigning	30
11. Complexity of decision-making; lack of information	78
12. Criticisms of present power distribution and policy output of the House	38
13. Lack of time [b]	39
14. Other	9

[a] Source: Table V in Michael O'Leary (ed.), *Congressional Reorganization: Problems and Prospects—A Conference Report* (Hanover, New Hampshire: Public Affairs Center, Dartmouth College, 1964, pp. 22-23).

[b] "Because 'lack of time' is such an obvious and commonplace problem, we excluded it from analysis whenever a Member mentioned his quota of ten other problems. It is therefore underrepresented in this table." *Ibid.*

As Table 1 clearly shows, by far the largest number of responses (78 percent) came under the category of "complexity of decision-making; lack of information." The same evaluation of the importance of this problem was expressed publicly by congressmen attending a conference held early in 1964 on the role of Congress in the American democratic process.[24] The summary of conference proceedings states:

Many members stressed that the quality and quantity of legislative output is jeopardized by the problems of gathering information. One Congressman expressed the conviction of most conferees when he stated that a high-priority goal should be to improve the gathering and analysis of information and the detailed consideration of alternative policies by Congress. It is in these areas, he felt, that Congress is most deficient.[25]

[24] This was the first annual Orvil E. Dryfoos Conference on Public Affairs, held on the Dartmouth College campus, March 7-8, 1964.

[25] O'Leary, *op. cit.*, p. 45.

Thus, lack of adequate information for developing knowledge and making decisions is recognized by scholars and legislators alike as one of the major problems confronting Congress. Various recommendations have been made to cope with this problem in one way or another. Recommendations for home rule for the District of Columbia would, for example, reduce Congress' work load and provide members with more time to become informed about other legislation. Suggestions for electric voting machines to record roll call votes would also save time and presumably free congressmen for reading and otherwise informing themselves. And, of course, all proposals for increasing Congress' professional staffs are directed toward the information problem.

Despite the variety of these proposals, they are all curiously restricted in range. Basically, they can be divided into two types: those which offer the congressman more *time* and those which offer more *help*. Few offer him more *information*. Although these various recommendations impinge upon congressmen's lack of information, they do not attack it *directly* as an information problem. They are restricted in failing to propose information processing solutions to an information problem.

Many scholars and legislators have apparently resigned themselves to the inevitability of inadequate information. This thinking is revealed in the Dartmouth Center analysis of congressmen's own opinions about their problems:

> . . . an examination of [Table 1] leads to the important conclusion that most of the problems perceived by Congressmen relate to conditions which are only marginally, if at all, susceptible to reform. The most frequently mentioned set of responses relates to the complexity of decision-making—the problem of obtaining adequate information and of selecting the proper alternative from among many conflicting courses of action. This group of problems—about one-fifth of all those mentioned—is probably a concomitant of policy-making under any set of rules or organizational form, rather than a manageable, "reformable" situation.[26]

Dahl and Lindblom display a similar fatalism in conceding, "Probably the problem of the modern legislature cannot be solved. But it can be reduced by changing and simplifying the agenda of legislators."[27]

---

[26] *Ibid.*, p. 23.
[27] Dahl and Lindblom, *op. cit.*, pp. 322-23.

By failing to view the lack of information as an information problem, one is led to recommend oblique rather than direct solutions. In this era, however, direct solutions to information problems are available through the use of automated information processing systems.

Present Use of Information Systems in Government

THE relatively recent development of methods and equipment for information processing may account in part for the failure to propose information processing systems as a solution for Congress' problem. Real advances in mechanical means of information processing did not come until the advent of electronic computers, which were not marketed until the early 1950s. Then there is always a lag between technological innovation and its application to practical problems.

Nevertheless, the paucity of recommendations for introducing information systems within Congress is still hard to understand, for automated information systems have been used in business and industry since the late 1950s. Moreover, as we will see, executive agencies of the government have long been engaged in programs of research and development of information systems to meet their own needs. Yet, the idea of information systems for Congress has still not caught on.

Consider the recommendations recently published in the *Interim Report* of the Joint Committee on the Organization of the Congress.[28] This document summarizes results of hearings conducted from May 10 through June 25, 1965. During this period, testimony and statements were received from 12 senators, 51 members of the House of Representatives, 17 political scientists, and representatives of 13 different voluntary associations. The recommendations advanced by congressmen, political scientists, and organizational representatives

---

[28] U. S., Congress, Joint Committee on the Organization of the Congress, *Interim Report,* Senate Report No. 426, 89th Congress, 1st Session, 1965.

are summarized, respectively, in Appendices A, B, and C to the *Interim Report*. Within each Appendix, the recommendations are classified into categories of proposed reforms. Table 2 summarizes the total distribution of recommendations within each category.

From hundreds of recommendations [29] summarized in the *Interim Report,* only three can be classified even liberally as proposals for providing Congress with integrated information processing systems. Under the category "electronic aids and television," the *Report* listed Representative Ed Edmondson's suggestion for establishing "a public information center in the Capitol with an electronic board providing information on matters under consideration on the floor, name and

TABLE 2: Distribution of Recommendations for Suggested Reforms of Congress Made in Hearings of the Joint Committee on the Organization of the Congress,[a] May-June 1965

Category of Reform	Number of Recommendations [b]
Committee Chairmen	18
Committee Jurisdiction	25
Committee Meetings	21
Committee Staffing	16
Office Staffing and Workload	17
Housekeeping Functions	23
Research Services	14
Fiscal Controls	45
Scheduling	14
Floor Procedures	26
Electronic Aids and Television	13
Oversight	14
Elections and Campaigns	10
Ethics	13
Foreign Policy	8
Leadership Policy	10
Total	287 [b]

[a] These data are compiled from the enumeration of suggested reforms in Appendices A, B, and C to the *Interim Report* (Senate Report No. 426, 89th Congress, 1st Session, 1965) of the U.S. Congress Joint Committee on the Organization of the Congress.

[b] Recommendations by congressmen, political scientists, and voluntary associations in each category have been summed without regard to duplication. Because some recommendations by the three groups may be substantially the same, the amounts in the table do not necessarily represent numbers of *different* reforms. Some overlap exists, but the effort required to eliminate duplicates was judged greater than the gain in accuracy to be achieved.

29 See footnote b in Table 2.

location of committee hearings, etc." [30] The same category contained the Council of State Governments' proposal to use "automatic data processing for bill indexing, statutory search, budget preparation, etc." [31] (Most of the other recommendations under this category dealt with such items as television, filming, and recording floor proceedings and installing electric voting machines.) The third and most comprehensive recommendation for an information system was listed under "research services," where Professor Alfred de Grazia referred to the use of computers and information processing methods for developing "an adequate intelligence and research system." [32] (Other recommendations for "research services" dealt with expanding the Legislative Reference Service and forming a scientific advisory commission for Congress, among other things.)

The *Report* contained other recommendations intended to increase the information flow to Congress, but these neglected to include means for *processing* the information before use. In one sense, Congress has quite enough information available in the form of bills, reports, speeches, testimony, regulations, decisions, and so on. Congressmen are swamped with documents produced by Congress itself, and they are deluged with publications of executive agencies. On the one hand, not all this information is needed by Congress, while, on the other hand, Congress still needs much information it does not get. Speaking more properly, Congress' problem is one of obtaining *relevant* information. What Congress really requires is a procedure for acquiring the information it needs and a method for processing that information in order to learn what it wants to know. This conception of the problem suggests that far more is required than just increasing the information flow to Congress. It suggests information processing systems that are integrated with congressional tasks, functions, and activities.

Although the hearings did not produce many recommendations for automated information systems, some members of the Joint Committee on Organization expressed a personal appreciation of their possibilities. The statement of Representative Jack Brooks is particulary relevant:

> My experience as sponsor of legislation dealing with the streamlining and centralization of the Government's automated data processing equipment and procedures leads me to believe

---

[30] *Interim Report, op. cit.,* p. 18.
[31] *Ibid.,* p. 28.
[32] *Ibid.,* p. 23.

that the committee should explore the services of modern technology as it can assist the legislative process, especially in the areas of ADP [automatic data processing] and other electronic devices. Such innovation is not to be shunned if it would help the individual legislator to better fulfill his role as an informed representative.[33]

Representative Brooks' statement refers to the successful use of data processing techniques within the executive branch. The branch of government with the lion's share of informational resources has been increasing its information processing capacity while Congress, which sorely needs to develop these muscles, has been virtually inactive. This situation clearly emerges from a review of executive and legislative activities in research and development of information systems during the last eight years.

Widespread interest in information processing systems and their applications in business, industry, government, and academic research has developed only within the last decade. In July 1957, the National Science Foundation inaugurated its periodic survey of activities in information processing with the publication of issue No. 1 in its continuing series *Current Research and Development in Scientific Documentation*.[34] Each issue in the series not only discloses new projects underway but also updates earlier reports—providing a statement of work in progress at the time. The continuous expansion of information processing activities during the period from July 1959 to November 1964 is reflected in the steady increase in the number of pages in each issue. This trend is graphed in Figure 1, which shows an increase from 55 pages for issue No. 1 to 486 pages for issue No. 13.

Some indication of governmental activities in information processing can be obtained by reviewing the projects reported in these surveys.[35] Most of the projects reported on were undertaken by uni-

[33] U. S., Congress, Joint Committee on the Organization of the Congress, *Hearings,* Part 1, 89th Congress, 1st Session, 1965, p. 12.

[34] Issues in this series were published semi-annually through issue No. 11 dated November 1962. Publication had fallen behind schedule, however, and the eleventh issue did not appear until 1963. The series was resumed with issue No. 13, which was dated November 1964. That issue carried a notice stating, "No. 12 will consist of an indexed bibliography of all reports and publications cited as references in Issues Nos. 1-11. This report is scheduled for publication in early 1965."

[35] Perhaps a better source of information for such a review would have been the National Science Foundation publication series *Nonconventional Technical Information Systems in Current Use,* which reported on systems

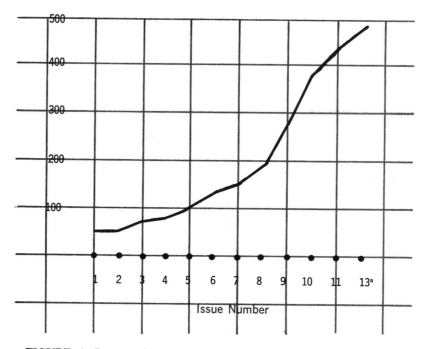

FIGURE 1: Increase in Number of Pages with Each Issue of Current Research and Development in Scientific Documentation, No. 1-13
ᵃ See Footnote 34 for an explanation of the absence of Issue No. 12.

versities and private corporations. From the beginning, however, some research work was conducted directly by the government—and almost exclusively by agencies in the executive branch.[36] Three of the 43 projects (7 percent) reported in July 1957 were conducted

that embodied new principles for the organization of subject matter or employed automatic equipment for storage and search. But according to my inquiries and my examination of the *Monthly Catalog of U.S. Government Publications,* this series terminated in October 1962, with issue No. 3. For the sake of continuity in reporting, I decided to use *Current Research and Development in Scientific Documentation* exclusively in this paper. Furthermore, it deserves to be noted that the term "scientific documentation" has been interpreted very broadly in the CRDSD series, which reported projects under such headings as "organization of information," "information needs and uses," "mechanical translation," and "equipment development."

[36] It is not always easy to decide what is and what is not an executive agency. Some of my decisions might be challenged. For example, the Rome Air Development Center was classified as an executive agency; the RAND Corporation was not. Disagreement with some of my classifications should not, however, be great enough to produce different interpretations of the data.

by executive agencies: two by the National Bureau of Standards and one by the U. S. Patent Office. By November 1964, 22 of 496 projects (4 percent) were reported by executive agencies. My compilation of the projects reported by all government agencies during this period is given in Table 3. Format inconsistencies from issue to issue and mistakes in tallying entries from tables of contents may have produced some errors in my tabulation, but the inaccuracy cannot be great.

TABLE 3: Projects Undertaken by Government Agencies as Reported in "Current Research and Developments in Scientific Documentation," Issues No. 1-13 [a]

Agency	Issue No.: 1	2	3	4	5	6	7	8	9	10	11	13[a]
National Bureau of Standards	2	2	3	6	6	6	4	4	7	7	8	7
U.S. Patent Office	1	1	1	1	1	1	1	1	1	1	1	
Rome Air Development Center	1										1	1
National Library of Medicine			1	1	1	1		1	1	1	1	1
U.S. Atomic Energy Commission						1	1	1	1	1	1	1
Armed Services Tech. Info. Agency						1	1	1	1	1	1	
U.S. Army Chemical Corps Res. & Dev.						1	1	1	1			
National Institutes of Health						1			1	1	1	1
Air Force Cambridge Research Lab.							2	3	3	3	3	1
Post Office Department								1	1	1	1	1
Department of Defense									1	1	1	
Library of Congress									1	1	2	2
U.S. Forest Service									1	1	1	
U.S. Naval Ordnance Test Station										1		
Walter Reed Army Medical Center										1	1	
U.S. Army Biological Laboratories										1	1	1
Department of Agriculture										1	1	2
Bureau of Ships											1	1
U.S. Naval Postgraduate School											1	1
National Agricultural Library												1
U.S. Public Health Service												1
Totals per issue: [b]	4	3	5	8	8	12	10	13	20	23	27	22

[a] See footnote 34 for an explanation of the issue sequence in this publication series.

[b] Some agencies reported progress on the same projects in each issue. Amounts at the bottom of the columns, therefore, cannot be summed so as to give the total number of different information processing projects undertaken by governmental agencies.

A word is in order about the nature of these government projects. Some of them—like the Post Office's attempt to devise an optical scanner that will read addresses and sort mail, and the Air Force

Cambridge Research Laboratories' work on pattern recognition and **speech** analysis—cannot easily be construed as giving the executive an edge over Congress in managing information and knowledge. But in general, experience in any type of automated information processing begets other applications, and such projects provide the requisite experience. Moreover, some of them clearly do contribute to the executive's ability to manage information. A case in point is the Defense Department's project "to design an all-computer document retrieval sytem which can find documents related to a request even though they may not be indexed by the exact terms of the request, and can present these documents in their appropriate order of their relevance to the request." [37]

The question may arise as to why Congress cannot be content with using the information systems developed within the executive. Why must Congress develop its own systems? This question deserves several answers. The first, of course, is that Congress' information needs are somewhat different from those of the executive and are unlikely to be fulfilled by any combination of systems prepared within the executive branch. Secondly, even granting that congressmen might use the executive's information systems upon occasion, they would not use them with the proficiency that comes from familiarity. And congressmen cannot be expected to familiarize themselves with every agency's particular system. Lastly, there is some doubt as to whether executive agencies would in fact grant congressmen unlimited access to their information systems. A staff report prepared by the Senate Committee on Government Operations in 1960 revealed such reluctance by an executive department to share its information resources with Congress:

> The staff was informed by officials of the Department of Defense that the Library of Congress was not being fully utilized as a scientific and technological storage center by the Department of Defense because much of the Department's material is classified, and that it is the Department's position that a documentation storage center of this nature should be a part of the executive branch, and not under the jurisdiction of the legislative branch of the Government as is the Library of Congress. Further, it was pointed out that it is the practice of the Department of Defense and other agencies to withhold from the Li-

---

[37] Statement provided for the National Science Foundation report *Current Research and Development in Scientific Documentation*, No. 9 (Washington: U.S. Government Printing Office, 1961), p. 48.

brary classified and certain other information which is now being withheld from committees of the Congress under executive policy. This position is based upon the premise that such information should not be made generally available to any agency of the legislative branch, since it would then be available to committees of the Congress, and be inconsistent with Presidential policy. The executive branch of the Government has consistently held that officials thereof should not provide information to the legislative committees when it is considered to be in the national interest to deny such information, or when it is related to so-called internal affairs of the executive branch and not a legislative concern of the Congress.[38]

All these considerations argue strongly for the development of information systems *by* Congress for use *within* Congress.

In 1965 the same Senate Committee on Government Operations reported on interagency coordination of information systems and commented on the relevance of all this activity to Congress' responsibilities:

> It may be observed that, as the executive agencies better organize their intra-agency information systems and hopefully, interagency systems, they may thereby facilitate the studies of expert committees of the Congress.
>
> It may also be noted that for the fulfillment of its many duties, the Congress may wish to have the latest technological systems directly at its own command.[39]

What has Congress actually done so far to place such systems at its own command? In contrast to the work in progress by the executive branch, the National Science Foundation surveys disclosed only two projects conducted under authority of the legislative branch. The earlier project, first reported in 1961 was to survey:

> . . . the possibilities for automating large research libraries, with the Library of Congress as primary focus of the survey. The emphasis of the survey is on the information organization, storage,

---

38 U. S., Congress, Senate, Committee on Government Operations, *Documentation, Indexing, and Retrieval of Scientific Information,* 86th Congress, 2d Session, Senate Document No. 113, 1960, pp. 18-19.

39 U. S., Congress, Senate, Committee on Government Operations, *Summary of Activities toward Interagency Coordination,* 89th Congress, 1st Session, Senate Report No. 369, p. 27.

and retrieval functions of libraries whose collections number in the millions and which serve research through the availability of both current and retrospective literature.[40]

The later project, first reported in 1963, was designed to determine user reactions to the Library of Congress' *Monthly Index of Russian Accessions*. While the second project does not pretend to improve Congress' position relative to the executive in the struggle for information and knowledge; the suggestion for automating the Library of Congress, which resulted from the first project, may have real strategic consequences.[41] Notwithstanding this effort, Congress has hardly distinguished itself by exploring the applications of automated techniques to its information problems.

If Congress itself is not undertaking these explorations, perhaps it is contracting them out to other organizations? How does Congress come out on this standard? Beginning with issue No. 6 in May 1960, *Current Research and Development in Scientific Documentation* has indexed projects according to their sponsoring organizations. The index to issue No. 6, for example, discloses that executive agencies (mainly the armed services) sponsored a total of 36 projects, although they themselves conducted only 12.[42] Figure 2 graphs the total number of projects sponsored and undertaken by government agencies, as reported in each issue of *CRDSD* since 1960.

Although the armed services sponsor most of the government's information processing projects by far, many civilian agencies have also been listed as sponsors—including the Office of Technical Services in the Department of Commerce, Food and Drug Administration, Office of Education, Fish and Wildlife Service, and the Peace Corps —to mention some that have not reported their own projects. In

---

[40] Statement provided for the National Science Foundation report, *op. cit.,* p. 64.

[41] A report on this project is published in The Council on Library Resources, *Automation and the Library of Congress* (Washington: Library of Congress, 1963). Also relevant are the proceedings of a conference reported in Barbara Evans Markuson (ed.), *Libraries and Automation* (Washington: Library of Congress, 1964).

[42] The organization of the index in *CRDSD* did not facilitate checking for duplicate sponsorship. Because two or more agencies could sponsor the same project (and sometimes did), this does not mean 36 different projects. Moreover, there may be some additional overlap because of agencies mentioned both as sponsors and as conductors of a project. But my examination of these possibilities suggests that these occurrences would not significantly alter the pattern of data if taken into account.

The tally of projects supported by executive agencies does not include grants awarded by the National Science Foundation.

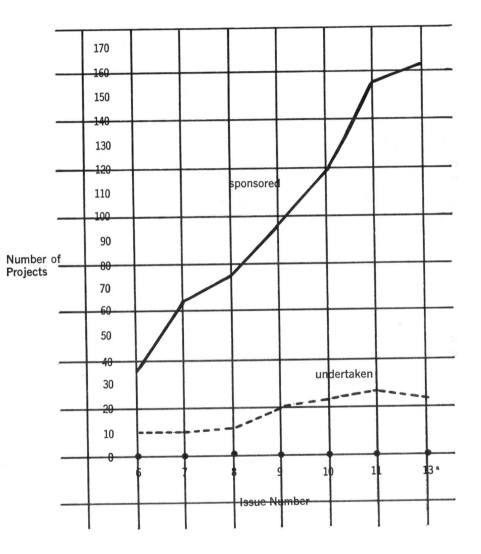

FIGURE 2: Growth in Number of Projects Sponsored and Undertaken by Governmental Agencies as Reported in issues No. 6-13 of Current Research and Development in Scientific Documentation.

[a] See footnote 34 for an explanation of the omission of Issue No. 12.

contrast to the support given by executive agencies for research and development in information systems, the National Science Foundation surveys disclosed *no* projects that were financed by Congress or its agencies. The projects undertaken by the Library of Congress mentioned earlier were *not* financed by Congress. The study of user reactions to the *Monthly Index of Russian Accessions* was supported by the National Science Foundation, and the more relevant investigation into automating large research libraries was supported by the Council on Library Resources, Inc.

The foregoing analysis of projects reported in *Current Research and Development in Scientific Documentation* was intended to illustrate Congress' lethargy in exploring the application of information processing systems to its information handling problems. By any standard, its activities in this area lag far behind those of the executive branch, which is already far ahead in informational resources. An extrapolation of present trends indicates a broadening, rather than a narrowing of the "information gap" that now exists between Congress and the executive.

The thesis of this paper is that this gap can be reduced substantially by retooling Congress with modern equipment and techniques for information processing. Before suggesting in some detail how this might be done, a few words are in order about some technical aspects of information processing systems.

Technology of an Information System[43]

I
T IS perhaps most important to point out initially what automated information systems are *not*. They are not devices for grinding out policy decisions, and they are not designed to replace human judgment. Rather they are intended to provide the human decision maker—here, the congressman—with knowledge for making informed choices. Automated systems for information processing, therefore, should not be confused with electronic schemes for solving complex social and political problems by putting them on a computer.

Dahl and Lindblom caution against sophomoric thinking that machines can replace man in decision making:

> Techniques regarded by some people as of great importance are mathematics and electronic calculators. Crudely stated, if there are too many variables for the human mind to handle at once in policy judgments, the problem is to reduce the variables to mathematical equations that can be fed into electronic calculators for a solution. Thereby, it might be suggested, an entirely new level of rationality in policy decisions would be possible, a leap

---

[43] This paper will not discuss technology of information processing in any detail, but there is a growing literature on the subject. On computers in general, see Bert F. Green, Jr., *Digital Computers in Research: An Introduction for Behavioral and Social Scientists* (New York: McGraw-Hill, 1963). Information processing is treated in Charles P. Bourne, *Methods of Information Handling* (New York: Wiley, 1963); Allen Kent, *Textbook on Mechanized Information Retrieval* (New York: Wiley, 1962); Joseph P. Spiegel and Donald Walker (eds.), *Information System Sciences* (Washington: Spartan Books, 1965); and Allen Kent (ed.), *Specialized Information Centers* (Washington: Spartan Books, 1965). Kenneth Janda, *Data Processing: Applications to Political Research* (Evanston: Northwestern University Press, 1965) may be helpful to the beginner.

forward roughly equivalent to the invention of language, writing, printing, or mathematics itself.

It is not really open to doubt that mathematics and electronic calculators can be of enormous aid in a number of specialized situations where quantification in comparable values is possible. . . .

Yet it would be easy to exaggerate what mathematics and electronic calculators are capable of. For as a substitute for decisions by human beings through social organizations the electronic computer suffers from several basic limitations.[44]

The limitations that Dahl and Lindblom recount deal with inabilities to reduce all variables to numbers, difficulties in assigning values to alternatives, uncertainties about consequences of actions and problems in controlling those who control the machines. All of these limitations, and others, attest to the absurdity of substituting computers for congressmen.

When Dahl and Lindblom published their book in 1953, computers were used almost exclusively for solving mathematical problems. Now, however, computers deal with words as well as numbers, with sentences as well as equations. They can therefore accept questions and provide answers. Computerized information processing systems are not designed to solve problems by means of mathematical equations but to provide information upon request. They propose not to eliminate the congressman as a decision maker but to increase his capabilities for making decisions by telling him what he wants to know.

A computer's ability to do arithmetic in a hurry is well known, but a computer can do other things as well. It can make logical decisions: if value A is larger than value B, do X; otherwise, do Y. It can also manipulate symbols, reading data in one way and printing them out in another. These capabilities enable computers to do more than just "compute." Speaking more broadly, they *process* data. The term "data" is usually associated with numerical values, and, strictly speaking, computers recognize and deal only with numerical values. But numbers can be made to stand for letters of the alphabet, which enables computers to process alphabetical as well as numerical data.

The term "information processing," in its broadest sense, applies to computer handling of either alphabetical or numerical information. "Information retrieval" is a somewhat more restricted term, fre-

---

[44] Dahl and Lindblom, *op. cit.*, p. 76.

quently reserved only for computer processing of alphabetical information. In an even narrower sense, "information retrieval" is sometimes applied only to computerized systems that store alphabetical information in memory, search the memory according to a set of instructions, and then retrieve items of information which satisfy the instructions. This paper will employ "information retrieval" in its narrower sense—meaning storage and retrieval—and "information processing" in its broader sense—including data processing and information retrieval.

Interest in computer processing of textual material first began with problems of information retrieval. Although librarians have always been engaged in storing and retrieving information, applying computers to these tasks seemed to breathe new life and interest into the methodology. Information retrieval technology now involves more than just computers, and considerable progress has been made with the use of microfilm and even purely mechanical devices. However, while product development in non-computer techniques of information retrieval seems promising, computers will clearly be the dominant force in information processing systems of the future.

Until recently, non-computer information systems had the great advantage over computers of being immediately accessible to the user: the system (e.g., a file of key-sort cards) could be at his side, available for use whenever he wanted an item of stored information. But few people could afford to maintain an electronic computer stationed alongside their desk at their beck and call. Economical use of the computer required that it be placed in a central location and fed a series of "jobs" assembled in "batches." The answers to a specific job, even a short one, could not be obtained until the entire batch had been processed and all the results printed out. The period of time required between submitting a job for processing and picking up the results—called the "turn-around time"—depended on the nature of the equipment and its work load. Even now, it is not at all uncommon for turn-around time to average about six hours, which is hardly quick enough to satisfy demands for immediate information. Recent technological developments in the computing industry, however, have brought the processing power of computers much closer to the user and his needs.

The development of "time sharing" and "remote terminals" has produced the first feasible desk-side information processing systems. "Time sharing," as its name implies, enables many different users to tap into the same computer at the same time. In actuality, the computer processes only a small part of one person's job at a time while rotating from user to user. But it returns so quickly that the wait is unnoticeable to the user, who feels he has sole use of the machine to answer his inquiry—thereby eliminating turn-around time completely. "Remote terminals" are input-output devices located in the user's office and connected to a central computer (usually on a time-sharing basis). These devices enable the user to communicate his inquiry to the computer (input) and provide for the computer to express its answer (output) without requiring a trip to the computing center.

Important advances in input-output devices themselves have also increased the value of computerized information processing systems. Typewriter keyboards now allow the user to type out his inquiry to the computer as if he were preparing a memo to his assistant. In due time, the user will even be able to communicate his request orally to the computer. And the perfection of optical scanning devices will empower the computer to "read" instructions typed, printed, or even handwritten on paper. Still more flexibility appears in types of computer *output*. The computer can answer by typewriting (for short replies) or through a high-speed printer. It can also display information on a cathode ray screen for viewing or photographing. If desired, standard oral messages can be recorded on tape and selected for response.

Not all of these devices have been fully developed, but perfection is close at hand. Time sharing and versatile remote terminals should certainly be incorporated in planning information systems for Congress.

Features of an Information
System for Congress

THE information processing system sketched out below is meant to illustrate ways in which electronic equipment and computers can help congressmen perform their job. Its various features presuppose a sophisticated level of technology. Although some features incorporate devices that have not yet been perfected, the system in its broad outlines can be put into operation with present capabilities. In any event, the task of recommending an information processing system for Congress should not be limited by the capabilities of today's equipment. Not only can we count on continuing progress within the industry to increase the performance and improve the flexibility of computing hardware in general, but we should also be aware that manufacturers are often able to design and build machines to meet customers' individual needs and specifications. This is already routinely done for agencies in the executive branch, most notably for the armed services. Preserving the strength and integrity of our national legislature—and thereby preserving the virtue of our government—is worth the price of some research and development to deliver the system that Congress needs.

The system outlined here is not necessarily the ideal one for Congress. It is suggested as a starting point for future thinking. Of necessity, the suggestions are not very specific, for specific suggestions would involve specific equipment, which is certainly premature. Instead the features of the system advanced here are primarily designed to illustrate how information processing can be tied directly to congressmen's daily activities.

Information systems for Congress probably should be organized on four different levels, serving Congress as a whole, each chamber

439

separately, committees within Congress, and individual congressmen. The levels of organization are not irrelevant to type and amount of computing equipment needed. It is hardly conceivable that a single computer, however gigantic, can service the combined needs of Congress, each chamber, scores of committees (standing, select, special, and joint), plus 535 individual members and their staffs. Some configuration of computers would probably be required to handle this load. Be that as it may, this discussion will largely ignore physical requirements and assume simply that each congressman and each committee will be served by a remote input-output terminal connected on a time-sharing basis to some central computing facility.

The proposed features of an information system for Congress will be grouped and discussed according to different levels of organization.

Congress as a whole: Certain kinds of information can best be collected and processed centrally for the use of both houses of Congress. Individual congressmen would tap into this centralized service.

1. *Informing congressmen of relevant bills:* Every congressman develops interests in particular legislative measures. These interests may develop from committee work, personal attitudes, or constituency requests; they may be permanent in nature, or merely temporary. At present, congressmen seek to locate bills affecting their interests by searching the "Daily Digest" of the *Congressional Record* and other publications about Congress, such as *Congressional Quarterly.* Sometimes the congressman finds what he wants; sometimes not. In any event, his search always requires time, and he seldom can be confident that he did not miss something relevant to his interests that was indexed under a different heading. Moreover, the congressman never has the information come after him; he must go after it.

An information retrieval technique called "selective dissemination of information" (SDI) has a very definite application here. SDI originally was developed to notify scientists as their library received new publications relevant to their research interests. In brief, SDI operates as follows.[45] The scientist personally prepares a list of the key terms describing his research interests. This list, which constitutes his "interest profile," is stored on magnetic tape, along with interest profiles from many other scientists. Meanwhile, as each new

---

[45] SDI is described in detail in *IBM, Selective Dissemination of Information* (White Plains, N. Y.: IBM Technical Publications Department, No. E20-8092, dated 1962).

publication comes into the library, a group of abstractors examines the document, describes its contents with a set of key terms, and prepares an abstract summarizing the research. Periodically this information is also recorded on magnetic tape. The computer then compares the scientists' interest profiles with the key terms describing each publication. When a document is found that deals with a term in a scientist's interest profile, the computer prints on a special form the name of the scientist and the abstract of the document. This form is then mailed to the scientist, notifying him that such-and-such a publication has been received in the library. If, upon reading the abstract, he decides he would like to see the whole document, he can return the card by mail to receive a copy of the original publication.

Much the same idea can be used for notifying congressmen of bills relevant to their interests that have been introduced in either house of Congress. Congressmen could establish their own "interest profiles," which could be changed or updated at any time, to be matched against abstracts of bills prepared soon after they have been introduced. Through a remote terminal in his office, the congressman could be notified of the bill, its sponsor, and the committee to which it was referred. He could then send for copies of the bills that especially interest him simply by typing the appropriate request on a keyboard input to the computer. At somewhat greater expense, the computer could actually print out complete bills upon his request.

If a congressman were to change his interest profile during the session, the system should be able to search the entire file bills previously introduced. In fact, the system should be able to search all the bills for specific key terms by any congressman upon request. The main advantage of using interest profiles in an SDI system is to disseminate information of interest to congressmen *selectively* and *automatically*. Relevant information is literally brought to their attention without their having to go after it.

2. *Disseminating information about lobbyists:* At present, lobbyists are required to register either with the Clerk of the House or the Secretary of the Senate. These registrations are required by law to be published quarterly in the *Congressional Record.* However, there is some question about how useful this reporting procedure is to congressmen.[46] For this reason, it is proposed that registration data on lobbyists could be stored on magnetic tape and made avail-

---

[46] Lester W. Milbrath, *The Washington Lobbyists* (Chicago: Rand McNally, 1963), pp. 318-19.

able for computer search and retrieval. Congressmen could then instruct the computer to search the lobbyist file for the name of any individual who has approached him with respect to legislation before Congress. Through its remote terminal, the computer could reply immediately whether or not the person is a registered lobbyist, whom he represents, with what particular piece of legislation he is concerned, what organizations he has represented in the past, his address, etc.

There is no doubt about the importance of the role in the governmental structure played by lobbyists, who constitute one of the most valuable sources of independent information available to Congress. The purpose of this recommendation is not to hamstring lobbyists' operations but to place congressmen in a more knowledgeable, and therefore more advantageous, position from which to interact with lobbyists. This proposal reflects the familiar thesis that "knowledge is power." Whatever increases the knowledge of individual congressmen increases their power, and thereby strengthens the position of Congress as an institution. Increments to knowledge can come from many quarters, and this proposal to keep congressmen informed about lobbyists is simply one possibility.

3. *Communicating with the Legislative Reference Service:* The Library of Congress and its Legislative Reference Service are already engaged in automating their information handling procedures. Congressmen's terminals could tap into these systems for routine interrogations of their information files. Specialized inquiries, however, might better be communicated through the terminals to a reference person in the Library of Congress or LRS, who would translate them into technical requests for computer searching. Results of the search could be routed directly back to the congressman through the terminals. This direct connection would again increase the amount of knowledge available at the congressman's fingertips.

4. *Searching the U.S. Code:* The entire U.S. Code of Laws has already been recorded on magnetic tape by the Health Law Center of the University of Pittsburgh and is available for computer processing.[47] The tape can be searched for laws affecting any given subject. The computer can retrieve all laws under that subject in the Code and also find laws dealing with one subject but entered under a dif-

---

[47] John C. Lyons, "Computers in Legislative Drafting," *American Bar Association Journal,* June 1965. See also Earl W. Brydges, "The Electronic Solon," *National Civic Review,* July 1965, p. 351. I want to thank John S. Appel for calling this citation to my attention.

ferent heading. It should be noted that at least one state legislature already has such a "legal retrieval" facility at its command. State Senator Earl W. Brydges reports on New York's system:

"Give me all the laws affecting banking that are not in the banking law," New York Senator Jeremiah B. Bloom recently asked the computer. The machine spewed forth 1,604 of them that this experienced lawmaker never knew existed. "This means," he said, "we have to bring sense out of this disorder. How can any bank possibly know its duties and obligations with so many laws scattered all over the legal lot?" And when Senator Bloom starts to modernize the law, the computer will point out duplications, obsolete sections and reorganize the laws into a logical order on command.[48]

Congress should provide itself with at least the same capability for conducting its lawmaking business that state legislatures have seen fit to develop.

Each Chamber of Congress: Some activities of Congress, particularly those of a scheduling and housekeeping nature, are best handled on the basis of each chamber. Applications of information processing techniques to a few such activities are illustrated below.

1. *Locating bills in the legislative process:* Congressmen should be able to learn immediately upon request the location of any bill in Congress, its status in the chamber, and its history of action to date, including amendments, committee votes, floor votes, and scheduling for future action. This information could be gathered within each chamber and immediately stored in the computer. It could then be recalled by the congressman simply upon keying the bill number into the remote terminal typewriter. The response should appear at the terminal in one of two forms: a printed message—if hard copy is desired—or visual display on a cathode ray tube—if the information is to be used immediately. In general, the use of visual display units in input-output terminals would substantially reduce the amount of paper messages generated by the computer, and would thereby result in savings on material and filing of documents with transient value.

2. *Providing information about votes:* One of congressmen's main complaints is that they find it difficult to obtain information about measures on which they must vote.[49] Summoned by sound of the

---

[48] *Ibid.,* p. 350.
[49] Clapp, *op. cit.,* pp. 145-49.

voting bell, congressmen sometimes rush into the chamber with little or no knowledge of what the vote is all about. Often the only information available is that supplied by a colleague on the floor or even by the doorkeeper. A chamber-based information system can substantially increase the congressman's knowledge of the vote as it is announced.

With the announcement of the vote, his office terminal can reveal the issue involved along with the bill number, sponsorship, legislative history—all of which could be taken from the information files proposed above. It would also be possible to build into the system, if desired, voting positions favored by the President and adopted by party leaders, including also perhaps the positions of individual congressmen volunteered in advance of the vote. At somewhat greater expense, announcement of the vote could include a summary of the issue and consequence of the vote for passage of the bill. The net result of these proposals would be to arm individual congressmen with relevant information in order to make more rational voting decisions.

3. *Providing for automated voting:* Voting itself can be viewed as an information process, with individual congressmen originating information instead of receiving it. But replacing traditional roll call voting in Congress with electronic voting machines is a controversial proposal—notwithstanding the fact that these machines have been used for varying lengths of time in 30 state legislatures.[50] The Dartmouth survey of congressmen's attitudes toward this innovation reveals 62 percent opposed to it and 35 percent in favor, with 3 percent undecided.[51] On the other hand, the *Interim Report* of the Joint Committee on the Organization of the Congress shows electronic voting advocated by five congressmen, two political scientists, and one organizational representative—while opposed by only one congressman.

The main advantage claimed for electronic voting machines, of course, is the saving of time. Galloway has calculated that record-

---

[50] Council of State Governments, *Book of the States: 1962-1963* (Chicago: Council of State Governments, 1962), Vol. XIV, p. 54.

[51] O'Leary, *op. cit.,* p. 58. The representatives were asked to state if they agreed or disagreed with this proposal: "Use electronic voting devices on the floor of the House, which would record a Member's vote on any measure on which one-fifth of the Members present request such a vote (that is, the present requirement for a roll call vote)." Conceivably, some congressmen might be in favor of electronic voting based on some other criterion or perhaps on all votes. Therefore these figures may understate support for electronic voting in general.

ing votes electronically would have saved the 78th Congress as much as two calendar months.[52] While virtually everyone concedes the timesaving advantages of automated voting, opposition to this innovation is sometimes rooted in the fear of what *else* it will do besides save time. The authors of the Dartmouth study of congressmen's attitudes toward reforms detected this apprehension:

> Some efficiency-minded respondents looked to electronic voting as a method of saving at least an hour of their time each day of a session; other Members, equally concerned with the demands on their time, explained their opposition to automatic voting by suggesting a "horror show" of unanticipated consequences of such an innovation.[53]

Probably the most vocal opposition to electronic voting stems from concern that installation of voting machines would limit congressmen's freedom to attend to business outside the chamber. This is the position taken by Representative Matthews, the single opponent of the innovation listed in the *Interim Report:*

> I think the fact that we have 20 or 30 minutes in the House— and I don't know, sir, what the time is in the Senate—to leave from attending to those myriad responsibilities at other places and yet get to the House to answer the roll is more of an advantage than the electronic voting device. . . .
>
> . . . it would seem to me that we have our committee responsibilities and can't always be right on the floor. We are over in our offices, or meeting with a delegation, for example. And the electronic system may not necessarily work here in our setup as well as it would work and as it does work in some of the State legislatures.[54]

The same attitude is revealed in the remark addressed to an advocate of electronic voting by Representative Robert P. Griffin, a member of the Joint Committee:

> . . . when you suggest that we have electronic voting and electronic devices for taking quorum calls, are you saying that committees should never sit while the House is in session?

---

[52] George Galloway, *Congress at the Crossroads* (New York: Thomas Y. Crowell Co., 1946), p. 80.

[53] O'Leary, *op. cit.,* p. 25.

[54] Joint Committee on the Organization of the Congress, *Hearings, op. cit.,* p. 130.

I raise that question because I think in order for it to be effective, all the Members would have to be on the floor in order to press their electronic button or whatever it is.[55]

It is true that voting machines in state legislatures require members to be present on the floor in order to cast their votes. But this condition can be eliminated through proper technology and, in itself, constitutes no real obstacle to automated voting in Congress. At the very least, congressmen could be empowered to cast their votes by direct connection from their offices.[56] Various electronic safeguards might be employed to insure that this power is not usurped by impostors voting in the congressmen's stead. One obvious protection against this would be closed-circuit television showing the congressman casting his vote. The action could be recorded on video tape and preserved to prove the legality of each vote. An even more ambitious step toward freeing congressmen to move about Washington without missing out on roll call votes would be to establish congressional "polling booths" in government buildings throughout Washington for their use while visiting executive agencies. These too could be equipped with closed circuit television and devices to protect against usurpation.

The point is that proposals to install electric voting machines should not be defeated merely by arguments that this would restrict congressmen's freedom. Under proper planning, it could very well increase their mobility while saving their time. On the other hand, electronic voting might deserve to be rejected for the reason that it would impair Congress' vitality rather than improve it. Other authors in this symposium, for example, fear the loss of personal contact and communication that now occurs when congressmen congregate for roll call votes.

The introduction of electronic voting would undoubtedly have many unknown consequences for congressional behavior. Perhaps additional assessment is required in order to predict its net effect upon Congress. But vague fears of unanticipated consequences alone should not kill this innovation. Virtually all change brings some unforeseen results. The task is to calculate carefully according to best available knowledge, and choose the means best designed to achieve a given goal. To do more is impossible; to do less, irrational.

---

[55] *Ibid.*, p. 37.

[56] There seems to be no constitutional requirement for congressmen to be present when casting their votes. The relevant passage states, "and the Yeas and Nays of the Members of either House on any question shall, at the Desire of one fifth of those Present, be entered on the Journal" (Article I, Section 5).

Individual congressmen: Congressmen vary in their legislative interests, constituency relationships, and styles of operation. Any information system for Congress should be adjustable to fit their individual needs. Here are a few suggestions of ways in which each congressman might use his own information processing facilities.

1. *Deciding how to vote:* Many pieces of information are important for congressmen's voting decisions. Some of this information can be furnished automatically by computer announcement of every vote, as described above. Yet there are many political factors, personally important to the congressman, that would not be included in the announcement but which he might like to review before voting. For this purpose, each congressman should be equipped with computing facilities to handle his personal file of information and his own retrieval system.

When a roll call vote is announced, the congressman could use this system to review his voting record on the subject; past votes can be stored in memory and recalled for study. He could also examine the attitudes of various groups in his constituency toward the issue; the computer could retrieve whatever constituency data he had read into storage beforehand. Exactly what he would put into storage would depend on what information he has collected and how his system has been organized. He might, for example, want to recall his own speeches and public statements on various issues. In the last analysis, the shape taken by the system would be determined largely by the imagination and resourcefulness of individual congressmen.

2. *Maintaining relations with his constituency:* Congressmen could use their computing facility for performing a variety of constituency-oriented activities. Constituents' names and addresses could be stored in memory along with other relevant data for automatic preparation of specialized mailings, e.g., to campaign contributors, labor leaders, businessmen, supporters of the congressman's party, supporters of the opposition party, and so on. Constituency mail might even be answered with the computer. Some printing devices now have both upper and lower case characters, which would give each computerized reply the appearance of an original letter, with the printing done at the rate of hundreds of *lines*—not words— per minute.

Obviously, this computing capability might also be used to analyze polling data and elections returns, thus helping the congressman in his continuous campaign for re-election. Here again, input to the computer would depend largely on the politics of the congressman's constituency and the ingenuity of individual congressmen. A man from a safe district might not bother with such analysis; one from a competitive district might cultivate it to a high degree.

3. *Reading and analyzing written material:* Modern congressmen are expected to devour daily an astounding stack of reading matter. In addition to the massive *Congressional Record* there are bills, committee reports, House and Senate documents, agency reports, constituency mail, newspapers, and so on. Much of this material need only be quickly scanned for occurrences of terms of interest before thoughtful reading begins. Other material has to be analyzed thoroughly, sentence by sentence. Automated equipment definitely can be used to scan documents for relevant passages marked by certain terms and—perhaps surprisingly—can also be employed for careful content analysis, sentence by sentence.

Some progress remains to be made in optical scanning equipment before computers are ready to assist congressmen with their reading load. Devices have already been built, however, that can read a variety of type fonts and enter the information into a computer for processing.[57] All the material to be read need not be stored in memory; this would soon exhaust the storage capacity of the largest computer. Instead, programs can be devised that would retain only material which satisfies search instructions that are given to the computer beforehand. In this way, the computer would not generate reel upon reel of magnetic tape for the thousands of pages it reads. It would analyze information in the process of reading it and be selective about what is communicated to the congressman.

Congressional committees: Most legislative work in Congress is conducted through committees, and at least the standing committees should serve as a basis for organizing a congressional information system. However, it is even harder to be specific about system features at the committee level, for the shape of the system will depend largely on the committee's jurisdiction and will have to be tailor-made to its workload. But a few general features readily suggest themselves.

1. *Compiling histories of committee action:* Over the years, each committee often considers many bills with identical or quite similar

---

[57] Work undertaken by the Post Office Department is quite relevant here, which underscores the fact that research and development in even purely "administrative" applications of technology can have broad consequences for information processing in general.

content. To a large extent, the combined memories of the senior committee members can recall important facts about similar bills that had been considered in the past. Upon occasion, however, their memories fail, and they forget results of previous hearings and actions on proposed legislation. More important, perhaps, is the inability of newer committee members to draw as extensively upon previous committee experience, which prevents them from functioning to maximum capacity as lawmakers.

To make previous experience generally available, the full history of committee action could be compiled on magnetic tape and made available to any committee member for computer processing. Upon request, any member could find all bills on a given subject that the committee had considered in past Congresses, the bills' provisions, whether or not hearings were held, relevant documents reporting the hearings, action taken by the committee, action taken in the chamber, action by the other chamber, whether the bill became law, and so on. Most of this information is available now through traditional methods of research. This proposal, however, would make the search and retrieval operations automatic, swift, and routine—thus eliminating the need for laborious study in order to locate basic information.

2. *Processing data on subjects under committee jurisdiction:* This is a general proposal for strengthening research capacities of committee staffs by equipping them with computers. It is difficult to say exactly how the computers would be used, for that would depend on the research needs of the committee. One example might be to use a computer for analyzing questionnaire data collected on special groups affected by governmental programs. The data could be processed and analyzed by the committee staff using Congress' own computing facilities. At present, committees do conduct such surveys, but they usually process their data on computers in some executive agency—which is usually only too happy to oblige.[58] This method of operation, however, hardly promotes Congress' independence of the executive. Congressional committees should be

---

[58] A good example of congressional use of executive computing facilities is provided by the Subcommittee on Domestic Finance of the House Committee on Banking and Currency, which used computers and computing time provided by the Federal Reserve Board and the Federal Deposit Insurance Corporation to analyze questionnaire data collected from some 3,000 commercial banks. This research is reported in several documents issued during the 2d Session of the 88th Congress, including *Correspondent Relations: A Survey of Banker Opinion* and *A Study of Selected Banking Services by Bank Size, Structure, and Location.*

given their own research tools so that they need not be beholden to the executive for information, expertise, or computing time.

3. *Controlling the administration:* One of the most needed areas of improvement for Congress lies in direction and control of the federal bureaucracy. In general, congressional committees are organized to parallel executive departments and to divide responsibilities accordingly for reviewing activities of given agencies. Committees can increase the effectiveness of their direction and control over the agencies through information processing techniques. One such application immediately suggests itself: analyzing past and projected budgetary expenditures for each agency.

Appropriating moneys and authorizing expenditures are cited together as the main weapon in congressional control of the executive. But it is generally conceded that Congress is underpowered to review effectively the enormously long and complex budget set before it by the executive. As Wallace has written:

> Congress does not now have access to nearly as much analytical data about the budget as does the Executive. Although there is probably a point beyond which additional information does not help to predict consequences of action, Congress has not yet reached that point. The present disparity between its information resources and those of the Executive means that effective control . . . is held in the hands of those who possess detailed information with respect to the various administrative needs and the adequacy of this or that amount of money for carrying out a particular program.[59]

Committees could use the computer for exhaustive and comprehensive analyses of current estimates according to past estimates and subsequent expenditures. The sources of increase and decrease (if any) can be pinpointed and subjected to closer scrutiny. Patterns of supplementary appropriations could be entered into the analysis. At the very least, the committee should be able to do fundamental arithmetic on a grand scale with executive budgets. This in itself would not insure economy and efficiency within the bureaucracy, but—coupled with other analytical procedures devised by the committees and executed on the computer—it should give Congress more punch to use in the battle of the budget.

---

[59] Robert Ash Wallace, "Congressional Control of the Budget," *Midwest Journal of Political Science,* May 1959, p. 152.

Issues in Automating Congress

IT WOULD be foolish to recommend an automated information system for Congress without considering some of the basic issues involved in this dramatic innovation. Four seem to be of paramount importance: cost of the system, smoothness of transition, mastery of the system, and effect upon the distribution of power. Each of these issues will be discussed in turn.

Cost of the system: I would not hazard a guess about the dollar cost of an automated information system for Congress, for this would be far beyond my competence. But I can roughly estimate the absolute outer limit of expense. Let us suppose that the physical and human facilities of a modern computing center at a major university were provided for exclusive use of *each* representative, *each* senator, *each* standing committee in both chambers, the House and Senate *separately*, and Congress as a whole. The total number of computing centers needed would be as follows:

Number of congressmen	535
Standing committees	36
Both chambers	2
Congress itself	1
Total	574

The annual operating budget of the computing center at Northwestern University can serve as a standard. Its budget for 1965-66 is $533,000. This amount covers rental cost of its basic machines, Control Data Corporation's new 3400 computer and its satellite, the CDC 8090; rental of a full complement of auxiliary equipment;

451

salaries of 17 staff members and wages of many hourly workers; and all associated supplies, cards, paper, magnetic tape, etc. Utilization of Northwestern's computing facilities has steadily increased over time. At present, the center serves 35 separate departments and schools in the University and has on file more than 500 active projects ranging in scope from nuclear physics to classical Greek. Even with this tremendous use by hundreds of students and faculty members and even with projected increases for the future, the present equipment will probably be able to handle Northwestern's demands for computer time for the next two years.

Suppose a vast computing facility like Northwestern's was made available to each of the users listed above. The annual operating cost for 574 such computing centers would be slightly less than $306 million. Given the magnitude of annual expenditures for some projects within governmental agencies, this does not seem like an astronomical figure. And a more sensible configuration of equipment using several very large central computers and remote control stations would bring the cost down to bargain prices for this contribution to democratic government.

Smoothness of transition: It would be folly to automate abruptly. Automation should proceed gradually, one step at a time, while maintaining traditional procedures to prevent bugs in the system from disrupting communications. Disseminating notifications of new bills might be tried first. This technique involves computer programs and procedures that are now almost routine in information processing. It could be introduced in Congress with relative ease and would give all congressmen a taste of innovation simultaneously. If their reaction is favorable, the next application might be in the committees. Some committee staffs already have had considerable experience in data processing with computers in the executive branch and thus can aid in the transition for Congress.

Authorization for establishing information systems at the committee level should, of course, be permissive—enabling committees to automate at their own initiative. The change would not be sweeping, but should provide for incremental expansion, committee by committee. Finally, similar arrangements should be made in establishing systems for individual congressmen. Those who want to automate their own information-handling activities should be enabled to do so. A gradual approach like this should allow the system to win acceptance on merits demonstrated through actual performance rather than promise. And if the system seems to be developing undesirable consequences, it could be altered or even scrapped—whatever the evidence indicates.

Mastery of the system: Further expansion of professional staffs is frequently recommended to cope with Congress' information problem. Congressmen are understandably reluctant to follow this advice out of fear that their own staffs would become bureaucracies and would, in turn, be difficult to control. They might also resist installation of automated information systems because of the same basic fear: losing control of their own tools. This fear may be all the more pronounced because the tools are space-age inventions unfamiliar to elected officials.

Installation of computing systems for Congress would clearly demand employment of persons trained in the technology. This means both computer operators and—even more important—computer programmers. Probably each chamber would have to maintain a small staff of programmers to develop and maintain its information processing systems. In addition, the standing committees would have to add programmers to their staffs, and eventually individual congressmen might themselves employ programmers on a part-time or job basis. These technicians will possess specialized knowledge. The question is: can congressmen make them work effectively and obtain the information they want and need?

Some people stand in awe of electronic computers, computer programmers, and men from IBM. The uninitiated imagine white-robed technicians communicating in a strange language and performing mysterious ceremonies around frightfully complex machinery. In short, computers and related things seem far beyond the ken of these ordinary mortals. Congressmen might find absurd the suggestion that they might learn how to use computers themselves. But it is not absurd; computers are tools that can be used, if not mastered, by intelligent and interested people.

I submit that congressmen can readily acquire a basic understanding of computers and computer programming for effective use of the system. A series of talks by capable instructors followed by equipment demonstrations should prove adequate for communicating this understanding. In time, this instruction could become part of the orientation for new members. My experience in teaching computer use and computer programming to college juniors and seniors in political science indicates that a working knowledge of the equipment is acquired very rapidly, once the initiation has occurred.

Effect upon the distribution of power: "Knowledge is power." Granting that premise, the question becomes, "Who gets the knowledge?" This is largely answered by disclosing the beneficiaries of the information system outlined above. Two groups will benefit: Congressmen individually and committees of congressmen. The fundamental belief underlying this whole proposal is that Congress can be strengthened as a legislative institution by improving the effectiveness of congressmen as individual lawmakers. Providing congressmen with more information and greater knowledge is a major way of doing this. Providing committees of congressmen with more information and greater knowledge also strengthens Congress, by promoting specialization and division of labor in lawmaking. As a consequence, Congress as a whole will become a far more effective force in our governmental structure.

This proposal studiously avoids concentrating remote terminals in the hands, say, of the elected leadership or perhaps party committees. Such concentration would produce no substantial increase in knowledge and information available to individual congressmen and would accelerate centralization of power within Congress. And centralization of power within Congress would have as *its* main beneficiary the party in control of the White House, which ultimately means the President. And we do not need recommendations which further strengthen the President's hand in his dealings with Congress.

The recommendations in this paper harbor no great or systematic alterations in the present distribution of power within Congress. Providing a quantum of knowledge to all congressmen across the board might hasten the effectiveness of newer members, but this effect, although welcome, is not likely to be substantial. Providing specialized information to standing committees simply recognizes and reinforces their current influence in the legislative process. Other things being equal, then, this proposal should benefit no political factions within Congress.

But other things are seldom equal, and some individuals may wring more knowledge, and therefore more power, out of the information system than others. I am certain this will happen, but I see no basis for alarm from any particular quarter—unless people in that quarter place little confidence in their abilities to compete successfully with others in using these tools. Some congressmen will work the system better than others, but it is impossible to forecast in advance who these will be—which means, again, no predictable change in the distribution of power.

Conclusion

WITHOUT doubt, establishing an automated information system within Congress will have many unanticipated consequences. Far-reaching changes have always accompanied the introduction of new technology into society. The automobile brought not only faster transportation but also giant shopping centers and drive-in movies. Television brought not only improved communications but also TV dinners and "family rooms." Technological innovation in society changes ways of living; in Congress, it will change ways of lawmaking.

It is impossible to predict in advance all concomitant outcomes of this proposal. No doubt, some changes will be evaluated negatively by congressmen and by students of the legislative process. But the final tally of pluses and minuses should find this innovation clearly moving Congress toward a more vital and independent role in our governmental system. The evaluation of a state senator who has experienced the application of computing techniques in New York's state legislature supports this estimate in full. Senator Brydges says:

> The computer places one of the greatest research tools in history in the hands of legislatures from coast to coast. Because it can do its work quickly, surely and extensively and print laws in quantity, it saves interim committees, research counsel and law revision agencies thousands of man-hours that would be consumed simply in trying to find all laws on a specific topic and reproducing them in quantities for scissoring, pasting and reshuffling. Its importance, however, lies beyond it ability to serve as a legal research assistant. The computer

455

becomes a means of restoring the legislature to its proper equal status with the judicial and executive branches of government. Today and in the future, control over facts—the ability to research in depth and quickly—can gain for legislatures some of the capabilities for leadership they have lost over the years.[60]

If computers can do this for state legislatures, why not for Congress?

---

[60] Brydges, *op. cit.,* pp. 351-52.

Strengthening The First Branch: An Inventory Of Proposals

Editorial Note

For the convenience of the reader, the various recommendations on the reform of Congress proposed in this symposium have been grouped into eight broad categories covering the main spheres of congressional activity. However, due to the meshing of the different aspects of Congress' work, absolute classification is not possible. For instance: fiscal initiative and control form but one aspect of oversight; checking and balancing the executive necessarily entails prowess in decision making; an increase in the flow of information would automatically benefit all spheres of activity, as would an increase in staffing. In consequence, many of the recommendations placed in one category could have been placed in another with equal relevance. Where this is the case, the principle guiding the placement has in general been a deference to the emphasis and context given to them by their own authors.

So that the reader may gain a complete picture of all the recommendations covering one subject, some cross-referencing has been introduced, though of course it has not been thought necessary to refer at the end of each section to, say, all the recommendations on information gathering or staffing. Only those recommendations that have a direct bearing on the section concerned have been cross-referenced. As a rule the cross-references have been placed at the end of each section. However, where recommendations in different categories either duplicate each other or represent a development of a particular proposal, the cross-references have been placed immediately after the appropriate recommendation or groups of related recommendations.

Although an effort has been made to use the author's own words, this has not been feasible in all cases. Where, for instance, the author did not frame his thought specifically in the form of a recommendation, or where, for lack of space, condensing was required, a new wording was supplied.

From what has been said, it should be clear that the organization of this inventory of proposals has been the work of the editor. The groupings cannot therefore be taken as in any way reflecting the views of the individual authors. Each author is responsible solely for his own recommendations, especially as they are made in the context of his own writing.

No attempt has been made to synthesize proposals of a closely similar nature, nor to reconcile with the whole those proposals, remarkably few in number, that are basically at odds with the general direction of the studies.

I. Checks and Balances, The Presidency and the Courts

Checks and balances

1. The traditional theory of legislative independence, whereby Congress is conceived as a bipartisan body with the leaders of the two parties aligning themselves to form a check on the executive, should continue to be the concept on which to base an evaluation of Congress' capacity to check and balance the other branches of government.

   (Robinson)

2. A Charter of Legislative Authority should declare the principle of legislative supremacy of Congress and the position of Congress with respect to the executive branch, and this Charter should be disseminated widely within and outside of the government.

   (A. de Grazia)

3. Exemplary Legislation should be made a regular feature of each session of Congress; it consists of laws with minimum scope

and substance but with vital principles asserting constantly congressional rights to employ a large range of devices—such as the legislative veto—in the full exercise of its powers and control of the executive branch.

(A. de Grazia)

4. All representative-type bodies formed by executive agencies should have the direct authorization of Congress, and all members of the hundreds of such agencies in the executive branch should be considered subrogated for Congress and should pass tests to assure their comprehension of the principles of government by legislature.

(A. de Grazia)

5. A General Counsel of Congress is the preferred instrument for expounding congressional intent and prerogatives at the bar; executive attorneys cannot always be relied upon for full support of congressional rationale.

(A. de Grazia)

6. The doctrine of check and balance should be restated in terms of the current social and political conditions and congressmen should articulate it as fully as possible to the public in terms of modern life. Organizational changes to assist Congress in checking and balancing the executive more efficiently will prove helpful only if there is a reinvigoration of the whole check-and-balance doctrine.

(Dexter)

7. The check-and-balance system can be used to correct the mistakes and errors of judgments of the specialists.

(Dexter)

8. To increase their capacity to check and balance, congressmen must regain their belief in their concept of Congress as an independent branch of government within a system of separate powers and having a definite function to perform vis-à-vis the other two branches, particularly the executive.

(Dexter)

9. Congress should recognize that part of its task of checking and balancing the executive is to thwart, hamper, interfere with, criticize and oppose its activities and thus hamper the making of mistakes, thwart the commission of errors, interfere with the imposition of one-sided or unfair decisions, and oppose the adoption of a wrong policy.

(Dexter)

10. Harassing the specialists ought to be a paramount task of Congress today. Check-and-balance operations must be performed by the standing committees since they are better equipped than any other legislative mechanism to perform the check-and-balance function. Congressmen should make themselves specialists on the kinds of mistakes the bureaucratic specialists make, the kinds of questions the bureaucrats ought to be asked, and the kinds of explanations the bureaucrats are likely to put forward in reply. In other words, they should acquire an *expertness* in challenging the specialists.
    (Dexter)

11. Since the congressman is dependent upon public support, every effort must be made to create a climate of opinion favorable to the operation of the check-and-balance principle in Congress.
    (Dexter)

12. Congress should hire its own specialists to counter the specialists of the executive, but it should make sure that they are indoctrinated in a congressional check-and-balance viewpoint. To this end, Congress should in hiring its own experts (a) develop a suitable program of indoctrination, (b) ensure that the specialists are exposed to adequate contact with the public and where possible have the same kind of contact that the congressmen themselves experience, (c) consider the use of personality tests to exclude specialists not sympathetic to the idea of Congress checking the executive, (d) develop regulations to prevent conflicts of interests arising and to insulate congressional experts from overexposure to their fellow experts employed in the executive.
    (Dexter) (See also VIII, 5)

13. The standing committees should be authorized to co-opt additional members, carefully selected so as to enhance effective check-and-balance operations. These persons would serve in effect as members of the committees, some on retainer and some serving as full-time members. Co-opted members could be drawn from the following categories: (1) ex-congressmen, (2) members of state legislatures, (3) journalists who have specialized in investigations, (4) certain types of professional specialists, e.g., fraud investigators, medical pathologists, (5) representatives of relevant special group interests which do not normally get a hearing in Congress—e.g., American Indians, representatives of the Maritime Provinces in Canada (on which

U.S. legislation has significant effects) to serve on committees such as Labor, Ways and Means, Interstate and Foreign Commerce, Merchant Marine and Fisheries. Procedures for employing co-opted persons should be left to the individual committees; some committees might not choose to co-opt additional persons. All co-opted members should be given positions of respect and esteem and permitted to select issues for investigation according to their particular interests and experience. Enforceable provisions would naturally have to be introduced to prohibit co-opted members from running for Congress themselves.

(Dexter)

14. Individual congressmen should deliberately plan their work in such a way as to enable them to check specialists and the administrators in the executive branch.

(Dexter)

15. Congress should consider the use of indoctrination courses on check-and-balance principles. Private foundations could provide a stipend for such courses especially designed to help the "congressman-elect" to think about the principles of check and balance and how to apply them to legislative issues.

(Dexter) (See also V, 26; VII, 18; VIII, 4)

16. Congress should make funds available for the use of members in soliciting countervailing arguments to representatives of the executive when necessary. Each member should keep a list of opinions of the people he has seen and heard from on a given topic; when it seems that the majority of these opinions espouse the executive viewpoint, he should then consider commissioning visits and briefs from specialists espousing the opposing view.

(Dexter) (See also VII, 19, 20; VIII, 3)

17. Supporters of check and balance should endorse the Roosevelt technique of leaving the jurisdictional lines of the various executive agencies unclear, thereby encouraging bureaucratic infighting and consequent clarification of issues. They should strongly resist the stress laid on harmony and consensus by Presidents like Eisenhower and Johnson.

(Dexter)

18. A Joint Commission on Check and Balance Principles should be established to serve as a central voice for ideas about how

Congress should more effectively carry out its work of checking and balancing, and to be a spokesman for congressmen in difficulties with the executive as a result of carrying out their tasks. From time to time the commission might undertake investigations and studies that do not fall appropriately within the sphere of any particular committee. It could also be assigned responsibility in those aspects of congressional management that bear on Congress' power to check and balance. In particular it might be made responsible for devising the general system for co-opting members for congressional committees, for establishing and supervising regulations on employment of ex-congressional employees in the executive departments, and for financing and locating experts for individual congressmen wishing to solicit a cogent brief on the case against a particular executive proposal. However, the commission should *not* be permitted to exercise general authority on other matters of congressional administration. The commission could be composed of co-opted members drawn from the general public and from the two houses of Congress (but where possible chairmen of important committees and subcommittees should be excluded). At least half of the noncongressional members should regard their commission assignments as taking one-third to two-thirds of their time, but all of them should have other work so as to prevent them from becoming too preoccupied with the work of the commission. Since the function of the commission is primarily innovative and creative and not concerned with the amendment of procedures, the professional experience of the staff it employs should *not* be in the sphere of congressional procedure, constitutional law, or the management of legislative bodies.

(Dexter)

The presidency

19. The President should serve for a term of six years and would not be eligible to succeed himself at any time.

    (A. de Grazia)

20. Limits ought to be set on the direct material benefits which the executive agencies are permitted to give any group of people in the period of six months prior to an election.

    (A. de Grazia)

21. Powers of the presidency attributable to past national emergencies should be reviewed and largely withdrawn.
(A. de Grazia)

22. Congress should present nonpartisan messages to the nation corresponding in time and scope to the President's State of the Union Message; Congress can employ special messages from time to time.
(A. de Grazia)

The courts

23. A Supreme Court of the Union, composed of members of the Supreme Court of the United States and of the several states, is needed to decide issues of constitutional law affecting the nature of the federal union.
(A. de Grazia)

24. The appellate jurisdiction of the Supreme Court requires review with regard to expediting the work of the Court on sheerly legal problems and in order to determine whether the Court can employ better types of social research in reconciling decisions with judicial objectivity.
(A. de Grazia)

25. The membership of the Supreme Court should be increased and divided into panels in order to increase its efficiency and discourage its participation in political ·affairs.
(A. de Grazia)

26. Congress should have the power to revise Supreme Court decisions that its statutes are unconstitutional, perhaps by re-enactment by two-thirds vote in two consecutive sessions of the legislature. Congress should also be permitted to review Supreme Court decisions invalidating state legislation under the constitution—i.e., by legislation incorporating reference to the state statute involved.
(Cotter)
(For other relevant recommendations see also II, 11; III, 11; V, 1, 2)

II. Top Leadership and Decision Making

1. Essential to the larger objective of the check-and-balance mechanism is the operation of Congress as a constructive or

positive instrument of national policy. In addition to checking the other two branches of government by merely amending or legitimating their decisions, Congress should also balance the executive and the judiciary by proposing original creative solutions of its own to both old and new public problems. An appraisal of the effectiveness of Congress is thus necessarily an appraisal of its effectiveness in contributing major decisions of government policy.
(Robinson)

2. Congress has to engage in long-range planning of the government by means of a better organized leadership working through a central office of both houses of Congress.
(A. de Grazia)

3. The internal process of lawmaking needs to be viewed and taught as the Process of Successive Majorities whereby every collective decision of Congress is passed through a multi-faceted representation of the nation.
(A. de Grazia)

4. In order to integrate the diverse work of the congressional committees, the party leadership of both houses of Congress should be centralized. One way of achieving this in the House would be to make it the responsibility of the leadership to determine the agenda (i.e., by removing all decisions concerning the agenda from the jurisdiction of the House Rules Committee). Another way of strengthening party leadership would be to provide it with more staff—if the majority leaders remain without adequate staff assistance, they will become increasingly dependent upon the White House Congressional Liaison Office.
(Robinson)

5. In order to minimize the risk to maintenance of legislative independence that increased centralization of party leadership entails, it is essential to maintain the present partial separation of congressional and presidential elections.
(Robinson)

6. The political organizations within Congress are not to be changed to strengthen party discipline in voting; their present state is satisfactory.
(A. de Grazia)

7. The American political party serves its country best in its traditional weak and decentralized form; the party should not be

construed as a military machine whose aim is the totalitarian government of its members and the eradication of opposition; it acts well as a catchall, a carryall, and a coverall.

(A. de Grazia)

8. For many years both Democratic and Republican campaign committees for both House and Senate have provided a variety of forms of assistance to members, ranging from raising campaign funds to helping them with their constituent problems; and in recent years the Democratic National Committee has launched an ambitious plan to assist freshman Democrats with the full support of the White House. Since this tends to increase the dependence of the freshman member upon the executive, the same plan could be advantageously, from the point of view of an independent Congress, taken over by the House leadership and the Democratic Congressional Campaign Committee. (Olson)

9. Congress as a whole may structure and restructure all agencies, down to their last unit, and can give and recapture all initiatives that it believes important to have.

(A. de Grazia)

10. The power to assess the organization and decision process of the executive branch is one of the few areas where Congress retains some of its former strength vis-à-vis the executive. Congress should take advantage of this special sphere of influence to make gradual improvements in the policymaking machinery throughout the government. This suggests an opportunity for Congress to be innovative and constructive instead of merely reactive and critical. In other words, it should raise its objectives from criticism of day-to-day decisions, on which it often has little information, and concentrate instead on finding organizational devices to encourage the executive to plan ahead in such a way as to represent the kind of values Congress favors. To help it perform this task, Congress could avail itself of a large body of extant research and the services of social scientists skilled in the necessary organization theory and techniques.

(Robinson)

11. All officials to whom has been delegated considerable legislative power are to be constituted into a Sub-Legislative Corps, certified by Congress as to their qualifications for such offices, and

required to acknowledge and act in terms of the legislative capacities of their office under Congress.

(A. de Grazia)

12. A Central Office of Congress, among its several functions, can command an array of talents to assist individual members of Congress in handling difficult cases of intervention with executive agencies.

(A. de Grazia)

13. Congress should recognize that arriving at creative decisions on public problems demands something more than knowledge just of the particular subject in hand. What is required is the combining of bits and pieces of information on many different subjects, or the relating of what is known about one aspect of a problem with what is known about the relevant aspects of other problems. Inventive problem solving requires integrative solutions.

(Robinson)

14. To achieve better integration of specialized knowledge on related subjects, Congress might create a National Security Committee, for instance, to combine consideration of foreign policy and defense policy which are at present handled by the Armed Services, Foreign Relations, and Foreign Affairs Committees. But if the proposed committee was to be formed as an *additional* committee, difficulties of attendance by already hard-pressed congressmen might be encountered. If, on the other hand, it was to be formed as a *substitute* committee, the total number of individual members in both houses acquainted with external affairs would be reduced, which in turn would be likely to undermine legislative-executive consensus and also the bipartisan character of congressional support for executive policies. Congress should understand that more integrative policies will probably mean less bipartisanship.

(Robinson)

15. Congress might create other joint committees similar to the National Security Committee proposed above.

(Robinson)

(For other relevant recommendations see IV, 2; V, 3, 5, 6, 13, 15; VII, 8-10)

III. Oversight of the Administration

General recommendations

1. The problem is one of perception of appropriate roles. Institutional changes will be worth the effort only insofar as they facilitate a change of attitude towards the oversight function. Congressmen should recognize that precisely because it is necessary in modern times to vest broad discretion in administrative officials, it is all the more necessary for them to envisage regularized and continuous oversight over the officials' activities if we are to avoid "uncontrolled and unaccountable power."
   (Cotter)

2. Greater use, indeed perhaps exclusive use, should be made of joint legislative committees, perhaps with the legislative committees performing the budget review process in addition to the authorization process for agencies within their purview.
   (Cotter)

3. The House and the Senate should establish oversight calendars, giving precedence at least two days in each month to committee reports pertaining to oversight of administration. Home rule for the District of Columbia would help to free legislative time for this purpose and for more effective and sustained oversight generally.
   (Cotter)

4. Congress could be assured of more effective oversight of emergency executive action, and the President assured more flexibility in response to emergency, if a generic statute applicable to all types of emergency were adopted. One provision of the statute could require that presidential proclamations of emergency and rules and regulations promulgated under such proclamations be subject to congressional veto by concurrent resolution.
   (Cotter)

5. Both House and Senate should experiment with a parliamentary procedure whereby a resolution would be offered for debate but without any legal consequence. Subjects of the debate would be national issues of importance as agreed by the leadership of the two parties. The debates would provide an opportunity for reviews of the administration of particular public policies (or appraisals of problems on which Congress contemplates eventual

legislation) by highlighting issues that the executive prefers not to raise. They could also furnish the executive with explicit guidelines as to the intent of Congress as a whole as opposed to the view merely of a single committee. This debate procedure is recommended in preference to instituting the British-type question period.
(Robinson)

6. Congress should revive Senator Kefauver's recommendation for a question period.
(Cotter)

7. The practice of permitting questions to be asked on occasion from the floor of either house and requiring their answer by agency chiefs then and there has little effect on the ultimate place of Congress in the government.
(A. de Grazia)

8. Legislation can be passed to require the canceling of an old activity whenever a new activity is begun, and to effectuate this policy, a periodical balancing of activities on a zero-sum basis can be performed.
(A. de Grazia)

9. A congressman or committee can justifiably intervene as advocate of a person being harmed by the executive branch in any way, or as advocate of a person receiving treatment that reveals corruption or abuse of administration. Penalties should be prescribed for officials wrongfully making allegations of conflict of interest against legislators.
(A. de Grazia)

10. Congress should consider establishing rules to ensure the just and legitimate conduct of its investigations, including the possible extension to legislative inquiries of the "due process" procedure that governs judicial inquiry.
(Robinson)
(For other relevant recommendations see II, 9-12; VII, 1-7)

Liaison as a means of enhancing oversight

11. Respect for the constitutional doctrine of the separation of powers does not entail Congress placing undue self-restraint upon the exercise of its traditional and legitimate prerogatives concerning the administration of the laws it has helped to pass and the oversight of the agencies it has helped to create.

Excessive self-restraint of this kind might work towards upsetting the balance of power and tip the scales irretrievably in favor of the executive arm.

(E. de Grazia)

12. From the point of view of Congress, liaison should be conceived as a network of two-way avenues through which the two branches of government can communicate with each other for the purpose of exerting a reciprocal influence upon their respective decision-making processes. Liaison should above all be regarded as a condition of *mutual* access with the objective of enhancing the legitimate functions of both branches.

(E. de Grazia)

13. Congressmen should adopt a more positive attitude towards the idea of liaison and develop more effective techniques of liaison both with the executive branch and with the public, thus simultaneously enhancing their capacity to oversee the administration and to represent their constituents.

(E. de Grazia)

14. Individual members, committees, and leaders together with their staffs should increase their direct contacts with officials of the various executive offices and departments. Liaison could thus become a principal means, rivaling committee inquiry, whereby Congress could gather information about and exert influence upon the executive's administration of the laws.

(E. de Grazia)

15. One way to increase congressional participation in administration would be greater cooperation with the President in the area of personal appointments in the executive; for this, reliable congressional liaison with the White House is required.

(E. de Grazia)

16. Increased direct liaison between Congress and the bureaucracy would help to repair the deficiency in political accountability frequently alleged to exist in the Army, Navy, and Air Force Departments where executive-defined and enforced security and secrecy regulations have weakened congressional oversight and control of the nation's military and defense programs. Consideration should therefore be given to the idea of establishing *within the Pentagon itself* congressional offices of executive liaison whose personnel have been cleared *by Congress* for access to classified data of the most sensitive categories. These persons could be attached to the staff of the government

operations committee; alternatively they could be attached to a new joint committee of Congress charged with handling matters affecting congressional relations with the other branches of government. The proposed congressional offices of executive liaison could convey informed opinions to Congress as to viable areas for changes in the military departments' critical operations; they should be armed with some investigative rights and probably linked to the offices of congressional liaison which each of the three Pentagon military departments presently maintains on Capitol Hill; eventually the congressional liaison offices could replace the departments' liaison offices.

(E. de Grazia)

17. The establishment of congressional offices of executive liaison, as proposed in relation to the military departments of the Pentagon, should be applied selectively throughout the executive branch.

(E. de Grazia)

18. Congressional Tribunes designated from a panel of qualified persons serving under Congress should be assigned to each agency of government and, each year, should assume the role of devil's advocate, proposing to the appropriate congressional committees that the agencies' activities, personnel, jurisdiction, and budget be eliminated, devolved to local governments or non-governmental groups, or otherwise reorganized.
(A. de Grazia)
(For other relevant recommendations see VII, 7; VIII, 6)

The service function (case work) as a means of enhancing oversight

19. Congress should recognize that its power to politicize seemingly routine administrative matters provides the major opportunities for members to relate the service function and casework to their supervisory and deliberative responsibilities. The knowledge gained by congressmen from the constant press of constituent requests can be used for remedial legislation and to initiate changes within the bureaucracy.
(Olson)

20. If properly developed, case and service work would provide Congress with important means and motives for oversight and with a mode for participation in the administration.
(E. de Grazia)

21. As far as oversight is concerned, much of the political value of casework is lost by the "shot gun" effect of having 535 members and several thousand staff employees serve as overseers. A modicum of systematization could, however, be introduced by following up Congressman Henry S. Reuss' proposal for establishing an Office of Administrative Counsel for Congress, consisting of perhaps 10-20 specialists to review cases of any person who believes his or her rights have been denied by the action or failure to act on the part of an officer or an employee of the United States. The office could be used to lift some of the burden of the more procedural aspects of case investigation from the individual congressman. Thus it could become an adjunct of a member's staff by helping to lighten the load in a far more expert way than would the addition of extra case-workers in the member's office. The office could also systematize the knowledge gained by individual congressmen from casework and report it to the congressional committees to assist them in their work of agency supervision and remedial legislation. The use of the office by members would be entirely voluntary, and it would be prohibited from handling cases at the direct behest of citizens; all contact with the constituent would be conducted by the member. As a consequence, the member could take all credit for success, while all blame for failure could be shifted to the administrative counsel.

   (Olson) (See also VI, 17-22; VIII, 6, 7)

Liaison as a means of increasing control of the regulatory commissions

22. Although congressional committee investigation can legitimately intervene in the processes of the regulatory agencies, effective oversight or participation by Congress requires more than occasional full-scale investigation. What is required are channels by which congressmen can constantly raise questions and get answers by the agency concerned. Congress' access to the executive, afforded by formal and informal channels of liaison, should be extended to the independent regulatory commissions.

   (E. de Grazia)

23. In view of the special concern that has gathered round the operations of the regulatory commissions, Congress should consider re-examining the basic question of the independence

of these bodies and their relationship to the President and to the legislative branch. It may be that some new institutional form of access by Congress to the processes of the commissions will have to be devised. In this connection, congressional experience with existing liaison offices in certain departments like the Department of State which have some quasi-judicial functions should be studied in greater detail.

(E. de Grazia)

24. Possibly all adjudicative operations of these commissions could be made over into a rule-making function and broadened up to oversight by Congress or control by the President and made accountable in some form to the public. If Congress were to assume a new responsibility towards the commissions, some type of consumer "Ombudsman" would probably be needed to provide properly representative institutional channels for public liaison.

(E. de Grazia)

IV. Fiscal Initiative and Control

General recommendations

1. The fiscal interventions of Congress are justifiable at several stages of financing and spending and in whatever depth of the executive hierarchy is needed to insure the achievement of congressional goals.

(A. de Grazia)

2. Increased fiscal control by Congress may well reopen the way to greater legislative initiative. The appropriations process is a critical area of legislation for long range *national* planning. This requires (a) projections of prospective tax inputs over a given future time span, (b) projections of existing and proposed agency activities over future time spans, (c) some means of achieving accord on the main areas of national needs and on the methods required to satisfy them. Improved input information, improved techniques of analysis, the development of internal congressional information collecting and analytic tools to reduce the number of policy options to a level manageable by parliamentary decision-making techniques would enable Congress in cooperation with the executive to prepare adequate-

ly conceived programs to be put into force at given times in the future.

(Dechert) (See also VII, Features of an Information System for Congress, d, iii)

3. The Bureau of the Budget should be made a joint agency of the President and Congress. Short of this, Congress should establish its own budget office, responsible to whatever officer of Congress, committee, or committees, appears most logical. (Cotter)

4. Steps should be taken (a) to computerize the budgetary and appropriations processes, and (b) to depart, on a selective basis, from the one-year, fiscal July 1-June 30, appropriation for programs which are not suited to this cycle. (Cotter)

5. Congress should require the executive to submit a two-year budget; this would enable it to take greater care in examining government estimates and appraising the relations between proposed expenditures and expected policy results. (Robinson)

6. Congress should assume greater control over the budget. (Robinson)

7. Steps should be taken to counteract the divisive tendencies on the House Appropriations Committee; at present none of its members serve on the legislative committees and the sub-committees are so highly specialized that each, out of concern for its own autonomy, zealously respects the independence of the others. (Robinson)

8. A major contribution to legislative information is supplied by the General Accounting Office, confirming by independent audit that all funds are disbursed in accordance with statute, making decisions that govern details of governmental financial practices, and required by Congress to undertake special investigations as requested. Congress should encourage and give the GAO increased funds to study the internal operations of federal agents within the broad terms of a "management audit" concerned with the overall adequacy and efficiency of operations in terms of the agency's statutory mission, and to develop measures of governmental effectiveness and quantitative tech-

niques for analyzing alternative patterns of organization and policy implementation. This would greatly enhance Congress' oversight capacities.
(Dechert)

9. Liaison between the GAO and individual members and committees should be improved.
(Dechert)

10. The personnel of the GAO might be organized into an independent or congressional civil service to accentuate their special congressional status.
(A. de Grazia) (See also III, 2)

Reform of budgeting

11. Under a system of *radical incrementalism,* the annual budgetary process as it is now known would be abandoned and be replaced by a continuous consideration of incremental changes to the existing base. Each agency would assume that the funds for its programs will be continued automatically and all appropriations would be continuous, except for a small number designed for a limited period. When an agency wishes to increase or decrease its funds for a program, or to eliminate an old program, or begin a new one, it will submit a request to Congress through the Bureau of the Budget. The President's budget would still go to Congress, but it would be used as a source of information and would not be the action document that it is now. Instead, the action on the President's requests would take place at the time he sends specific demands for specific items to the appropriations committees. For their part, the appropriations committees could call for testimony at any time on any budgetary matter, and change appropriations irrespective of the fiscal year. To ensure that Congress, in considering programs one at a time, would not lose track of the implications for the total rate of expenditure, a reporting service could be instituted to issue frequent statements on total approved expenditures.

To ensure that the more stable programs will not escape scrutiny over a period of several years, the agencies, the Bureau of the Budget, and the appropriations subcommittees of both houses could each agree to consider a few of these programs every year. Since each increment could be considered as it arises, attempts could be made to adapt the new policy, through successive approximation, to the major features of the environment as revealed by experience.

To facilitate strategic political knowledge of conflict between the different agencies' policies and preferences, a legal provision should be introduced requiring that the original request by the individual agencies be made public, together with a statement by the Bureau of the Budget of its reasons for making a change. Congress would still rely on the President's figures as a starting point and the agencies would continue to find it worth their while to seek the President's support for their requests. But the President could not maintain the fiction that the agencies uniformly endorse his budget, and Congress would be immediately alerted to the existence of any serious policy conflicts.
(Wildavsky)

V. Committee Organization and Internal Governance

1. The traditional committee functions do not exhaust the list of functions actually performed or possible. The Joint Committee on the Organization of the Congress ought to bring into the open, through an appropriate statement, those latent functions of committees that tend to strengthen Congress as a counterveiling power to that of the President and the bureaucracy—e.g., the congressional "veto" and the conflict-resolving function.
(Eulau)

2. Proposals designed to relieve committees of control over legislation should be carefully scrutinized from the point of view of whether they may not jeopardize an important function which is essential in a modern system of checks and balances.
(Eulau)

3. Congress should allocate funds for a continuing self-survey of its structures and functions to be conducted by a team of disinterested analysts, for the purpose of permitting Congress to reorganize and strengthen itself from session to session rather than from decade to decade. This would serve to alert Congress to the consistency or inconsistency—from the perspective of a strong legislature—of those piecemeal, incremental changes in structure and functions that inevitably occur.
(Eulau)

4. Caution should be exercised in creating or abolishing committees on the basis of some abstract principle. The number of committees and their names do not relate to any universal rule; an important activity, recognized as such, can even today find a committee home or achieve a new committee without much delay.

(A. de Grazia)

5. Not too much effort should be expended in attempts to clarify and sharply delineate committee jurisdictions, since this impedes just those conflict-resolving, bargaining processes which an elected legislative body is especially capable of performing. Moreover, most modern legislation is usually so complex that it cannot easily and unambiguously be assigned to one or another committee or subcommittee.
(Eulau)

6. The committee structure must remain sufficiently flexible to maximize political bargaining for which committees are the governmental instruments par excellence.
(Eulau)

7. Congress should experiment with a new type of committee—a kind of inter-committee committee—composed of members of those committees or subcommittees which claim jurisdiction over a piece of legislation. Its members would not be delegates from their standing committees and would not be required to report back to the committees from which they are recruited. On the other hand, the proposed inter-committee committee would have the power to bring bills to the floor according to whatever procedures are followed by the regular standing committees.
(Eulau)

8. There should be a biennial review of committee structures, functions, jurisdictions, workloads, etc., by the Joint Committee on the Organization of the Congress constituted as a permanent body, for the purpose of keeping the committee structure as flexible as possible and adjusting it, as nearly as possible, to the political contingencies of Congress. The review should be based on the continuing survey of Congress recommended above.
(Eulau)

9. The total committee process, including the special cases of committees of investigation, should be reviewed, not to limit com-

mittee activities but to derive principles of procedure more in accord with scientific research and the rules of legal discovery.
(A. de Grazia)

10. In the case of controversial legislation, each committee should be required to issue a report, accepted by the protagonists of both sides of an issue (and not necessarily party sides), which would inform the houses of the compromises that had been made and of the reasons for those compromises.
(Eulau)

11. A more formal designation of general representatives on all committees to prevent excessive special interest representation on the committee rosters is desirable.
(A. de Grazia)

12. In order to ensure that the wishes of the electorate will have an effect on congressional actions and decisions, members of sensitive committees such as the appropriations or ways and means committees ought to come from districts where sanctions can be effectively imposed. However, the burden of their responsibility should be equitably distributed among the variety of interests that constitute the congressional "quilt."
(Eulau)

13. The subcommittee structures should be so strengthened that each subcommittee can speak with authority in its own domain of expertise, in order that the function of bringing about coherence in programs, insofar as it is desirable, can be performed through the informal channels of deference and reciprocity rather than through central direction from the top of the congressional hierarchy.
(Eulau)

14. Congress should abolish the chairmanships as now constituted with their familiar rights and privileges. Instead, the housekeeping functions and the administrative work of the committees and subcommittees should be handled by a "presiding officer" assisted by a competent head of staff. This would allow the substantive work of the committee, especially the work on major legislation, to fall into the hands of those members who are capable of getting it done and so permit the committee to evolve a "natural" leadership team.
(Eulau)

15. Increased staff assistance does not automatically strengthen Congress vis-à-vis the executive agencies, nor does it automat-

ically lighten the workload of congressmen. However, some of the difficulties of workload would be overcome if congressmen were to do many of the things that are now assigned to the staff and if the staff were to do things now done by congressmen. That is, the staff should take on much of the routine work that now absorbs a good deal of the members' and chairmen's time—e.g., scheduling, investigation, hearings, markup, and even much of the liaison work with and oversight of the executive agencies. Thus the really creative aspects of committee work, now often delegated to the staff, would revert to where they properly belong, to the committee members. This kind of teamwork would enable the committee members to develop that broader perspective on problems, issues, and policies that a vigorous and innovative legislative body requires.

(Eulau)

16. Planning of committee staff work should be periodically accomplished, at which time proposals for action and research may be submitted by members, discussed and designated to receive aid.

(A. de Grazia)

17. Committees should be encouraged to produce policy and program statements on subjects within their jurisdiction, and to elevate these messages to the level of public reporting which has been achieved by many White House conferences, task force reports by executive and foundation groups, and agency studies.

(A. de Grazia)

18. Where minority-party staffing on committees is inadequate and the principle of check and balance is therefore threatened, provisions for giving over at least one-third of staff and facilities to the minority party as the convenient vehicle of honest opposition should be made.

(A. de Grazia)

19. The minority party represented in committees should be provided with a staff almost equal to that of the majority. Thus if the majority party becomes increasingly aligned with the executive branch, the minority party will be in a position to check the majority and in so doing provide the necessary legislative counterbalance to executive power.

(Robinson)

20. Committees should maintain a neutral and nonpartisan staff, equally available to majority and minority party members. (Eulau)

21. Proposals to make legislative committee meetings and hearings resemble fact-finding procedures (as in investigative or oversight situations) are ill-conceived. They ignore the fact that Congress is above all a political body whose vitality and maintenance as an independent branch of the government depends on the successful conduct of its political functions. Although the procedures could be improved in certain respects, hearings are the most effective devices for committees to inform themselves in a political context. (Eulau)

22. To offset or neutralize the forces of opposition to the passing of bills, discharge procedures should be eased and certain of the restrictive procedural rules now governing both House and Senate relaxed. In the House two helpful measures would be the complete removal of the Rules Committee from agenda-setting decisions and a reduction in the number of signatures required on petitions to discharge bills from committees. In the Senate, where there has already been some relaxation in the size of the majority required to vote cloture, further restrictions on the possibilities of filibustering could be introduced; a partial reform would be to relax discharge and cloture restrictions during the last six months of the calendar year, which would overcome the end-of-session advantage that normally accrues to the opposition in any legislative struggle. (Robinson)

23. Germaneness is not to be sought in Senate debate to the preclusion of the filibuster which, whether its verbiage is relevant or not, is the source of much of the power of Congress with respect to the President. (A. de Grazia)

24. The rules committees of both houses should undertake an examination of their respective rules of procedure in order to eliminate anomolies and "irrational procedures," particularly in rules governing amendments. (Robinson)

25. Due to possible unfortunate consequences of electrical voting— e.g., the possibility of having a duplicate voting board in the White House, uncertainty as to how the procedure would affect

leadership control over the houses, etc.—before considering introducing such a system, Congress should take a survey of the experience of those state legislatures where it is already in use and should perhaps contemplate experimenting with electrical voting for the duration of, say, one session.

(Robinson) (See also VII, Features of an Information System for Congress, b , iii)

26. First-term congressmen should be tendered greater orientation, apprenticing, and responsibilities in the operations of Congress. (A. de Grazia) (See also I, 15; VII, 18; VIII, 4)

27. From the point of view of the effectiveness of the service function, it is desirable to retain certain practices that have recently come under much criticism—namely, the practice of individual congressmen introducing private bills, the practice of patronage appointments, and the custom followed by certain executive departments of giving majority party members advance notice of contract awards in their states and districts.

(Olson)

(For further relevant recommendations see I, 10, 13; II, 4, 14, 15; III, 2, 5, 6, 7, 10; IV, 6; VI, 7-11; VIII, 5)

VI. Constituency Base and Relations With the Public

1. The poor image from which Congress suffers is the product of many causes other than its alleged "passivity" and "provincialism," most of the said causes being the by-products of the forces universally operating against the legislative way of life. The sense of inferiority that many congressmen have acquired in the face of the problems of contemporary society is quite unfounded in fact; but the performance of Congress suffers throughout in consequence. All recommendations should tend to reform this self-image.

(A. de Grazia)

2. Via a Central Office of Congress, congressional activities should be reported non-controversially to the press and public in popular language. Television and radio should be more extensively and imaginatively employed on the behalf of the Congress as an institutional whole.

(A. de Grazia)

3. Halls of Congress should set up in a central city of every state to explain the history and activities of Congress in tangible and graphic terms.
(A. de Grazia)

4. A National Civic Service should be formed to preserve and enlarge the independent public, which is essential to the survival of Congress; the same service could help enlarge and recruit members for the active constituencies that congressmen need.
(A. de Grazia)

5. A Joint Committee of Congress should be established to abstract and summarize by the internal use of survey research instruments the congressional viewpoint on the principal problems facing the United States as found in the flow of members' legislative recommendations. Besides serving a necessary coordinative function, the committee would also help to generate public interest and focus public attention on a manageable set of national issues defined as an alternative to the presidential perspective.
(Dechert)

6. A constitutional amendment is advisable to permit the states to experiment with theories of apportionment going beyond the sheer idea of equal-population districts, and to experiment also with other elements of providing representation for the future society.
(A. de Grazia)

7. As society produces new complexities in the congressional environment, it is necessary to ensure continuing representation of all interests through the standing committee system. A modest increase in the number of standing committees might therefore be contemplated; two immediate possibilities are committees on urban affairs and housing, and on education.
(Davidson)

8. Every effort should be taken to ensure that the various substantive committees do not become cabals of those most intimately affected by and concerned with the subject matter involved. As broad a representation as possible should be maintained on all committees; it is relevant, for example, to retain Brooklyn congressmen on the agricultural committees.
(Davidson)

9. *Ad hoc* congressional task forces should be created to study and interpret topics handled only tangentially by the standing com-

mittees. These task forces could either be given detailed *ad hoc* mandates or else they could be put on a study basis to deal with recurrent problems. They should range widely in their subject matter access, be empowered to commission research, hold seminars, and make field trips as appropriate.
(Davidson)

10. To enable congressmen to participate in the congressional task forces suggested above and to pay more attention to the representative aspect of their duties, some limitation on the number of standing committee assignments given each member might be a feasible prerequisite, together with the practice of granting leave from committee work without loss of seniority privileges.
(Davidson)

11. To assist legislators in their representative tasks, the congressional schedule should be formalized to provide for planned periodic recesses. This measure could be taken through an informal agreement between the party leaders at the beginning of each session. It would enable congressmen to spend substantial amounts of time in their home political base and to participate in the work of the congressional task forces proposed above.
(Davidson)

12. Bipartisan teams of legislators could undertake lecture tours to various communities throughout the country.
(Davidson)

13. Funds should be made available to permit legislators to convene public advisory groups in their states and districts to meet at frequent intervals to discuss mutual problems and interests.
(Davidson)

14. The practice of individual congressmen scheduling constituent meetings on specified topics should be encouraged and extended.
(Davidson)

15. Congress should direct the Bureau of the Census to make periodic reports on demographic trends on request.
(Davidson)

16. Congressmen wishing to employ survey research techniques upon issues in their constituencies should be enabled to draw upon competent professional advice.
(Davidson) (See also VII, 29)

17. In developing its channels of liaison with the bureaucracy, Congress should also concentrate on applying its new information and increased influence in the executive to serving the needs of

the constituents, to offset the impression that the congressman can no longer satisfactorily represent the people's interests which has been gained as a result of increased bureaucratic contact with the public.

(E. de Grazia)

18. Congress should not seek to counteract executive-public liaison by relying on the agency anti-lobbying law. Instead, by opening up its own liaison channels with the public similar to those already successfully developed by the executive departments, it should seek out ways of offering inducements to encourage constituents to refer their problems with the bureaucracy to their elected representatives.

(E. de Grazia)

19. Since casework is often too selective and is subject to the criticism that it involves special pleading, priority consideration should be given to the possibility of institutionalizing the service function and elevating it to the level of a formal comprehensive duty of the congressman.

(E. de Grazia)

20. Congress should forbid any agency or department from denying any request for a service, benefit, grant, award, loan contract, etc., without notifying the applicant's congressman in advance.

(E. de Grazia)

21. A congressional corps with loyalties and duties akin to those of the "Ombudsman" in Scandinavia should be established to investigate citizens' complaints against bureaucratic abuse.

(E. de Grazia)

22. Congressmen should authorize members to enlarge the number of staff available for case work, providing them with special funds for the retention of absolute contact, including legal assistance; thus making it plain to constituents that their elected representatives are in a position to provide them with more (free) services and to present cases effectively to the bureaucracy.

(E. de Grazia)

(For further recommendations affecting casework see also III, 19-21)

23. To increase representative effectiveness, unlimited travel allowance for travel to and from the member's state or district should be authorized.

(Davidson)

24. Congressmen should be reimbursed for up to 12 round trips to their districts annually plus 12 round trips for staff members whom they authorize to travel on official business.
    (Olson)

25. Since foreign travel is vital for every member, Congress should try to rectify public misunderstandings and misconceptions about "junketeering." One method would be to prohibit all official trips from "lame ducks" or retiring members; another would be to bring certain counterpart funds under the strict control of Congress with stricter reporting and accounting requirements.
    (Olson) (See also VII, 23)
    (For other relevant recommendations see I, 11; II, 8; III, 5, 10, 13, 21; V, 11, 12, 17, 27; VII, 12, 14, 15-18, 25; VIII, 6, 7)

VII. Increasing the Flow of Information to Congress

Access to information in the executive

1. Congress should improve the quality, standardize the format, and precisely define the information required from the executive agencies. Committee expectations from the executive should be clearly stated and arrangements made for routinizing transmission of requested material. Hence there would be a need to provide a facility to abstract and disseminate information of common congressional concern originating in the executive.
   (Dechert)

2. Congress must insure itself access to the operations and materials of the executive agencies, employing, however, some responsible internal machinery to screen its activities against abuse.
   (A. de Grazia)

3. Appropriate committees, e.g., the armed services committees, and the foreign affairs committees, should try to assure access to documentation systems in the executive branch, particularly the CIA's WALNUT system which provides a print-out of existing intelligence documentation on specific cases and issues.
   (Dechert)

4. To circumvent the lengthy "clearance" procedures normally required for congressional document procurement, Congress should obtain assent by heads of agencies for direct access to

files by an appropriate committee staff "historical" researcher inside the department or agency, as provided for in the 1959 Amendment to Executive Order 10501.
(Dechert)

5. Stern laws against secrecy are in order where secrecy cannot clearly be demonstrated to be vital to national security, as that term is defined by Congress.
(A. de Grazia)

6. To impose appropriate sanctions upon unwarranted refusal of information by the executive, Congress should establish institutionalized and automatic procedures for linking denial of information to future appropriations. The procedure envisaged involves establishment of a commission of notables to adjudicate cases of denial reported by Congress and to impose automatic sanctions. The function of the commission, which might be composed of nominees of the three branches of government plus independent members, would confirm legitimacy of the congressional request, authorize the use of congressional power of subpoena, and set a deadline for the handing over of the information requested. Failure on the part of the agency concerned to produce the material requested by that date would result in its being automatically notified that the relevant item or items of its program would not be authorized the following year and that it should terminate that part of its activity within the current appropriation.
(Dechert)

7. To assure that the fact of security clearance granted by executive agencies for congressional access to classified information may not be used at some future date to exclude congressmen from sensitive committees on purely political grounds, a Congressional Security Office should be established to engage in joint clearance procedures with executive investigative agencies; the office should have rights of access to executive files on all members of Congress and staff and it could also perform a classified document control function on the Hill.
(Dechert) (See also III, 16, 17)

Developing independent sources of information

8. Effective and independent decision making requires autonomous sources of information and analysis; Congress today is too de-

pendent on executive sources and on the President for the definition of problems and the development of decisional attitudes.
(Dechert)

9. Congress should organize itself in ways that anticipate the future and prepare for problems lying beyond the horizon.
(Robinson)

10. Congress needs to define problems, predetermine the range of consensus, provide alternatives to the executive program.
(Dechert)

11. A Congressional Institute should be established to conduct a RAND-type of study activity on a Congress-wide or committee basis for the development and application of sophisticated analytic techniques to the performance of congressional functions.
(Dechert)

12. A National University should be chartered under congressional auspices. This would provide members and committees of Congress with easy informal access to professional scholars in all disciplines. The university need maintain only a small staff on tenure appointment and could rely heavily on visiting professors and research associates on special leave from their own universities (as is the current practice in the Armed Forces Staff Colleges). The university could also be tied in with public and private universities in the District of Columbia, and with independent non-profit research groups.
(Dechert)

13. A Social and Behavioral Sciences Institute should be set up with grants from Congress to foster the development of pure and applied social science with respect to topics unconnected to immediate legislative needs.
(A. de Grazia)

14. A Sanctions Institute should study and recommend legislation and administrative practice in connection with the host of penalties that Congress and the agencies are constantly employing, often without scientific knowledge, to exact conformity to public policy.
(A. de Grazia)

15. An Inventory of Freedom and Restrictions can be built up and continuously maintained to keep accounts on how individual liberties of Americans are subtracted from or added to by governmental and non-governmental actions.
(A. de Grazia)

16. Congress should make greater use of external commissions to provide information inputs relevant to legislative and oversight functions. These commissions could conduct research and make legislative recommendations and could also serve a political function by providing a representation of the major interest groups in the problem area concerned. Thus in the very process of gathering data they could provide a forum for achieving a prior compromise between the varying demands made on the political system.

    (Dechert)

17. Congress should establish public commissions similar to those appointed by the President. The commissions could investigate and recommend on civil rights, health, etc., and would report either to particular committees or directly to the Speaker or the Vice President.

    (Robinson)

18. Academies of Congress should be established in association with universities throughout the country to prepare students for work in connection with legislatures and to do research on legislative problems. Freshmen congressmen should enter such academies for special courses directly upon election and before taking office.

    (A. de Grazia) (See also I, 15; V, 26; VIII, 4)

19. Congress should increase funds allotted to members and committees to commission external research on a consultative and contractual basis under the control of a special joint committee of Congress.

    (Dechert)

20. Congress should establish a consultants' fund to enable any member to call upon the expertise of non-governmental bodies at rates commensurate with private consultation fees in the same way as the executive departments do.

    (Robinson) (See also I, 6; VIII, 3)

21. Since members complain that the books they require are never available in the Library of Congress, a Capitol Bookstore should be instituted. Members should be afforded special allowances to enable them to buy books and periodicals.

    (Dechert)

22. Each congressman should be provided with an annual budget allowance say of $1,000 for the purchase of books, reports, and other published materials.

   (Robinson)

23. Congressmen should be encouraged to undertake foreign travel. Instead of relying as now on the legislative liaison office of the State Department to arrange these trips and on the use of the Defense Department's Air Force planes, Congress should set up its own travel office to make its own independent arrangements. Congressmen's foreign travel could be financed out of the United States excessive stock of local currencies that is at present lying idle, and the trips could be made at reduced rates on the commercial airlines (which are government subsidized).

   (Robinson)

24. Increase allowances for travel.

   (Dechert) (See also VI, 23-25)

25. Increase allowance for telecommunications to facilitate contact with knowledgeable persons in the member's home state.

   (Dechert)

26. Congress should allocate a larger budget and increased space facilities to both senators and representatives so as to enable them to augment their personal staff. However, the qualifications of these additional assistants should complement the members' own strengths and weaknesses not duplicate them. That is, since Congress as a whole does not generally possess technical and scientific expertise, the personal and the committee staff should be able to furnish this knowledge.

   (Robinson) (See also IV, 7; V, 21; VI, 5; VIII, 7)

Reform of the Legislative Reference Service and the Library of Congress

27. The LRS should be politicized by creating a separate division for the Democratic and Republican parties. Each party should be entitled to employ an appropriate number of qualified LRS researchers for its own exclusive use; both groups of researchers would be authorized and elected to prepare materials on issues that they themselves anticipate will arise, without waiting for

a formal request from any member of Congress. And both groups should frankly assist the parties in their partisan arguments.
(Robinson)

28. The Service's scientific personnel should be appreciably increased. To this end the Library could award a number of non-renewable fellowships of approximately three years' duration to scientists and equip them with suitable laboratory and other research facilities. The services of the fellows would be available to members of the House and Senate on the same basis as those of advisers and researchers in other divisions of the LRS.
(Robinson)

29. To assist congressmen in the work of polling their constituents' views on current issues, the LRS should be authorized to make available the services of two or three public opinion analysts or technical specialists in the use of survey methods and the interpretation of answers to survey questionnaires.
(Robinson)

30. The LRS should prepare abstracts of executive agency reports and other government publications in order to reduce volume of information and to permit members to exercise a greater selectivity in their choice of reading matter on subjects they wish to probe in depth.
(Dechert—proposal originally made by Representative Todd before the Joint Committee on the Organization of the Congress, May 24, 1965)

31. The LRS should be expanded so as to enable it to perform valuable in-depth studies tailored to the needs of individual congressmen.
(Dechert)

32. A panel of expert consultants on a full range of legislative subject matter could be established by the LRS, and congressmen could be authorized to call upon them for their services.
(A. de Grazia)

33. The Library of Congress should be given an increased budget to permit purchase by standing order of all books and significant periodicals published annually in the world, plus a corresponding expansion of staff and physical facilities.
(Dechert)

34. The Library should be made a center for research and development in the area of automated information, indexing, storage, and retrieval; that is, a center for research and development of policy documentation systems.
(Dechert)

Introducing automated systems of information processing

(An abstract of the proposal put forward by Kenneth Janda)

Definition of the Congress' information problem

Congress' problem is primarily one of obtaining *relevant* information; it requires a procedure for acquiring the information it needs and a method for processing that information in order to learn what it needs to know. This conception of the problem suggests that far more is necessary than just increasing the information flow to Congress. It suggests the need for information processing systems that are integrated with congressional tasks, functions, and activities. Each congressman and each committee should be served by a remote input-output terminal connected on a time-sharing basis to some central computing facility.

Features of an information system for congress

a. For Congress as a whole

Certain kinds of information can best be processed centrally for the use of both houses. Individual congressmen could tap into this centralized service which could perform the following functions:

(i) Keep congressmen informed of relevant bills by the use of an information retrieval technique called "selective dissemination of information" (SDI);

(ii) Disseminate information about lobbyists;

(iii) Communicate with the LRS to provide answers to specialized inquiries;

(iv) Search the U.S. Code (which is already on magnetic tape) for laws affecting any given subject requested by retrieving all laws under that subject and by locating laws dealing with one subject but entered under different headings.

b. For each chamber of Congress

Information on certain scheduling and housekeeping activities of

Congress would be best handled on the basis of each chamber. Processing systems could be used to:

(i) Locate bills in the legislative process, showing in each case the history of action including amendments, committee vote, floor vote, and scheduling for future action;

(ii) Provide information about the subject of the vote at the time the vote is announced, e.g., bill number, sponsorship, legislative history;

(iii) Provide for automated voting.

c. For individual congressmen

Any information system for Congress should be adjustable to suit the particular needs of individual congressmen who could use the system, as desired, to help them to:

(i) Decide how to vote by storing and retrieving data on their own voting record and statements on legislative issues, as well as data on the attitudes of various groups in their constituencies, etc.;

(ii) Maintain relations with their constituencies by storing constituents' names and addresses plus other relevant data for automatic preparation of specialized mailing, and by analyzing polling data and election returns, etc.;

(iii) Read and analyze written material by scanning documents for passages of interest and/or by making careful content analyses, sentence by sentence, as required.

d. For congressional committees

Since most of Congress' legislative work is conducted through the standing committees, these should serve as a basis for organizing congressional information systems. The specific shape of the system will depend in each case upon the particular committee's jurisdiction and workload, but in general the information systems developed for the different committees could be used to:

(i) Compile histories of committee action;

(ii) Process data on subjects under committee jurisdiction;

(iii) Improve control over the administration. E.g., by application of information processing techniques to make exhaustive and comprehensive analyses of past and projected budgetary expenditures for each agency, thus enabling the committees to pinpoint and subject to closer scrutiny sources of increase (and decreases, if any) and patterns of supplementary appropriations.

VIII. Staffing and Office Management

1. In view of limitations on money and space facilities to accommodate extra staff, consideration should be given to proposals to improve the effectiveness of office management and congressional personnel.

   (Olson)

2. Congress should establish an Office of Management Adviser to serve those members who wish to seek its advice on how to organize their office work more effectively and efficiently. The office could furnish professional consultants to provide, on request, guidance on setting up an office budget and records system, files for case materials, office layout, work systems, etc.

   (Olson)

3. To improve the quality of personal staff assistance, an Office of Personnel could be set up under the management of Congress to provide members of both houses with highly qualified personnel—professional, caseworker, secretarial—on a full-time or short-term basis as required; it could also maintain a roster of expert consultants available to members. The office would be available to any member who wished to use it, but no member would be compelled to do so. An additional use of the office could be for members to employ its service to help them select the most qualified applicants for patronage appointments.

   (Olson)

4. Regular programs of orientation sessions should be organized for members and their staffs, at which federal agency liaison representatives and congressional committee staff directors would discuss agency organization case procedures, and legislative problems. The series should be sponsored by the leadership of both houses and directed at freshman members and their staffs.

   (Olson) (See also I, 15; V, 26; VII, 18)

5. Qualifying tests to insure compatibility with congressional principles and suitable technical skills should be required of committee staff, but the direct responsibility of staff members to committee chairmen should not be disrupted.

   (A. de Grazia) (See also I, 12)

   (For other recommendations concerning the caliber and qualifications of staffing see also I, 12, 18; IV, 9; VII, 26)

6. The size of congressional staffs should be increased to provide necessary casework, legislative liaison, and committee agents for each congressman.

(A. de Grazia)

7. Certain staff problems cannot be solved without the addition of new personnel. In the Senate, provision should be made for at least one additional part-time committee staff assistant for each senator, responsible to him instead of to the committee. He could help on constituency problems falling within the committee's general area of jurisdiction, and his presence would release more of the senator's administrative assistant's time for constituency problems and supervising caseworkers. In the House, Congress should authorize each representative to hire an administrative assistant with salary, status, and responsibilities similar to his counterpart in the senator's office.

(Olson)

(For other recommendations concerning the increase of staffs see I, 12—more experts; II, 14—more staff for the Majority Leader; V, 17-20—on minority staffing; V, 22—more staff for casework; VII, 26—more staff with scientific expertise; and 27-29—more staff for the LRS)

CONGRESS, 1989*

Alfred de Grazia

When Congress convened in 1989, it was with all the pomp and circumstance of a 200-year old institution celebrating its anniversary in the full flush of its power and glory. The occasion had been long planned by a large Commission for the Bicentennial, composed of representatives of every element of the American community. The Commission symbolized in its completeness the quality of representation given the country by the most powerful legislature that the world had ever known.

A glance at the composition of the commission for the Bicentennial will give an idea of the scope of the celebrations Congress had in mind for the occasion. The Speaker and other members of the Plenary Council—that is, the major officers of the two chambers—were included. The President and Vice President were honorary co-chairmen of the commission, whose chairman was the Speaker of the House of Representatives. The 12 members of Congress of longest tenure were on the commission, including one congressman who at the age of 80 had enjoyed 56 years of service in both chambers. Also members were six representatives of the Sub-Legislative Corps (the special group of high government officials who possess rule-making powers in the republic); six delegates of the Center for Advisory Representative Councils; six governors, six

---

county leaders and mayors, six citizens delegated from the Civic Corps, six citizens chosen by lot from the 250 million Americans then living, and the Supreme Court Justice who headed the Administrative Law Panel of the Court and was a member of the Supreme Court of the Union (the special body that had in 1980 been created to cope with juridical issues of federalism and non-territorial associations of the largest size). Two members of the President's cabinet were also on the commission; but as heads of departments and therefore Sub-Legislative Corps officers, they were seated with their departmental associates.

It was this commission supplemented by three times their number of additional officials, judges, and citizens, and accompanied by representatives of the 130 nations of the world, who led the procession entering the Capitol to mark the opening of the Session of Congress. The Speaker delivered the opening address of the session. It had been advertised ahead of time that his speech would represent a collective address of the Congress. The task of composing the speech had been accomplished by the collaboration of the members of the Plenary Council of the Congress, the body which was formed in 1971 to represent Congress in its organic unity before the nation and the world on important issues and occasions.

The speech is worth repeating here in its entirety since it consisted in large part of a history of the major changes in congressional government which had taken place in the preceding 20 years.

CONGRESS, 1989

An Address by the Speaker of the House of Representatives to
the First Session of the One Hundred and First Congress on
the 200th Anniversary of the Meeting of the First Congress

No more than a generation ago doubts were being expressed in many quarters as to whether Congress would survive as the primary American governmental institution. Strong inroads into its functions in society had been made by new ways of conducting the government and by the deterioration of some of its traditional roles. Through the fault of no one, neither the courts nor the executive branch nor the presidency nor, for that matter, the public at large, many tendencies had gone on unnoticed which had eroded the basis for government by legislature. The crisis was all the more acute because the American Congress had long stood as the most popular and powerful legislature in the world. If its powers had been substantially weakened, within a short time thereafter the lights would have gone out on the legislative way of life throughout the world.

Happily such did not prove to be the case. On the contrary, the American system of government by legislature has been greatly strengthened during the past 20 years; and even in the Soviet Union and China, whose representatives sit here today, there has developed a quickening of interest in the possibilities of improving modern government by developing the conditions for legislative rule.

On the occasion of this anniversary of 200 years of congressional government, therefore, we shall highlight today a few of the critical events that within the lifetime of the last generation have brought about a strengthened model of congressional government in America.

It will be recalled, especially by those men of many years of seniority in the Congress who sit next to me, that the Congress of the 1960s faced a triple problem. There had been a sharp decline in the public estimation of the legislature and a gradual withering away of the roots of the legislative life in the everyday comportment of our citizens. The presidency had assumed a highly active role in lawmaking and rule making. In particular, it had come to regard military and foreign affairs, as well as the major domestic issues of the time, as virtually its exclusive preserve. Furthermore, the executive branch of government had waxed so large, and so dutiful, and competent, as to render the American system of government excessively centralized and bureaucratic.

The task facing Congress in those days thus became increasingly clear. It had to set aside a preoccupation with trivialities and short-range reforms, and concentrate upon developing new institutions to refurbish the original system of government that had been the fruit of the genius of the eighteenth century. How this task was accomplished constitutes an inspiring chapter in American history. The importance of that chapter is second to none, and is already part of the education and discipline of every youngster in the country. If I recite it here, it is out of a sense of pride and not because our citizens are ignorant of it.

We can recall firstly that this vast change in the organization and character of congressional government took place at a time when the country was undergoing a number of crises. Indeed, the struggle for changes in Congress was itself a recurring crisis during those difficult days of the past two decades. The country has developed in many ways at a disturbing rate throughout this 20-year period. In one generation its population has grown by over 50 million persons, adding one-quarter to the total in the 1960s. All but a few millions of our citizenry have come to live in metropolitan areas. But because the agricultural revolution has proceeded apace, we have not suffered for lack of food. Our water supply, though no better and in some instances worse than it was a generation ago, has had to be put under tight controls, and as a consequence serious pollution and shortages have been avoided. The nation has been covered by an ever denser network of highways in response to the desire of the people to get to places fast; but the roads are still choked with traffic and we have had to give constant attention to legislation for improved methods of transportation. The federal government, it must be confessed, has not yet been able to organize and plan sufficiently well to devolve this task upon local units. Nor have means been found to relate the needs and goals of the large transportation interests to the needs and goals of government. Here is a place for some ingenious planning on the part of representative government. The development of new means of communication by computers, by satellites, and by other means, has created many problems concerning the invasion of privacy; on the other hand, it has permitted many new forms of individual enjoyment of the facilities of our age.

Today practically everyone in America who is mentally and psychologically qualified by the minimum standards set by the decentralized educational authorities has a college education. We no longer have even the relatively small number of poor people that we had a generation ago. Yet in all honesty we are compelled to say that the people today are not a uniformly happy people. We have not solved the problems of mental health, which means that in general there are altogether far too many unhappy and anxious individuals in America. A solution to this problem, however, is in sight; partly, we believe, as a result of the same revolution in philosophy that has underpinned the reform and reorganization of Congress. That is, we have been learning more and more about the need to provide a sense of autonomy to small groups and to individual persons in their communities, so as to give them a sense of identity with and control of their environment. We have had almost unbelievable obstacles to overcome in this drive, but some success seems near at hand.

The problems of race relations are perhaps as troublesome now as they were a generation ago. The scientific experts of that generation predicted as much. At the time of the well-known Los Angeles rioting of 1965, it was acknowledged that as Negroes achieved important advances in politics, economics, and social affairs, they would not immediately respond by becoming happy and content. Like everyone else, they would wonder why they had not been permitted these benefits before; and then once the benefits were within their grasp, they would naturally be all the more impatient to achieve others and all the more critical of whatever obstacles were put in their way. So that, although there is practically the same proportion of Negroes as whites with a college education in America today, and the average annual earnings of Negro families are only 7 percent less than those of whites, there is nonetheless continual race friction; nor can we expect otherwise. However, it is already apparent that the emphasis of Negro demands has now shifted to a greater concern for the means by which legislation is enacted for their benefit. As a result, prospective legislation on welfare and civil liberties can be more easily controlled and adjusted within the framework of the philosophy that underlies the new structure of Congress and which stresses the value of community autonomy, individual initiative, and a common set of rules applicable to both Negroes and whites.

Business today continues to be on a large scale, and constant attention has to be given by the Congress to its overall policies. The monopoly threat which was felt very much a century ago is no longer viewed by economic experts as a serious danger. Partly this is owing to the fact that numerous big business corporations themselves have set up special organs to assess the social consequences of their actions. And partly it is due to the formal and informal liaison that has been established between congressmen and representatives of industry—in a country where the legislature rules there is normally a coincidence of morality between legislators and businessmen. The program of Congress for the enhancement of the number and activity of small businesses has also had some success; in economic terms this has meant greater initiatives and inventions and competition, and in political terms a stronger and firmer grassroots basis for the support of the legislative way of government.

Automation, so widely used in business, has kept the work week short and simultaneously raised the real wages of the people. But it has also caused a great displacement of workers. This has been partly compensated for by the creation of new industry. But a greater part of the adjustment has come through early retirement, through new provisions for leisure time, and especially through giving civic work to those who have reached the age of 55. Another factor contributing to the maintenance of full-time occupations has been the gradual extension of the years of education; today the average age of a man starting his career is four years above the average age in the 1960s. Adult education has become an integral part of the lives of one-third of the people over 30 years of age.

A good deal of the energies of those who have extensive leisure time is now being devoted to a wide variety of local and voluntary activities. It is to be hoped that our urban areas, which are scarcely more attractive today than they were 20 years ago, owing particularly to the population increase, will soon show the beneficial effects of new, locally-initiated programs. In other areas of life that have hitherto been dominated by ancient institutions some changes are also beginning to occur, though not very rapidly and not always in line with the desires of many people. It would be difficult to say that the churches in America today, for instance, are better organized or play a more vital role in the national or social scene than they did in the sixties. Principally this failure has its origins in a century of neglect of the social role of the churches on the part of government authorities, who have been all too eager to enforce a rigid separation of church and state without regard to the huge competitive advantage that the secular government could gain by taking over the problem of revitalizing the churches. Here was a case where the benevolence of government suffocated for a time the useful philanthropic activities of private groups. Apart from its large spiritual cost, the dollar cost of atrophied church welfare has been in the billions. However, in the next few years I think we may be able to devise new methods of promoting the social work of the church, if only by removing the traditional psychological obstacles that remain in the minds of secular civil servants.

The family in America is now reduced to the basic unit of parents and children, in which the rights of children are freely expressed at a very early age. This, we can appreciate, is a situation that was little desired by most Americans of a generation ago. In those days it was thought, with regard to both Negroes and whites, that the ideal family should be a large one with all the members knit together by ties of economic necessity and affection. However, there are now many studies which show that the basic family unit of today continues to maintain relations with grandparents, grandchildren, cousins. Moreover, these relations are on a higher level of affection and social intercourse than was the case a generation or more ago when economic necessity held together people who would really have preferred to live their own separate lives. Our legislative policy is therefore primarily concerned with ensuring the integrity of the basic family unit, and indeed all small units of mutually supporting persons. Our objective is to encourage them to plan and carry on as far as possible their own activities. Ultimately this means a strong society—and I might add, a strong infrastructure for Congress.

The most that can be said about the international scene is that atomic warfare has been avoided to date. Relations among the nuclear powers of the world have improved, even while general hostility must be said to exist among and between numerous sets of large nations. We must not let our guard down. Since international relations have become increasingly close, both economically and socially, we must beware that seemingly small incidents might provoke a nuclear holocaust that mankind has feared for two generations. It would be a great blessing for our children if they do not have to carry with them the horrible memories of partial genocide that would result from nuclear warfare.

Yet this same period of relative international calm saw a series of crises abroad that, as always, threatened the juridical defenses of congressional rule in America. Democratic institutions will never be safe in times of military crisis. Take, for example, the dangerous situation that was created when, at the very moment the United States was embroiled in a serious conflict in Southeast Asia, a second South American country threatened to fall into the hands of a regime of the type that once occupied Cuba. Strenuous efforts had to be employed by the congressional leadership to make certain that the

President would not wittingly or unwittingly accumulate vast powers as a result. It was then that Congress, in a set of "Resolutions on the Immediate Situation," took over for the first time some of the initiative as wartime leader of the nation which the President had monopolized for a century or more. In retrospect, historians will agree that the institution of the presidency was not harmed thereby. And, it has to be acknowledged that the United States survived the situation without the ups and downs of crowd psychology and dangerous explosions of public sentiment that had usually accompanied previous international crises.

Let me recall other crises that have affected the American Congress and people of the past generation. We recall the recession of 1971, and the special Plenary Council of Congress that was set up at the very beginning of the crisis in order to guide public opinion and affirm the positive role of Congress in attacking its economic and social causes. It may be said that this was the first economic depression in American history that did *not* result in increased regulation of the population, in a decline of federalism, and in the strengthening of the executive forces of the country. Much of the credit for this achievement was due to the well-developed research facilities of Congress (installed in 1967) that enabled it to put forward positive plans from the very outset of the recession. It has since become impossible for the President or anyone else to offer cut-and-dried solutions of the old kind for every national problem, in the expectation that a distraught and irrational legislature will swallow them whole.

We also recall with pride the great Federal Restoration Act of 1972 that granted all federal lands to the state governments. As a consequence of it, the states were given real and important work to do. A greater variety was introduced into the recreational facilities of the people and the land usage practices of the country. The national government was unburdened of much responsibility, and one great step taken toward achieving the ideal of a self-governing people. It is not at all a source of regret that the Federal Restoration Bill could be passed only by tying it in with the equally significant Metropolitan Self-Rule Bill of the same year. The latter bill, strongly supported by the urban interests now dominant in the country, enabled the metropolises of our land once and for all to set up an effective self-governing apparatus covering their entire areas. Thus what the states lost on the one hand, they made up on the other; also the urban interests were fully satisfied that they themselves would have a chance to exhibit their own willingness and capacity for local self-rule.

Other major efforts of Congress to institute a new philosophy of government did not have as prompt a success as the Federal Restoration Bill and the Metropolitan Self-Rule Bill. We recall with some dismay the ten years of struggle, largely with the federal civil service agencies, over turning education back to the localities, once the federal government had occupied this enormous field. We recall a similar struggle in respect to the problem of compulsory desegregation of neighborhood facilities and housing. After the far-reaching federal legislation on this issue in the early 1970s, it took another decade before it became possible to persuade leaders of the many groups involved to devolve upon the various communities the great task of social reconstruction and improving race relations economically and environmentally.

These two great struggles were part of the effort to establish a constant and formidable local basis for the power of the legislative branch of government. But there were other struggles of a more purely political and legal character which were of equal importance in the drive to strengthen the legislature. We recall the instance in 1968 of the first Exemplary Legislation Bill, and the refusal of the President to sign that bill and the ensuing attempt to overturn the veto. It was a struggle the likes of which had not been seen since President Jackson jousted with the United States Bank. That first Exemplary Legislation Bill hit at several sore points in presidential, executive, and congressional relations; it insisted upon the right of Congress to intervene in all administrative offices no matter how small, and to have access to all information of whatever minor character. The debates on that bill today constitute one of the richest sources of the theory of administrative control of government. When a version of the bill was finally enacted in 1971 and the Plenary Council of Congress was established in consequence, we were at last able to coordinate numerous joint functions of the Congress in relation to government and society. The Plenary Council has since performed a very useful task in taking up all cases where the executive branch has refused to cooperate with or give information to the Congress, whether to the congressional committees or individual congressmen. Moreover, the fact that the council has acted as arbitrator in these cases has ensured that the interventions have been confined to critical instances. Further, whenever the council has decided that a congressman should be delivered such information by the executive agency, it has succeeded without difficulty in obtaining presidential cooperation. The Exemplary Legislation Bill has been indeed one of the most important events in our constitutional history.

Again that struggle led to another of transcendent importance. The Supreme Court, in nullifying the Exemplary Legislation provisions, impelled an extraordinary majority of the Congress to provide for a drastic revision of the machinery of the rule of law in the United States by a constitutional amendment creating a larger Court of 24 members, with special panels for administrative law, and instituting a Supreme Court of the Nation.

We will note finally in our historical survey the tragic assassination of yet another President by a demented pensioner who suffered from the delusion that the President was personally responsible for his private economic troubles. It may be that the President occupies too exposed a position in our society and that death in office, whether by accident or by evil intent, will always be the fate of some proportion of such leaders. Insofar as the President has today come to be more widely recognized as being only one of a number of popular leaders who are responsible for the decisions of the country and the safety and happiness of its inhabitants, he will be likely to be the target of less hatred, as well as perhaps less personal affection, in the future.

I hope that this review of the main events of the past two decades has conveyed some sense of what Congress has achieved, and of the sweeping social changes that have taken place within a short period of time. Certainly America has not achieved Utopia. But things might be much worse. And it is unlikely that any political system, no matter how perfected and how ingeniously contrived, can solve the personal problems of citizens. Ultimately each man stands on his own feet in this world in relation to his loved ones, his country, and his God. What government can do, and what our government has been trying to do in recent years, is to make the social and political conditions for living as satisfactory as possible.

Now since we are on this important occasion privileged to have as guests men and women from every part of the world and from every walk of life, and from all parts of the United States of America, I should like to explain some of the basic principles of the Congress that you see convened here today and which will shortly begin its regular session of work.

Probably the most important of all the changes that have occurred in the congressional system are the least obvious ones. These are the changes in the character of the constituencies. The publics of Congress have been enormously strengthened in comparison with their condition of a generation ago. This has been the result not only of a heightened public interest fostered by the leadership of a more active Congress, but also of deliberate steps taken by a succession of Congresses to bolster their grassroots support. For one thing, congressmen have been provided with more services and assistance than they had formerly and can therefore maintain more elaborate offices in their districts. More important, the establishment of a Civic Corps has given special privileges to persons engaging in a modest amount of civic work. Participation in civic work has now produced a substantial body of citizens who know something about the workings of Congress and the importance of Congress as a channel of ideas and initiative. Today six million people in the country belong to the Civic Corps. Of these, only one-third are holding actual civic office; the rest have at one time held office or may do so in the future, or they may simply be citizens who have always worked outside of government and will continue to do so. Yet all of these people constitute the "politists" of the country today—that is, those men and women who are occupied more than the average citizen with the problems of running our great society. I think we can say that with the innovation of the Civic Corps the United States now has the largest public in history that is active in government.

Without these locally effective citizens there would be no basis for a strong legislature, but only the basis for a sheer despotism arising sharply out of the apathetic mass of people. With the Civic Corps we have a large variety of talents, skills, and energies to draw upon to keep the total circulation of government throughout its million offices healthy and alive.

The elections of congressmen are now held, as you know, separately from the election of the President. As a result, we do not get the severe fluctuation in the personnel of Congress that occurred when a larger number of people were voting blindly for congressmen on the basis of their choice for President. Now we have a somewhat smaller voting participation but a much more informed vote and a much more careful judgment of the character of congressmen themselves. The work of Congress has greatly benefited thereby. It is gratifying, in retrospect, to realize how much support sprang up for the constitutional amendment required in this case.

Little formal change has taken place in the apportionment of the vote for Congress. Congressmen today are elected from territorial districts of equal populations. Some states may soon experiment with a system of proportional representation which will produce equal population constituencies that are not based on territorial boundaries. Also, there has been an increase in the number of intermediary organizations partly connected with, and arising out of, the Civic Corps. These organizations signal a new tier of the public, which is better organized to undertake to speak for and reflect the economic, social, and cultural interests of the public. So while it is as true today as it was after the Supreme Court announced its decision in the case of *Wesberry* v. *Sanders* (1964) that equal populations, indifferently shaped, are the rule of apportionment, a typical congressman now has a set of middle-tier councils growing out of the Civic Corps to which he responds and which lend him support. Opposing groups of the same kind provide the opposition. The disorganization of communities and the abuse of minorities that were expected by many observers to follow the Court decisions did not materialize, largely because of fundamental but unofficial changes in the character of the electorate. We have today a double electorate in fact if not in law. The incumbent congressman is thus so closely connected to a variety of interests and so independent of political party and the President, that he can take more meaningful positions on community and national interests than he might otherwise take.

Over the last generation the types of congressmen have also been changing somewhat. In our membership today, for instance, we find more men and women who were formerly governmental officials, especially elected ones, and more former teachers and professors; congressmen of rural background are less numerous. This should not be surprising, since we have far more teachers than farmers and miners. The average tenure of congressmen has extended somewhat; but despite some good consequences of this fact, we still have the problem of providing effective opposition to candidates without at the same time favoring a single party or person, or interfering in elections. Nevertheless, we can say that today an opposition candidate has a great deal more help from public sources than he had heretofore. Not the least of this help has been provided by making available to him the rosters of the Civic Corps and assigning to him a free printing budget. New laws have also helped by prohibiting excessive use of certain kinds of advertising such as billboards, whose effect is to hypnotize people rather than to stimulate thought about the candidates. Codes of ethics formulated by associations of persons engaged in political campaign work as a profession have also helped.

Congress has, moreover, been strengthened in the country at large by the installation of institutes for legislative research in every state university in the country; by Halls of Congress ·in every state, containing exhibits, projections, information, wire television, and personnel all providing the public with a chance to understand Congress; and by the awarding of congressional fellowships in all the colleges in the country, which have helped to provide citizens in every community who understand and are able to participate in the affairs of Congress. We are pleased to say that after only a few years' operation of the system, 16 congressmen here today have at one time enjoyed such fellowships.

Information of the most varied kind is easily available nowadays through the data storage and processing systems that Congress has set up. I need only step over to this panel board which you see on my left here to dial an inquiry concerning a piece of information that I need for my speech at this point. When I dial L 49-49-A1, I am inquiring of our central computer system what is the latest statistic regarding the number of proposals that have been initiated by congressmen compared with proposals originating in the executive branch of the government, and how many of both types have actually been passed into law. This is a calculation of a different order, the end result of research by our Legislative Reference Service. While I have been talking, the response has been presented on the screen just next to the panel here; I read that during the last 30 years an increasing proportion of all bills passed has originated with Congress and that at this date their number in fact represents three-quarters of the total.

This is as it should be in government by legislature. We do not say that the participation of the presidency or of the executive branch or, naturally of many other elements of the country has not contributed to the making of these laws. But what we do say is that there can be no doubt any longer that legislation can and usually does begin in Congress.

I should pause for a moment to remind you that many other aspects of our daily work in Congress have been aided by automation. For example, we vote electrically now. I think you all appreciate that this saves a certain amount of time. It is an efficient procedure because we have learned how to use well the time we have saved. In fact we have cut down by one-half the research and chasing about for information that we used to need to do in order to carry out our work. Now the business of research is almost entirely accomplished by the electronic data processing and information retrieval centers that were instituted in the late sixties and which are constantly being improved as new techniques are developed.

There are literally millions of facts that are stored in these systems for instantaneous retrieval whenever an individual congressman wants them; and each congressman has in his own office, for his use and the use of his authorized staff, tabletop machinery that ties in with the total system. We can now truly say that Congress has equaled the presidency and the administrative agencies in the use of up-to-date machinery of information and intelligence.

That this is an important factor in the control of administration should of course be apparent. Thus I can dial for information on any item of the federal budget, that huge tome which used to discourage every student and practitioner of government. And I can very quickly discover, for instance, that a certain office which specializes in the procurement of road equipment has had less money to work with this year than in the previous fiscal year. Similarly, trends in the number of personnel employed throughout the government can be made instantly apparent.

The computer center also stores information on what agency activities are due to be phased out, or are being proposed for phasing out, according to our Zero-Sum Activity Formula. The use of this formula has led to a balanced activity program under which for every new activity undertaken by the federal government an old one either is devolved onto a non-federal organization or else is discontinued. The proposals for devolution, as you may know, come largely from the Congressional Tribunes who are attached to each agency of government and who have specific instructions to report back annually to Congress with proposals for phasing out or devolution. Their word is not taken as final; in fact, since their inception, only 1 percent of their recommendations have been favorably acted upon. But the system gives us an adversary proceeding on the budget of an agency that we have never had before, and a built-in method of controlling bureaucratic growth and extending the range of government thinking and planning.

Other techniques have added to congressional control of administration. All of them depend for some of their effect upon a psychological recasting of mind about the government. The history of the Sub-Legislative Corps, established by law in 1969, exemplifies what I mean. The idea behind the Sub-Legislative Corps was born out of a new interest in the study of Congress in the universities of the country. A new group of scholars conducted detailed research studies which systematically exposed the extent to which most of the officials, teachers, and opinion leaders of the country had come to regard the executive branch as the exclusive preserve of the presidency. The very word "executive"—which has two meanings, "administrative" and "member of the presidency"—served to confound people into thinking that administration of government is synonymous with control by the Chief Executive. This group of scholars also pointed out that the rule-making powers delegated to non-elective officials were in effect turning them into congressmen. Several hundreds of officials were rapidly assuming powers greater than those of the members of state legislatures, heads of giant corporations, and judges, as well as congressmen.

It was to combat this trend that we instituted the Sub-Legislative Corps. The idea is a simple one. Congress is the chief legislator. All other legislators are sub-legislators and have to acknowledge the legislative supremacy of Congress. Congress convenes the Sub-Legislative Corps once a year and determines the ideological as well as the material fitness of its members.

As might have been expected, there was a prolonged legislative struggle over the establishment of the corps. The executive, including the President, stood as adversaries to the will of Congress, at least for some time. But finally the appropriate legislation was enacted, declaring that all persons who had rule-making power of any kind in the federal government must subscribe to a statement in which they acknowledged that they were responsible as much to the Congress as to the President. The statement also required them to recognize the legislative nature of their jobs and the need to reconcile their legislative decisions with those of the Congress as the supreme legislator of the land.

This formal acknowledgement of the obvious proved to be critical in opening up the whole psychology of the legislative way of government. The results have been most gratifying. Today no responsible rule-making official in the government thinks of himself as a member of a kind of pyramidal hierarchy or old-type of army in which he is responsible only to one boss, the President (which as we know means too often no boss at all). Instead, he believes and recognizes that in his legislative capacity he owes as much discipline and self-control and accountability to Congress for his actions as to the President. The establishment of the corps thus brought about a mental restructuring of the executive world and a fresh outlook throughout the whole government. The new outlook on life among top administrators has even encouraged some of them to go out and become politicians themselves. In fact, 22 members of the present Congress have at one time or another been in the top grade of the civil service that coincides with the Sub-Legislative Corps. There could be no healthier relation for the country as a whole than this intermingling of groups that were once mutually hostile.

Related to the Sub-Legislative Corps is the Center for Advisory Representative Councils. As the twentieth century progressed, executive agencies came to employ more and more special forms of representing the views of the publics or clienteles for which they were responsible. They organized hundreds of little legislatures to reflect public opinion to agency officials. Often these groups were used as instruments of the agency to compete with Congress and all too often they were creatures of the agencies. Finally in 1969, Congress passed the Advisory Representative Council Bills which recognized the fact that such forms of functional representation were becoming an important feature of the republic. It gave them a definite status and role to play as an arm of Congress as well as a source of help to the agencies. Consequently a center was established and a charter adopted to cover all instances in which agencies believed that some form of special representation of views was needed in their work. The thousands of members of such councils now recognize that they are in a real sense assisting the work of Congress in giving fuller representation to the myriad interests of the nation.

It was also discovered in the course of the revival of research on Congress that the functions of our committees had hitherto been described in a one-sided manner. Emulators and adulators of the then existing executive organization of the government had tended to regard committees as a kind of meaningless obstacle course. (That was in the days when people thought to turn Congress into a streamlined executive pyramid dominated by a strong party system that was subordinated in turn to the President.) But then it was more properly reported by the new group of scholars that the committees were essentially furnishing various ways of looking at legislation. Furthermore, a single committee rarely gave an absolute verdict; instead, its judgments were summed up along with a lot of other views in the final product of Congress. The committees were for the most part instruments for the processing of different kinds of majorities through the legislative process itself.

Nevertheless, starting in the sixties, Congress did several things to improve the effectiveness of its committees. It made them a little more responsive to majority sentiments in the Congress than had formerly been the case. It did so by instituting the present dual system of apportionment, in which the Speaker and party leaders propose three names and the members of the committee choose the chairman from among these three. This system has not deprived the chairmen of committees of their function nor of much of their power. Today the chairmen of committees of the House and Senate are still the most powerful members of the Congress and they are intended to be so. It is owing almost entirely to a re-education of the public and to the reforms that have been passed during the past two decades that the legitimacy of the chairmen of committees and the importance of the role they play in the operations of the American government are recognized by public opinion.

Our chairmen, specifically speaking, are still elderly gentlemen and we make no apology for this; for they are men of long experience and deep knowledge of legislative processes. But they are more than that. I would warrant that there is not a chairman of any committee in either house of Congress who is not as justified in holding his position as anyone occupying a similar position of respect and power in any voluntary association, local government, or business corporation of the country.

Every committee now has an annual program, a budget, and a research program development staff, as well as several Congressional Tribunes reporting to it. The chairmen direct these elements, but each member of the committees has a considerable appropriation of his own that he can distribute as he wishes.

We continue to support a lively party system, but it is now apparent to the public that the parties do not and should not rule Congress. The parties suggest positions that congressmen may take and they present alternatives to congressmen and to the country. They agitate but they do not rule. The Congress of 1989 is nonpartisan. This is so, even though practically all of its members bear partisan labels.

I realize that it is difficult to explain this situation to those peoples of the world whose governments are controlled by one party—or in a very few cases by two well organized parties, one of which commands the government. We in the United States value our parties. They perform useful functions of public instruction and of group alliances. They help organize Congress but they do not smother the independence of the congressmen. We feel that this is the ideal reconciliation of the role of parties with the complicated interests of a modern democracy. In America what governs are the freely organized and flexible groupings of congressmen that form around the various issues confronting the nation, as well as the programs designed by successive Congresses. At the beginning of each session the congressional leadership presents to the country a consensus on what this Congress expects to accomplish during its term of office. That statement says much; yet it says no more than congressmen can agree to. Thereupon, the Congress breaks into groups naturally forming on those major issues or combinations of issues on which action is sought.

The budget still constitutes a matter of central concern for Congress. But the Second Budget Act of 1980 radically revised the concept of a single annual budget. The budget today consists of 694 individual budget processes, continuously maintained, revised and forwarded as congressional machinery and executive machinery, in parallel operations, develop their sections of the total budget. There is close coordination nowadays, too, between the substantive committees of Congress that occupy themselves with such matters as urban affairs, agriculture, and foreign relations, and the appropriations committees and subcommittees dealing with the fiscal aspects of those substantive issues. The lightning-like calculating and reporting capacities of our central computing system enables us readily to control the overall as well as the particular processes in the giant operations of government.

Although the appropriations committees retain their detailed functions with respect to the budget, the substantive interests are strengthened by the interposition in the substantive committees of the reports of the Congressional Tribunes—those men who are placed in each agency of the executive branch of government with the task of performing as devil's advocates in the agencies to which they are assigned. Despite the difficulties the Tribunes have encountered (for this has been a truly new institution in the history of government), these men have largely succeeded in winning the confidence of the Congress and the country at large for the work that they have done. It has been estimated that in the last ten years, $32 billion of annual expenditures have been shifted out of federal budgets into local governmental or non-governmental expenditures; and that a total of 134 major and minor projects have been thus devolved. This achievement, which is chiefly due to the activity of the Tribunes, has helped greatly in controlling the size and character of the federal executive establishment. It is not surprising, therefore, that when on occasion men who have been Congressional Tribunes have run for office, they have been cordially welcomed by the electorate. Six members of the present Congress have had such experience. Altogether some 14 former Tribunes ran for congressional seats in the last election. It is understood, of course, that if they do run for office, they are disqualified for five years from reinstatement on the panel of qualified persons from which Congressional Tribunes are appointed by the Plenary Council of Congress.

No body of men and women who have such strong and varied roots in the communities of the country as congressmen have can escape frequent problems of conflict of interests. At one time it was thought that strict laws governing conflict of interests would somehow produce a completely objective and well-disposed body of legislators. More recently the country's lawmakers have abandoned that approach as tending to deprive the nation of the services of some of its most skilled people and as tending to make neuters, politically speaking, of leaders. This problem, therefore, has been attacked by means of laws requiring the publication of income and property holdings of congressmen, and laws governing outright corruption.

Thanks to such restraint in imposing restrictions on operations and activities, and to various rules and laws promoting both old and new functions, congressmen today are more independent than they have been in a century. They are freed from a great deal of routine that used to be the burden of congressmen. They have not, however, cut down on the amount of casework—that is, the much needed social work at which congressmen are expert. Rather, they have recruited more staff to take care of the many cases that each year require the individual congressman to intercede with one of the agencies of the government on behalf of his constituents or for some other worthy cause. The congressman's staff today is on the average double what it was a generation ago. The number of personal intercessions by congressmen has now exceeded 4,000,000 per year

—this is an admirable extension of American "government for the people." Adequate travel privileges are nowadays guaranteed every member of Congress, both in America and throughout the world. (The word "junket," like the word "lobby," no longer has any unfavorable overtones.) No longer do congressmen need to "bum" rides from the President or armed forces; they have unlimited access to charter and regular air travel facilities.

Congressmen and their staffs do not depend nowadays upon executive agency officials for security clearance. The Central Security Office of Congress, established in 1974, clears congressional personnel for whatever activities may be required of them, and for access to whatever classified information they may require. The legislature thus will never be at the mercy of the police state through such means. (I know that this system must mean a good deal to some of our foreign guests here today.)

There has been a large increase in expenditures for research facilities external to personal staffs. The Congressional Sanctions Institute, the Institute for Social and Behavioral Research, and the annual Inventory of Freedom and Restrictions have all added to the congressional budget. These three new institutes are primarily designed to extend the range of congressional intelligence, planning, and control. Together with a much enlarged Legislative Reference Service, they form the Institute of Congressional Research and involve an average annual expenditure of over $100 million. This money we regard as well spent; and we cannot help looking back with a certain amazement at a period earlier in the century when Congress was trying to run the greatest economy and power center in the world with research and intelligence facilities that were less adequate than those of any one of the government's 30 separate administrative agencies.

It may be, indeed, that these research efforts have been one of the principal causes of the comparative decline of overall national government expenditures, despite continuing heavy obligations abroad and the assumption of a number of new activities at home. For it is now possible for any individual congressman to command a first-class research machine to investigate any theory he may have as to the better organization or operation of any agency of the government. Of course it is just as difficult as it always has been for a congressman to be an expert on more than a few of the subjects that concern the nation; but the congressman today does a much better job in respect to his particular special interests than he has ever done before. For he has truly taken advantage of the expansion of technical and social sciences in the twentieth century.

We who have supported the development of the new model of Congress offer no apologies for the trouble that has been stirred up by the necessary reforms. In a number of significant instances we have even found support for our labors within the administration, courts, and presidency; and we are grateful for that support. Moreover, we feel, on this two hundredth anniversary of the first Congress, that there is greater appreciation of our work among the officials and the public of the land than has ever been given us. It is only because of the will, initiative, and the power of Congress that the President of the United States is today both a democratic and republican leader. He is *primus inter pares;* we would even go as far as to say that he may very well be a greater leader than any of us. But he is in his place, and Congress is in its place; and the American Republic retains its place, in turn, as the most stable and powerful republic that the world has ever known.